THE POULANTZAS READER

THE POULANTZAS READER

Marxism, Law and the State

EDITED BY JAMES MARTIN

VERSO

London • New York

First published by Verso 2008
'Marxist Examination of the Contemporary State and Law and the Question of the "Alternative"'
first published as 'L'examen marxiste de l'état et du droit actuels et de question de l'alternative' in
Les Temps Modernes, nos 219 and 220, © *Les Temps Modernes* 1964. 'Sartre's *Critique of
Dialectical Reason* and Law' first published as 'La *Critique de la Raison Dialectique* de J-P Sartre et
le droit' in *Archives de Philosophie du Droit*, no. 10, © *Archives de Philosophie du Droit* 1965.
'Preliminaries to the Study of Hegemony in the State' first published as 'Préliminaires à l'étude de
l'hégémonie dans l'état' in *Les Temps Modernes* nos 234 and 235, © *Les Temps Modernes* 1965.
'Marxist Political Theory in Great Britain' reprinted by permission of the publisher from *New Left
Review* 43 (May–June 1967), © New Left Review 1967. First published as 'La théorie politique
marxiste en Grande Bretagne' in *Les Temps Modernes*, no. 238, © *Les Temps Modernes* 1966.
'Towards A Marxist Theory' first published as 'Vers une théorie marxiste' in *Les Temps Modernes*,
no. 240, © *Les Temps Modernes* 1966. 'The Problem of the Capitalist State' first published in *New
Left Review* 58, © *New Left Review* 1969. 'On Social Classes' reprinted by permission of the
publisher from *New Left Review* 78, © *New Left Review* 1973. First published as 'Les classes
sociales' in *L'Homme et la Société* 24/25, © *L'Homme et la Société* 1972. 'Internationalization of
Capitalist Relations and the Nation State' reprinted by permission of the publisher from *Economy
and Society*, vol. 3, © *Economy and Society* 1974. First published as 'L'Internationalisation des
rapports capitalistes et de l'Etat-Nation' in *Les Temps Modernes*, no. 319 © *Les Temps Modernes*
1973. 'On the Popular Impact of Fascism' first published as 'A propos de l'impact populaire du
fascisme' in M. Macciochi, ed., *Elements pour une analyse du fascisme*, Union Generale d'Edition
1976, © Union Generale d'Edition, Paris 1976. 'The Capitalist State: A Reply to Miliband and
Laclau' first published in *New Left Review* 95, © *New Left Review* 1976. 'The Political Crisis and
the Crisis of the State' reprinted by permission of the publisher from J.W. Freiburg, ed., *Critical
Sociology: European Perspectives*, Halstead Press, New York 1979, © Halstead Press 1979. First
published as 'Les transformations actuelles de l'état, la crise politique, et la crise de l'état' in N.
Poulantzas, ed., *La Crise de L'Etat*, PUF, Paris 1976, © PUF 1976. 'The New Petty Bourgeoisie'
reprinted by permission of the publisher from A. Hunt, ed., *Class and Class Struggle*, Lawrence &
Wishart, London 1977, © Lawrence & Wishart 1977. 'The State and the Transition to Socialism'
first published as 'L'état et la transition au socialisme' in *Critique communiste*, no. 16 © *Critique
communiste* 1977. 'Towards A Democratic Socialism' reprinted by permission of the publisher from
New Left Review 109, © *New Left Review* 1978. First published as the postscript to *L'Etat, le
pouvoir, le socialisme*, PUF, Paris 1978, © PUF 1978. 'Is There a Crisis in Marxism?' reprinted by
permission of the publisher from *Journal of the Hellenic Diaspora*, vol. 6, no.3, © *Journal of the
Hellenic Diaspora* 1979. 'Research Note on the State and Society' first published in *International
Social Science Journal*, vol. 32, no. 4, © *International Social Science Journal* 1980.

1 3 5 7 9 10 8 6 4 2

Verso
UK: 6 Meard Street, London W1F 0EG
USA: 180 Varick Street, New York, NY 10014-4606
www.versobooks.com

Verso is the imprint of New Left Books

ISBN-13: 978-1-84467-200-4 (pbk)
ISBN-13: 978-1-84467-199-1 (hbk)

British Library Cataloguing in Publication Data
A catalogue record for this book is available from the British Library

Library of Congress Cataloging-in-Publication Data
A catalog record for this book is available from the Library of Congress

Typeset in Sabon by Hewer Text UK Ltd, Edinburgh
Printed in the USA by Maple Vail

CONTENTS

ACKNOWLEDGEMENTS

I owe a debt of gratitude to a number of people for their assistance in the production of this volume: the Nicos Poulantzas Institute in Athens for financial assistance to procure a number of the translations; Bob Jessop of the University of Lancaster and Stathis Kouvelakis of Kings College, University of London for offering information and advice on the writings and biography of Poulantzas; Bob was also splendidly generous in supplying some vital materials and, along with my colleague at Goldsmiths, Sanjay Seth, kindly passed comment on a draft of the Introduction; at Verso, Sebastian Budgen and, formerly, Jane Hindle kept an improbable project going; and the staff at Goldsmiths Library arranged numerous inter-library loans with typical speed and efficiency. Finally, I'd like to thank Susan for not asking any questions.

James Martin

Acknowledgement is due to the following publications and publishers for permission to reproduce Poulantzas's work:
Archives de Philosophie du Droit, *Economy and Society*, Halstead Press, *International Social Science Journal*, *Journal of the Hellenic Diaspora*, Lawrence & Wishart, *New Left Review*, *Politis*, *Les Temps Modernes* and Union Générale d'Édition.

INTRODUCTION
James Martin

Nicos Poulantzas (1936–1979) was one of the leading Marxist theorists of the late twentieth century. From the mid-1960s he developed seminal analyses of the state and social classes and, during the crisis years in post-war capitalism, contributed uniquely to the theoretical extension of radical political analysis. Born and educated in Greece and resident in Paris, initially as a scholar of law, he was closely engaged with the philosophical currents of the age. Influenced first by Sartrean existentialism and, soon after, by Althusser's structuralism, Poulantzas brought a formidable depth and complexity to the Marxist understanding of politics.

The articles collected in this volume offer a representative range of Poulantzas's scholarly interests throughout his career. Undoubtedly, however, he remains most well-known for his theory of the capitalist state whose 'relative autonomy' from class interests endow it with a distinctive, unifying purpose. This theory, which had important implications for conceptualizing the permutations of bourgeois class domination and for the formulation of revolutionary socialist strategy, brought him into controversy with other Marxists in whom he detected a tendency to 'economistic' reduction. His debate on the state with Ralph Miliband in the early 1970s was, for a while, a central reference point for all students of social and political theory.

Yet, as the writings gathered here demonstrate, Poulantzas's original approach to the state was a theoretical project under constant development. Indeed, the nature of the state could not, he insisted, be separated from the ongoing conflicts, contradictions and compromises of the struggles that permeate capitalist societies. In this, Poulantzas, much like Gramsci before him, brought to his Marxism an awareness of the strategic variations and reversals that often characterized politics on the capitalist periphery. 'A theory of the capitalist State', he argued, 'must be able to elucidate the metamorphoses of its object'.[1] Today, what is taken to be Poulantzas's 'theory of the state' might, then, better be understood as a developing reflection on the space of the political opened up by capitalist relations of production. For, built-in to this space is a potential for novelty and change that is often better demonstrated by 'exceptional' states, such as fascism, than the classic, parliamentary-democratic model.

Poulantzas took it upon himself to acknowledge this potential for variation without losing sight of the principal reference-points found in the Marxist 'classics' (Marx, Engels and Lenin). Yet, at times, reconciling the two took him to the limits, perhaps limitations, of Marxist theory itself. By the time of his suicide in 1979, the Althusserian moment had passed decisively, as had the burst of revolutionary enthusiasm and the explosion of interest in Marxism catalyzed by the events in Paris of May 1968. The tragic end to Poulantzas's own life seemed to mirror the wider exhaustion of Marxism's influence on popular struggles.

Yet, thirty years on, interest in Poulantzas persists, sustained in part by the efforts of those who fell under his influence in the 1970s but also by a renewed concern for some of the themes on which he wrote. If, reasonably, a good part of Poulantzas's preoccupations seem *passé* to a contemporary audience, there is nonetheless much in his work that remains instructive: for example, his conceptualization of the state as a material 'condensation' of struggles, his focus on the changing forms of state power in contemporary capitalism, or his interest in the authoritarian tendency in late capitalist politics.

In the remainder of this Introduction I outline, in broad terms, the arguments contained in the articles that follow and sketch some of their intellectual and political background. My aims here are merely to survey Poulantzas's evolving theoretical concerns and offer a guide to interpretation so as to illuminate his writings and help locate them alongside his other, book-length texts.

Philosophy and Law

It has been Poulantzas's fate to be associated closely with the structural Marxism of Louis Althusser which dominated French intellectual life for around a decade from the mid-1960s. Yet this association has done much to obscure Poulantzas's own, independent, development both before and after the high-point of Althusser's influence in the late 1960s. Prior to taking up Althusser's problematic, Poulantzas had been a scholar of law and a devotee of a more 'humanistic' philosophical

style, influenced by Jean-Paul Sartre, György Lukács and Lucien
Goldmann. Let us begin, then, with this early period in his formation.

Poulantzas was born in Athens on 21 September 1936. He grew to
adolescence during a turbulent period which encompassed the authoritarian regime of General Ioannis Metaxas in the late 1930s, followed
by the Nazi puppet regime during the war, the civil war of 1946–49 and
the Western-backed, conservative democracy of the 1950s.[2] Graduat-
ing in law from the University of Athens in 1957 and, following
compulsory military service, he set off in 1960 to undertake doctoral
studies in German legal philosophy in Munich. That decision was
soon aborted, however, and Poulantzas relocated to Paris, the home of
a large Greek diaspora that included figures such as Kostas Axelos,
Cornelius Castoriadis and other exiled left-wing intellectuals.

Poulantzas enrolled as a teaching assistant at the Université
Panthéon-Sorbonne and continued his research on law, submitting
a *mémoire de doctorat* in 1961 on natural law theory in Germany after
the Second World War. By 1964 he had completed his doctoral thesis,
published in the following year as his first book, *Nature des choses et
droit: essai sur la dialectique du fait et de la valeur.*[3]

In *Nature des choses*, Poulantzas undertook a synthesis of phenomenological approaches to law and existentialist philosophy to produce
a theory of natural law grounded in the 'dialectical unity' of facts and
values. For natural law theorists, obligations to obey legal prescrip-
tions depend upon law's coincidence with moral intuitions, that is,
with the 'nature of things'. By contrast, followers of legal positivism
(such as Kelsen, Hart, and so forth) argue that law must be obeyed
regardless of its moral character, simply because it is law. Poulantzas
broadly followed the first path, aiming to develop an approach to law
that overcame both the ahistorical, 'transcendental' enquiry into
moral values associated with Kant, and the dualism of fact and value,
or 'is' and 'ought', common to legal positivism. Inspired by Hegel,
Marx, Heidegger and Sartre, Poulantzas argued for the 'immanent'
grounding of legal values in the ontological 'fact' of human freedom:

> A legal universe is 'valuable' . . . to the extent that it constitutes,
> historically, a step in the human struggle against the given facts
> which alienate and reify man, and towards the creation of a 'human'
> universe where man can create his own dignity and realise his own
> generic being.[4]

At first glance, Poulantzas's philosophical approach to law appears at
some distance from his later work on the state. Yet, if the explicit

objective of *Nature des choses* was to defend a species of natural law, its focus was not moral philosophy but, rather, what in the Anglo-American world is called 'social theory'. Having established a broadly Marxian anthropology of legal values – tracing values to a conscious human interaction with the practical, material dilemmas of collective existence – Poulantzas devoted the second half of the book to the 'sociology of law'. Here he drew upon Sartre's analysis (in the *Critique of Dialectical Reason*) of relations of 'interiority' and 'exteriority' to conceptualize the interaction of legal structures with the economic base. Thus Poulantzas produced a global theory of the legal order conceived, following Lukács, as a 'reified' social structure generated, at various levels of mediation, through human 'praxis' founded in the social struggle for economic subsistence. Feeding existentialist insights into sociology, he developed a comprehensive 'meta-theorization' of the place of law in the social development of human existence, one that avoided the crude reduction of law to class interests and cleared space for grasping the complex variation of social orders. If, later, he was to drop his interest in legal philosophy, this comprehensive theoretical approach and anti-economism nevertheless remained.

Poulantzas's earliest published articles mirrored the concerns of his legal studies, surveying academic literature on phenomenological and existentialist approaches to law and 'juridical ontology'. In Chapter 1, 'Marxist Examination of the Contemporary State and Law and the Question of the "Alternative"', published in 1964 in Sartre's *Les Temps Modernes* (a frequent outlet for Poulantzas in the 1960s and 70s), the sociological concerns of the second part of *Nature des choses* are set out with an enhanced political accent. Here Poulantzas again elaborates a Marxist approach to the state and law, based on the 'internal-external' method and defending the 'relative autonomy' of legal superstructures against Marxist economism.

Refusing the dismissal of superstructures as 'unreal', Poulantzas reconnects juridical norms to the economic infrastructure by emphasizing their mediation by values grounded in material praxis. Thus modern property law is related to economic conditions, not *directly* as a class instrument, but through values such as liberty and equality, in addition to market values concerning contract and exchange. It is precisely these values that grant legal norms a wider validity, independently of any instrumental advantage to the bourgeoisie and despite their 'reified' status and role in sustaining alienated relations throughout civil society. Indeed, for Poulantzas, the significance in noting this crystallization into legal norms of certain values lies precisely in the radical possibilities engendered when the proletariat recognizes the contradiction between its real and ideal existence. Without such recognition, an alternative set of values – elaborated through the existing values of liberty and equality – could not come into play.

Marxist analysis, claims Poulantzas, cannot rest at merely noting the internal unity of law and the state. Its purpose is to *criticize* the reification of law by exposing its mediated relationship to the economic base, whilst respecting the specificity of law in its historical genesis. For instance, Poulantzas himself notes the significance of 'calculability' and 'predictability' in contemporary Western states, values which correspond to a period of monopoly capitalism in which strategic forecasting has become paramount at the level of the state. These values give rise to legal norms based on generality, abstraction, formality and codification, which result in a 'systematization of law' and a 'formal hierarchy of state bodies'. A critical Marxist analysis, he goes on, must expose the contradictions at work in this legal order by simultaneously grasping the specificity of a normative model of law (an internal analysis of 'the state as an organization') *and* the dialectical relation of the legal superstructure to the base (an external analysis of 'the state as body or instrument'), so establishing the various, complex degrees of proximity of legal norms to class exploitation.

For the early Poulantzas, this model of analysis provided the basis for a strategic assault on the state by gauging the extent to which a revolutionary advance must adapt and/or relinquish elements of the bourgeois order. His debt to Sartrean existentialism in developing a non-economistic, Marxist sociology of law is illuminated in Chapter 2, 'Sartre's *Critique of Dialectical Reason* and Law'. In a review of the philosopher's lengthy effort to fuse Marxist theory and existentialist philosophy, Poulantzas sets out the relevance of Sartrean Marxism to legal analysis.

Sartre's advance over phenomenological approaches, claims Poulantzas, lies in his effort to develop categories that shift ontological analysis from the level of the individual to that of society. The dialectic, in Sartre's hands, entails an ongoing process of 'totalization' whereby man as a meaning-creating subject exists in a constitutive, interactive relationship with the material world, encompassed in the experience of labour. This originary 'praxis-totalization' – whereby man makes himself as he labours on the world – is the basis to an 'existentialist ontology of law' that, in Poulantzas's view, surpasses the ahistorical and de-contextualized approaches of established legal phenomenology.

Poulantzas goes on to sketch Sartre's account of the different modes of social being – 'series', 'collectives', 'fused', 'statutory' and 'institutionalized' groups – as moments in the 'structuration of the social'. These represent different stages of dialectical praxis in which group members relate to each other through a shared experience of being. Juridical relations fundamentally express, therefore, a form of collective identity grounded in social 'needs' and 'labour':

> Law is thus the specific 'ontological' dimension of the cohesion of a social group . . . organized for its permanency through the pledge, demanding a predictability on the part of its members, and necessitating a differentiation of tasks in order to achieve a common objective.[5]

If Poulantzas adds a critical note of caution concerning Sartre's own philosophical starting point – not in socio-economic structures but in an 'ahistorical' and solitary individual praxis – which significantly distances his enterprise from classical Marxist analysis, the tenor of his article is nevertheless supportive. Sartre offers a non-reductionist approach to juridical relations, underlining the autonomy of law and the state from economic interests, one that is broadly compatible with Marxism, as Poulantzas sees it. At this stage, the young student of law looked forward to a further and deeper engagement with Sartre on these issues.

Althusser and the Revival of Marxism

Just as *Nature des choses* was published and its various offshoots found themselves in print, Poulantzas began to switch intellectual allegiances from Sartre to Althusser, moving from a paradigm based on existentialism and phenomenology to one based on structuralism. This was not an overnight conversion, by any means. Althusser's presence had first taken form as a brief footnote in *Nature des choses* and developed into more substantial but still unelaborated references in the journal articles. Between 1964 and 1966, Poulantzas gradually abandoned both his direct interest in law and his existentialist Marxism, adopting, instead, a focus on the state as a distinctly political, rather than strictly juridical, object of Marxist analysis. This phase of transition also saw Poulantzas shifting attention to debates within contemporary European Marxism, whilst at the same time reassessing the Marxist classics. Whilst still concerned with the autonomy of the political realm from simple or direct class influence, Poulantzas began

to incorporate into his own analysis the more refined and philoso-
phically rigorous language of Althusser.

Althusser's impact on French Marxism had been underway since his
seminars in the early 1960s. The theoretical work undertaken there
was published in 1965 in the collection of essays, *For Marx*, and the
jointly-authored *Reading 'Capital'*.[6] The promise of these works was
no less than a wholesale revival of Marxism as a 'scientific' enterprise,
founded on a structuralist-inspired reading of Marx's 'epistemological
break' with the 'humanism' of his early years, and directed towards
returning Marxist theory to a deeper, more radical political engagement than Soviet orthodoxy permitted. There is no room here to
discuss the details of Althusser's enterprise, so I shall sketch only some
of its key claims as they relate directly to Poulantzas.[7]

Althusser's reading of Marx offered a route between what he saw as
the mechanistic economism of Stalinist orthodoxy – which construed
history as the linear development of modes of production based on the
inexorable expansion of productive forces – and its 'mirror-image', the
Hegelian Marxism of Lukács, Korsch and Gramsci, which made
history the journey of a subject overcoming its alienated essence.[8]
The first was viewed as a crude, dogmatic assimilation of Marxism to
the model of the natural sciences, whilst the second lapsed into
'historicism', that is, the reduction of knowledge to its own conditions
of existence, thus abandoning altogether Marxism's claim to genuine,
scientific status. Building on the structuralist orientation underway
since the mid-1950s in the work of figures such as Roland Barthes and
Claude Lévi-Strauss, Althusser proposed to reconstruct Marx's 'problematic' as an autonomous scientific practice whose object was the
complex 'mode of production', consisting of several autonomous
structural levels whose overall interdependence was determined by
economic relations only 'in the last instance'. Economism, historicism
and humanism were castigated as unscientific enterprises that either
reduced history to a single cause (economism) or the expression of a
subject (historicism and humanism).

Althusser's fundamental challenge had been to draw a line between
a rigorous, scientific historical materialism and the unscientific,
'ideological' forms it had taken in previous interpretations. If he
concentrated on the philosophical grounds for this enterprise in his
reconstruction of the later Marx, it remained to be seen how a more
concrete socio-political analysis could be drawn from it. It was
precisely that wider extrapolation that Poulantzas undertook to
explore. His first, elaborate engagement with Althusserian categories
– although not with Althusser himself – arrived in a mammoth

discussion of the concept of 'hegemony', 'Preliminaries to the Study of Hegemony in the State' (see Chapter 3). Here, Poulantzas explores the significance of hegemony – Gramsci's strategic-theoretical concept then popularized by the Italian Communist Party – for a 'scientific' analysis of the state and class struggle. Rejecting once more the economistic reduction of the state to an instrument of the dominant class, he underscores the link between economism and voluntarism as part of 'a Hegelian conception of the Idea-totality' and proposes a more complex understanding of the 'political level' that draws on a distinction between the young and late Marx. These points of reference are clearly Althusserian in origin and Poulantzas's objective was, accordingly, to sketch the basis for a theory of the state and politics that dispensed with a Hegelian-inspired philosophy of the subject.

Poulantzas conceives hegemony not now as the reified projection of an alienated class consciousness – broadly, the 'humanist' view represented in his earlier work – but as a political practice which, in the capitalist mode of production, has as its object the structures of the state. The autonomization of the political in capitalism allocates to it the task of organizing the 'universal' interest under the leadership of the dominant class or class 'fraction'. A hegemonic analysis takes into consideration the variable capacity of a class fraction to structure the political realm by bringing together, in varying degrees, subordinate and allied classes and fractions. Hegemony denotes, therefore, a complex field of political practice opened up by the mode of production, but not reducible to the contradictions within it. The state is characterized both by its global function in guaranteeing the economic-corporate interests of the dominant class (that is, it is a class state) but this is achieved indirectly, via the mediation of a hegemonic leadership in which the dominant class articulates its immediate interests as the general interest.

This schematic, theoretical outline was supplemented the same year by the more concrete focus on 'Marxist Political Theory in Great Britain' (Chapter 4), published originally in *Les Temps Modernes* and in translation the next year in *New Left Review* as Poulantzas's first English-language publication. As the title suggests, the topic of this article was the recent developments in Marxist political analysis in Britain: more precisely, the historical 'theses' developed by the editors of *New Left Review*, Perry Anderson and Tom Nairn. In a series of articles focused on the development of the British state, Anderson and Nairn had set out to explain the backward nature of class politics in the UK which accounted for the relative decline in British economic and political significance after the war.[9] This decline was traced to the early bourgeois revolution in the seventeenth century and the compromise between the aristocratic landowning classes and the emergent bourgeoisie. This compromise, it was argued, left the aristocracy as the hegemonic class until the nineteenth century, its feudal trappings remaining in place and preventing the full development of an independent bourgeois class consciousness. Likewise, the absence of a bourgeois-led hegemony disabled the formation of a distinctive and revolutionary working-class consciousness.

Anderson and Nairn's analyses sparked a furious response from the historian E.P. Thompson who disputed, largely empirically, their interpretation of the limited presence of the bourgeoisie and the inadequacies of the British proletariat's revolutionary potential.[10] Poulantzas, by contrast, sought to clarify the theoretical terms of the dispute and correct the conceptual apparatus employed by Anderson and Nairn. In keeping with his analysis above, he argued that Anderson and Nairn had succumbed to both historicism and subjectivism in associating hegemony exclusively with a unified class consciousness. This led them to confuse the absence of a distinctly bourgeois ideology with the failure of that class to properly achieve political domination. On the contrary, Poulantzas argued, hegemony is not exclusively an ideological phenomenon but primarily a political practice that unifies different class fractions. So long as the political function of hegemony is achieved, its ideological content may reflect various different elements. The bourgeoisie therefore remained the politically dominant class in so far as its interests, grounded in the capitalist mode of production, were secured by a hegemony that, in this instance, took aristocratic form. Similarly, the success of the British proletariat depended not merely on projecting 'its own' class consciousness as universal through some vague, ideological 'synthesis' but, rather, in securing the political unity of a bloc of objectively positioned class forces.

Throughout Poulantzas's critical reading of Anderson and Nairn, he insists on the distinctiveness of a 'Marxist type of unity' in conceptualizing the social formation. This unity is the complex unity of an over-determined structure with autonomous levels, not an 'expressive totality' in which interests at the base are directly transmitted, via class subjects, to the superstructures. Poulantzas wants therefore to retain a degree of complexity to class political analysis but insists, persistently, on the 'objective' correspondence of this complexity to the structure of the mode of production.

Already, then, Poulantzas had begun to elaborate the form of political analysis for which he will later gain renown. However, in

'Towards a Marxist Theory' (Chapter 5), he confronts directly and critically the philosophical source of his new insights: Althusser. Poulantzas later spoke of his 'agreement and disagreement, from the beginning, with Althusser'.[11] Here, he sets out to clarify the advance Althusser made in his attack on the Hegelian concept of 'totality' and his alternative conceptualization of structural causality. He lists as the most important consequences of Althusser's enterprise: the restoration to theory of its scientific status; the effort to account for economic determination only in the last instance; and the complex variations in socio-economic and political development this account helps illuminate. Yet Poulantzas finds Althusser's work insufficiently clear in its account of the relationship between structure and history, unable to reconcile the claim to economic determination in the last instance whilst permitting variation in the dominance of the economic level. He warns of the danger of functionalism in Althusser and points to his confused conceptualization of the political level, suggesting that even Althusser might tend towards the historicism he has so vehemently rejected.

Despite these reservations, Althusser's influence remained firm and culminated in the 1968 publication of Poulantzas's book, *Pouvoir politique et classes sociales* (*Political Power and Social Classes*).[12] Although not published in the book series edited by Althusser (who is reputed to have objected to its Gramscian – purportedly 'historicist' – leanings),[13] *Political Power* took his project as the inspiration to an ambitious study which, in its introduction, declared as its object the political 'region' in a 'capitalist mode of production'. What followed was a bold, comprehensive theoretical reconstruction of the role and function of the capitalist state, drawing upon and, in Poulantzas's words, 'completing' the texts of the 'Marxist classics', and underlining the errors of historicist forms of Marxist analysis which tend either to reductive and/or 'over-politicized' interpretations of class politics.[14]

The essential starting point of Poulantzas's reconstruction was the formal separation of the political from the economic sphere, which established the relative autonomy of the state and the function allocated to it of securing social cohesion. As the 'point of condensation' between various class contradictions, the state was regarded as structurally positioned to secure the interests of the dominant class by virtue, not of the interests of its immediate 'occupants', but of its capacity to articulate various class demands at once. Poulantzas also developed an account of the nature of social classes, again rejecting their reduction to self-aware subjects emanating from 'pure' economic structures. Instead, classes represented 'effects' of mutually limiting economic, political and ideological structures; constituted through conflicting 'practices' which lead to their dissolution and fusion into various form of class fractions, groups and other categories.[15] Thus, Poulantzas insisted, 'political struggle' – the struggle to unify these groupings through the competition for state power – 'is the *over-determining* level of the class struggle'.[16]

These arguments concerning the relative autonomy of the political level permitted Poulantzas to examine numerous features of the capitalist 'type' of state, to note its different periodizations and regimes, the varying forms of hegemonic 'power-bloc' uniting the dominant classes, the roles played by 'state apparatuses' and a legitimating ideology in relation to this bloc, and the status of a ruling élite and bureaucracy. *Political Power* was a kind of Marxist encyclopaedia of political analysis, building extensively on the work of Gramsci and elucidating a range of variable components and conditions within the parameters set by the capitalist mode of production. Although Poulantzas would retreat from the structuralism that inspired it, in later writings he repeatedly referred readers to the analyses originally developed there.

The Debate with Miliband

Political Power presented an overwhelmingly theoretical account of a Marxist approach to politics and the state, and Poulantzas himself later admitted its tendential 'theoreticism' and relative lack of concrete, empirical analysis. At stake for Poulantzas, however, was the question of an autonomous Marxist theory of politics, one, he believed, could escape the narrow horizons of bourgeois political science and provide a vital, objective foundation to revolutionary strategy. His strong commitment to developing this theory therefore explains, to some extent, his part in the celebrated 'debate' in *New Left Review* with the UK-based Marxist, and editor of *Socialist Register*, Ralph Miliband. That encounter – which later involved the Argentinean political theorist, Ernesto Laclau, also based in the UK – has served as an exemplary marker of the differences between 'Continental' and British Marxism. Arguably, however, it provided only a snapshot – and perhaps a crude one at that – of Poulantzas's concerns.

The debate began in 1969 with a review by Poulantzas of Miliband's book, *The State in Capitalist Society*, at the time a refreshingly clear dismissal of post-war Anglo-American political science, whose analyses of government and politics were criticized for endorsing a

mistaken, liberal view of the state as a 'neutral' umpire to the freely
articulated demands of a pluralist society.[17] Miliband's book was
replete with empirical detail and drew widely upon Marxist classics to
make the case that, far from being neutral, in capitalist society the
realms of the state and politics were deeply pervaded by the interests of
the dominant class.

Fresh from publishing his own book, in 'The Problem of the
Capitalist State' (Chapter 7) Poulantzas took issue with Miliband's
'procedure' which, in his view, too easily accepted the terms of
bourgeois epistemology. This led Miliband simply to invert the claims
of political scientists rather than challenge their theoretical basis. For
Poulantzas, Miliband's critique reduced to an exposé of the empirical
presence of class interests among élites. That, however, was to treat
political power as a matter of inter-personal linkages, that is, as
'subjective' rather than objectively structured relations. Bereft of an
independent and distinctively Marxist analysis of the mode of production, Miliband was compelled, sometimes erroneously, to attribute
interests to the motivations of state personnel which led, effectively, to
an instrumentalist conception according to which the state, essentially
neutral as regards class interests, was 'taken over'.

In a now-familiar line of argument, according to Poulantzas there
was no necessity for class interests and the functions of the state
always to coincide. The state served class interests by virtue of its
function as the 'factor of cohesion'. That there might be such a
coincidence is a consequence of variations among classes distributed
in relations of production, and of the outcome of ongoing class
struggles. The state was, therefore, capitalist from the start, and
not, as Miliband apparently implied, an institution inserted into
'capitalist society'.

Miliband responded twice to Poulantzas's charges. The first, brief
reply followed in the subsequent issue of New Left Review (January–
February, 1970), whilst the second, slightly expanded response came
later, in 1973, in the form of a review article of the English translation
of Political Power and Social Classes.[18] In the first, Miliband set out a
brief defence of his work against the criticism that he had neglected a
properly Marxist class analysis by employing an empirical mode of
enquiry. He attacked what he saw as the functionalism of Poulantzas's
alternative approach, that is, its tendency to abstraction without
'empirical validation' and what he coined 'structural super-determinism' where 'what the state does is in every particular and at all times
wholly determined by these "objective relations"'.[19] For Poulantzas,
he argued, 'the state élite is . . . totally imprisoned in objective

structures' and thus 'it follows that there is *really* no difference between a state ruled, say, by bourgeois constitutionalists, whether conservative or social democrat, and one ruled by, say, Fascists'.[20] Furthermore, Miliband accused Poulantzas of blurring the boundaries between the state and the wider society by including as 'ideological state apparatuses' institutions entirely outside the command structure of the state.

In the second response, Miliband repeated these critical themes, but now underscored what he regarded as the relentlessly obscure 'linguistic code' of *Political Power* and the tendency of its author to avoid concrete analysis. Developing his earlier thesis, Miliband identified Poulantzas's fundamental weakness in his 'structural abstractionism': the tendency to be concerned with abstract levels and structures that 'cuts him off' from the possibility of examining actual historical conjunctures and forms of state.[21] In particular, Poulantzas was unable to clarify what was distinctive about such features of the bourgeois state as its 'separation of powers' or the role of political parties. Indeed, for all his criticism of economism, claimed Miliband, Poulantzas had effectively presented his own instrumentalist account of the state. By failing to discriminate between class power and state power, the state was in effect permanently functioning in the interests of the dominant class.[22] Surely this was simply to presuppose the very relationship between classes and the state that Poulantzas needed to explain?

Finally, returning to a point already noted in his first reply, Miliband disputed Poulantzas's appeal to Marx and Engels as support for his approach. Here, Poulantzas was said to be guilty of over-generalizing their account of Bonapartism as a form of state in which the 'general interest' has separated off from any specific class interest. There was little evidence, claimed Miliband, either that Marx and Engels believed this form to be constitutive of the bourgeois state as such, as Poulantzas had claimed, or that such a form is found in historical reality in anything other than exceptional circumstances.[23] On the contrary, Miliband suggested, there was much to be discerned in analyzing the empirical differences among various forms of state.

Laclau's contribution took as its object the Miliband-Poulantzas debate itself and the epistemological positions adopted by each author.[24] More sympathetic to Poulantzas's enterprise, Laclau defended the critique of empiricism in so far as Miliband had failed adequately to set out the terms of his own analysis, suggesting that the adequacy of a theory can be ascertained by the degree to which it meets the 'facts'. Poulantzas's Althusserian epistemology was, undoubtedly, 'radically different' to that presumed by Miliband.[25] Here, facts are produced by theory and the validity of theory therefore depends not on its adequacy with 'real objects' but, rather, on its internal consistency. That is, the theoretical contradictions posed by concrete problems had to be resolved on the terrain of theory, something Miliband had failed to do by assuming that facts speak for themselves.

Nevertheless, Laclau argued, Poulantzas's argument in *Political Power* remained unsatisfactory and Miliband's criticisms, especially his charge of 'structural abstractionism', still had considerable bite. Poulantzas's problem was not, however, his lack of attention to empirical variations but his failure to 'demonstrate the internal contradictions of the problematics which he rejects'.[26] Instead, argued Laclau, Poulantzas restricted himself merely to describing differences, castigating 'historicist' and 'humanist' orientations without accounting for their weaknesses. This failure to engage his opponents revealed the absence of 'a dialectical conception of the process of knowledge' and a tendency to treat theoretical problematics as 'closed universes'.[27]

In Laclau's view, Poulantzas's analyses exemplified a 'formalism', that is, a tendency to invoke concepts with predominantly 'symbolic' rather than logical functions, describing a unified content rather than explaining it: 'his attitude when faced with a complex reality is to react with taxonomic fury'.[28] Behind this formalism Laclau detected a more fundamental 'theoretical attitude', traceable to structuralist ideas concerning a determining 'mode of production'. Pitched at an improbable degree of abstraction, these ideas functioned primarily as metaphors without theoretical content: 'At this altitude we are now in the realm of complete mythology, in an abstract world of structures and levels in which it becomes impossible to establish logical relations between the concepts'.[29] Without properly interrogating the concept of the mode of production, Poulantzas merely restated it and, as a consequence, was unable to theorize the process of historical change. To this extent, Miliband's accusation of structuralist abstraction remained fair.

Poulantzas made a final reply to both Miliband and Laclau in his *New Left Review* article of 1975 (see Chapter 11). Six years on from his initial review, he was eager to register the developments in his own research and dispel what had become a popular image of the debate as a crude confrontation between structuralist and instrumentalist Marxisms. With the splintering of Althusserianism in France and further afield, it was also an opportunity to take stock and mark out some important differences in his approach. Poulantzas's 'Reply' to Miliband and Laclau stands, therefore, both as a partial *mea culpa* as regards his earlier work and also as a review of the new, more nuanced directions his theoretical work had begun to take since the publication of *Political Power*.

In restating his criticism of Miliband's empiricism, Poulantzas is nevertheless prepared to accept Laclau's interpretation of the excessive formalism of his early work but defends the general thrust of his argument that the state must be understood fundamentally in terms of the essential separation of economic and political realms. If, as he admitted, his theoreticism led to certain misleading statements, his purpose had never been to subsume all reality within the abstraction of a mode of production. This error had been rectified in his later work on fascism and his analyses of classes (examined below) which explored important variations in the form of the state and which placed class struggle rather than the mode of production at its centre.

Poulantzas now underscores the distinction between the mode of production and a specific, concrete 'social formation' in which the contingencies of history play out. The structuralist error, he argues, alluding primarily to the contribution of Balibar, was to have read all determinations from a static and ahistorical concept of the mode of production and its distinct levels, something he had always sought to avoid, if only with partial success. In fact, he asserts, 'I have attempted to break definitively with structuralism'[30] by embedding the division between the economic and the political in conflictual class relations rather than an abstract structure. As such, the state's role as a 'factor of cohesion' never sits outside class 'practices' as some autonomous subject-like entity with a will of its own but was 'the condensate of a relation of power between struggling classes'.

The weakening of an overt structuralist presence in Poulantzas's work, his effort to capture the variations in the forms of state by reference to changing relations of production and class struggle, and the conceptualization of the state as a relation whose form was inseparable from the political and ideological dimensions of struggle, these were all hallmarks of his 'mature' theory. The debate with Miliband had eventually brought to the surface these aspects, even if it had never itself adequately conveyed the breadth and potential within Poulantzas's enterprise.

Fascism and Political Class Analysis

In 1970 Poulantzas published his study on what he called the 'exceptional' form of capitalist state, *Fascisme et dictature: la troisième internationale face au fascisme* (*Fascism and Dictatorship*).[31] A com-

prehensive synthesis of recent research on the nature of German and
Italian fascisms, the book was at once an examination of a concrete
form of state and an original, theoretical critique of Marxist approaches to fascism, principally those of the Communist International
(or 'Comintern') in the 1920s and 30s, which still remained influential
on the left.

Much of *Fascism and Dictatorship* was devoted to a thematic
inventory of the class relations that, argued Poulantzas, were the
primary determinant in explaining the conjunctures during which
fascism arose. In opposition to a simple class reductionism, which
usually overstated the linkage between fascism and the dominant
classes, Poulantzas fleshed out his claim that fascism produced a
distinctive form of state based on peculiar conditions of political
crisis during the transition to monopoly capitalism. Understood that
way, Poulantzas discriminated between the different phases of struggle
that gave fascism its opportunity to intervene, the role of the fascist
state in reorganizing the power-bloc of dominant classes through both
repression and ideology, and the different routes both Italian and
German fascisms took in securing the dominance of big capital
through the revolt of the petty-bourgeoisie.

Fascism and Dictatorship was a lengthy redescription of the rise of
fascism; not a narrative history but a summary and interpretation of
recent sociological research. Dedicated to surveying a specific historical conjuncture, and hence not as overtly theoretical as *Political
Power*, its openly critical view of the Comintern's errors (that is,
its economistic interpretation of fascism and its consequent failure to
promote a 'mass line' until very late on), as well as its effort to
distinguish fascism from other kinds of exceptional regimes such as
'Bonapartism' or military dictatorships, was nevertheless directed at a
wider Marxist audience for whom such errors still remained common-
place. Poulantzas's analysis provided a sophisticated apparatus of
concepts to unravel the complexity of class politics in the phenomenon
of fascism but also, more generally, to enable a detailed periodization
of political conjunctures. It also began the work of distinguishing his
sociological approach from the theoretical positions of Althusser.[32]

Examples of this effort to inject greater nuance into understanding
class ideological and political relations, specifically in connection with
exceptional regimes, can be found in Chapters 6 and 10, both of which
demonstrate the type of class analysis developed at greater length in
Fascism and Dictatorship. In 'The Political Forms of the Military
Coup d'État', published in 1967 directly following the Greek military
coup, Poulantzas asks whether the coup is accurately understood as

being fascist. Whilst his analysis is clearly provisional, he argues in the negative because of the absence of popular support channelled through a fascist party. In 'On the Popular Impact of Fascism' of 1976, by contrast, he sketches a response to what he sees as the frequent misunderstanding of the nature of fascism's popular appeal, common amongst those who looked exclusively to its ideological features and hence disregarded its differential impact upon social classes. Uppermost in his approach was an effort to unravel the diverse relationships – ideological, political and economic – with fascism among various classes both within the dominant power bloc as well as among the dominated classes who took the brunt of fascist repression.

Poulantzas's analyses of exceptional regimes permitted him to expand on the theoretical claims laid down in *Political Power*. In particular, they underscored his view of the continual presence of class ideological and political struggles over the state's function to secure social cohesion, struggles that constantly permeated the state apparatuses, which were therefore never guaranteed success. This view challenged the 'structural-functionalist' interpretation of Poulantzas's approach. Rather than subsume the capitalist state under a conception of its generic function – thereby misperceiving important variations (Miliband's criticism) – Poulantzas sought to differentiate the forms the state took under capitalist relations of production as it was configured under diverse conditions of class struggle. This focus on the internal class contradictions and compromises laid bare in exceptional regimes was also central to his book-length essay on the military dictatorships in Portugal, Greece and Spain, *La Crise des dictatures* (*The Crisis of the Dictatorships*) of 1975.[33]

If his analysis had taken a historical direction in *Fascism and Dictatorship*, Poulantzas's next book turned to the question of class relations and political power in contemporary conditions. *Les Classes sociales dans le capitalisme aujourd'hui* (*Classes in Contemporary Capitalism*) was published in 1974 and brought Poulantzas into another series of critical engagements with other Marxists.[34] Versions of the pieces contained in that book are published here as Chapters 8 ('On Social Classes', which was revised as part of the book's Introduction) and 9 ('Internationalization of Capitalist Relations and the Nation-State', which became 'Part One' of the book). Issues rising from the book were also taken up in a published conference paper, 'The New Petty Bourgeoisie', reproduced here as Chapter 13.

In 'On Social Classes' Poulantzas sketches a theoretical overview of his approach to social classes, conceived not merely as locations within economic relations of production but also in terms of their distinctive ideological and political relations, too. He criticizes 'economistic' approaches to class which define it narrowly by technical criteria. A properly 'objective' understanding of the 'structural determination' of class, he argues, must acknowledge the ideological and political relations that determine classes and also, perhaps fundamentally, the importance of class struggle, for 'classes have existence only in the class struggle'. Yet, Poulantzas also insists that, in defining class, 'an economic criterion remains determinant'.

This confusing layering of theses is designed to paint a composite picture of classes at different levels of abstraction and in different moments of their constitution but, inevitably, it results in a lack of clarity when trying to conceive the relation between classes in the abstract as 'objective' coordinates and classes as political agents in specific conjunctures. It is not always certain which dimension of social class Poulantzas wishes to emphasize. For instance, he talks of the 'contradictory' position of technicians and engineers who, in a technical sense, contribute to the production of surplus-value, but who may also align ideologically and politically with the bourgeoisie in so far as they exert authority over the labour process. And yet, even if they did align with the working class, claims Poulantzas, strictly speaking (that is, in narrowly economic terms) 'they are not workers'.

The problems of defining classes had, of course, an explicitly strategic dimension: exactly which other classes could join the proletariat in a popular alliance? In his paper on 'The Petty Bourgeoisie', Poulantzas turns directly to this question by way of a defence of his arguments in *Classes*. There he had devoted space to a discussion of the emergence of a new form of petty bourgeoisie, or 'salaried non-productive workers'.[35] But, in arguing that the new petty bourgeoisie constituted a distinct class – albeit one that lacks specific class interests and hence may, in certain instances, align politically with the working class – Poulantzas was accused of holding to a narrow, economistic definition. If class-definition turned, fundamentally, on the role played in *producing* surplus-value (as opposed to merely 'realizing' it at later moments, or suffering exploitation in other, non-productive functions), then the working class, it could be argued, counted for a surprisingly small sector of industrial economies. Poulantzas defends his argument by insisting on the importance of ideological and political factors in the wider con-stitution of classes, factors which override any abstract definition of class based exclusively on economic criteria. Again, his composite view sought to grasp both the minimal, 'economic' definition but also expand upon this with an awareness of the nuances of ideology and politics which could not be collapsed into the economic.

The wider context of Poulantzas's essays on classes is set out in 'Internationalization of Capitalist Relations and the Nation-State' where he examines the changes in international relations of production and their impact on the post-war nation-state. These changes are understood in terms of an 'imperialist' expansion of American monopoly capital throughout the world, but specifically to European states. Contesting other Marxist interpretations (such as those of Ernest Mandel and the French Communist Party), Poulantzas argues that the importation of American capital has created a new type 'interior bourgeoisie' that is neither simply internal nor external to the national capitalism in Europe but has its own national base alongside complex links and dependencies with American capital. By consequence, the expansion of American capital cannot be assumed to overwhelm the functions of the national state so much as impose upon it new responsibilities based around the 'interiorization' of this new fraction of imperialist capital.

In comments that precede but substantially prefigure later debates over the role of the state under conditions of 'globalization', Poulantzas notes that, although the transformations brought by greater internationalization of capital disrupt the unity of the nation-state (witnessed in the emergence of regionalist and nationalist political movements) and bring a greater role for co-ordination among states (via the European Economic Community: now the European Union, or EU), the economic, political and ideological functions of the nation-state nevertheless remain central. Drawing out the consequences of this situation for revolutionary politics, he warns against Communist Parties taking up strategies of national liberation by allying with a so-called 'national bourgeoisie'.

State Crisis and Democratic Socialism

The theme of state crisis and its implications for radical socialist strategy dominated Poulantzas's work from the mid-1970s. In Chapter 12, 'The Political Crisis and the Crisis of the State', he reflects directly on the dislocations brought by the internationalization of monopoly capitalism and set out an agenda that was developed in more detail in L'État, le pouvoir, le socialisme (State, Power, Socialism) of 1978.[36] In this chapter, originally an introduction to a collection of essays on state crisis he edited himself and published in 1976,[37] Poulantzas offers an overview of the complex relationship between economic and political crises, a topic then under wide discussion on the left.[38]

Setting aside reductionist or 'teleological' concepts of crisis that 'dissolve' the specificity of the current situation, Poulantzas argues for a nuanced view of the linkages between the economic crisis brought by changes in monopoly capitalism and the ruptures they impose on the hegemony of the power-bloc. Maintaining his view of the separation of the economic and political realms, vital to all capitalist states, Poulantzas argues the state must be regarded neither as a neutral instrument to be occupied nor as a subject with its own independent will. As a 'relation' between classes, rather than a self-contained instrument that 'holds' power, the state cannot constitute an 'agency' with homogeneous purpose of its own but, rather, condenses the relations of the classes it seeks to unify. This means that it contains within its own apparatuses the contradictory interests of both dominant and dominated classes. As such, the ongoing crisis of this state entails a series of dislocations among its allied classes, the ideological and political forms that unify them, and the branches where class compromises have crystallized. The direct intervention in the economy by the state, a distinctive feature of monopoly capitalism, ensured that the ongoing internalization of international capital (examined in Chapter 9) is felt even more deeply, at an ideological and political level, as contradictions expand within the state apparatuses.

Poulantzas also touches upon one, key repercussion of the crisis: the emergence of an authoritarian type of state, not merely as a temporary measure but as an enduring form in itself. Among the elements of this new form, he lists: limitations increasingly placed on individual liberties, the displacement of parliamentary politics in favour of the executive authority, and the overturning of the 'traditional limits' of public and private relations in favour of either violent repression or new forms of social control. Briefly engaging with Foucault's work on surveillance, Poulantzas suggests the diffusion of a new 'micro-physics' of power directed at shaping the 'social body'. Some of his projected repercussions – such as the 'overthrow of the legal' system – may appear somewhat apocalyptic, yet this image of the 'strong state' emerging from the crisis of post-war social-democratic settlements is, on the whole, not so wide off the mark.[39]

In *State, Power, Socialism*, Poulantzas developed these insights into a new, and eloquent, theoretical statement on the capitalist state. Not by any means a systematic or comprehensive work, the book nevertheless demonstrated Poulantzas's significant departure from Althusserianism and his interest in Foucault's 'anti-essentialist' conception of power. Poulantzas wrote of the 'institutional materiality' of the state, that is, the way power is inscribed into, not 'possessed' by, state apparatuses. He took up Foucault's idea of power as a 'positive' phenomenon, with the state productively shaping subjects through the organization of knowledge and the 'individualization' of bodies, rather than by repression alone. He also underscored the diversity of 'discourses' that permeate the fragmented network of state activities.

Yet, if Poulantzas accepted many of Foucault's insights concerning the materiality of power, he remained critical of the latter's failure to acknowledge the 'determining role' of economic relations of production in separating out the state as an independent entity. Nor did he grasp the primacy of class struggles, and hence of class contradictions, in the inscription of state power.[40] Foucault, he argued, 'tends to blot out power by dispersing it among tiny molecular vessels'.[41] His analyses advanced a 'strategic' conception of power but, for Poulantzas, social classes were the central elements of this strategic field. The state, he claimed, possessed no power of its own but, as the 'strategic site of domination of the dominant class', it is 'a *site* and a *centre* of the exercise of power'.[42] Foucault, claimed Poulantzas, missed this class 'basis' to power and could not therefore properly conceive the nature of 'resistances' operative within the state.

In his encounter with Foucault, Poulantzas aimed to return the discussion of power back to a Marxist terrain that was, arguably, incompatible with Foucault's analyses. That did not diminish, however, the originality of Poulantzas's enquiries in *State, Power, Socialism*, which also contained discussions of the 'spatial matrix' of the nation and a further elaboration of 'authoritarian statism'. If his fundamental points of reference remained classically Marxist, it is clear nevertheless that Poulantzas was still looking beyond the parameters of that tradition. His posthumously published 'Research Note on the State and Society' (Chapter 18) gives some indication of the questions that for him remained to be asked in a period of state crisis and socio-economic transformation.

Poulantzas's comments on the crisis of the state and the class alliances that underpinned it were inseparable from his views on political strategy. A member since the early 1960s of the Greek Communist Party, he aligned with the anti-Stalinist, so-called 'Party of the Interior' when it formally split in 1968. Poulantzas was a left-wing critic of Soviet policy, as *Fascism and Dictatorship* demonstrated from an historical perspective, and, from the late 1960s, he was keen to highlight the potential for democratic alliances in the face of authoritarian regimes. This was so especially in relation to Greece during the dictatorship of 1967-74, but also in France during the crises of the 1970s. Poulantzas therefore abandoned his early orthodox Leninism, with its dismissal of 'illusory' bourgeois-parliamentary freedoms in favour of a dictatorship of the proletariat, for a more pluralist position which acknowledged the importance of popular and class struggles in and through the state.[43] His writings of the 1970s were persistently critical of the policies of the French Communist Party and the theory of 'state monopoly capitalism' in so far as these failed to acknowledge the contradictions inside the state itself. Poulantzas supported an inclusive strategy of left unity in Greece as well as France and underscored the need for parliamentary democratic institutions in the transition to socialism.

Issues of strategy and democratic representation are central to the interview with Henri Weber of 1977, 'The State and the Transition to Socialism' (Chapter 14). Weber, then a Trotskyist sympathetic to a strategy of left unity, takes issue with Poulantzas on how a revolutionary socialist strategy ought to negotiate a transition from capitalism. For Poulantzas, it is improbable, given the extent to which class contradictions and struggles permeate the state, for socialists to effectively organize an oppositional alliance wholly external to it. In that respect, the Bolshevik model of revolutionary assault and the development of alternative institutional forms (the question of 'dual power') no longer apply. It is necessary, he argues against Weber, to struggle both inside and outside the terrain of the state, simultaneously seeking to democratize it from within *and* to develop alternative apparatuses to replace it.

Poulantzas also contests Weber's view of the centrality of direct democracy to socialist struggle. Whilst in principle an advocate of socialist self-management, Poulantzas nevertheless affirms the need to retain parliamentary forms of representation, to guarantee certain civil liberties and to uphold party democracy. These issues, famously debated in Italy in the 1970s between the radical left and Norberto Bobbio,[44] reflect Poulantzas's concern to avoid the degeneration of socialist democracy either into workerist corporatism or party centralism. For him, a socialist democracy must maintain 'pluralism and liberties' whilst, simultaneously, radically transforming the state in a socialist direction.

Similar issues are taken up in Chapter 15, 'Towards a Democratic Socialism', which also supplied the final chapter to *State, Power, Socialism*. 'Socialism will be democratic', argues Poulantzas, 'or it will not be at all'. Here, again, he takes issue with an anti-democratic tendency of the Bolshevik tradition from Lenin through to Stalin. Like social democracy, he claims, that tradition distrusts popular initiatives and rank-and-file democracy; both preferring 'state-worship' in the form of rule by an enlightened élite. Yet, he continues, it is also necessary to avoid the illusion of directly counterposing to this statism the ideal of the workers' 'self-management'. 'Today less than ever is the state an ivory tower isolated from the popular masses. Their struggles constantly traverse the state, even when they are not physically present in its apparatuses.'[45]

If it is to avoid its own tendency to authoritarian statism, democratic socialism must be a long process of transforming the state from within and without, not an 'occupation' or a 'seizure' of power dedicated to replacing wholesale the apparatuses of parliamentary representation.

Poulantzas aligned himself with the 'Eurocommunist' strategy of the Spanish and Italian Communist parties, which accepted the need for a parliamentary rather than insurrectionary road to power. As his interview in *Marxism Today* of 1979 (Chapter 17) indicates, he saw himself on the left of this orientation, insisting on the importance of rank-and-file democracy and the radical transformation of – and hence a 'moment of rupture' in – the state apparatuses. However, he also acknowledges that having abandoned the idea of a 'sudden clash' with the state, 'the distinction between reformism and the revolutionary road becomes much more difficult to grasp, even if nevertheless it continues to exist'.[46]

If these remarks on strategy seem defensive or imbued with a hefty dose of realism, it is because, like other Marxist intellectuals, Poulantzas was increasingly conscious of the decline in the radical left's fortunes both in Europe and internationally. A loss of momentum – signalled, for example, in the disappointments of the Italian Communists' co-operation with the governments of 'national unity' and the electoral defeat of the Socialists in France – was also registered in the resurgence of anti-Marxist polemic in Europe, particularly the work of the *nouveaux philosophes* such as André Glucksmann or Bernard-Henri Lévy, which associated Marxism with the Gulag and Soviet repression.

In Chapter 16, 'Is There a Crisis in Marxism?', Poulantzas seeks to defend Marxism from its critics, whilst conceding its vulnerability on certain grounds. If there is a crisis in Marxism, he argues, it is primarily a crisis in the dogmatic Marxism-Leninism of the Soviet Union, around which an intellectual 'counter-attack' has formed. Poulantzas regards this attack as part of a resurgence of the dominant ideology following recent defeats of the working class, a neo-liberal ideology which lends itself to authoritarianism and irrationalism. To advance, however, it is necessary to cultivate an 'undogmatic and

creative' Marxism, one assured of its own object (the class struggle)
and yet prepared to engage other disciplines with a view to the
generation of new concepts and the abandonment of the old. Among
the areas he regards as in need of development along Marxist lines, he
notes the concept of ideology, a theory of justice and rights, and an
approach to nationalism.

Poulantzas leapt to his death from a tower bloc in Paris on 3 October
1979. This sudden and violent end to his life was met with shock and
incomprehension by those who had followed his career. Later, however, Althusser would speak of a previous suicide attempt, suggesting
deeper currents to Poulantzas's personal difficulties.[47] In the years that
immediately followed, there was certainly recognition for his contribution to Marxist political theory[48] but, for a thinker whose
originality was, in part, propelled by his engagement with others,
his profile inevitably diminished, even if his concepts and his concerns
continued to resonate in the analyses of the radical left.[49]

In the writings collected here there are, undoubtedly, many flaws.
Poulantzas was attached to a Marxist class analysis that, for all his
efforts to insert various nuances, could not throw off the accusation of
economism. His approach to ideology and to non-class social movements remained, as a consequence, deeply problematic.[50] For those not
interested in resurrecting debates concerning the epistemological
'primacy' of economic relations of production in the 'determination'
of society, these aspects of his work will seem profoundly dated. Yet,
as recent efforts to re-engage the legacy of Poulantzas demonstrate, his
analyses of the capitalist state and its evolving form retain a value that
exceeds their original formulation.[51] Poulantzas denied there could be
a 'general theory' of the state, either in Marxism or elsewhere, only a
theory in relation to specific modes of production and their different
stages of development. As a consequence, there is no 'last word' on the
capitalist state, only a constant requirement to develop analyses
adequate to its perpetual 'metamorphoses'. In this respect, Poulantzas
has bequeathed a uniquely open-ended legacy for political theory and
practice.

1

MARXIST EXAMINATION OF THE CONTEMPORARY STATE AND LAW AND THE QUESTION OF THE 'ALTERNATIVE'

If, in the highly industrialized Western societies, the problem of the transition to socialism, of reform or revolution, is also posed in terms of the political level of the state, law and institutions, then a Marxist examination of that level is of major significance. As with any study of the superstructures, the important thing here is the *specificity* of the juridical and state superstructure.

However, we must beware: analysis should not start out by considering the beautiful, the just and the good and their relations with the base. Their specificity *as such*, far from being pre-given as a transcendental category or as eidetic, can only be revealed to us in the course, or at the end, of the theoretical-practical process of knowledge. When they involve the superstructures, as in the case of art, law and the state, or morality, the most universal-concrete, general-particular – in short, simple-complex – concepts cannot be directly referred to the base: they can only be captured by preliminary research into their *historical* relations with the base. What analysis can set out from is, on the one hand, the specificity of the superstructure in general and its fundamental dialectical division – for it refers to a historically determinant division – from the base; and, on the other, the specificity of a *certain* law or state, a *certain* art, a *certain* morality, situated in time and space. And yet, the problem of definition is essential when it

* First published in French as 'L'examen marxiste de l'État et du droit actuels et la question de l'alternative', in *Les Temps Modernes*, no. 219–20 (1964), pp. 274–302. Translated by Gregory Elliott.

comes to the level of law and the state. In the transition from socialism
to communism, the other domains of the superstructure – art,
morality, philosophy, the humanism of religion – will be gradually
stripped of their ideological phenomenality and enter into a new
process of relations with the base, becoming ever more closely
integrated into the fundamental level of history. By contrast, law
and the state will wither away. This will involve not some process of
their translation into a world, of their death-rebirth, negation-realiza-
tion, but precisely their 'extinction' in the strong sense of the term: in
what sense, to what extent, and from what moment onwards, will it be
impossible to *define* their residue – for as long as a residue persists – as
law and state?

But here we are concerned with an essay in Marxist analysis of the
contemporary law and state in industrialized Western societies. And,
to revert to the methodological problems indicated above, we note in
Marxist authors two main tendencies as regards conceptions of the
juridical and state level as part of the superstructure.[1] One, represented by Reisner and Vyshinsky, regards law as a *set of norms*
decreed by the state, and geared towards the exploitation of the classes
oppressed by the dominant class, whose state represents volition-
power. The other, represented by Stuchka and Pashukanis, regards
law as a *system or order of social relations* ratified by the state; for the
former, these correspond to the interests of the dominant class, while
for the latter, they correspond, more especially, to the relations
between commodity owners. Neither of these tendencies would appear
to have succeeded in capturing the precise meaning of the fact that the
juridical and state level pertains to the superstructure.

The first tendency restricts itself to a descriptive emphasis on the
superstructural character of law and the state, as a conceptual
ensemble of behavioural norms and rules. Having correctly registered
this basic characteristic of law and the state, Reisner and Vyshinsky
regarded juridical-state norms as data-facts and, in a sense, 'confined'
them between brackets as 'normative objects', thus separating them
from the concrete values they express. In fact, any sphere of norms, of
practical commands, *presupposes* a crystallization – whether explicit
or not in this sphere – of the values according to which the normative
hierarchy is structured. The distinctive characteristic of those superstructural domains that comprise a normative ensemble – morality,
religion, law and the state, even art (albeit in a different sense) –
precisely consists in the fact they express what should be socially.
These domains are thus *genetically structured*, and must be methodologically grasped, according to the concrete historical values,

themselves engendered from the base, that they embody. In other words, the *condition of existence* of a rule or institution at the juridical-state level consists in the historical values that it specifies juridically, in as much as these values have, in a given historical context, taken on the *distinctive mode* of expression that is the juridical domain. The very notions of juridical rule, norm or institution, as historical realities and objects of analysis, are only captured genetically and are therefore only operative to the extent that they are given concrete expression axiologically. To do that, it is not sufficient, in the manner of Reisner and Vyshsinsky, to place these norms in a direct, external relationship, as *already* structured objects, with the class struggle, restricting their axiological content to their de facto character as 'norms-geared-towards-the-exploitation-of-the-oppressed-classes'. Exploitation there certainly is; but through the mediation of what concrete values? For example, how do the present-day values of equality and liberty – which, *as values*, precisely make the state appear to be a 'higher order' reconciling different interests – operate as *forces* of exploitation? And in what sense does such exploitation, by virtue *also* of these values, assume a *particular* character?

The need for genetic reference to the structuring factors represented by the concrete historical values expressed in them was stressed by Marx in connection with law and the state. When Marx says that '[t]he state is the form in which the individuals of a ruling class render their common interests *geltend*',[2] the term *geltend*, in German and in juridical and political science, has a dual meaning: it signifies both *effective* and *valid* – effective because, and as such, valid. The validity of a complex of norms, which is distinct from sheer effectiveness conceived as a direct power relationship, precisely consists in the relationship between these norms and the values they crystallize. Their effectivity as law and state consists in a power relationship mediated by certain historical values.

Furthermore, Reisner and Vyshinsky's conception does not make it possible to define the dialectical relations between the juridical-state sphere and the economic base concretely. Establishing an external, direct relationship, in the indicated sense, between law and the state and class struggle, which (let us not forget) is situated on the level of social relations of production – not on the economic level of forces and modes of production – this conception shuts off access to the economic level. It is not a question of simply observing that law and the state embody the volition of the class in power, but of understanding why and how a *certain* mode of production, generating a *particular* class struggle, is crystallized in *these* legal norms and state forms, not others. To establish an external, direct relationship between a domain of the superstructure and the class struggle is, in fact, to neglect the *specificity* of this domain at a moment in history – a specificity that is itself related to the historical values crystallized by this domain. *By the same token*, it is to exclude the possibilities of transition, generating meaning for this domain and with regard to it, of class struggle at the economic level: a transition that can only be effected *for this domain* through the mediation of the values engendered *on the basis* of the forces and modes of production. The relationship between the normative systems of the superstructure that pertain to what should be socially and the infrastructure, while including that of signifier to signified or of language to reality, *is determinant and significant as a relationship between what should be and what is, value and fact* – these terms being conceived not in their essential idealist irreducibility, but in their relationship of dialectical totality. The process of genesis of historical values represents the mediator between the economic base and these superstructures, for the base, *also* understood as 'practice', as needs and objectifications that are structured – within the relationship between the dialectic in nature and the dialectic in history that is *praxis* – in the mode of production, already involves an outline of what is possible and legitimate, a creation of values. This makes possible the axiological dialectical transition, within a totalization-*praxis*, from the economy to the class struggle and thence to normative systems.

Stuchka and Pashukanis, who regard law and the state as an *order or system of social relations*, mainly corresponding (for Pashukanis) to the relations between commodity owners, are situated at a quite different level. At first sight, their conception seems to make it possible to establish the relationship between the juridical-state level and the economic base. In fact, however, in accordance with a simplistic economism, they *reduce* law and the state to the base. They disregard their specific character as a coherent system of norms and thus completely ignore their relative autonomy.

Now, it must be acknowledged that this reduction is much more tempting when it comes to examining the juridical-state level than in the case of the other superstructural domains. Given that social classes are basically defined according to their position with respect to *ownership* of the means of production, law and the state, which *inter alia* ratify a particular mode of property, might appear to be situated directly at the level of the relations of production, of class struggle over this property. Pashukanis's view can be explained by the miscomprehension of the relationship between base and superstructure that persisted in Marxist thought for a long time, notwithstanding Marx and Engels; but also by the suspicion which this author – in touch with the Western thought of his time – harboured towards the very notion of superstructure. As is well known, especially between 1900 and 1920 Kantian neo-criticism had attempted with Vorländer – refuted by Max Adler – and, in the theory of law and the state, with Stammler – refuted (less paradoxically than it might seem) by Max Weber – to appropriate the base/superstructure schema-reality. The superstructure was envisaged as the transcendental form, the rational, ideal and necessary structuration of a 'material', real base-content, essentially distinct from it, and subject to the laws of mechanical causality. The indifference of the form to the content, introduced by Kant at the theoretical level, but which he had sought to cancel at the practical level – by deducing the *very content* of moral and juridical rules from their a priori, categorical form (an endeavour criticized by Hegel) – was immediately transposed by Kant's exegetes, who were sensitive to this criticism, to the level of practice: 'Natural law – ideal form of law and the state – with variable content', as their preferred formula had it. To reduce law and the state to the relations of production seemed to Marxist theory the only way of subtracting ownership of the means of production from some sphere of *ideal* transcendence, by demonstrating its genetic relationship with the *reality* of class struggle, and of preserving the *real* character of this struggle.

What ensued in the Marxist science of the state political level was an identification of the superstructure with the *ideal* and of the base with the *real*, which, formulated on the basis of the Kantian problematic, truncates the very question. It persisted despite the rediscovery of Hegel's thought. In fact, here it would be appropriate to return to the latter and to the famous key phrase in his philosophy of right: 'what is real is logical, what is logical is real'. Marx's monism of contradiction cannot be regarded as 'analogous' to Hegel's monism of identification, now based not on the logical-*ideal* but on the *real*. This would in fact be to pose the problem on idealist bases. Conceiving his monism on the basis of the terms 'logical' and 'real', Hegel grounds it in the primacy of the concept-idea (logic). It is true that, for Hegel, every economic and sociological datum *in principle* – as an objectification of the concept – remains *real*, the primacy of the concept being a primacy between *two* distinct, dialectically totalized terms. However, by means of the dialectical and *historical* intervention of the relationship of totality between subject and object of history, the concept-subject of this history, in unveiling what it *already* was at the outset, *ends up* being a self-development of the idea – man-as-subject having access to it 'after the event'. The idea is thereby *identified* with the logical concept and the *real* is therewith phenomenally *reabsorbed* into the *idea*; it is essentially identified with it while being severed from its material residue, which is ignored *historically*. In short, in Hegel there is ultimately no reality; only the idea exists. In this sense, we do not find in Hegel, within this idea-totality (identity), a primacy of the concept over the other domains, which have all become idea-domains. It is inaccurate to say that what corresponds in Hegel to the Marxist superstructure has primacy over what corresponds to the Marxist base.[3] In Hegel, there is no basic level – state, philosophy, religion – that is the motor of history. The motor is the idea-totality in progress, its various *domains* (not *levels*) being situated – identified – on the same dialectically unilinear level. For Marx, in contrast, monism, the 'inversion' of Hegel, is situated – and this is what matters to us here – *within a starting-point* that is at the antipodes of the position at which Hegel *arrives*, in making an absolute idealism of his thought. For Hegel, everything ended up being an idea; for Marx, every social datum is not materiality, but *reality*. However, *within this global reality*, he discovered the *primacy* – hence his monism of contradiction – of the *real-material* (the base) over the *real-ideal* (superstructure). The primacy of materiality, *which led him* to a revolution in the notion of reality, is thus epistemologically possible in Marx. Moreover, even when Marx refers to ideology, and in the pejorative sense, as a phenomenon distorting the base because it no longer corresponds to it, ideology is not thereby unreal: it too is genetically integrated into the – Marxist – totality, in praxis starting out from the base.

Thus, when Marx *emphasizes* the 'real' character of materiality, it is not in order to establish the unreality of the superstructure, but to *underscore, by positioning himself on the terrain of the problematic* of the maxim 'what is real is logical, what is logical is real' – the terrain of the left-Hegelians' critique of Hegel – what radically separates him from Hegel. It is in this accentuation of the reality of the base that the 'polemical' character – *contra* Hegel and his critics – of his language consists, and not (as people are often happy to say) in an allegedly abusive employment of the term 'materialism'. Meanwhile, in his early works, and even in the context of this polemical problematic, Marx already acknowledged the reality of the superstructures and ideologies.[4]

If I stress these remarks, it is because it seems to me essential for a Marxist analysis of the juridical-state level to arrive at a precise conception of the *reality of ideal social phenomena*, of the state sphere of juridical norms – a reality that is not essentialist, but grounded in their division from the base and their historical effectivity. It will then not seem necessary, in order to establish the *reality* of law and the state, to reduce them purely and simply to the *materiality* of the infrastructural levels, regarding them either as direct relations of production, or as mere 'factual' and 'coercive' realities – as if these infrastructural levels were the only ones to attain the dignity of the real, the only ones that could have a historical function that is exercised on them(selves) – in short, as if history progressed exclusively through the infrastructure's self-structuration. Thus, when Marx envisages the juridical and state level as the *ideal* expression of conditions of existence, and not directly as social relations at the level of the relations of production, he simultaneously conceives this level as ideal-axiological (values), as ideal-being (a normative ensemble), and often even as false norms and values, given that they are no longer *adequate* to the base. But he never conceives it as unreal-ideal. It is because this system of norms and values is real (real-ideal) that it can *effectively* influence the real-material levels of the base, through its axiological and normative specificity, and not simply as the brute force of the state. The juridical and state level thus emerges as a *specific* axiological-normative totality geared, by means of state repression, to the exploitation of the oppressed classes by the dominant class.[5]

Marx provided us with the keys to an analysis of the juridical and state superstructure – an analysis whose basic characteristics we have defined above – especially in his examination of modern, capitalist bourgeois society. We need not dwell on the familiar features of this period: the gradual expansion of markets and expanded reproduction of the commodity economy; increased commodity fetishism, whose consequences invade the whole of social existence; a marked replacement of qualitative labour by quantitative labour, with labour itself assuming a commodity form of existence; the autonomization and isolation of individuals, producers and consumers, in a sphere of social relations mediated by things that depreciate into commodities. These socio-economic realities generate a series of juridical realities. In property rights – so-called real rights, or those bearing directly on things, the means of production and commodities – these realities give rise to private property in the modern sense: the *jus utendi, fruendi, abutendi*. Through this private ownership of the means of production by a limited number of individuals, the means of production become capital and the individuals a capitalist class. In the sphere of rights bearing on the obligation on the part of one person to pay another – essentially on the transfer of private property in things – these realities engender modern exchange. We are no longer dealing, as in ancient

Greek law and Roman law, with a source of obligations consisting in
the performance of certain ritual, typical acts; or in the concession by
judges to plaintiffs, according to criteria of equity based on their
immediate needs 'as they stand', of 'shares' that permit them to obtain
a certain provision – according to the Roman adage that 'shares are the
mother of obligation'. Now it is the duly expressed will of the
individual, abstract subject of law, that constitutes the juridical source
of obligation.

Thus we note that, for Marx, it is not a question of establishing an
external relationship between juridical realities and infrastructural
realities, but of relating them through the mediation of the fundamental *reality-value* for law of *individualistic voluntarism*. In the
exchange relationship, the individual will was in fact the potential
common field of '*recognition*' – a Fichtean and Hegelian notion that
Marx renovates by constituting it on the basis of modes and relations
of production – of individuals, producers and consumers, who are
numerous, autonomous and heterogeneous. In the property relationship, this volition was precisely what made possible its privatization,
dictated by infrastructural realities. In fact, it is not possession – the
corporeal and material relation of appropriation of a thing by a subject
– that is established as (private) ownership by law. Only a possession
that is pre-juridically accompanied by a voluntaristic element-value,
by an *animus dominandi*, by an intention to own, can be elevated to
the status of private property.

It is onto this element-value of volition, already apparent in market
societies preceding capitalist society, that the new values of formal,
abstract liberty and equality have been grafted in *modern* law and the
state, on the basis of the infrastructural realities of capitalist society.
They represent so many mediations between the state sphere and the
infrastructure; and Jean-Marie Vincent, presenting Umberto Cerroni's
work in this issue of *Les Temps Modernes*, clarifies the point
admirably. Concrete men, fixed by the juridical sphere – division
between the state and civil society – in their social reification, are
regarded as abstract numerical entities. Their social relations, and the
juridical regulation of these relations, are subject to a reified sphere of
relations between goods, realities, or systems of relations that assume
the form of 'things': between labour and commodities, between labour
and capital, between capital and commodities, between commodity
and commodity. The liberty and equality of these men, phantom
entities, are *abstract* and *formal* in as much as they constitute values
that are *simply postulated as required for the structuration of the
norms* regulating modern private property – absolute: hence liberty

and equality; the exchange-value of a wholly quantified labour – hence equality; the universal circulation and expanded reproduction of commodities – hence liberty and equality; the specific extraction of surplus-value – hence liberty and equality in the work contract; the private accumulation of capital – hence the liberty and equality of capitalists between themselves; and so on and so forth.[6] Postulated in the state sphere, these values, by virtue of their formal, abstract character – division between the state and civil society – and the infrastructural realities that dictate this characteristic – this division – in reality manifest themselves in civil society as their polar opposites.

Thus, Marx and Engels in particular studied the juridical level of modern capitalist society, where the new values of liberty and equality make their 'state' appearance, while noting that these structures make it possible to understand this level in earlier societies. It is not correct to claim that for them modern law and the modern state are identified with law and the state *tout court*, as a *specific* domain of the super-structure; and that, as a result, law and the state 'proper' are the product of capitalist society. Starting out from this society, Marx and Engels in fact discovered a *process* of genetic structuration. Primed by the division of *societies producing for the market* into classes, it led, engendering the structural values of formal, abstract liberty and equality, to the modern juridical-state level. However, this process had already been set in train *by abstract juridical voluntarism* – for example, ancient law and the city-state – in the privatization of property and the universalization of exchange in market societies. And theories of juridical and state voluntarism have long based their conceptions of the state and law precisely on will-as-value, mystifying it and considering it independently of the base, not as a private individual will, but as a 'collective' emanation of the people. Take, for example, the series of theories of the state as social contract, which had their repercussions even in Hegel and the historical school of law. The 'universal' will seemed necessary, *as a value*, to make the state and law appear to be a 'higher order' reconciling various interests. This same process of genetic structuration introduces a *qualitative* turning point in modern societies, in accordance with the new values of liberty and equality.[7]

The material negation in modern society of the values of liberty and equality, which the state and law postulate abstractly and formally, is nevertheless only one aspect of the problem. Marx and Engels did in fact acknowledge a positive side to bourgeois law and the bourgeois state in comparison with those of previous history.[8] How precisely is this to be understood? In fact, the historical infrastructural process, which on the side of the dominant classes engenders the *alienated* values of formal, abstract liberty and equality, presents another – *positive* – aspect on the side of the oppressed classes. This consists in the gradual genesis in these classes, as lack and need, of the ever more concrete and material values of equality and liberty, in the maturation of 'human' demo-cratization as a possibility and imperative. Marx and Engels em-phasized this *aspect* of the historical infrastructural process: through man's progressive mastery of nature by means of technique; through increased labour productivity, which brings out its economic effi-ciency and its essential role in the humanization of nature; through the pronounced division of labour and the universalization of exchange, which discloses the possibility of 'organic' human rela-tions; through the industrial concentration of labourers in the workplace – hence through the 'economic' socialization of the forces and modes of production – in short, through what Marx refers to as the recession of natural relations in favour of social relations, the oppressed man/worker/classes have been able to experience and conceive their generic relations with others. In this way, they have been able gradually to open up the prospect of their communal existence, their 'real' – concrete and material – liberty and equality. The same economic infrastructural realities that in the modern epoch engender the alienated state expression of liberty and equality, hasten the human, democratic positive realization of the oppressed classes. In this sense, the political positivity of the bourgeoisie – for it possesses an economic positivity (technique, etc.) – derives from the fact that, by alienating 'human' values themselves, it makes exploitation *obvious* to proletarians. The positive political element of bourgeois society is the proletariat.[9] As regards the specific domain we are concerned with here, the proletariat: (a) is already the bearer in its economic and sociological conditions of existence of the *positive* ideal-real existence of genuine liberty and equality; (b) endures, in these conditions of existence, the total negation by the bourgeoisie of those values, which, in their bourgeois state form, represent *total* exploitation for the proletariat. Through its universality, functionally articulated at this level with *both these aspects*[10] – not merely (as is often believed) the second – the proletariat will be able to make these values *material* in two senses of the term: by extracting them from their formal and abstract character, while transforming them; and by making them, thus transformed, effective in the material sphere of the base. This process will take two paths: expanding liberty and equality will embrace all men and will relate them in a thoroughgoing way to generic human reality, labour and concrete needs: from each according to his abilities, to each according to his needs.

Examination of the specificity of *present-day* Western societies at the juridical and state level will start out from an analysis of the *particular* character of the modern values of formal, abstract liberty and equality in our time. There is, however, a new structuring factor in this contemporary specificity: *the need for calculability and forecasting*. This no longer represents a mere imperative of 'rationality' in the case of an economy (re)producing for a comparatively large market. It was in this form that Max Weber studied it, regarding it as the framework for a rationalization of law and the state that had been underway since the Roman period – although elsewhere such rationalization was not due exclusively to infrastructural realities, but essentially to the advent of a caste of specialist jurists. Calculation and prediction are currently assuming a *qualitatively* different meaning and importance. In these societies, the operation of justice, legislation and administration must take the form of predictable acts, judgements and decisions, and thus be calculable in advance. This need is itself created by, and manifest in, current infrastructural realities – a society of monopolies and concentration of large capital; the importance of the interests at stake; the accumulation characteristic of this capital; the increased amount of initial investment as a result of technical progress and the need to recover it macro-chronically; the rigidity of fixed capital, machines, and so on – capital which, on account of the high degree of its technical specialization, becomes difficult to switch between the various spheres of production; the need to determine the cost of production and the sum of wages in advance; and so on. As a result, the margin of juridical-state uncertainty must be particularly limited in these societies, starting from certain strictly predetermined coordinates of systematization. The need for calculation and prediction thus arises as the common, simple *end product* of various partial and complex infrastructural imperatives of predictability in their concerted influence on the juridical and state superstructure. It assumes a relatively autonomous importance for this superstructure in as much as it is currently established, in its global character, as a *specific value* of 'calculability' and 'predictability'.

If we situate ourselves at the level of the economic *behaviour generated by this particular mode of production*, we will be able to observe the strategic significance of forecasting. In an economy of *speculation for profit*, the economic activity of the capitalist in a sense constitutes a 'game'. Now, if the essence of games consists in the element of risk and unpredictability, the role of the rules of the economic game – to be specific, juridical and administrative rules – consists in ensuring this element of risk – by leaving a 'free' field for the activities of the players – while limiting unpredictability. The rules of the game represent the same set of information possessed, in whole or in part, by the players at the beginning of the game, eliminating their uncertainties and facilitating prior calculation. The operation of forecasting, which is a given imperative of the current mode of production and a framework for capitalist economic behaviour, does not change significantly as a structuring factor in Western law and the state in a planned economy. The plan – and this is what its basic antinomy consists in, *from the standpoint of capital*, in contemporary capitalist society – will tend to strengthen the forecasting required for growth and real capital accumulation. However, by virtue of its variability, its adaptation in the more or less long term to concrete economic realities, on the one hand, and its infringements of the liberty and equality of capital-owners, on the other, it cannot perform the precise role of predictability that the coordinates of capital and capitalist behaviour assign to the juridical and state level. It cannot constitutively assume the *particular* formality and abstraction of a 'fixed' framework which, while ensuring predictability, must nevertheless guarantee the margin of speculation in an economy involving competition between oligopolies. That is why it is difficult for the plan to attain the status of a juridical-state rule possessing the force of law, the *rule of the game*, and instead itself remains an *element in the game* – an element of speculation that each fraction of capital seeks to tip in its own favour.

Thus, the formality and abstraction of the values of liberty and equality, combined with the particular value of calculability and predictability, constitute the structuring factors in the present-day specificity of the complex of juridical-state norms. These norms present themselves as: (a) *general*, contrary in this respect to individual dispositions that only concern a specific case or person; (b) *abstract*, constructed by means of concepts that are autonomous from concrete reality; (c) *formal*, stripped of concrete, 'material' content; and (d) *strictly codified*: by this we mean the specific structuration whose goal is to preserve the existence – and thus *also* guarantee the predictability – of a normative order, by allowing for its 'complete reversibility'.[11] It consists in a linking and interlocking of the various elements of a normative system, such that a change can occur within the framework of this system without leading to its break-up. In other words, every product of operations within the juridical-state order must always constitute an operation of this order – for example, decrees, laws and constitutions that anticipate and provide for their own alteration and transformation.

These characteristics – generality, abstraction, formality, and co-dification – far from being situated in a context that is immanent in any conceptualization and normative regulation, constitute a reifying break with concrete reality and are *consequently* established as *specific* elements of the current juridical and state level. Their purpose is, in the first place, to ensure the values of liberty and equality and the margin of action required for capital accumulation. Secondly, they are ne-cessary for the operation of forecasting. In fact, codification geared towards the predictability and survival of a normative system can anticipate its own alterations, so that they do not undermine the whole system, only if the partial norms themselves evince a significant degree of abstraction, generality and formality. It is only thus that they will be able on the one hand to encompass the maximum possible number of particular cases and realities, and on the other to operate in isolation, immunized against concrete contact with material reality, thereby excluding any significant alteration of a basic rule in the formal hierarchy of the system – and this because such an alteration would risk the overthrow of the whole system.

For contemporary law and the state, the result is a very strict, complex, and phenomenally coherent systematization, according to the rules of formal normative logic, based on the reified independence of forms and concepts vis-à-vis material content and data – even a formal *axiomatization* of law and state institutions. This development in law and the state had already been sensed by Engels: 'In a modern state, law must not only correspond to the general economic situation and be its expression, but must also be an *internally coherent* expression which does not, owing to internal conflicts, contradict itself.'[12] The juridical sphere thus appears to be a normative (logical-formal) hierarchy of rules and institutions, with each norm assuming, in its reified insulation from its substratum, the form-function of applying a logically and normatively higher norm – more abstract, general and formal, and thus possessing a more fundamental role in the codified systematization. Any norm is *legally* valid by its attribu-tion, within the insulated system, to the higher norm. It in turn is presented as the legal validation of lower-level norms – more concrete, particular and material. From this point of view, the state itself, while remaining the exploitation of the oppressed classes by force, takes the form of a complex of norms and institutions, of the juridical order considered as a whole. Thus, a systematization of law corresponds to a formal hierarchy of state bodies, whose relations of subordination are governed by the formal rule of competence and the logical-normative intervention of the delegation of power.

The specific structuration of the juridical and state sphere has already been noted in part by logicians and theoreticians of law and the state. Their analyses have been criticized by thinkers identified with Hegelianism or Weberian sociology. According to the latter, it is a question of replacing – methodologically – the current formal concepts-rules by concepts with a concrete content, notably the concept of 'concrete universal' or 'ideal type'. By substituting, at an intellectual level, concrete concepts for this formal reality, by thus fashioning at a 'logical' level concepts-models-essences that this reality would subsequently simply realize, we could (according to them) discover the *essential* structuration – the truth – of law and the state, this structuration being in keeping with the idea-concept of the subject. For Marxist thought, the task is quite different. In the first instance, it involves *criticizing* the theories that study the formal, general and abstract specificity of law and the state. At best, these theories cannot go beyond phenomenal description to uncover the genetic structuration. Far from considering the characteristics of the institutionalized juridical and political as they are engendered from the base, and hence far from being able accurately to study their precise functioning, they regard them as an idealist eidetic of law and the state in general. However, *in the second place*, Marxist thought has to uncover the mediations between the base and this superstructure *while respecting its current specificity* – that is to say, in and through this very specificity. The 'dialecticization', the concrete study of this superstructure will not occur in Hegelian fashion, by absorbing and internalizing the phenomenon in an essence at the same real-logical level (idea) as it, but by reference to the concrete dialectical relations between formal, abstract specificity and the material base. Thus, Marxist dialectical logic both contains and supersedes formal normative logic. The significant totality does not consist, as it does in Hegel, in a mediation of unilinear conceptual contradictions, but in the dialectical totalization of *real* contradictions between *two* domains of *reality* – between ideality-superstructure and materiality-base. These remarks also concern the methodological tools, structures, institutions and so on that will serve Marxist analysis of the realities of a capitalist state superstructure. These concepts-tools, which in so far as they are employed on an axiological terrain and are adequate to it are both *real schemas* and *normative models*, will have to be capable of establishing *the axiological-normative specificity* of the superstructure, while capturing it, *in their own structuration as methodological concepts*, in its relationship with the base.[13] In this way, we will be able to understand the specific logic of the capitalist superstructure, its particular degree of endurance, and the precise functioning of its relative autonomy, and thereby accurately assess the prospects for working-class *praxis* at this level.

This particular aspect of a dialectical examination of the juridical and state sphere can be characterized as an 'internal-external' process of analysis, with the relations of interiority and exteriority – relations (as Hegel demonstrated) of totality – being conceived in accordance with the Marxist dialectic and totality. Given that this sphere constitutes a formally coherent system of rules, institutions and hierarchies of powers – internal viewpoint – aimed at exploiting the oppressed classes through repressive state power – external viewpoint – any particular norm or institution, generated out of concrete infrastructural realities – external viewpoint – will be integrated into it by embracing the specific characteristics of this sphere and being inserted into its *modus operandi* – internal viewpoint. For example, we currently observe that the principle of the autonomy of the will, an expression of formal and abstract liberty, is subject to progressive restriction as a result of the requirements of a state-regulated economy. However, in order to be able to understand the internal meaning of this restriction for the overall juridical and state order and its distinctive coherence, we must, aside from cases where it is immediately apparent – membership contracts, control of present-day types of company by large capital, and so on – identify its repercussions in the degree of de-personalization, formality and abstraction of the seemingly most varied norms and institutions: for example, in the rules regarding defects in contractual volition, objective responsibility for a factual state of affairs – that is to say, bound up with the damage caused by some 'thing' that is private property – and even in the concrete modalities of the delegation of power – forms of centralization of the exercise of power and responsibility – within the administrative and bureaucratic hierarchy.

In the *external* relationship between the juridical and state level of the superstructure and the base, we can, in line with Marx's thought, proceed to divide it into several stages of structuration. It will be via the mediation of the stage which concretely presents itself as 'closest' to the base that we shall begin the process of *comprehension* and *foundation* – validation or legitimation – of the more remote stages. The external degree of distance of a stage of structuration from the base is not, in its turn, correlative to a process of formal induction, whereby the more concrete, particular and material a rule is, the closer it is to the base and thereby constitutes the validation of a more abstract and formal rule. For example, the bodies of 'property law' and 'law of liabilities', based on the fundamental economic and sociological relations between subject and things and subject and others, might be more closely linked to the base than a logically narrower legal structure – a certain type of company or contract – and, *in this sense*, constitute the starting-point for understanding and grounding the latter. However, the reverse process can just as easily occur: in the precise case of 'property law', it is the structure-institution of private property which, although logically narrower than this corpus, in contemporary juridical-state orders constitutes the legal foundation of the other laws bearing on possessions – the real easements, usufruct, and so on *granted* by the owner. If the given realities of the base are transposed into this structure with greater immediacy, it is not *because* it is logically more concrete, and *thus* closer to these realities. It is a matter of dialectical relations, transpositions, and mediations: from the external point of view, the juridical-state order does indeed constitute a coherent whole, but not a whole that is logically organized, inductively or deductively. It constitutes a dialectical totality of meaning, containing contradictions, highs and lows, and multi-dimensional tensions between the ensembles that structure it.

Nevertheless, if the internal linkage of juridical-state norms according to formal normative logic does not *in itself* have a significant role as regards the external relationship between superstructure and base – that is to say, as regards the external distance of a stage of structuration from the base – it can indeed have such a role *if this form of linkage is itself due to infrastructural realities*, as is the case in contemporary Western societies. In fact, in these societies the more abstract, formal, general and codified a juridical-state structure is, the closer it can be to the base, by virtue of the formal, abstract liberty and equality that it crystallizes and the calculability that is grafted onto them. And the more it can therefore have a historically preponderant role, expressed as a *superior* position in the systematized hierarchical logic, in governing the axiological-normative foundation and validation of the *logically* narrower, more concrete structures. *By the same token*, however – *and this is what* the phenomenon of reification of contemporary superstructures consists in – the more a norm or institution is *structurally* – through the mediation of its current *specificity* (abstraction, etc.) – consonant with the needs and interests of capital, the more it becomes impervious – through its abstraction and so on – to concrete materiality, to the new forces and new modes of production. In other words, the closer it is to the *capitalist* side of the base, the more incapable it finds itself of capturing the *true meaning* of new infrastructural realities and the more unwieldy, but necessary, it becomes for capital itself. Let us take the example of the firm. Concrete infrastructural realities – automation and so on – are registered in the superstructure as the need for a distinction between *ownership* and *control* of a production unit. The only means of harnessing this *economic* socialization of the mode of production, while integrating it into the juridical-state systematization – that is to say, subjecting it to other abstract and formal concepts and norms – was to depersonalize property while privatizing it still further, by means of an extreme formality and abstraction that lead to a fetishistic personalization of capital as *direct* subject of law. What follows is the development of the juridical and state institution of the 'firm' and the outline of a 'company law' whose contradiction with the reality of the firm at the base is flagrant. Every current state norm, corpus, hierarchy or institution is thus *simultaneously* in an external genetic relationship with the base *and* in an internal normative relationship with the system as a whole. The discrepancies between these two relationships, seemingly resolved in the system, precisely constitute its profound contradictions.

Such internal-external investigation is also appropriate in the Marxist analysis of the state proper, of the relations of public law. From an external point of view, it will be possible to study the relations between economic and sociological realities, the level of the class struggle, civil society on the one hand and the state on the other. The complex levels of mediation between the base and the state political superstructure – professional bodies, trade unions, political parties – will be underscored: the state and its institutions will be regarded as particular repressive instruments at the disposal of the class in power. However, this examination will be *dialectically combined* with a study from an internal point of view, according to which institutionalized power emerges as a tool in the service of the interests of the dominant class through the mediation of a highly and specifically structured complex of norms and values. For example, let us take the case of the administrative bureaucracy in capitalist society. This 'caste' cannot actually function as a factor totalizing private interests and the general interest, as Hegel believed; or as a 'neutral' mediator between social classes, as the neo-capitalist doctrines of the welfare state would have it. This is *not only* because,

from an external viewpoint, it collaborates as a caste with the class
in power in the infrastructural domain – economic interests, social
relations. It is *also* because from an internal point of view, *even
supposing* that in its substratum at the base this caste could operate
with autonomy and independence, the axiological-normative sphere
which forms its operative framework of existence – for example, the
internal logic of the formal delegation of powers through the rule of
competence, the formal distinction but actual confusion between the
three powers, the abstract and formal distinction between the
'governmental' and 'administrative' acts of executive power, and
so on – would not allow it to play this neutral role. In fact, contrary
to what Weber thought, the specificity of this sphere is not attributable to this bureaucratic caste even when 'rationalizing', but to
the systematization, which has its own internal logic, of an axiological-normative ensemble based on the interests of capital. From
this, moreover, derives the illusionism of a neo-capitalist imperative
for a 'rejuvenation' of the technocratic bureaucracy's operational
framework. In actual fact, this framework is congenitally 'old'.

Let us further consider the problems, for example, of centralization
and decentralization. From an external point of view, we can study the
infrastructural realities that govern these modes of state organization
and the forms they take in capitalist societies. From an internal point
of view, we will be able to examine the importance of the systematic
structuration of norms-institutions as regards the form, framework
and degree of decentralization that it can accept by virtue of its own
functioning. This framework appears to be restricted, on account *both*
of the particular form of normative hierarchy by delegation of power
from a 'systematic' centre, *and* of the modality of the normative interlocking of functions within the executive. What is more, we will be
able to appreciate the inflexibility of current structures, which are
resistant to real decentralization – i.e. not a mere administrative
decentralization at the stage of implementation, but a *local autonomy*
extending to local decision-making, local legislative power. In fact,
because of the internal relations between legislature and executive and
the axiomatization of the system, such autonomy, occurring at this
systematic 'point', would afford the opportunity – or, in the capitalist
version, the risk – of a serious break-up.

At the end of this analysis, we observe the *historical* identity, at once
genetic and *specific*, of the state and law, signalled by Marx, Engels
and Lenin. From an internal point of view, the state emerges as the
axiological-normative order of juridical rules and institutions taken as
a whole (state as organization). From an external point of view, the

state is the repressive force which, through juridical rules and institutions, is directed towards class exploitation (the state as body or instrument).

This internal-external analysis, which makes it possible to situate with precision a component of the current state superstructure as an element in the balance of forces in the class struggle, and in working-class *praxis*, is more than ever of great practical importance today. On the one hand, it is not a question, here and now, of seizing power by direct armed struggle – from the very beginning – but of conquering power. On the other hand, still more than in the case of any seizure of power, this conquest can and must be carried out by a *hegemonic* organization of the working class, by an organization which, from its subaltern position, raises itself up to the level of a class that already envisages the concrete exercise of power, while struggling to conquer it. The ultimate goal of this power in the hands of the proletariat is to impart to the 'democratic' values of liberty and equality, negated by the contemporary state and its division from civil society – the base – a concrete, material content and meaning that are 'human' and 'true', extending to all levels. Now, to the precise extent that the seizure of power – the *replacement* of a 'given' power through armed struggle (seizure) – becomes conquest, the development of plans for the exercise of power proposed by the working class through its hegemonic organization assumes fundamental importance. It is not simply a question of envisaging *in the here and now* the preservation of the same state structures for *later on*, so that, passing into other hands via a change in power, they can continue – even if they are to be abolished later – to perform the same function for which they were originally created: basically, a 'dictatorship'. Nor is it a question *simply* of studying what must be 'smashed' (to use Lenin's terms), and what must be preserved, in the structures of the capitalist state, with a view *solely* to a dictatorship of the proletariat over the bourgeoisie, anarchists, and so on. For, as Lenin has clearly shown,[14] the socialist state presents two aspects: an aspect of popular dictatorship – novel – over the bourgeoisie; and an aspect of popular democracy for the oppressed classes. And the structures of the capitalist state must precisely be contested in *the here and now* in their *specific* essence, with this *doubly* novel plan for the exercise of power in mind. For it is not a question of these structures simply permitting dictatorial power at a later date, even if it means discovering the schemas of a popular democracy once the working class is in place, *but of their being envisaged globally in this class's strategy of hegemonic organization.*

The working class will have to fashion its own models, structures, concepts and political forms with a view *both* to a popular, revolutionary democracy, *and* to a positive realization of the concrete values of 'true' liberty and equality. For it is not a matter of this class, at its current core level of development (maturity), which makes a new road to power possible, only losing its subaltern character *afterwards*, and thus constructing its models of democracy solely through the exercise of power as dictatorship.

As regards the democratic-political domain of concern to us here, this hegemonic organization must thus prime itself strategically – and, in the first instance, on the totality of infrastructural levels, especially at the economic level: production units, firms, professional bodies, trade unions, or the various present-day sociological levels mediating between the economic and the political. However, *in so far as* this organization must not be content with trade unionism, must not restrict itself to these levels, but must in addition extend itself to the overall political level *now*, it must involve a positive challenge, through the prospect of a new and different exercise of power, to the juridical-state system as a whole. The internal-external investigation of the capitalist system we have proposed thus proves useful, for it *concretely* demonstrates the degree of *radicalism* that must characterize the strategic models constructed by the working class. It concretely demonstrates the precise degree to which, and through what mediations, the formal and even specific framework of this capitalist sphere – its concepts, *modus operandi*, its state core – are bound up, from an external point of view, but also from the standpoint of its own internal logic, with the interests and values of capital. It demonstrates the decisive extent to which it is not a question of borrowing a form while tempering it in a new context, but of revolutionizing the very forms in the development of new models proposed by the working class. It demonstrates how far these strategic models of organization must, in the here and now, be parallel, but not analogous or homologous, to those of capitalism.[15]

In this 'positive' task, working-class *praxis* already has some reference-points. In fact, the very infrastructural realities that prompt the contemporary capitalist state and law to an absolute negation of the values of liberty and equality in the base are, by the same token, the substratum of a positive realization of these values in the conditions of existence of the working class. The process of the democratic positive realization of the oppressed classes, which Marx and Engels (as we have had occasion to emphasize) observed throughout the pre-history of humanity, becomes more pronounced, since it is the case that infrastructural realities, today as ever, have two sides to them: that of capital, the dominant class, and that of the working class, the oppressed class. Today, the exploited classes are alienated both in the process of production – alienation of labour – and in the process of consumption – the discrepancy between needs and their satisfaction. And yet, the increased concentration of manpower in the workplace, the intensified process of expanded reproduction, the enhanced relations between the various sectors of the division of labour, the beginning of automation and the 'economic' possibility and necessity of the technical control of labour by the workers, mean that, *in the process of production*, the democratic values of real, concrete liberty and equality – this particular expression of the generic socialization of man – are increasingly experienced as a pressing lack, because they are a lack that can be made good. And if the hegemonic organization is also a strategic channelling of this *'material force'*; and if this channelling consists in proposing models to this *already existing* positivity at the global political level – i.e. *historically* objectifying it by suggesting objectives that suit it – it is through the concrete study of organization in the production process (firms, unions) that these models-objectives must be constructed. It is in the concrete positivity of working-class *praxis* that its positive political realization must be sought, while taking account of the mediations required to transpose a democratic economy into a revolutionary political democracy.

Such internal-external analysis will equally be of use when it comes to the problems of tactics and their relations with strategy. For, while taking care not to slip into illusions, we must not forget that if revolutionary strategy must determine concrete tactics – which to that extent are not reform – a strategy can only exist where particular tactics, with this strategy in mind, are possible. If the strategy *must be*, it is because tactics consonant with it *can be*, thus making it the case that the working class only poses as a strategic real-ideal those problems that it can tactically resolve as an initial realization of this ideal. And, in fact, the basic realities of working-class struggle, but also of the formality, abstraction, generality and codification of present-day state rules-institutions – which precisely make a 'fascisization' of power 'from above' so easy – can offer real tactical possibilities for revolutionary *praxis*. For example, through the 'gaps' that they contain structurally; through the relatively 'neutral' fields that can allow for initial organization of working-class *praxis*; or through the relative fragility that this system, by virtue of its specificity, presents as the reverse side of its inflexibility, so that a decisive tactical assault on one link can seriously affect the whole chain by

activating its contradictions, which have been reconciled phenomenally; or, again, through the liberty and equality (even when formal and
abstract), by means of which, as a result of the enhanced positivity of
the oppressed classes, this system seeks to claim the support of the
masses. But whoever says tactics in accordance with a strategy says
clear understanding of the balance of forces. In what sense, and to
what extent, can a particular demand or change challenge the specific
internal-external operation of the overall superstructural system? How
will this demand-change be experienced in the system and how can we
predict the concrete form that the reaction will take inside the system?
What should be the order of priority, the practical articulation of
means and end, of one objective of struggle over another – an order
mainly dictated by the basic facts of working-class struggle, but also
taking into account, as the enemy to be fought, the internal-external
operation of a system this is to be used in order to destroy it? And,
above all – *something that remains the fundamental problem* – to what
concrete extent might a particular tactic at the level of the system not
be absorbed into its own internal-external functioning, *in immediate
or mediated fashion*, but practically function in a sense conducive to
the revolutionary strategy? On concrete answers to these questions
depend revolution or reform, the advent or non-advent of socialism.

2

SARTRE'S *CRITIQUE OF DIALECTICAL REASON* AND LAW

In this paper I have no intention of offering an exhaustive account of the analyses contained in the *Critique of Dialectical Reason* and their implications for the field of law. There are several reasons for this. First, this massive book is intended as part one of a work in progress. Second, Sartre's project is precisely to furnish *concrete analyses of highly specific situations*: the whole of Volume One is intended as a critique of what Sartre regards as the 'uncritical' and 'abstract' studies of contemporary Marxists. This means that the best way to understand our author is to refer to the text itself. Thus, I simply wish to offer some remarks here that might help jurists to situate Sartre's enterprise with respect to the field of law.

It is appropriate to emphasize at the outset that Sartre (mark II) claims to situate the contribution of the existentialist current he represents *within Marxism*. Indeed, in the first instance, his aim is to *found*, in the 'philosophical' sense of the term, the main assumptions of the materialist dialectic, to account for the validity of Marxism in the domain of human practices and the sciences of these practices – in short, to assign an ontological, meaning-creating status to the type of intelligibility represented by 'dialectical reason'. Why, asks Sartre, does the conceptual system of Marxism actually form the only adequate explanation of the history *and* mode of existence of human societies? His second aim is to enrich contemporary Marxist theory with certain categories, concepts, methodological procedures, and examples of concrete analysis. In accordance with its author's project, any examination of the potential contribution of the *Critique*

* First published in French as 'La *Critique de la Raison Dialectique* de J-P Sartre et le droit' in *Archives de Philosophie du Droit*, no. 10 (1965), pp. 83-106. Translated by Gregory Elliott.

of Dialectical Reason to the juridical domain must be conducted with reference to Marxism; and this what we shall attempt to do in schematic fashion.

To try to respond to the question signalled above, let us begin by placing ourselves at the level that Sartre refers to as 'ontological'. This signifies the *immanent, primary and original structures of reality, the 'basic' matrix that generates all meaning.* Contrary to Kant, the type of intelligibility of 'human reason' *presupposes* the existence of these pre-categorial or ante-predicative meaningful structures, which constitute not logical axioms, but philosophical *conditions* of possibility and meaning. For the original Sartre, the structures immanent in reality consisted in *a certain mode of practical and original insertion of man in the world* – his being-in-the-world. Generically, man was already 'openness' towards the world, a project striving to transcend the nothingness and the lack that he is as pure subjectivity in existence through action, through *practical experience* – as opposed to the *'intentionality'* of phenomenology's transcendental Ego – in the world. The essential dimension of human beings is their permanent self-distantiation towards the external world. Human existence cannot be conceived in itself, enclosed in the quintessence of its being, but only with respect to a non-self. Every concrete human experience participates in the mode of being that is its defining relationship with non-selves who, themselves *organized* 'with respect' to human experience, constitute the world.

This is the main route by which Sartre, with Hegel's mediation, tends to coincide with Marxism as his *oeuvre* develops. Obviously, this rapprochement goes through several stages that I cannot examine in depth here, but which I shall have to restrict myself to encapsulating very schematically. First, let us note the meeting points between existentialist and Hegelian theory. For the Hegelian 'onto-logic' or conceptual dialectic, man is a being situated in a historically determinate 'worldly' situation by virtue of his dialectical status. In his pure subjectivity, man is privation, lack, need, *desire* for what is other than himself – a nature that he must conquer in order to satisfy his needs and desires. Nature, the world, negates man, is hostile to him at the initial dialectical moment of human existence, at the moment of pure subjectivity. In the second moment – the antithesis – man *externalizes and objectifies himself* in his acts; he negates the world, conquers it, subjects it to his ends. His consciousness 'returns to itself in the third moment – the synthesis – enriched by its objective signification; it recognizes itself in its works and deeds and is reconciled with the world.

Now, the dialectical conception of human existence occurs in Hegel as a phenomenal expression, or particular realization, of an absolute abstract principle: the Concept or Idea, whose self-development towards self-consciousness engenders nature, humanity, history, and society. The laws of this logical dialectic govern every stage of being's development; and we are familiar with the dialectic in action in the sphere of law and the state, which Hegel set out for us in his *Elements of the Philosophy of Right*. The result is a dialectic of abstraction that seeks to account for human phenomena by uncritically deforming them and bending them in such away that they can be integrated into the concept's essential self-determination as its phenomenal expressions. Ultimately, that self-determination is dependent on the arbitrariness of the philosopher's thought. There is no better example of this than those peaks of Hegelianism, the *Elements of the Philosophy of Right* and the *Logic*, in whose light the concrete historical analyses contained in the *Phenomenology of Spirit* must be interpreted.

The reaction to Hegel's idealist dialectic found expression in the so-called left Hegelians with Feuerbach, Ruge, and the writings of the young Marx. Feuerbach, for example, sharply criticized Hegelian philosophy.[1] In the course of his work, he attempted to lodge the creation and unfolding of the dialectic not in the conceptual sphere, but in the 'concrete individual' and 'generic man' – that is to say, universal man as realized in each individual at grips with a historically determinate, concrete, 'material' situation. Contrary to Hegel's abstract conceptual logic, in Feuerbach the 'rational kernel' of the Hegelian dialectic takes the form of a *concrete humanist anthropology*, in which 'man is god for man'. The dialectic is in a sense inverted and put back on its feet. The meaning-generating structures of reality are grounded in a primary ontological soil, in which man's historical itinerary is inscribed: *the concretely situated, material relations between man and his fellow creatures* – relations which, in their authentic form, result in the mutual creation of man by man in 'love'. (The influence of this current on Werner Maihofer, in his article in the *Archives* two years ago, is well known.)[2]

This is the standpoint initially adopted by Marx, in what are called the works of the 'young Marx', which (it should be stressed) are essentially *concerned with the critique of the state, law, and political ideology*.[3] Still influenced by the humanism of Fichte, who was the first to speak of an original social 'reciprocity' between I-You (*Ich-Du*) as grounding the meaning of social relations, and of Feuerbach, he is close to the latter in so far as he sets out to discover the dialectical meaning

immanent in the *real-material* – the meaning correctly described by
Hegel, although he turned it upside down by lodging it in the Idea –
through an investigation of the situated relations between 'concrete
individuals'. This research takes material form in the 1844 *Manuscripts*,
where Marx emphasizes the *meaning-creating standpoint of human
reality, the ante-predicative ground of any concrete human experience*
represented by 'concrete material labour'. This conception is linked to a
critique of Hegel. For the latter, labour also constituted the 'mediation'
between man and nature – the quintessential act through which man
fashions himself by objectifying himself, by transcending the negativity
of his needs, by recognizing himself in his works, which aim to master
the world. In his famous analysis of the Master and Slave – the 'ontological' dimension that is immanent in any historicized human relationship to various degrees – it is the Slave who conquers his substance, his
authentic existence. For it is he who objectifies himself in the practical
struggle in nature through his labour:

> The importance of Hegel's *Phenomenology* and its final result – the
> dialectic of negativity as the moving and producing principle – lies
> in the fact that Hegel conceives the self-creation of man as a process,
> objectification as loss of object . . . as alienation and as supersession
> of this alienation; that he therefore grasps the nature of *labour* and
> conceives objective man – true, because real man – as the result of
> his *own labour*.[4]

However, Marx criticizes the abstract concept of labour in Hegel, for
whom this human practical and 'existential' activity *par excellence*,
this 'ontological fact' which defines the 'humanity' of the natural being
that is man, is reduced to an *a priori* self-determination of the concept,
to a manifestation of Spirit. For Marx, the negative moment of man in
search of his humanity, which is a *'concrete need' in a determinate
situation*, is superseded by labour that is materially situated and in
dialectical correspondence, in a given society, with this need – labour
through which man fashions himself by humanizing and conquering
nature. In Marx, labour appears to take on an existential ontological
dimension: from the outset, it signifies the active presence of man in
the real-material; it is identified with human existence; it represents
the especial openness of man towards the world, towards material
realities and the sphere of others, the point of their 'practical' contact,
which remains decisive for man as a natural being in a natural world.

    From *The German Ideology* and the introductory 'Theses on
Feuerbach' onwards, Marx changes viewpoints. He moves towards

a profoundly original problematic, which goes far beyond a simple 'inversion' of Hegel's dialectic and its location in the structures immanent in a 'humanist anthropological' reality, whose thematic centre is the concrete-individual-in-a-given-material-situation.[5] Marx discovers his original concepts of *scientific* explanation and understanding: namely, forces of production, mode of production, relations of production, social class and class struggle, base and superstructure, ideology, and so on. With respect to the human sciences, his endeavour now is to uncover the laws of historical development *in the dialectic that is specific to materially structured social totalities, specific to a particular contradictory unity, composed of numerous levels of specific social practices under the dominance, in the last instance, of the economic.*

Now, what is the problem of the 'foundation', generally posed by the Marxist dialectic, with which Sartre, like many Marxologists before him, is concerned? As rational intelligibility, as 'meaning', the Hegelian dialectic was founded in so far as it consisted in the *absolute beginning* that is the principle of the Idea: in the beginning is the Idea. This principle is ultimately identified, as the *object* of knowledge, with the *subject*, who is the thinker, the philosopher. Meaning, dialectical logic, reside in the Spirit, the Idea, the Concept. The thinker is *himself* Spirit, Idea, Concept. This relationship of identity, in the last instance, between subject and object establishes an *a priori* permeability and transparency between the meaning immanent in reality (i.e. objective Spirit) – reality as entirely absorbed into Spirit, as a simple manifestation of Spirit – and the thinker. In short, we encounter here both the blossoming of the Christian tradition, for which meaning is Spirit – Hegel as the last 'Christian' philosopher, who made us live the death of God – and the resolution of the Kantian aporiae, which risked obscuring everything by posing the problem of the *conditions of possibility of man's rational knowledge as 'subject'*. Reality, the *Elements of the Philosophy of Right* tells us, is logic, Spirit and Concept, in as much as logic, Spirit and Concept are reality. In short, according to the ancient idealist tradition, thought can only understand what it has itself produced. In as much as the Marxist dialectic considers *rationality* – that is to say, a 'meaning' which *is not reduced to mechanical causality* – as immanent in materiality itself, the problem of the foundation becomes that of discovering *on what basis* and *how* this meaning emerges as the immanence peculiar to this materiality: in ontological terms, what is the *'material' original ground of the genesis of meaning?*

Two currents stand out among the many responses to this question. The first is what might be identified as 'anthropological philosophical

Marxism'. It is bound up with the work of the 'young Marx' – with a certain interpretation of it – which is taken to be the basis for all of Marx's subsequent work. Its point of departure is a set of coordinates already laid down by the young Marx – needs in a material situation, the concrete individual, negativity and objectification, concrete labour, and so on. It attributes an 'existential' significance to him and discovers the genesis of dialectical meaning either on the model of Husserl's phenomenological enterprise – that is to say, as a basic standpoint of 'practical intentional negativity' on the part of the concrete Ego towards the material world (the *Lebenswelt*), in which society and history are inscribed;[6] or on the model of Heidegger and the early Sartre's existentialism – that is to say, as the essential existential 'openness' of *Dasein*,[7] the concrete, temporal individual, towards the world, the dimension through which society and history exist. Obviously, this occurs with the stress on the *materiality* of the Husserlian *Lebenswelt* and the existentialist world and on the *practical* aspect of phenomenological intentionality and existential openness. However, regardless of the basic reservations that might be expressed towards them, the various tendencies grouped in this current fall without exception under the blade of a fundamental objection – i.e. the impossibility of a *coherent* transition from a 'concrete', even *empirical* ontology of the *individual*, who thus reveals himself to be an abstract anthropology, to historically determinate *levels of social structuration*. For example, how, and through what mediations, can a dialectical existential dimension of 'need' or 'interest', of 'labour' and 'practical objectification' of an ontological social relationship of reciprocity between 'I-the Other', and so on, *which can be regarded as initial elements of a juridical ontology*, be transposed into *socio-economic needs and interests, concretely historicized and structured within the totality of a society at a determinate moment of the development of the mode of production and the class struggle, which for Marx precisely constitute the foundation of the superstructure of law and the state?* In short, what is the concrete relationship between the individual and society, man and history, the ontological and the socio-historical?

What makes Sartre's enterprise interesting is that, despite the fact that he is by far the most important representative of existentialism, he has not remained taken in by his philosophical youth. Leaving existentialist exegetes to their debate in the mazes of a pure and simple existentialization or phenomenologization of Marxism, he attempts, through a considerable effort of adaptation, to transform the ontological coordinates of existentialism in such a way that they can account for the problematic of the ante-predicative ground of the social material practice that creates meaning. This problematic is posed by Marxism and clearly formulated by Desanti:

> But perhaps also what has been sought for under the name of original ground, what has been posed as the first, constitutive relationship of man to the world (*Da-sein*), can be attained and named in its own, concretely real being. Perhaps, in effecting for good this 'migration of the spirit' that Marxism has necessitated, we shall precisely be in the presence – in the flesh, without transfiguration – of the original ground that has been so sought after, the essential relationship to the world which has so often been asserted.[8]

Sartre will not attempt to add materiality as mere facticity, as mere datum of the situation that human activity encounters in its unfolding in the world, to some original – pure – existential human activity. He will seek to discover the 'constitutive' dialectical relations between human practice and materiality that establish these two terms as meaningful coordinates of society and history.

Thus, for Sartre, the dialectic is a type of intelligibility that is defined as a process of totalization, as specific to organized 'wholes'. For Hegel already, the concept of totality was the central concept of the dialectic. Let us stress this key principle, which governs the dialectical understanding of phenomena pertaining to the human sciences – and which, moreover, is evident in *Gestalttheorie*, structuralism, and so on.

For Hegel, Being, the Idea (absolute Spirit) constitutes a totality evolving dialectically. The Idea contains in itself, *in potentia*, all the various moments or expressions of its dialectical development. It is present in any phenomenon or concrete reality, which only becomes meaningful when integrated into *the whole* constituted by the Idea en route to realizing itself. It is precisely on account of this category of totality of Being that we can speak of its dialectical development. It has been remarked that for Hegel the dialectical schema of thesis-antithesis-synthesis is to be found at each level and manifestation of juridical reality. Take the example of property rights. Man in himself, in his very subjectivity, constitutes the thesis. He objectifies himself, externalizes himself from the moment he turns towards an external object whose appropriation he regards as a means of his externalization. This objectification, representing the antithesis, is 'recognized' by others; and the consciousness or will 'returns' to itself enriched, as synthesis, as property right.[9] The same schema can be applied to all juridical phenomena, large and small.

However, this dialectical dynamic can form a synthesis transcending the moments of thesis and antithesis *only if the three dialectical moments move as a totality*. Only by virtue of this totality is the negation of the negation (of the antithesis) itself an affirmation (synthesis), and not a further negation and so on ad infinitum, in the Spinozist sense, for which *omnis determinatio est negatio*. On account of this totality, consciousness, enriched by its objectification in the thing, returns to itself as property right, and not as a mere negation of appropriation or possession, in order for the whole process to restart with another objectification, and so on. This is how the dynamic towards an ever larger totality is outlined, one that ultimately coincides with the Idea, with the Idea achieving self-realization. The synthesis transcends (*aufhebt*) the elements of thesis and antithesis while preserving them, precisely because these three dialectical moments form a totality. The latter itself constitutes the thesis of a larger, higher level of totality, once again comprising three dialectical stages, and so on. Dialectical development thus consists in a process of ongoing totalization within the absolute totality that is the Idea – a process of totalization through which the potential totality actually totalizes itself in becoming conscious of itself.

However – and this is a point of fundamental importance – for Hegel this totality constitutes a purely conceptual category. This amounts to saying that it is conceived as external to human activity, which is thus 'subject' to it. The totality is a category of dialectical *logic*; it is itself grounded in the metaphysical conception of a universal totality, the Idea. In the global alteration of standpoint towards the Hegelian dialectic effected by Marx, this 'totality' is transposed into the domain of social structures and practices; for example, Marx tells us that the relations of production constitute a 'whole'. Here, I cannot attend to the basic differences which, over and above the fact that Marx discovers the dialectic in the domain not of the concept but of practical materiality, differentiate the totality and categories of the Hegelian dialectic – for example, negation, synthesis, and so on – from those of Marx's dialectic. But let us note that for Marx social reality at a determinate historical moment constitutes a *global unity* composed of several *ensembles* which, in their own specificity, themselves form structured 'wholes'. In this global dialectical unity, we can distinguish between two particular ensembles: the base and the superstructure. The base – the material structures of social and historical practice – is itself composed of particular ensembles: the mode of production – the

economic in the strict sense – and the social relations of production –
the class struggle, the social in the strict sense of the term. *Starting
from* the base, the *particular, specific ensembles* that are the domains
of the superstructure are built up, including the state and law – which
are in no sense mere 'reflections' of the base, as a gross vulgarization of
Marxism would have it. These levels of structuration, these degrees of
totalization – to employ Sartrean terms – can only be deciphered in
their genesis and specific effectivity within a global type of historically
determinate society, a 'type' – for example, capitalist – whose unity is,
in the last instance, dominated by a scientifically defined 'mode' of
production.

Sartre, *who expressly accepts this thematic of Marx's as absolutely
self-evident and indisputable*, asks how it comes about that this
dialectical totality, which is no longer a logical category of Being-
as-Idea, is immanent in human, 'material' reality? *It is because it
essentially constitutes an ontological dimension of man-as-action*:

> If dialectical Reason exists, then, from an ontological point of view,
> it can only be a developing totalization . . . It is therefore necessary
> for the critical investigation to ask the fundamental question: is
> there a region of being where totalization is the very form of
> existence?[10]

However,

> there would not even be the beginnings of partial totalization if the
> individual were not totalizing *through himself. The entire historical
> dialectic rests on individual praxis in so far as it is already
> dialectical*, that is to say, to the extent that action is itself . . .
> the determination of a present totalization in the name of a future
> totality.[11]

The dialectic is thus founded on the ontological structures of practical
individual existence, on 'human labour' – privileged ontological site
and original *praxis* whereby man produces and reproduces his existence. In so far as man's concrete experience represents not an
expression of his pre-established essence, but a project whereby he
transcends and supersedes the given situation, this experience *totalizes*
the external realities of the world that it plans to transform. In that it
represents the ontological site of his existence, man's practical activity
consists in the totalization through human labour of the 'practical
material field' of this activity; it consists in the organization of the

world into a structured ensemble by the dialectical finality of human
activity – totalizing *praxis*. Nature negates man; man is lacking in
himself; he negates natures and through his acts transcends this lack.
Through his practical act, these disparate 'moments' are established as
the 'means' of a future 'end', in the developing, active totality that is
human existence.

*Sartre's ontological enterprise with respect to Marxism is, however,
fundamentally different, in two respects, from those of the other
Marxological supporters of a 'humanist anthropology'; and these
points are of crucial importance in his numerous analyses of the state
and law.* First, Sartre seeks to go beyond the starting-point of an
'individual' *praxis*, by stressing the *real mediations* that bind the
individual to the social group. He attempts to integrate the individual
into society by underscoring the fact that the dialectical dimensions of
individual *praxis* are, by virtue of their ontological status, inscribed in
the integral totalization that is a society – a common *praxis*-totaliza-
tion which is always underway and active. His enterprise thus consists
in the establishment of an *ontology of the socio-economic* from a
Marxist standpoint.

Second, Sartre seeks to uncover the profound dialectical relations
that unite the ontological dimension of *praxis* and the 'materiality' of
the external world. Sartre attempts to consider this 'materiality' and
the meaning immanent in socio-historical realities – which are both
natural data and the crystallization of a human historical *praxis*, and
in which there is to be found a *praxis* that strives to transform them –
not merely as a coordinate external to human activity, as a datum that
this activity, already ontologically constituted, encounters in its externalization. He regards them as something which determines it, on
account of its ontological status, in its practical core: need, interests
and labour do not exist outside or prior to a material ensemble of
natural and socio-economic given realities, *which constitute their
ontological condition of possibility*.

These two points, which distinguish Sartre's enterprise from other,
similar ones, are underlined by him thus:

> I have simply tried to establish without prejudice . . . the basic
> relations between *praxis* and the material environment (in so far as
> it organises a practical field and defines the relation between men
> through their objects, and the relations between objects through
> men) in which a rational foundation for the certainty of dialectical
> investigations . . . which any reader of Marx can experience, can be
> found.[12]

There are numerous passages in the *Critique of Dialectical Reason* of relevance to law.[13] I shall attempt schematically to highlight the most characteristic of them. In order to underscore the originality of Sartre's contribution, let us begin with certain reference-points as regards attempts at an existentialist ontology of law.

Attempts at a legal ontology on existentialist principles are not new. The first part of Maihofer's work, which is beginning to become known in France, represented the first undertaking of this kind.[14] Emphasizing the primary ontological *reciprocity* of I-Other, which supposedly constitutes the initial foundation of any social relation, the ontological substratum of an original sociality, Maihofer grounds the main coordinates of a juridical ontology in it. More specifically, this involves human existence from the angle of '*Als-sein*', of 'being-as' for another, within a specific correlative relation between concrete existences. In the social world, we observe men in reciprocal existential relations: seller-buyer, creditor-debtor, doctor-patient, and so on. Depending on the particular concrete relationship, men feature with different skills and functions. The latter are not deduced from a supposed a priori – phenomenological – eidetic of a contract or institution. Nor do they constitute manifestations of a supposed human 'essence' or 'nature'. Instead, they are *existential* ontological 'openings'. In such a relationship, each of the persons involved tends correlatively towards the other. Out of this ontological existential independence, a certain mode of reciprocal behaviour is engendered on the part of subjects – a mode specific to the relationship they are involved in. Each 'expects' behaviour from his partner in accordance with his role in the concrete relationship, in the absence of which he would himself be destroyed. From this 'expectation' a 'natural' interest is born – a 'requirement' that the other perform his particular role within a relationship. 'Directly' transposed to the juridical level, this interest constitutes the substratum of the bond of obligation, real rights, and juridical relations pertaining to public law and so on – in short, legal rights and duties, norms and values.

In this journal, I have previously levelled certain criticisms at Maihofer's conceptions,[15] which can be baldly summarized in two points – the precise points on which Sartre's endeavour is focused in the analyses of law and the state contained in the *Critique of Dialectical Reason*. First, I challenged the idea that this ontological conception of law could allow for a coherent integration of the original coordinates of law into the socio-economic structures of a society at a historically determinate moment of its development – when only such integration (according to us) makes it possible to *account for* the specificity of the social superstructural phenomenon of law, within the dialectical materialist conception founded by Marx. Maihofer's view seemed to me – and still does, despite the author's evolution towards a humanist materialism, inspired by Feuerbach and the interpretation he offers of the young Marx[16] – to lead to an abstract, a-historical ontology of juridical phenomena. For example, the seller-buyer relationship only assumes significance within an ensemble of structures that both engender this relationship and assign it a concrete historical meaning, which *generates the founding value of legal norms.* Maihofer's theory seems to me to lead to a simple *'relational' theory* of law and the state, in which social legal relations appear as the 'inter-personal' relations of individualized monads, insulated in a socio-historical vacuum.

My second criticism concerned the fact that Maihofer's conception did not take account, in the original constitution of the juridical phenomenon, of the importance of the *material dialectical* praxis *of man* engaged in a given situation, of men's *practical freedom to fashion* – labour – which, starting from their concretely socialized and historicized needs and interests, organizes the practical material field that is established, through numerous mediations, as a specific sphere of *values*: law or, at least, modern law. As I saw it, Maihofer's theory succeeded in explaining law only in its dimension of power relations, by 'directly' transposing given factual relations into juridical values and norms, by virtue of an imposed human 'openness' and 'condition', on the model of the Hegelian Master-Slave relationship – relations stripped of the socio-historical context that precisely explains why, in the case of the modern state and law, power relations are scientifically 'comprehensible' only within a normative ensemble. This failure to take dialectical *praxis* into consideration further leads, at the historical level, to an 'immobilism': the eternal return of the same – the same ontological situations-relations of the human condition moving in a circular perpetuity.

Now, it is precisely these two points that govern the analyses of law and the state by Sartre mark II. First, he establishes the original ontological coordinates that govern every specific domain of human practice and, consequently, every superstructural sphere, including law. These are *needs* and *labour*.[17] In line with the general exposition I have given above, human activity consists in a totalizing dialectical praxis. On the basis of man's needs and the lack they determine in his subjectivity, it organizes by means of his labour – original existential dimension of man's practical externalization, by which man makes himself man – the unity of the material field of action.[18] In its structural ensemble, this field comprises both objects and others. *If, at this level, we sought to establish the outline of a Sartrean ontology of the juridical*, we would already have underlined an important observation – i.e. that the meaning-generating matrix of the juridical phenomenon does not consist in the 'phenomenological' attitudinal relations between subjects involved in a given relationship, relations of a subjectivist stamp correlative to an intentionality. We would have to search for the guiding thread of the advent of law in a substratum *constitutively rooted* in socio-economic materiality: needs and labour, in the broadest sense of the term. In fact, for Sartre, these notions of need and labour do not constitute abstract notions of a humanist anthropology of the Feuerbachian variety. Needs only exist in the form of *concretely socialized and historicized needs*, in a *material* world governed by a *scarcity of goods, and in the historically determinate totality formed by a society at a certain stage of its development*. And this stage is itself determined by a concretely socialized and historicized mode of common labour, constituted by the process of production, which precisely structures the 'material situation' that a concrete individual is situated in. The particular totality of needs and labour – the primary ontological substratum of a concrete juridical relationship – thus structurally refers to a given socio-economic ensemble that forms, moreover, the foundation of the sphere of juridical values and norms. We might note what is at stake in these coordinates of Sartre's thinking – and it is considerable: it involves an *ontological* refutation (i.e. of a 'philosophical' kind and status, not merely a 'sociological' one) of the tendencies of *Begriffsjurisprudenz*, legal phenomenology, normativism, and so on. It is not a matter of socio-economically complementing an idealist view of law, considering it 'from a socio-economic standpoint', criticizing it 'from without'. *Situated on the same terrain and within the modern thematic of these theories*, it is a question of demonstrating their philosophical 'impossibility'.

However, Sartre appears to be acutely conscious of the fact that these ontological coordinates of needs and labour integrated into a unity in a given material field do not yet account for the '*ontological' specificity of the juridical phenomenon*. That is to say, although these coordinates have always existed in every form of sociality, the phenomenon of law – and, as we shall see, of the state – does not, contrary to the somewhat vulgarized opinion that *ubi societas ibi jus*, pertain to every human grouping. This means that the *social relations* inscribed in the basic structure of these primary ontological coordinates can take the form of exteriority represented by sheer force and violence. Such force can be invested in religious and moral values of a magical and sacred character, but it escapes the 'diffuse power of jurisdiction' that is particular to a certain moment in the process of social structuration – within any historical society – and which, for Sartre, constitutes the framework of law. Needs and labour can only become established as law, *can only generate juridical meaning and 'value' on the basis of a framework of certain facts of sociality.* Within this framework, these coordinates, through the mediation of their transposition to socio-economic interests and so on, will be able to form the substratum of a 'juridical sphere'. In their *juridical* embodiment, these coordinates are overdetermined by the existence of this framework – a framework that constitutes the embodiment of these coordinates as juridical elements. However, this reference framework is not, in the first instance, situated at the level of *overall social structures*; it thus does not constitute the object of a sociological theory, strictly speaking. It is essentially captured at the level of 'ontological' relations of original sociality between I-the Other, such as they materialize at a given moment in the process of social structuration. The interest of Sartre's enterprise precisely consists in this attempt at a *structural integration* of ontology into the socio-historical, a coherent transition from the inter-individual to social structure.

In order to establish the ontologico-social framework of the juridical, let us briefly set out the social structures whose ontological status it is Sartre's object to establish. He distinguishes between 'practico-inert ensembles' and 'groups'.[19] In the first category, he distinguishes between *series* and *collectives*; in the second, between *fused groups*,[20] *statutory groups*,[21] and *institutionalized groups*.[22] Practico-inert ensembles are characteristic of forms of sociality in which, *as the function unifying individuals*, as the common material field, the 'instrumentalization of material reality'[23] is predominant – a simple form of *external* cohesion that consists in a simple objectification – alienation – of man 'working' matter in common. Series and collectives – serial ensembles – result from the mediating role of the human in the matter worked by man. Human relations at this level are passively mediated by objects; man's dialectical experience is alienated in objects; man becomes 'bewitched matter'.[24] The 'serial' is thus composed of a 'plurality of separations'; it is, 'quite simply, the practical existence of men among men';[25] it constitutes 'ways of being-outside-oneself'. Thus, in line with his project, Sartre develops a *dual* viewpoint for formulating the *ontological status of the serial*: a certain relationship, itself 'alienating', of man to matter, to the scarcity that structures his passively 'imposed' socio-economic interests – we shall return to this; *and* a certain I-Other relationship in which, more particularly, 'everyone becomes himself (*as Other than self*) in so far as he is other than the Others, and so, in so far as the Others are other than him'.[26] Here, we are still dealing with the *ontological dimension of 'reciprocity'* that Sartre established as early as *Being and Nothingness* – such reciprocity being merely a 'reciprocity of separation' which resembles the *mechanical contact of social atoms as relations of force*, on the Hobbesian model.

In contrast, to put it schematically, groups are social ensembles characterized by a 'common *praxis*', by a cohesion grounded in an internal reciprocity between human beings, who in some concrete material field undertake in common to supersede their socio-economic situation in the direction of a shared goal. Hence the character of groups as *'organic totalities' in totalization*, as distinctively dialectical moments of the structuration of the social, as *specifically 'organized'* with a view to a logic of *social and historical action*. Groups likewise possess a *dual ontological status*. On the one hand, they have an ontological relation to concrete material realities, to the determinate socio-economic ensemble, but where this ensemble is no longer a site that human practices get absorbed into – the site of an 'exis' – but is integrated into their totalizing *praxis* as an element in the standpoint of men who make their own history. On the other hand, groups evince an ontological relationship of sociality consisting in a 'mediated reciprocity', where the individual is extricated from his passive separation and integrated into a totalizing organization as a 'common individual' *recognized* by others, as a being with a specific role in the collective action of the 'group':

> The mediation of functions is the common *praxis*: the group produces me as the power to realize a certain detail of the common *praxis* so that this *praxis* can be realized in its totality and differentiate itself . . . in objectifying itself.[27]

The members of a group are not Others in 'direct' external relationships, but *third parties*, mediated and recognized in reciprocity by all the other members of the group: 'the members of the group are *third parties'*[28] – which is not alterity, but mediated reciprocity.

Let us make it very clear that these *ontological* moments in the structuration of the social – series, collective, fused group, statutory group, institutionalized group – do not, *in their ontological status*, represent stages in a general historical evolution or in the evolution of a type of society. They coexist in fact as *particular ontological instances of a given social totality*, as (to put it inaccurately) super-imposed within a single totality. In a given social ensemble, we can distinguish between the practico-inert – serial or collective (ensemble of series) – and the group. The *serial* – or collective – exists in every similar ensemble and constitutes the initial substratum, the passive determination by socio-economic 'facts', of every form of sociality, with groups representing 'the erosion of a seriality'.[29] Absorption into the practico-inert is a constant menace for *praxis*, which represents its historical transcendence. For example, a social class pertains to the serial and the collective in so far as it is a syncretic and passive mass of interests 'imposed' as 'fate' by the external facts of socio-economic materiality. But it pertains to the fused group to the extent that it establishes itself as unorganized common *praxis*; to the statutory group as 'diffuse power of jurisdiction' and organization, for example, in a party; and to the institutionalized group to the extent that it becomes the dominant class, with its own institutions, and so on. Hence, 'ontologically', the practio-inert is ever-present. The group *can* also be present – it thus possesses an ontologically aleatory existence – the practico-inert being ontologically *overdetermined* in this instance by the group. As for the three moments of the group, they can be conceived as temporally successive – the fused group that becomes a statutory group – and as ontologically coexisting: for example, the statutory group that is also an institutionalized group.

According to Sartre, it is at the ontological point when a group makes the transition from the rudimentary stage of an unorganized common dialectical praxis to the stage of statutory group that one can capture the juridical in its ontological specificity. The organizational moment of a group translates into an attempt by its members to preserve its existence with a view to achieving a common objective, by an ontological dimension that tends to *guarantee the functional permanency of the group* which, without it, is constantly in danger of disintegrating. This dimension is the 'pledge'.[30] By means of the pledge, which is not a historical act here but an ontological dimension – similar, for example, to the social contract that theoreticians assume (as fiction) as the foundation of a given society, but which (in fact) is the real ontological substratum of every statutory group – the *third-party* members of a group 'swear' the group's permanency to all its other members, mortgaging their practice as integrated to a framework that guarantees the group' s future. It is by means of the pledge that individuals arrive at that form of mediated dialectical reciprocity – pledge of all recognized by all – which characterizes the moment of socialized man's practical freedom. Through the pledge – a 'free relationship between free commitments', common individuals integrated into a *praxis* rooted in a concretely historicized material situation – external relations of force and violence between isolated individuals alienated in objects are ontologically invested in internal relations of freedom:

> The intelligibility of the pledge derives from the fact that it is a rediscovery and an affirmation of violence as a diffuse structure of the fused group and that it transforms it reflexively into a statutory structure of common relations. In fact, to precisely the extent that the relations of the third parties are mediated, that is to say, to the extent that they pass through all, the character of violence cannot be detected in them: they are the free common relations of members of the group as such. But as soon as the danger of disintegration appears, every third party produces himself for everyone else as the one who passes sentence in the name of the group . . . And Terror comes to everyone . . .[31]

The ontological peculiarity of the pledge precisely inheres in this pair 'Fraternity-Terror' and 'Freedom-Violence'. Moreover, to the extent that its ontological horizon is to guarantee the permanency of the group, the pledge is also an organic framework of *predictability* regarding each person's conduct for all the others.[32] In as much as it forms the substratum of an organized common *praxis* in a material situation, it constitutes the *ontological* presupposition of a social form where *the division of labour and a differentiation of tasks is possible*: 'through the pledge, the statutory group *becomes capable of differentiation*; to put it differently, it makes itself such that *not only* do differentiations not destroy its unity, but also practical problems *can reveal themselves to it through differential problems*'.[33]

It is precisely these ontological components and results of the pledge that determine the genesis of the juridical for Sartre:

> It is impossible to derive juridical power either from individual freedom, which has no power over reciprocal freedom, or from a social contract uniting several entities, or from the constraint imposed on the group by some differentiated organ, or from the customs of a community in so far as they appear to involve an *exis*.[34]

The juridical is a new form of social 'totalization', which derives from the fact that the members of a group engaged in a common *praxis*

realize that their action cannot be enclosed in itself, but can only exist
as a constant 'totalizing' objectification. Hence their permanent integration into the group cannot derive from a 'closed' collective
consciousness, superior to all the members of the group, a consciousness totalized once and for all as a form, as *Gestalt*. This integration
can only be grounded in a pledge that guarantees the group's permanency and its organization in ongoing, active totalization through
pledged common practices.

   Thus, this pledge is the substratum of a diffuse power of jurisdiction
of all over all – reciprocal rights and duties – which consists in the
constant affirmation and reaffirmation of the pledge whenever a
particular practice tends to rupture the group's unity or dissolve its
permanency: 'The *common* characteristic of the individual (or his
being-in-the-group) becomes everyone's juridical power over organic
individuality in himself in every third party.'[35] On the other hand, the
ontological necessity of the 'pledge' arises at the stage of an *organized
differentiation* of social tasks and *'functions'* – a differentiation which,
within a pledged group, assumes the form of a diffuse power of all
over all. This power correlative to mutual commitments is immanent
in the ontological structuration of rights and duties:

> Function is both negative and positive: in the practical movement, a
> *prohibition* (do not do *anything else*) is perceived as a positive
> determination, as a *creative imperative*: do *precisely that*. But in the
> milieu of the pledge, *doing that* is the right of each over all, just as it
> is a right of all over each: the definition of *power*, in so far as a
> concrete function particularises it, is that for everyone it is the right
> to carry out his particular duty.[36]

*The ontological framework of the pledged group thus furnishes, by
means of the genesis of a primary power, the matrix of a multiplicity
of rights and duties of third parties*:

> Now, all these abstract moments of concrete exigency are given
> together in my way of acting, of realizing my function through my
> action and of basing my action on my powers: the right which the
> group has through me over all, and the duty towards the group as
> defined by all, the reciprocity of right (I have the right that you
> should assert your rights), that of duty (my duty is to remind you of
> yours), that of right and duty (I have the right that you should allow
> me to do my duty), that of duty and right (I have the duty to respect
> your rights) – the infinite complication of these reciprocities . . . all

these lines of force constitute the web of what might be called power as reality lived in and through *praxis*. According to circumstances, one or other of these lines of force may appear, as a form, against the synthetic background of all the others; but if they are not all present, the group will break up.[37]

Law is thus the specific 'ontological' dimension of cohesion of a social 'group' – hence of an ensemble where social practice vis-à-vis things takes the form of a *'common praxis'* and social relations assume the form of 'free' internal relations – *organized for its permanency through the pledge, demanding a predictability of practices on the part of its members, and necessitating a differentiation of tasks in order to achieve a common objective.*

Now, these rights and duties in mediated dialectical reciprocity are still captured here in their formal ontological structure: their content depends on the totality of socio-economic realities within which the social *needs* and *labour* of a group engaged in a historically determinate common *praxis* are situated. The ontological dimensions of need and labour retain all their importance, signalled above, as the ontological substratum of law, as of any particular social sphere – morality, religion, and so on. *However, only the needs and labour inscribed in a framework of dialectical praxis of a pledged group can assume the specific form of the juridical.* In fact, the only form of *needs* and *labour* that exist are concretely socialized and historicized ones, integrated into the totality of a given society at a determinate stage of its development. The concrete content of rights and duties precisely depends upon the materialization of needs and labour in the historical material circumstances *in which the praxis of a pledged group is situated.* However, the needs and labour of series and collectives – already present at the moment of the practico-inert – are not directly transposed, through their materialization as such in the pledged group, into rights and duties. Sartre in fact highlights a form of sociality, *situated at the level of the serial and the collective*, which represents the ontological form that needs and labour pass through in order to take concrete form in rights and duties: *these are socio-economic 'interests'.*[38] This point must be stressed, because it is fundamental – as the current of *Interessenjurisprudenz* demonstrates – for the structuration of law. The unity of the serial and the collective – of the practico-inert – which, as we recall, is purely *external, imposed and absorbed in objects*, precisely materializes in interests, of which Sartre undertakes a highly elaborate ontological analysis. Interest is 'being-completely-outside-oneself-in-a-thing', in as much as it conditions a certain

practice or labour by the series when confronted with matter that is to
be instrumentalized. Interest is a certain relationship between man and
things in a social field. It exists wherever men live within a material
ensemble of tools dictating their techniques. In this rudimentary
relationship between man and social objects, these objects – social
materiality – are not considered in the process of a group practice that
transcends the fact of working matter to satisfy momentary needs in
the direction of a common project for the future. Instead, social
materiality forms the limit of man's dialectical freedom, the alienation
of the horizons of human labour in matter – in short, 'real subser-
vience to "natural" forces [and] to "mechanical" forces'.[39]

The common interest of the series or the collective is thus a form of
purely external cohesion of their members, an inter-human unity
imposed as 'fate' by material necessity and by the 'common condition'
of the members of practico-inert ensembles in their passivity in the face
of social objects. This ontological form of practico-inert unity – serial
or collective – is sanctioned by pure relations of *force* and *violence* in
so far as human relations are, as in the group, 'freely mediated' by all
the third-party members, but conditioned by the mediation of matter.
At this level, the common interest is ultimately the *survival*, as such, of
a social ensemble; and the conformity of an individual in his practice
to this interest is imposed by sheer Violence and Terror. *Now, we have
noted that the ontological realities of the practico-inert, of the series or
collective, coexist ontologically in the group – a group whose primary,
'perennial' substratum is formed by the practico-inert.* This is to say
that in the pledged group, 'interests' – these forms of social materialization of need and labour in the practico-inert – are 'established' by
the process we have expounded as rights and duties, as the juridical
phenomenon. *The specifically juridical is needs and labour materialized in serialized interests, themselves transposed into pledged group
relations. Hence the dual dialectical ontological status of law* – as of
every group reality – which simultaneously pertains to serial or
collective recurrence and to group recurrence: a relationship of force
invested in a relationship of freedom; a socialized relationship of
direct, external reciprocity invested in a socialized relationship of
mediated, internal reciprocity; a relation of *exis* – a relation alienated
in socio-economic materiality – invested in a relation of *praxis*
superseding this hitherto passively endured materiality; a relationship
of necessity invested in a relationship of freedom.

Before proceeding to a discussion of Sartre's views, let us merely add
a few words on what he characterizes as the third moment of group
structuration: the institutionalized group with its specific institutions

and state.[40] We have noted the constant threat to the group represented by the underlying series – the danger that, notwithstanding the
pledge, the group will dissolve into seriality. Institutions precisely aim
to strengthen the *guarantee of the group's permanency, its specific
unity and cohesion*, by crystallizing it. Yet for that – and this is where
we register the emergence in Sartre of a historical circle of human
societies, grounded in ontological coordinates – institutions must, in
order to be able to constitute themselves as 'Power', be able to sink
their roots in the seriality that they act against, the role of institutions
being to preserve the group. Power and state institutions – *and this is
their ontologically contradictory character* – derive their *authority*,
their *sovereignty*, their establishment, from the inertia, the impotence,
the isolation, the passivity, the violence and terror which, in every
social ensemble, form part of its invariable, underlying dimension of
seriality. Institutions are the rebirth of seriality in the organized group,
to the precise extent that they functionally exist to preserve it from its
dissolution into seriality. *This is the return of seriality and violence,
but in a new form, for it has already taken the form of the pledged
group's 'mediated reciprocity'.* Force is a legitimate force, a sovereign
authority. This mediation is no longer the free mediation of all by all
on the part of the pledged. It passes through the 'single mediator' who
is the sovereign, the sovereign who preserves the group's unity while
grounding his 'unsurpassable mediation' in the external relations of
seriality, which always underlie the relations between the group's
members. The state itself is definitely not a supra-functional group
integrating all the other groups, as conceived by Hegel; or an organ of
arbitration and reconciliation between the particular *praxes* of social
groups, as conceived by theoreticians of the welfare state. In short, it is
not a structure that integrates men's *praxes*, but a specific group, with
its own internal unity, which tends to perpetuate itself by dissolving
the organic unity of the other social groups. The state's function is to
reconcile the irreconcilable contradictions between social classes, by
breaking the internal bonds between members of the dominated
classes – which it strives to reduce from classes-as-groups to
classes-as-series-or-collectives – and crystallizing the bonds of the
dominant classes as bonds that are themselves external – i.e. based
on *domination* of the oppressed classes, on 'what can be called the self-
domestication of man by man'. The

> institutional ensemble, cloaked and reunited by the sovereign in-
> stitution, by the State . . . as a small group of organisers, admin-
> istrators and propagandists take[s] on the task of imposing

modified institutions within collectives, as serial bonds which unite serialities.[41]

We have concluded our exposition of Sartre's text. Given that it is a work of eight hundred pages, whose style is admirable in its *clarity* and conceptual rigour, but which is hard to understand, it is more than likely that various errors have crept into my critical interpretation. Even so, on this basis let me venture some general observations.

In the first place, as regards law and Sartre's ontological interpretation, what is important is the author's attempt to provide an *ontological interpretation of the social character of law*. Having situated the juridical phenomenon at the level of the group – i.e. the level of ternary social relations (third parties) – and not merely inter-individual (binary) relations, as a long philosophical tradition dating back to Fichte, which grounds the juridical in the ontological substratum of original I-Other sociality, would have it, Sartre essays an ontological interpretation of the juridical that can integrate the individual into a social totality. (I stress: an *ontological* interpretation.) In Sartre's project, we are not dealing with an inter-individual substratum of law *complemented* by an additional sociological theory, modelled on the original I-Other relationship. We are dealing with the ontological substratum of *various degrees of structuration of the social, even various degrees of structuration of the juridical*.

The *ontological* interpretation Sartre provides of those fundamental characteristics of law that are permanency, predictability, differentiation of tasks, and hence the division of labour and the division of society into social classes, will not be lost on the philosophical or methodological jurist. At the same time, throughout his ontological analyses Sartre emphasizes two basic aspects of the juridical: i.e. the fact that law has the characteristic of *freedom-praxis*, which transcends its residue of sheer force and coercion; and the fact that, as a social phenomenon, it is *constitutively* engendered in its very specificity by the socio-economic materiality of a given society. Having captured the ontological specificity of law on the basis of the dialectical, meaning–creating coordinates of needs, labour, interests, the pledge, and *praxis*, in their relationship with the given socio-historical situation – in short, *starting out from ontological coordinates structured in the manner of the dialectical materialist totality* – his project is to establish through concrete analysis the legitimacy and conditions of possibility of an interpretation of law by means of the Marxist schema – reality and method – of base and superstructure, in a historically determinate given society.

Accordingly, the distance that separates Sartre's enterprise in this respect from those of a juridical ontology with 'phenomenological' leanings – see Gardies's essays[42] – or the 'philosophical humanist' tendency of the Feuerbachian materialist variety – see the development of Maihofer's thinking – is sizeable. Regardless of any other criticisms that might be directed at them, these are characterized by the fact that the ontological framework of law which they establish cannot explain the distinctively *social* phenomenon of law in its internal coherent unity. Hence a *hiatus irrationalis* between their ontological conception of law and sociological theories, which they address *afterwards*, in order to account for law as a *historical* phenomenon in human societies.

As for problems of juridical epistemology, certain solutions can be derived from Sartre's ontology – for example, in connection with the fact-value relationship or that between what is and what should be. As a specific phenomenon, law consists in the moment of group structuration when common *praxis* integrates these two terms into a dialectical totalization. Facts, material realities, serial facticity are precisely constituted as value through the *praxis* of a group, whose members undertake in common, starting out from a certain objective-ideal, to transform them with a view to realizing this goal. It is this investment of necessity in freedom, of separation in community, of violence in mediated reciprocity, which engenders certain values that constitute the juridical. And we also come across some shrewd analyses of concrete juridical problems here – for example, of 'subjective law', a notion Sartre criticizes by stressing the complexity of mediated reciprocities in the juridical, which connects up with the notion of 'juridical situation' as a complex of intertwined rights and duties. A further example would be juridical 'normativism': the original stage of the juridical, of the *specificity* of the juridical, is prior to the crystallization of rights and duties in a coherent, more or less institutionalized sphere of juridical rules or norms. Before the structuration of the normativist sphere, we can already speak of 'rights' and 'duties' *in the juridical sense of the term*, of which these rights and duties form the substratum. Yet another example would be the factor that generates these legal rights and duties, and which consists in the diffuse power of jurisdiction in the pledged group. This is an *ontological* conception close to Charbonnier's ethnologico-sociological position, which precisely maintains that the original element defining the juridical consists in *judiciarity*.[43]

On the problematic of the relations between law and state, let us limit ourselves to noting that juridical relations appear to Sartre to be ontologically prior to the state, as its presuppositions and conditions of possibility. Their relationship is not *genetic and constitutive*, but aleatory. Once the state is in place, and on the basis of a society's socio-economic evolution, it 'institutionalizes' rights and duties, which are henceforth in a historically determinate relationship with the state. The upshot is that even in this latter relationship, the juridical cannot be completely reduced or absorbed into social relations, which are more or less mediated by state 'institutions'. On the one hand, there is an 'adjoining' juridical zone which is in a sense 'external' to the state – that of the pledged relations escaping statification. On the other hand, the pledged group's juridical relations show through under the institutionalized relations of the group-institution which, except in the event of an absolute 'mystification' on the state's part – for example, a dictatorship pure and simple – *overdetermines* the pledged group that underlies it, superimposes itself on it without completely reducing the group to seriality. By reference to the account we have just given of Sartre's doctrine, we can see that his anti-statism, in the tradition of Proudhon and Marx, does not extend to an anti-legalism, in the ontological sense of the juridical employed by him.

However, the significance of Sartre's text should not be limited to these analyses. I have sought to stress that Sartrean theory *aims to contribute something original to Marxism*. Sartre – and it is appropriate to emphasize this point – does not offer us a new theory of law and the state or other social phenomena, but adheres to a Marxist interpretation, to which he subscribes unreservedly, even if means establishing its ontological presuppositions and possibly refining or enriching it. According to Sartre, his analyses are productive and operative only to the extent that they are considered in the framework of dialectical materialism.

An objection then occurs to readers: only on the condition that these analyses can be integrated into that framework. Can they? Yes and no. Throughout the *Critique*, we witness the constant effort of a philosopher who is returning from afar – from phenomenology and existentialism – to adapt, correct himself, catch himself just in time, stop himself in the middle of stylistic slips of the 'good old subjective individualism' variety, only to re-offend shortly afterwards and re-cover once again, so as to integrate his analyses into Marxism. Sartre's work is a *dramatic* work in the etymological sense of the term. For the fact remains that Sartre still takes the individual *praxis* of the 'solitary' man as the starting-point for his ontology; and that he regards the dialectical totality as peculiar to human history and denies its immanence in nature, of which man forms part. This often renders his analysis incompatible with scientific Marxism, which takes as its starting-point the *socio-economic structures of a society* at a historically determinate stage of its development – structures whose immanent dialectical meaning is an unfurling, albeit a qualitatively different one, of the dialectical meaning of nature.

Thus we note that in the course of this book Sartre ultimately uses very few of the basic conceptual tools fashioned by Marx in his intellectual maturity; or at least he uses them in a far from explicit manner. More specifically, his analyses of law and the state – which often explicitly criticize Marxist analyses of this domain – appear to result more from the development of certain 'ontological' coordinates than from a Marxist scientific investigation of the objective socio-economic reality of a historically determinate society. Indeed, the general coordinates of the pledge, interests, labour, *'praxis'*, and so on do not seem to us as such to be useful for capturing the 'internal', specific characteristics of a *certain historically determinate sphere of law and a certain state* – for example, the characteristics of generality, formality, abstraction, systematization, and predictability associated with modern law – and accounting for them. They lead Sartre to endeavour to establish *the presuppositions of any possible law or state*. Thus, the *diachronic* dimension, the *historical* perspective, does not end up being integrated into the internal structuration of the phenomena of law and the state – which is the basic issue for the Marxist method – and instead seems to be added on afterwards, as a simple factor of variations, to a certain a-temporal, 'ontological' framework immanent in the domain of social practices and structures formed by law and the state. And yet, in a Marxist analysis of superstructural phenomena, analysis should not start out by considering 'art', 'morality', 'law and the state', and their relations with the base. Far from being pre-given, as a transcendental category, as eidetic, or as an a-temporal ontological framework, the specificity of these phenomena can only be disclosed to us in the course, or at the end, of a process of knowledge that takes as its starting-point a *certain* art, a *certain* law and state, a *certain* morality, concretely situated in time and space and maintaining a determinate relationship with certain structures of the base in a given society.

And thus we arrive at the problematic formulated by Sartre's enterprise of an ontologization of Marxism – that, in short, of a *primary*, meaning-creating *foundation* of the type of intelligibility represented by dialectical reason. Sartre has frequently been criticized for the *idealist* character of his enterprise, for the Kantian problematic that governs it. That is to say, the problem of the 'philosophical', meaning-creating foundation is only posed in a conception of the world where the *rational* subject, the 'subject of knowledge' – man – is presented as 'transcendent' and, in a sense, as external to the world whose intelligibility is to be deciphered, whose conditions of possibility of existence are to be established – conditions that are also the conditions of possibility for man's rational knowledge of the world. For Marxism, by contrast, for which man – a natural being – is originally integrated into a concrete natural materiality, for which human rationality is regarded as a dialectical extension of the rationality of this natural materiality, this is a false problem: meaning is ever-present. It would be presumptuous to seek to discuss this question in the space of a brief essay. But it may be remarked that in so far as, according to Marxism, the dialectical rationality of history – history considered as a 'product' of a natural being, man, who is qualitatively differentiated from other natural beings – contains features that are qualitatively different from those evinced by the rationality – the dialectic – of nature, one can *legitimately* pose the problem of the primary, anthropological – ontological – origins of the particular quality of meaning represented by the dialectic of history. However, the problem posed in this instance is to arrive at a meaning-creating ground that is *different* from the Sartrean matrix of social phenomena, which is ultimately a-historical. In Sartre this matrix is presented as the foundation of social phenomena at all levels – a foundation that in a way *duplicates* socio-economic structures in the Marxist sense. To take only one example, in Sartre the state emerges as '*founded*' on the socio-economic structures of the base (mode of production, social relations of production, and so on) and, *at the same time*, on a certain ontological (a-historical) mode of sociality (Fraternity-Terror, even Master-Slave, and so on). Moreover, this ambiguity consistently arises in Sartre at every level of concrete analysis of juridical phenomena. By contrast, in terms of this enterprise the original ground to be discovered is a simple *starting-point*, but one that would make possible the *historical* scientific operation of the categories of dialectical materialism: a difficult undertaking that Sartre does not as yet seem to have confronted in all its complexity.[44]

By way of conclusion, we may add a remark on Sartre's position on the problem of *juridical positivism*. This issue cannot be treated definitively in the framework of a book that Sartre himself considers to be the first part of work in progress. In Volume One of the *Critique of Dialectical Reason*, Sartre tries to show how, and through what mediations, certain socio-economic structures of the base are transposed into superstructural phenomena, including the state and law.

However, the question as to whether *a certain given juridical universe*, engendered starting from the base, is thereby historically *valid* – that is to say, whether it is legitimated by virtue of being a *fait accompli* – remains open. As is well known, this is a basic issue in the Marxist theory of the state and law. To know Sartre's answer to this question, we shall have to await the second volume of the *Critique*, which will be devoted to the problems of a *historical ethics*.

3

PRELIMINARIES TO THE STUDY OF HEGEMONY IN THE STATE

Generalities

The success currently being enjoyed by the concept of hegemony is well-known: hegemony of the proletariat, hegemonic power, hegemony in the state, hegemonic class, and so on. In short, we often find the concept being used in a way that is either too broad or too narrow – at all events, too vague as long as no attempt is made to define its *scientific status*. This concept, developed by Gramsci even though it had already been explicitly employed by Plekhanov, can be used in two domains which, notwithstanding the relations between them, are distinct: the objective political function and strategy of the proletariat – which poses the issue of the relationship between hegemony and the concept of the 'dictatorship of the proletariat' – and the structures of the capitalist state and the political constitution of the dominant classes in modern society. I am going to situate myself on the latter terrain in order to capture the novelty, the presuppositions, and the operative possibilities of the concept of hegemony in the Marxist analysis of the state.

The concept of hegemony actually forms part of a whole distinctive problematic of dialectical materialism concerning the issues of the base/superstructure relationship and the specificity of the political and state domain in a historically determinate social formation. Contrary to a widespread tendency, its contribution cannot be restricted to some domain of 'ideology' in general, indicating the role of a ruling class which, by means of its intellectuals – ideological functionaries – succeeds in getting its own world-view accepted by the whole of a

* First published in French as 'Préliminaires à l'étude de l'hégémonie dans l'État' in *Les Temps Modernes*, nos 234, pp. 862–96, and 235 (1965), pp. 1048–69. Translated by Gregory Elliott.

society and thereby rules more through conditioned consent than domination in the strict sense of the term. There is in fact no need to introduce a new concept designed merely to highlight the specific effectivity of ideologies, in the broad sense of the term, on the base – something that has always been accepted by Marxist analysis. If the concept of hegemony has a distinctive scientific status, it is because it allow us, when applied to the capitalist state and the classes to whose interests it corresponds, to elucidate their particular historical characteristics in their relations with a historically determinate mode of production. In short, it makes it possible for us to investigate the 'specific logic of a specific object' – the concrete relationship between the capitalist state and the dominant classes – by thus constituting a *determinate-abstract scientific* concept.[1]

In order to assess the contribution of the concept of hegemony, we need to consider what long remained the model of Marxist analysis of the state by 'authorized authors', Vyshinsky at their head. It was governed by the key formula: state = will of the dominant class. First, the state was regarded as an ensemble whose institutional specificity was reduced to its normative aspect – rules of conduct, laws, and so on: this ensemble thus presupposed a certain subject transmitting these norms and personified in a class will. Secondly, and correspondingly, it was considered to be an instrument of repressive violence, which assumed a certain actor deploying and exercising this violence, who could be none other than the will of the dominant class. In fact, this absolutely idealist and voluntarist conception of the state, which identifies it with a 'machine' or a 'tool' invented and created solely for the purposes of domination by a class 'will', is utterly contrary to Marxist scientific analysis of the state. It has numerous consequences that eventually materialize in two currents. On the one hand, the state is genetically regarded as the product of a class will, even a 'consciousness', an abstract entity and a subject transcending history, whose objective relations with the structures of a particular mode of production cannot be elucidated, in as much as it is an ideological concept. On the other hand, the class interests that constitute the state's substratum in its relations with the specific domain of the class struggle, are treated in vulgarly economistic and uncritical fashion as transposed into their institutionalized political expression 'without further ado', without any other mediation. Thus, to the precise extent that this concept of will cannot form the genetic link between the state and the ensemble of objective relations of a mode of production, within which these interests are themselves constituted, no dialectical relationship can be established between those 'socio-economic inter-

ests' and the 'class political will'. This invariant structure of 'voluntarism-economism' is to be found in all the concrete consequences
produced by the formula state = will of the dominant class. They are
as follows:

(a) The state is regarded as the exclusive property of 'a' dominant
class. The class will, the determining principle of the mediation and
production of the superstructures and ideologies on the basis of the
infrastructure, is presented as the expression of an indivisible, abstract
essence of a *single* class-subject of the 'will' of domination and the
state.

(b) This class-subject of the state is *itself* regarded in its relations
with the state as abstractly *unified* exclusively 'by' its will to dominate.
The problematic of a scientific investigation of the internal contradictions of this class, in their transposition to the level of the state, is
dissolved in treating it as a *unity of will*.

(c) The distinctive internal unity of the state corresponding to its
relative autonomy and specific effectivity is itself directly related to the
dominant class's unity of will. The dialectical relations between the
state and the dominant classes, founded on their respective constitution as particular political units, thus boil down to a reduction of the
state's unity to that of the dominant class, which is presupposed.

(d) The state is regarded as the instrument, the machine, the tool,
the apparatus invented and created by this class for the purposes of its
domination and as *manipulable at will* by the class will.

(e) The state is one-sidedly regarded as an 'oppressive force' and
'organized violence', concrete expression of the class will. The generating principle and effectivity of the state are crystallized in violence,
treated as a corollary, of a psycho-social sort, of the class will – which
leads to a whole series of voluntarist theories of the state, from
Hobbes to Sorel.

(f) The problematic of the *historical specificity* of a determinate
state is dissolved into abstract consideration of the state in general. To
the extent that this concept of class will does not allow us to establish
the *historical* genetic link between the institutionalized political level
and the particular ensemble of a 'type' of mode of production – forces
and relations of production – which form the base of a given social
formation, the different types of state are ultimately characterized by a
mere difference in 'expressing' or 'presenting' oppression with a
dominant class and by an identity in the historically undifferentiated
will to dominate and the baton blows dealt out by its organs. This
results in anarchist conceptions of the state and the Hegelian conception of Master and Slave.

It is all too clear that the consequences of the theoretico-historical conception of the state as the 'product' of a 'will' on the part of 'the dominant class' render concrete analysis of a particular, historically determinate state an utter impossibility.

Indeed, this conception of the state is itself bound up with a whole purely instrumentalist treatment of the status of the superstructures and ideologies – a conception that finds a spectacular formulation in Stalin. In its *genesis* and *particular effectivity*, the superstructural domain supposedly constitutes 'what is useful to the base'.[2] And the employment of the term 'useful', which is not (in its ambiguous meaning) accidental, is itself bound up with a whole 'voluntarist' and 'subjectivist' conception of the superstructures. Men 'know' and 'become conscious' of the base through the superstructures and therefore 'want' and 'construct' 'useful' superstructures. Or, again, the latter supposedly represent the element for men's access and action as subjects – voluntarism – on an 'opaque', 'recalcitrant' base – economism – which can only be dealt with through the intermediary of superstructures that can be made and unmade at will. The base allegedly poses problems that it cannot itself resolve – economism – and to which only the superstructure can furnish solutions – voluntarism. The Marxist problematic of an objective relationship between the objective structures and practices of the base and the superstructure is conjured away in favour of *a radical division in the respective status of the base – economism – and the superstructure – voluntarism*. This *division cannot but lead to simplistic monisms*, precisely in so far as these two anti-dialectical conceptions, *which are necessarily linked*, complement one another by turns and constitute a global conception of the historical process. In this finalist vision of history, the superstructural domains, products of the will of a class-subject of history, ultimately possess no objective reality of their own engendered from the base. In the historical process of an idealist will-subject of history as a whole, a subject that produces and totalizes the various levels of social practices, the superstructures have the status of a simple objectification of the consciousness-will of a class whose own effectivity on the base can be explained by the circular return of the phenomenon into the essence, in the distinctive unfolding of the subject. The superstructures appear alternatively and indifferently – *at the same time* – either as simple phenomena – objectifications reducible to the base, itself the 'product' of a voluntarist '*praxis*'; or as the determining factor in the social formation as a whole – witness the conception of the Stalinist state. *The determining role can in fact be inverted in the unilinear relationship between these two domains constituted by the praxis-will of the class-subject of history.* This is because economism – the invariable corollary of voluntarism – cannot but lead to a comprehensively voluntarist conception of the ensemble of relations of a social formation. Indeed, in an economistic conception of Marxism, corresponding to a vulgar monism, the objective relationship between the various levels of reality of social practices – which is precisely what founds the historical dialectical process – is abandoned in favour of a unilinear determinism: the superstructures are *reduced* to the base and practice is dissolved in favour of a mechanistic account of the productive forces. In this case, the historical process can only be explained to the extent that it is 'set to work' by the introduction, following the Hegelian example, of a totalizing, driving will-consciousness-subject. This will-consciousness is no longer simply a mediating link between the base – in its economistic conception – and superstructure, the generating principle of the superstructures starting from the base, but necessarily assumes the role of agent, 'producing' – *through* the superstructures – the objective structures even of the base. In short, this invariant theoretical structure 'voluntarism-economism' is globally situated within the logic of a Hegelian conception of the Idea-totality. In it, base and superstructure appear indifferently interchangeable in their role of *determining instance* in the dialectical process, given that within this will-consciousness-*praxis*, motor of the spherical and circular process, there is in fact no need for a *determining instance.*

Now, in order to situate the original Marxist problematic of the state, it is appropriate to return to Marx's early works, where he is concerned with the modern political state, and to see what their relationship with the development of his thinking is – in particular, as regards the problem of the base/superstructure relationship. In fact, this is the only way that we can define the presuppositions of the concept of hegemony.

As is well known, in the *Critique of Hegel's Doctrine of the State* and the articles in the *Franco-German Yearbooks*, where his viewpoint still attests to the influence of Feuerbach and Fichte, Marx criticizes Hegel using the model of political-anthropological alienation – the relations between subject and predicate, essence and phenomenon. For Hegel, the state constitutes the subject, the essence of civil society – the sphere of needs; for Marx, this subject and essence are concrete individuals, generic men – civil society – and the state represents the alienated expression – the political religion – of their essence. For Hegel, therefore, the state has created the ensemble of civil society and contains it, whereas for Marx it is the ensemble of civil society – generic people-men – who have created the state, but without containing it, for what is involved is a political alienation – the phenomenon of this essence. Now, I am not going to return to the discussion about the young Marx here, but I want to indicate the kind of issues posed for investigation of the state by Marx's transition from his youth to maturity. Marx develops scientific concepts of mode of production, class, class struggle, base and superstructure, and so on. The state – a particular domain of the superstructure – no longer takes the form of a mere phenomenon, an 'alienation', or predicate of an essence, of civil society-concrete individuals, but that of an *objective, specific reality with its own effectivity*, which is engendered starting from the base, scientifically defined as class struggle in a historically determinate mode of production: the conception of the 'class state' makes its appearance. But what has been attempted by the most serious Marxists who have sought to harness the undoubted evolution and originality of the mature Marx with respect to the young Marx when it comes to the relations between base and superstructure and the particular problem of the state? In fact, they reduce the distinctive reality of the state as a specific domain of the superstructure, not to the particular *ensemble* constituted (for Marx) by a historically determinate mode of production, *but to the political practice* – not the 'will' – *of a class* – the dominant class – thus wholly misjudging the meaning of 'class state'. In fact, for the mature Marx, Engels and Lenin, the state is the state of a *class-divided society* (I shall deal with the problem of the state in the Asiatic mode of production below). It comprises a particular ensemble of objective structures that are created and function in connection with the contradictions specific to a particular *ensemble*, a 'type' of unity represented by a social formation on the basis of a determinate mode of production. In his own intellectual development, Marx retained from his early writings the conception of the state as an organic ensemble corresponding to another ensemble constituted by civil society, whose structuration as a *unity* in its own right he uncovered in his later work. The state *corresponds* to the interests of the dominant class in so far as these interests are themselves structured in an *objective site* constituted by the unity of an ensemble – the base – which means that there is one dominant class or certain dominant classes, that there is a given state, and that this state corresponds to the interests of the dominant class or fraction. Even though the state is in no way the 'product' of these classes, this correspondence is not due to the coincidence of some ruse of Reason. And this is because the state, while possessing its own objective reality, is constituted starting from the same place as class struggle and the relations of exploitation and domination are situated. Thus, in its own unity, and by virtue of its creation starting from the unity of the base, the state crystallizes the *relations* of production and *class relations*. The modern political state does not translate the 'interests' of the dominant classes at the political level, *but the relationship between those interests and the interests of the dominated classes* – which means that it precisely constitutes the 'political' expression of the interests of the dominant classes.

To return to the originality and scientific content of the Marxist theory of the state, we must break with any purely 'descriptive' conception that perceives the state as the product or instrument of the dominant classes. Or rather, we must not confuse the descriptive expressions of the Marxist classics – which understandably abound in the political field – with scientific concepts. And the scientificity of a concept precisely depends upon the theoretical location in which it is situated in its constitution. We cannot 'abstract' one of Marx's theoretical concepts – 'class' – and elevate it, thus isolated, into a historical subject producing superstructures-objects, thereby neglecting the fact that this concept can only be theoretically constituted in an objective ensemble designated by the 'mode of production'. If we therefore wish to go decisively beyond any conception that *necessarily* results in a voluntarism of the Lukácsian variety, it will not be by replacing the notion of 'concrete individuals' by that of 'class', or the notion of class 'consciousness' or will by that of class practice, or by uncritically juxtaposing as the factors which engender superstructures the 'subjective factor' – class will – and the 'objective factor' – the objective ensemble of the base. It will in fact only be by definitively abandoning any viewpoint that simultaneously reduces the structuration of a given social formation and the sequence of these formations to a subject – be it social labour, *praxis*, social class, or concrete individuals. Indeed, it can easily be demonstrated – something which is perfectly clear, moreover, in the work of the young Marx, where the subjectivist standpoint is adopted – that this standpoint necessarily assigns the status of alienation to the domain of superstructures and ideologies; and that, vice versa, the problematic of *alienation* is invariably bound up with the introduction of the *subject*. In this case, we *unfailingly* encounter a pair of *superimposable* statuses involving, respectively, base and superstructure, which in fact reduce the dialectical materialist viewpoint to an empiricist Marxist one. I am referring to the pairs subject-objectification, real-ideal, concrete-abstract, essence-alienation, material-consciousness. As a result, the superstructures and ideologies are presented both as having the status of an abstract 'ideal' phenomenon – even false and deceptive – *and* as instrumental 'products' of the subject. Because of the invariant theoretical structure that is voluntarism-economism, which ultimately comes down to introducing the subject, it would be no exaggeration to regard the 'Stalinist' instrumentalist problematic of the superstructure and ideologies as an inverted image of the young Marx's subjectivist viewpoint.

Furthermore, we should not forget the problematic that led Second International Marxism to neglect investigation of the state, and which Lenin combated with *The State and Revolution*. On account of the Hegelian perspective predominant in the Marxist movement at the time, and because of an interpretation of Marx and Engels's texts in accordance with the young Marx's schema of alienation-consciousness, the state was demoted to the status of an ideal phenomenon, the alienated content of consciousness, which led, in the case of the anti-revisionist tendency, to the conception of an anarcho-syndicalist strategy situated at the strictly socio-economic level. This reaction is clearly evident in the work of Karl Korsch who, himself adopting the subjectivist Hegelian standpoint, vainly sought to demonstrate the real character of the state, while ultimately regarding it as a product of class consciousness.

In the scientific Marxist perspective, the subjectivist problematic is abandoned in favour of a system of objective relations between objective structures and practices, constituting specific levels of reality with their own unity, within the unity of a determinate social formation – a unity that can itself be referred to the 'typical' unity of a mode of production. Consequently, the problem of historicity is in no way reduced to a subject-agent-totalizer, but to the *succession* of and *transition* between systems of relations – social formations – that as such form systems of governed transformations. This assumes a *complex* sequence at every level, not a *unilinear* one, as in the Hegelian or voluntarist historicity of the subject, or in economistic historicity grounded in the unilinear development of the productive forces.

The constitutive features of the political structures of the modern state, in contrast to those of the 'economic-corporate' state, were signalled by Marx in his early works, where he drew attention to a crucial fact for the investigation of the modern state: the separation between civil society and the state. In sum, Marx tells us, Hegel had observed – following Locke, Kant and so on, and even though the observation was variously formulated by them – a real problem and sought to resolve it in mistaken fashion: the separation of the modern bourgeois state – constituting the sphere of the *universal* and the *general* – from civil society, or particular, private socio-economic needs. The French bourgeoisie, Marx argues, had carried out a

> partial, *merely* political revolution . . . What is the basis of a partial and merely political revolution? Its basis is the fact that one *part of civil society* emancipates itself and attains *universal* domination, that one particular class undertakes from its *particular situation* the universal emancipation of society.[3]

Unlike the slave and feudal types of state, the political state does not take the form of the simple ratification by force of the socio-economic interests, in the strict sense, of the dominant classes or class fractions. In their relations with the objective structures of the state, these interests are not transposed in their 'direct' form of private interests, but must assume a *specifically political* mediated form and appear to embody the general interest of society as a whole. The state does not emerge as the site where the 'public' domination of a privileged 'private' realm is constituted, but as the expression of the universal and, through the political constitution of the dominant classes, as the guarantor of the general interest. Precisely to the extent that the universalizing political structures of the state arise, the state splits off from civil society, which remains the site of contradictions between private interests. Its characteristic of universality, based on reconciling different private interests, on synthesizing their contradictions, is nothing but an illusion and a pure 'deceptive' formalism, which is in fact correlative not to its real status and function with respect to civil society, but to its *alienating abstraction* from the coordinates – concrete individuals – specific to this society. The modern state's political characteristic of universality constitutes a 'political act of complete trans-substantiation', an 'ecstasy', an act whereby civil society is divided in itself as civil society: 'the abstraction of the state *as such* belongs exclusively to the modern age . . . the abstraction of the *political state* is a modern product'. Thus the modern state, while corresponding to the private interests of the bourgeois class, 'claims', through a strictly mystificatory 'ideological' projection, to be the sphere of universal interest.

This notion of the separation between civil society and the state remained a constant in Marx's thinking despite its evolution, which led to his conception of the 'class state'. It is precisely in his subsequent work that Marx was to discover the scientific foundation of this 'separation', which no longer emerges as a result of the 'alienation' of generic men – a phenomenon separated from the essence – but as a characteristic reality of the *objective structures* of the political state engendered on the basis of a determinate mode of production. Far from abolishing the distantiation between the state and civil society, the conception of a 'class state' is itself situated within it; and in this way Marx sought to discover what had to be the distinctively political structuration of the interests of a social class, interests to which the objective structures of a state 'separated' from civil society correspond.[4] Obviously, the specificity of these structures will not consist in the fact that the state, on the Hegelian model, realizes the reconciliation of private interests in the 'universal'. It will consist in a real, but 'formal' and 'abstract' universality, whose abstraction and formality will have to be defined *scientifically*. The abstraction and formality of the universalizing structure of the modern state will not be conceived as constitutive characteristics of a political 'alienation', as features of a phenomenon 'abstracted' from its 'concrete' essence. As the characteristics of a specific real structure, they will be related to the objective realities of the base.

Thus, the separation between state and civil society – that is, the *specifically political* character of the capitalist state – manifests itself in Marx's subsequent work in the characteristic of universality assumed by a particular set of values. These constitute the objective structuring factors, the specific mediation between the base and the political superstructure of the institutions of a state that is engendered by a particular 'type' of mode of production characteristic of the capitalist, exchange-based social formation. This set of 'values' does not merely exercise an ideological role of justification; it functions as a condition of possibility of the objective structures of the modern representative state: structures that themselves constitute the conditions of possibility of the coordinates of the base in a capitalist, exchange-based society. They are the 'universal' values of formal, abstract liberty and equality. In societies based on expanded reproduction and generalized commodity exchange, we observe a process of privatization and autonomization of men as producers. Natural human relations, founded on a hierarchy involving the socio-economic subordination of producers (witness slave and feudal states), are replaced by *'social' relations between 'autonomized' individuals*, located in the exchange process. *Marx and Lenin underscore this evolution of natural relations into social relations*, the autonomization of individuals corresponding to a division between concrete labour and 'abstract' labour, between use-value and exchange-value, that underlies the constitution of commodity-value and labour-value and exploitation in capitalist, exchange-based society. The process of 'abstraction' and 'equalization' within the labour process, the autonomization and privatization of individuals inside the exchange process, and the forms of private ownership and competition that derive from it, correspond, at the political level, to the values of *abstract, formal liberty and equality* and to the 'separation' between civil society and the state.[5] This appearance of social relations in the capitalist system of production in fact presupposes, as a necessary precondition, the characteristic atomization of civil society and goes hand in hand with the advent of specifically political relations, in so far as the capitalist mode of production is incompatible with a division of labour subject to a 'public' hierarchy that might obstruct the formation of the relations required by a stage of development of the productive forces, which might prevent the molecularization of society. In slave and feudal societies, the producers were in fact directly subordinated by 'natural' bonds, which, as a result, assumed a 'public' character. In short, the relations of exploitation overall took on a *mixed* character, socio-economic and political. The relationship of the producer to the hierarchical community – the *public status* of the slave, the serf, the peasant, and so on – grounded in a mode of production where exchange did not play a determining role in the process of reproduction, directly conditioned his socio-economic position in the production process. Socio-economic relations and public relations as materialized in state institutions were thus assimilated and identified within the global relationship of naturalness. Social classes – unlike mobile, open modern classes – were simultaneously '*political' castes*; and the state was a ratification by 'public' force of socio-economic relations 'as such', whose relationship with the state stemmed from their being considered 'natural' or 'sacred'. They were reputed to be determined in advance by a human 'nature' – a projection of existing social relations – and thus to derive from a 'natural inequality' between human beings, or – and in fact at the same time – as ethical-religious relations established by some divinity, by the god-given nature of society.

In the framework of slave and medieval societies, the 'political' does not constitute a *specific* level, with its own internal logic, of 'autonomized' structures and practices, because man's membership of a public community is identified with his socio-economic function – transposed into a 'sacred' mythology – in economic-corporate bodies within a social formation that is wholly and strictly hierarchical. The concept of the '*specifically political*', and the concrete consequences

that follow from it for politics-as-power and politics-as-practice, is in
fact linked in Marx and Gramsci[6] to the separation between the state
and civil society in the context of the gradual constitution of the
modern bourgeois state. The autonomization of the producers in
capitalist society, the particular forms assumed by competition, and
the mode of production that engenders the distinctive form of the
'private' and 'particular' correspond, on the side of the state, to its
properly political 'universal' character – treated by political theory as
the state's *rationality* – based on formal, abstract liberty and equality:
all men are free and equal in as much as all men are private individuals.
The state assumes the 'secular' form of an abstract normative regulation of the relations between individual wills engaged in exchange and
competition, takes on the objective function of establishing the formal
framework of external cohesion for a practical field of competitive
encounters involving exchange in a civil society fragmented into a
multiplicity of centres of autonomized 'wills'. The modern juridical
system, distinct from feudal regulation based on 'privileges', assumes a
'normative' character based on the values of equality and liberty, and
expresses specific relations in the sphere of generalized exchange and
competition. The state thus establishes an 'order' in the anarchy of
inter-individual relations, an order that possesses a dual objective
function: preserving and maintaining the fragmentation of civil society
and organizing it with a view to its operation within a capitalist,
exchange-based mode of production. The state's legitimacy is no
longer based on the divine will embodied, for example, in the
monarchical principle, but on the abstract set of individuals who
are formally free and equal – separated, in other words, from their
concrete determinations in civil society – on popular sovereignty and
the state's secular responsibility towards the 'people'. The people is
itself established as the principle of the state's political determination,
not as a set of individuals occupying a particular place in the
production process, but as an empirical, abstract mass of indivi-
duals-citizens whose mode of participation in a national political
community as expressed by the state is manifest in universal suffrage.
The modern state presents itself as embodying the *general interest* of
society as a whole, as the substantiation of the 'will' of the 'political
body' that is the 'nation'. By comparison with other types of state, it
thus possesses the fundamental peculiarity that it presents itself as the
sphere of the universal and the general, that it liberates political
individuals-persons from the natural hierarchies which obstruct their
integration into a 'universal' community – and this in as much as its
objective function is to impose a kind of unification on molecularized,

exchange-based society. The atomistic separation of civil society precisely constitutes its condition of possibility: the state separates itself from civil society for, based on this molecularization, it can only attain the sphere of the universal through an abstraction and formality that make it possible politically to harness human beings/the governed as political individuals/persons, separated from their concrete socio-economic determinations.

Thus, study of the objective structures of the state in their relationship with the basic framework of the mode of production, on the basis of which social classes, class interests and class struggle are structured, makes it possible to move on to the political level of the class struggle and to examine the relationship between the particular – political – structuration that is assumed in capitalist society by the socio-economic interests of the dominant class or classes and the objective structures of the state which 'asserts' those interests – in short, the relations between political class struggle proper and the political state proper. The structure of domination is not some unchanging 'socio-economic interests of the dominant classes + state as repression', but corresponds to a universalizing, mediated form which these interests must assume with respect to a political state that at the same time has the *real* function, while remaining a class state, of representing a formal and abstract 'general interest' of society. In the economic-corporate state of the feudal or fascist type, the socio-economic interests of the dominant classes enjoy in their empirical immediacy, just as they are, the sanction of the state as force, invested in a literally imaginary 'justificatory' ideology. Civil society and the state, the economic and the political are closely interwoven in as much as the state imposes the 'private' economic-corporate interests of the dominant classes through 'direct' officiation and domination of society. In contrast, the modern state corresponds to the specifically political interests of the hegemonic classes; the socio-economic interests of these classes, in their relationship with the 'universalizing', objective institutions of this state, are conceived and presented as the driving force of a universal expansion, a development of all 'national' energies.[7]

We can thus define the scientific field of constitution of the concept of hegemony: it is situated in the theoretical field that corresponds to the particular 'site' represented by the 'political' level; and it presupposes, as a theoretico-historical condition of its constitution, the basic coordinates of a determinate mode of production which underlie the emergence of the political as a *specific* level of structures and practices, 'autonomized' through the mediation of the separation between civil society and the state that they engender. To adopt Lenin's characteristic formulation, we can summarily divide social practice into economic practice, political practice and ideological practice. From this standpoint, in the context of a class-divided society we can characterize political practice in general as the practice that has as its object the state, whose constitution as an objective institution corresponds, even in the Asiatic mode of production, to the emergence of a 'public power' – a force separated from a population organized under arms. However, in the context of pre-capitalist formations, these various practices and structures emerge as *closely interwoven* and do not form specific levels with their own internal logic – sites that might represent the *specific objects of corresponding specific sciences*. And, without wishing to enter into the debate about the relations between scientific theory and its object, we can nevertheless see that one of the reasons why economic science and political science – the latter emerging with Hobbes (politics as power) and Machiavelli (politics as practice) – first emerged in the capitalist formation consists in the basic characteristic of this formation in this respect: the various levels of social structures and practices emerge as relatively autonomous in it. As regards the autonomization of the economic from the political, in pre-capitalist formations – even market societies – based on slavery and the *corvée*, production and reproduction are determined by public relations of domination; in the capitalist formation, the determining factors in production and reproduction are exchange and surplus-value as the 'immediate aim and decisive motive in production', as Marx points out. As regards the autonomization of the political from the economic, we witness the modern separation between civil society and the state, not in the sense of the separation between the state as force (public power) and the armed population – which does not prevent the imbrication of the political and the economic: quite the reverse – but in the sense we have just explained. This is to say that the political, as a result of such autonomization, takes on specific features in the capitalist formation when compared with the characteristics that constituted it in pre-capitalist formations – a process that is, moreover, homologous to the differentiation, with respect to economic science, between the capitalist mode of production and pre-capitalist modes of production. Thus, the concept of hegemony, referring to the 'most openly political phase', contains the distinctive constitutive elements of the political in the capitalist formation and precisely signals the *moment* when these elements attain such importance that they emerge as determining factors in

the 'balance of the situation' or 'balance of forces' in the current social
formation. The concept of hegemony therefore has as its field of
application both the domain of institutionalized political structures
and the domain of the political practices of the dominant classes –
namely:

a) *The domain of institutionalized political 'structures'.* Here the
'political' comprises the structures of a state separated from civil
society. It designates a specific form of power (hegemony-power),
materialized in objective superstructural institutions, including the
instance of 'universality'. This universality itself has two aspects. The
modern state represents a specific factor, with relative autonomy and
specific effectivity, structuring a real general interest of the dominant
classes or fractions under the aegis of the hegemonic class or fraction
and appears as the representative of the formal, abstract general
interest of the nation. Here the concept of hegemony refers to the
phase of objective process of structuration of the modern state, when
the concrete consequences of this instance of universality – consent,
ideological functions, organizing role, role of intellectual and moral
leadership, and so on – attain a decisive role in the particular relations
of domination crystallized by this state.

b) *The domain of the political 'practices' of the 'dominant classes' in
capitalist, exchange-based society.* Here the 'political' refers to a
particular practice with its own autonomy – distinct, for example,
from ethical-religious practice – whose specific object is the preservation or conquest of power. In the first instance, this is the institutionalized form of power – the political state now stripped of its 'sacred
aura' – but also a particular form of non-institutionalized power, only
to the extent, however, that this latter form of power goes beyond
domination or a position of 'strength' of a strictly economic-corporate
kind, and appears correlative to a universalizing structuration of
socio-economic interests – leadership of subordinate groups by a
group, and so on – in their constitutive relationship to the political
state. Extending to the complex domain of ideologies, political
practice is thus related to the degree of 'homogeneity, self-consciousness and organization' achieved to this end by the dominant classes
and itself includes the instance of universality, in its dual aspect. The
dominant class or fraction that maintains itself in, or which strives to
conquer, political power will have to organize itself through a
structuration of its *specific socio-economic interests* such that they
can represent a real general interest of the dominant classes or

fractions, presented and conceived as the general interest of the 'nation'. Here the concept of hegemony (hegemony-as-political-practice) refers to the moment when the political structuration of the dominant classes – ideological function, organizational function, leadership, and so on – assumes decisive importance in class relations.[8]

Thus defined, the concept of hegemony can be of use to us in several respects. In the first place, considered in the 'typological' problematic concerning a type of state, this concept, when applied to the type of state that corresponds to the capitalist, exchange-based formation, makes it possible to account for its specific unity and distinctive development. The Marxist 'typological' problematic consists in identifying a concept-type that can explain the 'typical' unity of the specific structures of a level of the social reality which constitutes them as an 'object' of scientific analysis, in their relations with a 'type' of mode of production which constitutes the basis of the unity of a historically determinate social formation. In short, it identifies a concept which, in contrast to formalist and formalizing models of the 'ideal type' variety or the 'concrete-universal' concept, constitutes a 'determinate-abstract' concept: these are precisely the characteristic features of the concept of hegemony. In this sense, the hegemonic state must be conceived in its *gradual* structuration. This has taken highly diverse concrete forms depending on the national ensemble considered, and so on – the *'transitional'* form pertaining to this 'type' of state being the *absolutist* state – but which, in general, evince the typical characteristics created by the separation between civil society and the state.

This will enable us to define certain problems. We shall be able to conceptualize with precision the evolution of this type of state towards its hegemonic constitution, which itself assumes different concrete forms; and thus appreciate that such diversity, or the transformations in forms of state or political 'regimes' within the capitalist mode of production, does not fundamentally call into question the objective framework of the hegemonic state. They correspond to the specificities of this mode and the concrete dimensions assumed by the political class struggle, *even to the different forms of a 'hegemonic' class exploitation – to the content and concrete form of this hegemony.* It is in this context that we shall be able to pose the question as to whether the particularities in the development of the productive forces and relations of production that characterize 'imperialism' or 'state monopoly capitalism' constitute differentiated unities of a mode of production, corresponding to new 'types' of state. In fact, these peculiarities do indeed evince a unity of their own, but within the capitalist 'type' –

witness, for example, the whole issue of the transition within the capitalist mode of production from manufacture to large-scale industry. However, this unity, at least as regards its relations with the specific internal unity of the state, by no means represents a 'typical' ensemble, yielding a new 'type' of state, but simply contradictions within the basic framework 'type' of state. The so-called 'welfare state' or 'technocratic state', and so on, can in fact only be accounted for if they are considered, *in accordance with developments in class hegemony*, as forms of state or regime within the modern class 'type' of state. This is because these particularities in the mode of production are themselves situated, as contradictions, within the 'type' of the capitalist social formation, as Lenin clearly demonstrated.

Thus, without going into an analysis of the key differences between the contemporary state and the liberal state, I will restrict myself to indicating that the rigorous application of the concept of hegemony to the type of state corresponding to the capitalist social formation makes it possible to situate these differences within the historicity that is peculiar to a type of state corresponding to hegemonic class exploitation. Developments in the contemporary state are situated *within a separation between civil society and the state*, despite the transformation of the democratic liberalism theorized by Locke, Montesquieu, Humboldt, Constant and so on, in the direction of a 'strong state'; *within a specific internal unity* of the state corresponding to its separation from civil society, despite certain 'corporatist' developments in the state; *within a molecularization of civil society* maintained by the state, despite the new forms taken by the progressive socialization of the productive forces; *within a specificity of the political level vis-à-vis the economic-corporate level*; *within a relative autonomy of the state* with respect both to the socio-economic ensembles of civil society and the dominant classes or fractions, despite the phenomenon of monopolistic concentration – in short, *within a specifically political, even hegemonic, class exploitation*. And here we can recognize the themes and hobby horses of the whole neo-capitalist 'corporatist-institutionalist' theoretical current of the state. In fact, the basic coordinates of the hegemonic class state are still present in the current form of a state that corresponds to changes in hegemonic domination in the context of monopolistic concentration. And here we should possibly stress the crucial 'ideological' phenomenon that occurs in connection with neo-capitalist theories of the state, which presuppose the basic theoretical coordinates of the 'functionalist' current. Because of the monopolistic concentration of capital on the one hand, and

the progressive socialization of the productive forces on the other –
i.e. because of the concrete form currently taken by the principal
aspect of the contradiction between private appropriation of the
means of production and progressive socialization of the productive
forces – we are witnessing real changes in the state, aimed at
containing this contradiction. These real phenomena, which in the
production process itself disclose the concrete relations between the
individual, centre of liberal-democratic thought, and the social
ensembles in which he is integrated, even constituted – at once
individual-proprietor and individual-producer – while opening up
possibilities for a scientific problematic, are theoretically extrapolated through a purely ideological use of the thematic generated by
the real process. We may advance as a working hypothesis that the
real phenomena indicated above generate at the theoretical level, and
via numerous mediations, the theme of the totality – the problematic
of 'institutions', 'structures', 'corporations', 'masses', and so on –
which replaces that of individualism. The ideological extrapolation
of this thematic consists in subjectivist materializations and applications, dating back to Weber , of the 'totality' in the current of
'functionalism' – theoretical framework of the neo-corporatist-in-
stitutionalist current of the state – in the very notion of 'structure' or
'system' and the relations between its elements that it employs. In
short, it consists in the 'political' thematic of the social formation
conceived, in the last analysis, as a *circular subject-set of equivalent,
balanced and integrated 'empirical' elements* – powers and counter-
powers, veto groups, and so on. And this is in contrast to the Marxist
notion of totality, indicating at the political level the contradictory
objective unity of elements that are simultaneously 'functional' and
'dysfunctional', *under the dominance* of the hegemonic class or
fraction. Hence, moreover, the fact that functionalism is situated
within an invariant ideological problematic of 'subject-totality-em-
piricism'. Thus, I am simply signalling that using the concept of
hegemony makes it possible correctly to grasp both the framework of
the liberal state and current developments in the state, situated
within the basic coordinates of the capitalist type of state and the
new forms assumed by hegemonic class exploitation.

The State in the Relationship between Dominant and Dominated Classes

We may thus seek to define more precisely the particularities of the
modern state that the concept of hegemony allows us to identify – and

in the first instance, as regards the relationship between the dominant classes and the dominated classes.

a) First, this concept indicates that the modern state cannot unequivocally ratify the specific socio-economic interests, empirically construed, of the dominant classes. If its hegemonic function of universality, as the organizing framework of molecularized society, conforms to the interests of capital, it nevertheless necessarily contains, at the specific political level of class struggle, a guarantee of certain of the dominated classes' economic-corporate interests – a guarantee in accordance with the hegemonic constitution of the class in power, whose political interests are asserted by the state. What matters here is that the integration of the economic-corporate interests of the dominated classes into the political state does not have the character of a mechanical 'compromise' within a socio-economic balance of forces, as is the case in the economic-corporate state. In the latter, the interests of the dominated classes are in general only guaranteed in so far as they are compatible with the strict economic-corporate interests of the dominant classes and can be incorporated into the small margin of 'mechanical' compromise permitted by the balance of the opposing economic and social forces. Indeed, in the framework of this state, every *particle* of social-economic power shifted from the dominant class to the dominated classes counts as such – in other words, it 'automatically' reduces the power held by the dominant class. *Socio-economic power in fact emerges here as a set of 'bastions of power' whose internal unity is not realized, through state mediation, at a specific level* – the 'autonomized' political level – with its own internal logic – corresponding, moreover, to the specific unity of the hegemonic state – and which precisely allows for the 'assimilation' of a relatively broad swathe of the dominated classes' socio-economic interests to the political interest of the dominant classes. Thus in the case of the modern state, to take only one example, certain working-class 'conquests', such as social security at the outset, in fact conform to the strict economic-corporate interest of capital, in as much as they ensure the reproduction of labour-power. Others, however, when assessed on the economic-corporate level – the issue of the welfare state – can be regarded as contrary to the strict interests of capital, even though they correspond to its political interests. The modern state is in fact frequently in the service of the political interests of the hegemonic classes against their own economic-corporate interests, in the service of the general interest of the dominant classes or fractions, politically constituted as society's general interest.

b) The concept of hegemony assumes major importance in connection with the study of the function, the specific effectivity, and the political character of ideologies in the context of hegemonic class exploitation. And this is so in as much as it is constituted starting from the specifically political level of the capitalist formation. It is well known, in a somewhat popularized version of Gramsci, that hegemony refers to the characteristic of a class that succeeds in imposing on a whole social formation the ideology, the world-view, the 'way of life', the taste, and so on, constituted on the basis of its own position in this formation. *However, this general reference does not situate the specifically political function of ideologies in the contemporary social formation with precision.*

To do that, we must return to one of the presuppositions of the constitution of the concept of hegemony. We have already mentioned the fact that the general conception of hegemony presupposes wholly abandoning the 'subjectivist' perspective. We know that the young Marx conceived the problematic of ideology, like the problematic of the superstructures, on basis of the subject-alienation model. The subject was dispossessed of his concrete essence in reality itself and ideology constituted the projection into a fantastic, imaginary world of his 'mystified' essence – in short, the alienating 'ideal' reconstruction of his essence that had been objectified-alienated in socio-economic reality. Ideology, tacked onto the schema of alienation, was identified with false consciousness. The respective separations between state and civil society, superstructures and base, ideology and reality, abstract phenomenon and concrete subject, and so on, were reduced to a status that was at once monist – the subject being the real foundation – and radically autonomized – division between the real and the ideal, and so on.

There is no doubt that a subjectivist viewpoint, whatever it may be, necessarily identifies ideology and alienation, resulting in a voluntarist status for ideologies, which are regarded as 'products' of a class consciousness or a freedom – the alienated *praxis* of the subject. This status presupposes both an alienation, and an incomplete alienation, of the subject in 'reality'. In the case, for example, of communist society, because of the recuperation by the subject of his essence, ideologies will have disappeared, giving way to a scientific 'transparency' of consciousness to its objectified existence. In the event of a total alienation of the subject in reality, ideologies would themselves have toppled over 'into reality' in as much as, with consciousness wholly 'bogged down' in the real, any possibility of a relatively coherent 'alienating' projection – or an 'emancipatory' one in the

exclusive case of the proletariat, the privileged class in the 'real' – of
the essence in an 'ideal' world would have disappeared. *And this
invariant relationship between ideology, alienation and reality* is clear
in all 'subjectivist' *marxisant* conceptions, from Goldmann to Adorno
and Marcuse, who interpret current social developments in accordance
with the schema of a total reification-alienation of the subject in the
real, resulting in an 'absorption of ideology into reality', a de-ideologization, correlative to a de-politicization, in contemporary societies.

From Marx's scientific viewpoint, ideologies themselves take the
form of a specific objective level with their own reality, comprising a
relatively coherent set of concepts, representations, values, and so on.
(On account of the very status of the ideological, ideologies cannot,
strictly speaking, constitute 'systems'.)[9] Their status and their function
consist in 'expressing' men's 'lived' relationship to their conditions of
existence, the way men live these conditions. They in fact constitute
the point of men's insertion into an objective system of relations –
comprising both the base and the superstructures in the strict sense of
the term – with ideology in a sense constituting the 'material of
cohesion' between the different levels of social practices and structures. This means that ideologies refer, in the last analysis, to human
lived experience, without thereby being reduced to a genetic problematic of the subject-consciousness. They consist in 'real' structures,
which, in so far as they refer to the relationship between men and their
conditions of existence, do not constitute the simple expression of this
relationship – of the signifier-signified, symbol-reality variety – but its
imaginary investment. This social imaginary, possessing a real prac-
tico-social function, is thus in no way reducible to a problematic of the
subject – hence to that of alienation: ideologies are always required, no
matter what the social formation. In so far as they are constitutively
imbricated in this function of the imaginary, they are necessarily
adequate-inadequate to objective social relations. However, the particular relationship of ideology and these relations to reality is not
given in unequivocal fashion and for all social formations. *The
function, the effectivity, and the particular political role of ideologies
in fact depend in the capitalist formation on the specific relationship
between ideology and reality in this formation.*

In these formations, the state must present itself as guarantor of the
general interest of society at all levels, as the contract between free and
equal individual wills, despite the fact that it ratifies the class division
of society, inequality, and slavery in civil society. Consequently, the
dominant classes and the political state, structured into hegemonic

classes and a hegemonic state, must develop a whole distinctive
political ideological ensemble, which has a specific objective function
when compared with that of ideology in other types of state: the
precise function of 'resolving' the basic contradiction between two
levels of reality, between men's real relationship to their conditions of
existence in the state and their real relationship to their conditions of
existence in civil society – a contradiction that itself derives from the
separation between civil society and the state transposed to human
'lived experience'. The objective function of ideologies, which assigns
them a key role in the political class struggle over the modern state,
cannot be explained solely by reference to the political structuration of
the dominant classes in the political class struggle as empirically
conceived – consciousness and political organization of their own
interests – while ignoring the particular structures of the 'institutionalized' political level. For that we must refer to the relations between
the dominant classes and the dominated classes as they are expressed
in the hegemonic state. In other types of state, ideology took the form
of justifying the global real relationship between the dominated classes
and the dominant classes. Men entered into relations at every level as
naturally unequal, enslaved beings; and ideology's function of domination consisted in simple rationalization and justification of this
inequality and enslavement, expressing in a coherent 'imaginary'
sphere the 'reasons' why human relations were – and had to be –
what they were. Ideology exercised no mediating function in the very
'interior' of real contradictions. It constituted a purely 'mystifying'
transposition of 'assimilated' structures of public and socio-economic
domination to an illusory world. In the modern state, politically men
exist differently from the way in which they exist in the sphere of civil
society. This fixing of political human man as a free individual, equal
to all others, does not as such constitute a mystifying 'ideology'. It
consists in a real relationship between men – albeit an abstract and
formal one – but only in the political sphere, in an objective structure
required by relations of class domination in the capitalist formation.
The specific role of ideologies consists in resolving, through numerous
mediations, the real division of men-producers into private beings and
public beings, in presenting – and this is what their 'mystifying'
character consists in – their real relations in civil society as a replica
of their political relations, in persuading them that what they are
globally is their political relations in the state.

Ideologies thus currently exercise a major objective function, a
specifically political one, in the operation of the modern state – the
state's ethico-political function – and in the hegemonic constitution of

the dominant class: 'substituting' a different relationship for the real
relationship – replacing the socio-economic relationship by the political relationship – and thus reconstructing at an 'imaginary' level the
ideal unity of what is a real division between two levels of reality: the
state and civil society. Accordingly, this ideological ensemble has the
role of imposing on society as a whole a world-view in which the
hegemonic classes are presented as actually representing the general
interest of society at every level, as entities possessing the keys to the
universal in the face of private individuals; in which these individuals
are presented as abstractly unified in that they participate on a free and
equal basis, at all levels, in a 'national' community under the aegis of
the hegemonic classes, who are supposed to embody the popular will.
Rather than emphasize the concrete content of these ideologies as
currently expressed in the mass media, in ideologies of consumption,
abundance, and so on, let us signal their political connotations. Their
political common denominator consists not only in the fact that they
justify, through numerous mediations obviously, the hegemonic
classes' 'economic-corporate' interests, but that they presuppose,
compose or impose the image of a formal equality – in civil society
itself – between 'identical', 'disparate' private individuals, who are
abstractly unified in the ideal political community of the nation-state;
that they induce an 'identification' by the individual, through his real
participation in this political community presented as his own society,
with society as a whole and his integration into relations of class
domination. The specifically 'political', objective role of these ideologies thus consists in the fact that they both privatize civil society, by
preserving its molecularization – thereby depoliticizing the dominated
classes – and indicate their abstract unification through the objective
institutions of the political state, thereby structuring the hegemony of
the dominant classes. In modern society, the hegemonic political
constitution of the dominant classes precisely consists in passing
themselves off, on the basis of their own interests and by means of
'ideologies', as unifying and actually 'organizing' the whole molecularized society at all levels under their aegis. The constant tendency
towards a depoliticization of the dominated classes is the determining
factor in a politicization of the current hegemonic classes and corresponds to the objective structures of the hegemonic state.

   In this specific context, Gramsci's analyses of the role of ideologies
in the hegemonic constitution of the dominant classes assume their full
significance. In effect, because of the particular relationship in the
capitalist formation between ideology and reality, and because of the
concrete function of ideologies, whose political connotations are

particularly mediated in capitalism, we can clearly observe the specifically political effectivity of the whole ideological domain in such
formations – in short, a necessary over-politicization of ideologies,
which is seemingly expressed by their depoliticized character. Moreover, the political character of ideologies is clearly evident in present-
day ideologies of 'mass society'. The real changes in the framework of
state monopoly capitalism, consisting in the heightened contradiction
between socialization of the productive forces and private appropriation, far from inducing a de-privatization, even a 'reification' of the
individual in the 'mass-reality' – a reification that would remove the
molecularization of civil society and establish the thematic of 'mass
society' as a science, connoting a de-ideologization (even a depoliticization) – are in fact located within this molecularization. The
relationship between ideology and reality in ideologies of 'mass
society' is homologous to that in the ideologies of the capitalist
formation in general. The specifically political function of these
ideologies consists in replacing the molecularized relations of civil
society with a different relationship, articulating a putative 'unity'
presupposed in the 'godlike image' of the dominant-hegemonic class.
The political function of ideologies of the mass-nation is precisely
homologous, taking account of current changes in civil society and the
state, to that of ideologies of the people-nation.

So, the concept of hegemony, stressing the role of the dominant
classes in the domain of ideologies, presupposes the objective coordinates that determine their particular content and function in the
political state. The significant role of 'intellectuals' in the hegemonic
structures of this state can be explained not only by the imperatives of
increased labour productivity – evident in the educational function of
the educator-state – or by the need, in the political class struggle, for a
group that has given a specific homogeneity and cohesion, abstractly
and empirically conceived, to the dominant classes, but also by the
function and concrete content of these ideologies as regards the
dominated classes in their relationship with the state. In this respect,
we know that Gramsci paved the way for a Marxist conception of
intellectuals as a group, by seeking to define this group through an
analysis of intellectual practice. In particular, he established the
importance of the dimension of 'leadership' and 'organization' in
such practice. In this sense, the term 'intellectuals' undergoes an
extension whereby it comprises both the group regularly referred
to by this term and those who are referred to as the 'technocratic
caste', the 'bureaucratic caste', and so on. If the current importance of
intellectual practice thus conceived is itself created by the totality of

the system of relations into which this practice is integrated, and in particular by the role assumed by organization in the current mode of production and power relations, nevertheless it can only be precisely defined in its relations with ideological structures, themselves considered in their relations with the base and their specific political importance in the modern state. In short, the significance of the role of intellectuals and ideologies in the relations of hegemonic class domination has to be related both to the leadership and organization characteristic of intellectual practice, and to the content and function of the ideological structures that this practice involves, in their constitutive relations within the ensemble of relations of the present-day social formation.

c) The concept of hegemony further allows us to account for a particular feature of *political power* with respect to the dominated classes: the relations of 'consent' combined with those of coercion that it crystallizes. This is because, on account of the conception of the relations between superstructures and base presupposed by the concept, it revives the original Marxist conception of the state, which never reduced this institution to a pure 'repressive force', an 'instrument or apparatus of violence', a 'physical' oppression that is the psycho-social corollary of a class will. This element of 'force' and 'violence' constitutes a general, undifferentiated characteristic of social existence as a whole, in a class-divided society grounded in exploitation. As such, it cannot account for the genesis, specificity, and particular effectivity of a particular superstructural domain.

In fact, as regards the question of *force*, in the modern state we observe the outcome of a process initiated with the very emergence of the state – a result that seems to be bound up with the modern separation between civil society and the state. Engels and Lenin clearly indicated that the emergence of the state corresponds to the formation of an institution of 'public force', which no longer coincides with the population organizing itself as an armed force. This concentration of the exercise of organized material violence in the hands of the state is completed in the modern state, which has a monopoly on such violence – in contrast, for example, to medieval society, where the church and various castes of a mixed (economic-corporate and public) character still retained the privilege of exercising it. This monopolization of organized violence thus appears to be bound up both with the strengthening of the public institution of the state separated from civil society; and with the fact that, precisely because of this separation and the consequent privatization, the socio-economic bodies consti-

tuting civil society have been stripped of their 'public' character –
which precisely conferred the privilege of exercising organized force on
them – to the exclusive benefit of the state. The exercise of violence
thus appears to be bound up at all the stages of development of the
production process with the objective structures of domination, which
result in the constitution of the modern state. The objective institutions of this state are in a sense 'derived' from relations of force. The
monopoly on organized violence corresponds to the emergence of the
political state and, to this extent, expresses itself through the mediation of the particular structures of a '*Rechtsstaat*'. The monopoly on
violence, and the concrete forms its exercise takes, in fact presuppose
the modern political relations of 'liberty-slavery', 'equality-inequality',
in which present-day class exploitation is invested in the general
framework of modern institutions. Contemporary 'political' relations
of domination thus present themselves, at all levels, as relations of
consent and leadership 'armour-plated' by the specific form of violence that is the 'constitutionalized' violence of the *Rechtsstaat*.
Relations of direct oppression develop into political relations of
hegemony. In a state that corresponds to the formation of a hegemonic
class, objective institutions cannot actually function without a certain
'consent', armour-plated by coercion, on the part of 'citizens'. This
consent is merely the concrete expression, as regards the dominated
classes, of exploitation by a state that consists in a popular-class
representation. The concept of hegemony thus assumes a key function
in as much as it makes it possible for us to study, in all domains, the
contradictory unities characteristic of present-day class *political* exploitation, whose emergence corresponds to the objective structuration of the modern state – unities such as leadership-domination,
organization-force, legitimacy-violence, consent-duress. This concept,
precisely because it presupposes an adequate relationship between the
objective structures of the modern state and the coordinates of a 'type'
of mode of production as a precondition of its constitution, makes it
possible to discern the particular role of violence in its historically
determinate relations with the structures of this state and paves the
way for a scientific study of today's 'institutionalized power' of
exploitation. Applied to 'non-institutionalized political power', it
makes possible an examination of the concrete forms assumed, in
their exercise, by the contradictory characteristics of 'political power'
in general, in a society governed by the separation between civil society
and the state. And we know the importance of what is at stake: is not
one of the fundamental problems of contemporary sociology and
political science to refine a concept of 'power' (of 'authority', in

particular) as it applies to the state, or to non-institutionalized 'human relations', or to both – a concept which, through its formal characteristics of organization, consent, leadership, and so on, could challenge the specificity of political power and the character of class domination of any 'political power' in a class-divided society?

In fact, in this respect Gramsci's error was that he wanted to restrict the concept of hegemony and distinguish in principle, in modern society's structures of domination and exploitation, between the *direct power of domination – force and coercion –* exercised by the state and the 'legal' government – in short, by political society (a term used not in the Marxist sense of the political state, but borrowed from general political science) – *and the indirect power of intellectual and moral leadership and organization-hegemony*. The latter was exercised by the hegemonic class in civil society through the set of organizations usually deemed to be 'private': the church, education, cultural institutions, and so on. Sticking with the descriptive Marxist conception of the state as an 'instrument of coercion and violence', even though he was able to identify the importance of the hegemonic character of the power to exploit, Gramsci could only conceive these two aspects of power as having relations of a complementary kind:

> The greatest modern theoretician of the philosophy of praxis [Lenin], on the terrain of political struggle and organization . . . gave new weight – in opposition to the various 'economist' tendencies – to the front of cultural struggle, and constructed the doctrine of hegemony as a complement to the theory of the State-as-force.[10]

This relationship of complementarity – a rather vague term – was not situated by Gramsci in the relations between the various *aspects* (principal, secondary) of the power to dominate in all domains, within its specific contemporary constitution as 'political power'. In fact, he divides 'political' power into political power as institutionalized force and political power as institutionalized hegemony, thereby dissolving the specificity of the 'political'. Yet the term 'political', whether applied to the structures of institutionalized power or non-institutionalized political relations, must possess theoretical-practical specificity, which itself comes down to the contradictory unity of the coordinates of the power of 'domination' in the current social formation. The concept of hegemony partakes of the specificity of the ensemble of political relations that constitute its field of application and constitution. It can account both for the characteristic of organization and leadership of state power and for the characteristic of 'coercion' of non-institutionalized power. Thus, as regards the political state, 'institutionalized' power, as we have shown, appears at all levels as a contradictory unity of leadership and violence, organization and coercion, and so on. And this is so with respect not only to its exercise in political relations in the formal sense of the term – suffrage, elections, and so on – but also to its direct action as a power-as-institution that is already 'politically' constituted in civil society. In cases, for example, where the state 'intervenes' in the socio-economic sphere, this intervention, which is violent or regulatory in kind, is presented as conforming to the general interest of the 'nation', as the 'legitimate' activity of a *Rechtsstaat*. On the other hand, in the case of the 'non-institutionalized power' of the hegemonic class *exercised* in civil society, we must make distinctions. It can involve *'force' pure and simple* – for example, relations in general within firms – which is directly bound up with the dominant socio-economic position of this class and which, in this instance, does not pertain to the domain of the political strictly speaking: relations of force (and here we might mention the distinction between *Macht* and *Herrschaft*), notwithstanding the 'dual function' of the capitalist within the firm – the exploitation and domination, but also the organization and direction, of labour. As Marx says, 'It can . . . be laid down as a general rule that the less authority presides over the division of labour inside society, the more the division of labour develops inside the workshop, and the more it is subjected there to the authority of a single person.'[11] In the context, however, of the exercise of *political power* by 'private' organizations, which escape 'institutionalization' and the 'stranglehold of the state' – the church, 'private' education, various cultural organizations, and so on, or, in short, hegemonic power in the Gramscian sense – this power is a contradictory unity of organization and intellectual and moral leadership on the one hand *and of coercion* on the other. In this instance, such 'coercion' stems neither from some division of labour, nor some psycho-sociological necessity and effectivity of human relations, nor the application of the 'public violence' exclusively deployed by the state. In the various forms it takes, it is bound up with the hegemonic class's socio-economic position of *strength* in civil society, which is *transposed* in this instance into non-institutionalized *political* power – and this to the precise extent that the object of such power is the preservation of the hegemonic class in, or the conquest of, the 'hegemonic' state, which comprises a unity of violence and organization, coercion and leadership, and so on. Moreover, this characteristic – the 'dual pertinence' of the hegemonic

power of leadership – is apparent if we refer to its exercise as
'intellectual practice'. In reality – and leaving aside for one moment
bureaucratic and technocratic practices as intellectual practices – the
'pedagogical' relations between teachers and taught and the relations
between the priestly 'ministry' and believers pertain in this sense to the
political, not only on account of the particular content and function of
the 'ideologies' they involve, but also because of the forms of 'power'
they express as practices – that is to say, because of the relations
between these practices and the ensemble of social relations and,
consequently, because of the 'power' relations that they realize with
hegemonic political power, whether institutionalized or not, expressed
in the ensemble of those social relations. Their 'coercive' character,
which is combined with intellectual and moral leadership or organization, cannot be explained solely by reference to these practices as such
– to some technical division of labour – or by their possible 'institutionalization', or by their 'ideological' content and its possible
differentiation from 'science'. This would be the temptation if,
following Gramsci, we excluded from intellectual practice, regarded
as hegemonic power, its 'moment' or 'aspect' of coercion, reserving it
for state power. It must be related, via numerous mediations, to the
contradictory character of the 'political power' of the hegemonic class
exercised in civil society.

The State in the Relationship between Dominant Classes

The concept of hegemony cannot be limited to the use we have just
made of it – in sum, its application to the specificity of the modern
state and the distinctive characteristics of the domination of the
hegemonic class or fraction over the dominated classes. *In fact, it
can be extended to an examination of the relations of socio-economic
and political interests between dominant classes and fractions* in the
capitalist social formation and lead us to the construction of a
theoretical schema that makes it possible to account for the political
problematic of such formations. The concept was not employed thus
by Gramsci; nor has it been by those who have subsequently used it. In
the case of Gramsci, this can be explained by the fact that, influenced
by Croce and especially Labriola, whose thought is situated in the
theoretical context of the Second International, his analyses of hegemony still sometimes smack of 'subjectivism-voluntarism', which
often leads him to reduce the application of the concept to the domain
of the superstructures and ideologies. It is this schema that we are
proposing as a scientific hypothesis in the brief remarks below. In

actual fact, the dominant classes or fractions in the capitalist formation emerge as structured into a particular ensemble, *via state mediation*, by 'the hegemony of one social group over a series of subordinate
groups'. The objective function of the hegemonic state cannot be
grasped by an uncritical, descriptive conception that regards the state
as an instrument created by the will of the dominant class. When
applied to the relationship between dominant classes and fractions of
dominant classes, such a conception has consequences that we have
already signalled and which we shall have to return to in more detail.

The first is that there can only exist *one* dominant class with respect
to the state – something that either automatically reduces the other
classes to the rank of dominated classes, or implies that the dominant-
dominated relationship is situated at the 'institutionalized' political
level between two classes. There is no need to labour the fact that
Marx, Engels and Lenin in no way reduced the class struggle into a
dualistic conflict, finalist in character, between two classes – dominant
and dominated – but conceived it as the objective site of a complex
relationship between several classes and class fractions, which are
defined according to their position in the process of production and
their relationship to private property in the means of production.
Although, in capitalist society and at the level of class struggle, the
basic economic contradiction between capital and labour is focused in
the relationship between capitalists and proletarians, it is constituted
at this level within a complex relationship between several classes and
class 'fractions'. However, *at the political level of power relations and
through the mediation of the objective institution of the state*, this
complex relationship assumes the relatively simple form of relations
between the dominant and the dominated, governors and governed.
This form does not itself derive from a *simple transposition* of the
multiplicity of classes and fractions in play in the class struggle from
the level of socio-economic relations as a whole to that of political
power relations, and through the surreptitious emergence of two
'political classes', one dominant and the other dominated. In other
words, this simplification of class relations at the level of political
power is not a mere reproduction of the 'simple' economic contradiction between capital and labour. In fact, as regards the 'dominant'
classes or fractions, it consists in their concentration at the political
level, through the 'specific' interests of the 'hegemonic' class or
fraction and by means of the state, into a 'power bloc'. *Situated at
the specifically political level, this power bloc actually constitutes a
contradictory unity 'under the dominance' of the hegemonic class or
fraction.* At the 'autonomized' political level of capitalist formations,

it expresses the Marxist type of unity that characterizes both the social formation as a whole and each *specific* level of structures.

The fact that certain classes or class fractions are structured into a 'power bloc' thus assumes particular significance in the objective conditions that engender the modern state and its feature of *universality*. On the one hand, the structures of the hegemonic state and the constitution of a hegemonic class or fraction permit several classes or class fractions to accede to, or participate in, power. On the other hand, in capitalist social formations we register a basic phenomenon as regards the bourgeois class, which Marx analyzed in *Class Struggles in France* and *The Eighteenth Brumaire* – i.e. the fact that, *on account of the phenomenon of competition*, it emerges as a class subject to profound *divisions* by virtue of its very constitution. Furthermore, there is no need to stress the fact that monopolistic concentration, far from cancelling competitive contradictions, only serves to reproduce them at a different level – a phenomenon described from Hilferding to Luxemburg and Lenin. However, in the analyses by Marx that we have mentioned, and bearing in mind their micro-chronic scale, we already note a crucial fact – i.e. *that the class fraction which accedes to institutionalized power only attains it by constituting itself as a hegemonic fraction. In other words, despite the contradictions that separate it from other dominant fractions, it succeeds in concentrating them 'politically' by organizing its own specific interests into the common general interest of these fractions.*

This unitary process of constitution of a 'power bloc' thus ultimately seems possible and necessary only in the general context of the separation between the modern state and civil society and the class struggle that it determines. In the case of an economic-corporate state, we are not faced with a class struggle such that it corresponds to the emergence of a hegemonic class or fraction – a phenomenon of competition and the emergence of a specifically political level – operating, by means of the state, as the pivot of 'unitary' concentration of various dominant classes or fractions. Nor, on the other side, do we have the objective institutions of a state with *its own internal unity* – something that, strictly speaking, exists only in so far as it is separated from civil society – and whose constitution precisely answers, on the side of the dominant classes or fractions, to the particular unity of a power bloc. In fact, in the economic-corporate type of state – and when it is not a question of class domination by sheer force – we observe between the castes-classes in power a mechanism of compromise, 'tactical' *share outs* or *alliances*, syncretic in character, between purely socio-economic interests. In the case of the hegemonic state and the hegemonic class or fraction, the constitution of a power bloc evincing internal unity becomes necessary and possible to the extent that this class or fraction, situating itself at the specifically political level that corresponds to the objective structures of the state, 'organizes' a politically structured general interest of the classes or fractions in power. The contradictions between these classes and fractions remain profound, but, through state mediation, they are 'contained' in and unified by the hegemonic fraction's '*universalizing*' political interests.

These reflections, while giving concrete substance to the dualistic Marxist schema that makes it possible to decipher the political struggle within capitalist formations, have, so one would imagine, some importance in the current conditions of class struggle and the working-class strategy of 'alliances', enabling us to avoid certain errors. For the consequences of the voluntarist schema 'state = will of the dominant class' have not finished making themselves felt. Indeed, even if we accept the simultaneous participation of several classes or class fractions in the structures of domination, we might be tempted to regard the state as the product of a will to dominate on the part of one of them. In that case, we would in a sense transpose the schema of domination to the relations between the class or fraction that is the *creator* of the state and the other classes. And the latter, despite their participation in the state, would be regarded as being dominated to all intents and purposes by the former. The unity of the ensemble in power would be regard as based solely on a deceptive mystification of the dominant classes or fractions by the superdominant fraction; the cleavage between the dominant and the dominated would be obscured by the admission into the politically dominant group of a broad swathe of the dominated, who are unawares and who, with a nudge in the right direction, might have switched over to the side of the proletariat.

These observations immediately pose the fundamental problematic for Marxist theory of the state's specific internal unity and relative autonomy within the capitalist formation – a problematic that has scarcely been developed and which, in the context of this article, we can only table. It is well known that 'autonomy' broadly recognized by Marxism at each level of social practice and social structure, has nevertheless only been indicated in an incidental, circumstantial manner in the case of the state. It is accepted only in the context of what has been called 'Bonapartism' – that is to say, in cases where the classes and fractions engaged in struggle are close to counterbalancing one another. In other instances, the state is identified with the predominant class or fraction. Now, if Bonapartism represents a case where the state's specific unity and relative autonomy with respect both to civil society and the dominant classes and fractions are especially clear, it is itself situated within the general framework of the relative autonomy of the political state in capitalist formations. Moreover, just as the Bonapartist form of state is not in fact *independent* of the hegemonic fractions – something Marx clearly perceived in *The Civil War in France* – the modern type of state is not *reducible* to this fraction. This 'type' of state in fact presents an internal unity of its own, corresponding to its relative autonomy both from civil society as a whole and from the dominant classes and fractions, owing to two principles of external unity that emerge as correlative in the set of objective coordinates of these formations. *The state constitutes a specific internal unity enjoying relative autonomy in as much as it represents the factor of unity of the non-unified dominant classes or fractions, whose relations are governed by their characteristic division in the capitalist mode of production.* In this respect, the problematic remains the same in the context of mono-polistic concentration and state monopoly capitalism. And it is pre-cisely in this theoretical context that we find the scientific analyses of Marx's maturity concerning the role of the 'bureaucracy' in the modern state: analyses that cannot, any more than can those con-cerning the unity and autonomy of the state, be reduced to the *ideological* thematic of some 'alienation' of the society-subject in the phenomenon of the state-bureaucracy, or to that of a 'dysfunc-tionality' of the bureaucratic autonomy of the state vis-à-vis the 'whole' of society (in the gestaltist sense).

We can therefore schematically define the current political role of the state and the hegemonic fraction in power. What is especially im-portant here is that the bourgeois class, the dominant class *par excellence* in the capitalist mode of production, currently appears profoundly divided – a division due, in its present exacerbated form, to monopolistic concentration – by internal contradictions that bring about its scission into several class fractions. However, these elements-fractions, masters of the contemporary state, do not form a disparate set that breaks the state itself up into a multiplicity of powers and counter-powers, decision-making centres, veto groups, or compensa-tory powers 'shared out' between dominant classes and fractions. Nor do they possess external unity on account of some quintessential dominant fraction imposing – by means of compromises and counter-compromises – its economic-corporate interests on the profoundly divergent economic-corporate interests of the other dominant classes and fractions. With respect to the state, these elements structure a political bloc within which the hegemonic fraction, to whose specific interests the class state 'corresponds', presents itself as guarantor of the general interest of the dominant classes and fractions, which it concentrates in their political expression. This concentration is not prior or external to a state created by the hegemonic fractions for its own ends. In its own objective unity and relative autonomy, the present-day state presents itself as the structuring factor politically in this contradictory unity, under the dominance of the hegemonic fraction.

At what remains a relative degree of monopolistic concentration, the important thing in any definition of the hege-monopolist state fraction is the relative fusion of large landowners and the bourgeoisie and the division of the bourgeois class. However, there is often a tendency to reduce the problems posed by an exact definition of the current hegemonic political fraction by describing it in economistic-empiricist and abstract fashion as 'large capital' or 'large monopolies'. This terminology is insufficient to situate the group that currently represents the hegemonic fraction in the political state with precision: *a concrete definition of this fraction is needed, because the concrete form of concentration of the interests of the dominant fractions under its aegis depends on the political constitution of its specific interests.*

Today, we note a new phenomenon in the process of concentration of industrial firms. This manifests itself not only in the process of capital production and accumulation, but also in the fact that a limited number of individuals concentrate the control levers of the economy in their hands. This fraction is not structured according to the classic 'type' of private ownership of the means of production and capital – a type which, in the framework of finance capital, allows for the distinction into fractions in accordance with the single criterion of the size of the property owned by the members of this fraction, and which would ultimately limit the hegemonic fraction to 'big finance capital' identified, in this respect, with banking groups comparable to monopolies. In his polemic against Proudhon, Marx had already warned against isolating a juridical 'paradigm-concept' of private ownership – for example, the concept of property in the civil code – in order to define classes or class fractions, thereby indicating that this concept develops in the socio-economic context of a particular mode of production, to which it gives juridical expression. As a criterion for distinguishing between classes and class fractions occupying a determinate position in the production process, private ownership itself constitutes a relation of production. At the present stage of monopolistic concentration in large joint-stock companies, a fraction of finance capital occupies a particular place that corresponds to current developments in the mode of production. In the process of industrial development, of the tendency for capital's rate of profit to fall, of the importance of growth rates and industrial productivity, of the imperative to organize the market and prices by monopolies, and so on, the *control* of initial investment and reinvestment in firms assumes vital importance. In and through the development of private property relations, the objective function of the managerial, technical and economic control of monopolistic firms-companies creates a particular fraction of financial managers. In addition to the property in finance capital it possesses – commercial capital and industrial capital – as share-holdings, this fraction harnesses, through the managerial and juridical intervention of firms' general meetings and boards, the industrial capital which forms part of minor finance capital, the shares held by numerous small and medium-sized shareholders. The latter are dispossessed of the share in the ownership of machines, equipment, and so on that pertains to their stock; they no longer have any power over decisions about the operation, output and productivity of firms. Managers concentrate the totality of industrial property in their hands to the extent that – through control, also exercised over others' property – they monopolize the socio-economic powers and prerogatives contained in the concept of property, the latter being regarded as the substratum of the *socio-economic position of strength* – '*power as force*' – that determines political domination.

Moreover, the concentration of economic power in the hands of this fraction of managers-controllers is enhanced by the procedure of self-financing. Through this procedure, managers-controllers acquire autonomy with respect to banking groups – large firms create their own banks. By means of control, they capture commercial capital – undistributed profits constituting part of firms' reserve funds – which corresponds to minor finance capital (the shares of small and medium-sized shareholders), thus possessing owners' prerogatives over the totality of the 'goods' – industrial capital and commercial capital – which make up a firm. The role of managers-controllers, far from constituting (as it is often represented as being) the 'revenge' of industrial capital over finance capital, on the contrary emerges as a corollary of the increased concentration of finance capital in contemporary monopolistic society. Economic power is concentrated in the hands of this particular fraction of finance capital, which at present constitutes the hegemonic fraction of the society based on state monopoly capitalism.[12]

Now, we are familiar with the incredible success enjoyed in neo-capitalist ideology by the notion of 'control', construed not in the sociological sense of 'social control' and so on, but in the sense that the prerogatives contained in the notion of 'private ownership', which for Marxist theory constitute the foundation of the socio-economic position of strength (power as force) – itself the substratum of political power – are concentrated in the hands of a 'managerial' or 'techno-cratic' fraction, independently of 'private ownership' in the classical sense of the term. In industrial or technological society, this fraction, while not being the 'owner' of the means of production, has suppo-sedly concentrated the 'exclusive' disposal of these means in its hands – 'technical' decisions on firms' output and productivity, and so on – and derives the material advantages bound up with this, in the shape of 'remuneration' and so on. It thereby supposedly occupies a socio-economic vantage-point that allows it to exercise political power and, at the same time, this power-as-force emerges as independent of 'profit', which in the Marxist sense is bound up with private own-ership. Now, and so as not to dwell on these economic considerations, if the power of exclusive disposal over the means of production, contained in the notion of private ownership, forms the basis of the socio-economic position of strength of a class or fraction for Marxism, it is precisely to the extent that, private ownership being conceived as a 'relation of production' within the ensemble of relations of a capitalist society, this power is bound up in it with the conversion of surplus-value into profit. It is impossible to isolate some technological power of 'control' and regard it as the foundation of political power, treating it as independent of private ownership-profit. It is superfluous to stress that Marx's celebrated analyses of the managers-supervisors of labour, concerning in the first instance the technical division of labour and the dual function – exploitation and direction – of the capitalist, in no way call into question the relations between capital and private ownership. In fact, this control represents not a particular function-power 'ex-tricated' from private ownership, which for its part is restricted exclusively to 'profit', but an evolution in private property as a whole as a relation of production – an extension and concentration of private ownership of the means of production. The managers-controllers actually represent a fraction that owns a large proportion of shares. In addition, on the 'institutionalized' basis of this ownership – that is to say, by virtue of their position in the process based on exploitation for profit – through 'control' they wrest the prerogatives (disposal of the means of production and profit) that are immanent in the private ownership of minor finance capital.

The mistaken conception of the separation between private ownership and control has led to a whole series of consequences. As a general rule, it both masks the major role of the current hegemonic fraction (despite its constitution *in accordance with the logic of private profit*) as 'organizing' fraction – a role that in fact forms its *hegemonic* function with respect to the dominant fractions of capital; and it conceals the 'organizing' role of the contemporary state as it corresponds to the specific interests of this fraction – a role that grounds its own hegemonic character as structuring the power bloc. This separation is in fact presented as surmounting the contradiction between the profitability of investment and productive development; between the private profit and interests of the dominant classes – fractions, on the one hand, and rational administration and the general interest of the national community, on the other; between the progressive socialization of the productive forces and optimal development of labour productivity, on the one hand, and the realization of maximum profit, on the other. We are thus witnessing attempts to define a new, general and undifferentiated form of 'power' – a 'functionalist' type – that would consist in an 'organization-administration' corresponding to the general interest of society 'as a whole'. The latter, in contrast to the *specific* political power of class domination, is allegedly based on the 'technical' power of various 'controlling' or 'managing' castes which escape the logic of profit immanent in private ownership, in an 'integrated' technological or industrial society that is liberated from class struggle based, precisely, on the contradiction between the private ownership of the means of production and their social character.

Now, what matters for the Marxist critique of the state by means of the concept of hegemony is to recall that the current hegemonic fraction of managers-controllers is a class fraction, grounded in a particular form of private ownership, but also that it displays certain distinctive characteristics. The effect of these is that the state, which corresponds to the specific interests of this fraction, while remaining a class state, has, as a result of its objective function and in its relations with the 'dominant fractions', a particular organizing role that currently structures its hegemonic particularity.

In the already superseded context of the predominance of banking groups, considerations of financial and commercial supremacy prevailed over those of productivity and growth. What mattered, for example, was more the hierarchy of joint-stock companies in terms of banking power and the establishment of close links with banks, than the promotion of standardization or the pursuit of optimum implantation for an industry. The spirit of the retrenchment and contraction of investment prevailed over that of productive ventures. Security of profits was sought much more by improving the strategic financial position of each firm, by obstructing and restricting opposing initiatives, than by developing and improving specific initiatives in the sphere of production. These characteristics of monopolistic production are far from having disappeared. Nevertheless, the hegemonic fraction of managers-controllers emerges as bound up with current developments in the mode of production that take concrete form in state monopoly capitalism. These, while remaining within the framework of a mode of production based on class exploitation and profit, determine an especially important function for industrial productivity, for the application of the technological revolution, for the rationalization of market anarchy, and so on. It is these particular features constitutive of the particular interests of the hegemonic fraction that allow it not only to present itself, through the mediation of the state, as embodying the 'general interest of society', *but also to structure a specific general interest of the dominant fractions politically.*

Perhaps there is no need to underscore the current manner of the hegemonic fraction's participation in the state: sufficient stress has been laid on the development of the structures of the contemporary state, which is evolving from a parliamentarism where 'popular' legislative power remained the dominant element of the state, into a state where executive power is dominant. This evolution corresponds in fact to ever increasing state intervention, in breadth and depth alike, in the domain of civil society, in the economy, and in social relations. Real political power is located in numerous specialist committees, connected to executive power, where the direct participation of the hegemonic fraction of managers-controllers proves decisive. However, the sway of the monopolies and oligopolies over the state concerns (in so far as it only affects the external relations between the economic and the political) only one aspect of the problematic of the contemporary hegemonic state. In actual fact, the particular relationship between the state and the major financial conglomerates, reinforcing in its turn the dependency of the political on the economic, *is itself only possible* as a result of an evolution in the state's *objective structures* – an evolution that corresponds to the concrete form currently taken by the specific interests of the hegemonic fraction. In fact, the interests of this fraction are structured within an overall process in which concerns that we shall for now refer to as 'technico-economic' assume a decisive importance as conditions for the current realization of profit by self-financing monopolies. The participation in the state of managers-controllers and their 'authorized representatives' thus appears to be necessary, not for the domination of the strictly economic-corporate interests of the hegemonic fraction, but for the 'rational regulation' of the process of production as a whole – i.e., at a phenomenal level, to the well-being of society as a whole, but in reality to a politically conceived general interest of capital as a whole.

Moreover, this specific function of 'technico-economic' regulation by the state is in no sense foreign to Marxist thought. As Marx, Engels and Lenin clearly indicated, the state corresponds to an objective stage of development of the productive forces. In the case of the Asiatic mode of production, for example, the need to carry out certain major 'public works' – canals, dams, and so on – essential at a particular stage of the production process for increasing labour productivity, corresponds to the emergence of a public, central and organizing power to undertake them: the state. The state's regulatory function is clearly articulated in the *Critique of the Gotha Programme*, where Marx stresses it, indicating that during the transitional phase from socialism to communism – that is to say, before the advent of the 'self-governed' society corresponding to a new development of the productive forces – forms of 'right', 'technico-juridical' norms will persist, in 'their capacity as regulator (determining factor) of the distribution of products and the distribution of labour among the members of society'. The state's regulatory-organizing function derives in fact from the very nature of the relations between base and superstructures. Conceived as a crystallization in objective structures of certain social practices, with respect to the practices of the infrastructural domain the superstructure possesses the distinctive characteristic that, while being integrated under the primacy of the base and, in the last instance, of the economic into a unity constituted by the ensemble of a social formation at a historically determinate moment, it assumes the function of regulatory principle within this unity. As Bukharin put it, 'the relationship between infrastructural practice (*Basis-Arbeit*) and superstructural practice (*Überbau-Arbeit*) consists in the fact that the latter, a magnitude of the second order, at the same time represents a regulatory principle.'[13]

And this is precisely the meaning of Gramsci's analyses of intellectual practice. However – and this is what concerns us here – when it involves a state based on class exploitation, this regulatory function, *always performed within the ensemble of relations of a social for-*

mation, itself reflecting the mode of production as a unity, corresponds very precisely to the structures of this exploitation. As practice, it is integrated into the structures assumed by this state with respect to the unity of the base. All the illusions of a power-structure – the state as technical apparatus in a 'customized' technological society; of a power-practice; of the replacement of the power of domination over human beings by an organization – administration of things and men-things reified by the technological society; in short, of a 'purely' *technico-administrative* function of the capitalist state – ideologies of development, consumption, industrial society, technological society, and so on – isolated from its 'political' structure as a class state, are precisely bound up with a technologistic conception of the economy. This separates off a particular level of the base – the level of the productive forces – and ignores the fact that a mode of production constitutes a unitary ensemble of several levels that can be grouped into forces of production and social relations of production. In the case of the Asiatic mode of production, for example, the technico-economic imperatives of productivity *correspond* to a certain 'political' relationship of *exploitation*, the state's regulatory function entering into its own structures of domination. Alternatively put, whether as labour productivity or as the history of technical instruments, the level of the productive forces, diachronically manifest in their development, possesses no intelligibility or rationality in its own right, which might, *at a certain level of this development*, constitute it as the sole, monist factor structuring a given social formation – the issue of 'industrial' or 'technological ' society – and thereby enable us to decipher superstructural institutions or their functions by direct reference to this level. Although, for Marx, the problem of the sequence of modes of production – of historicity – is connected with the level of the productive forces and their development, this always expresses itself, at the synchronic level, *within the ensemble of relations of the various successive modes of production*. In the capitalist mode of production, based on accumulation and exploitation for profit, each regulatory function – which definitely cannot be reduced to a 'technological' organization concerning the level of the productive forces alone, but necessarily includes the economic regulation of production in general – constitutes an optimal possible regulation of production, in the development of this mode as a whole, with a view to the maximum realization of profit for the hegemonic fraction. This function, entering into the political structures of the modern class state, itself assumes a specifically political character. The objective structures and functions of the hegemonic state in fact correspond to current developments of a 'technological' or 'industrial' kind, but considered within the mode of production as a whole. *In other words, they correspond to the political interests of the present 'hegemonic' fraction.*[14]

It is precisely the state's *regulatory* function, which is distinct from mere intervention on behalf of the *economic-corporate* interests of 'large monopolies', that currently grounds its distinctive hegemonic character within the state's global role in state monopoly capitalism. It is true that its directly interventionist role is constantly apparent: the state currently has the function of guaranteeing monopoly super-profits. In the context of an economy governed by the super-profits of self-financing monopolies, the intensive realization of the hegemonic fraction's super-profits presupposes an 'attempt' at rational regulation of the *economic process as a whole* and assumes the form of a general interest of the fractions of capital taken together. In the context of the hegemony of finance capital in the classical sense of the term, the state's role in the economic process as a whole predominantly came down to direct intervention. For profit realization through short-term banking speculation was not connected with some particular increase in productivity, with some particular technical progress, with some general macro-chronic stability, and so on, required for the super-profits of self-financing monopolies. In the context of the current hegemony of these monopolies, the specific conditions for the realization of their super-profits correspond, on the state's part, to a preliminary effort to fix and calculate wages and costs (in order to uncouple profit from the price mechanism), to programme industrialization, to plan with a view to forecasting, and so on – in short activities that aim to control the capitalist system's characteristic anarchy. These measures thus correspond to the specific interests of the hegemonic fraction. As such, however, they form a substratum of the political structuration of a 'general interest' of certain fractions of the capitalist class and are presented by the state as beneficial for all factions of the dominant class. The hegemonic fraction presents itself as realizing its own profits by seeking, via the intermediary of the state's regulatory function, to correct the 'catastrophic' conditions afflicting capital as a whole. And there is no doubt that this attempt at regulation, when considered at a certain level, has a real foundation on the basis of which it can be 'presented' and 'conceived' as corresponding to a general interest on the part of capital. For example, industrial capital – those medium-sized firms that still exist – and finance capital – small but especially medium-sized shareowners – themselves benefit from this 'regulation', to the precise extent that the general repercussions of capitalist disorder and anarchy affect them as much as they do monopoly groups. The involvement of banking groups in the super-profits of self-financing monopolies is ensured not by means of credit, but by penetration of their management by means of share portfolios. In this instance, the banking groups are themselves closely tied up with the particular rationalization required by the modus operandi of such monopolies. On the other hand, we should not lose sight of the current phenomenon of socialization of capital ownership within the capitalist class as a whole by means of joint-stock companies. Obviously, such socialization has nothing to do with the 'myth' of a so-called 'popular capitalism': by virtue of the generalization of joint-stock companies (monopolies), private ownership of the means of production possesses an authentically class character today. It no longer involves individual private ownership by members of a class, but a class private ownership that creates a network of intervention and solidarity between the interests of the fractions of this class. This network affords the hegemonic fraction of capital, in its political constitution as repre-sentative of the collective interest of capital, a wide margin of manipulation. We know, for example, that the interests of small and medium-sized shareowners, based on the distribution of divi-dends, conflict with those of the hegemonic fraction, which restricts dividends with a view to self-financing. However, it remains the case that, by virtue of the particular modus operandi of these self-financed firms in the current mode of production as a whole, the nominal value of such shares on the stock exchange often experience a spectacular rise that can offset this contradiction. Or again, the elimination of small and medium-sized industrial firms by their absorption into large monopolies is compensated for by the involvement of their owners-entrepreneurs in class private ownership through shares in self-finan-cing monopolies.

Thus, the state's 'rationalizing' regulatory function emerges as based both on the deep contradictions that divide the capitalist class, which correspond to the concentration of (self-financing) monopolies, and, at the same time, on a certain community of socio-economic interests among these fractions, which are politically supportive of the hegemonic fraction's interests in their rationalizing form. Such con-siderations do not prejudge the issue as to the extent to which this attempt at 'rationalization' actually succeeds in stabilizing the system of state monopoly capitalism. When it comes to its hegemonic character, what matters is that it is based on a community of socio-economic interests among the dominant fractions, such that it can politically present itself as the structuring substratum of a 'power

bloc', in as much as it is currently 'presented' as the way to achieve
general stability: a stability that is itself presented as corresponding to
the political interest of capital as a whole, under the aegis of the
hegemonic fraction.

Nevertheless, the state's 'regulatory' function with respect to infrastructural coordinates cannot, as such, be held to exhaust its hegemonic character. If it constitutes the substratum of the latter, it is clear
that, exercised within the state monopoly capitalist mode of production, it can only evince a 'stark' tendency towards extreme financial
concentration, in accordance with the developmental logic of the mode
of production as a whole – with all the risks that that entails for the
remaining fractions of the dominant class. In contrast to Weber's
'formal' conception of rationalization, a 'rationalization' that regulates the whole capitalist system can only be conceived within the
specific logic – 'rationality' – governing the ensemble of this system's
relations. It corresponds perfectly to the financial concentration of
self-financing monopolies. The present-day state thus has a particular
function which, situated at the *socio-economic* and *specifically political* levels, but grafted onto its *essentially technico-economic* 'regulatory' function, endows it with a distinctively hegemonic character:
that of establishing, in the very performance of its regulatory function,
an 'order' between the different fractions of the dominant class – an
'order' aimed at containing the contradictions between them.[15] In
actual fact, the contemporary state's political function of 'order'
cannot be distinguished from its regulatory function. In the context
of simple state 'interventionism' in the sphere of civil society, effected
in relatively limited fashion, the state's function as guarantor of social
'order' appeared separated from its role of technico-economic intervention. The latter, in turn, thus seemed to represent an 'exceptional',
'shamefaced' feature on the part of a state that proclaimed itself to be
nothing more than the 'political' guarantor of order in social conflicts.
In the context of the form taken by the state today, and the need for its
decisive action in all sectors of civil society, its function of 'order'
precisely constitutes an investment of its regulatory function in its
hegemonic structure: *it involves establishing a 'regulatory order' in the
strict sense.* Thus the function of the state is to 'order' the various
interests of the fractions of the dominant class by 'concentrating' them
politically, on the basis of their solidarity with those of the hegemonic
fraction – *i.e. to organize their political expression in the sites and
institutions where its regulatory function is elaborated.* In fact, this is
the only way in which this function can assume a properly hegemonic
form – that is to say, present itself as corresponding to the collective

interest of the 'dominant fractions – and adapt itself to the political
role of a sate in state monopoly capitalism. In this instance, it is
therefore not a question of simply recruiting the various fractions of
the dominant class, through their expression in the exercise of the
state's regulatory function, to the service of the economic-corporate
interest of the large monopolies – close examination of the contemporary state would demonstrate that, appearances to the contrary
notwithstanding, it cannot be identified with an economic-corporate
state of the fascist type, in the scientific sense of the term. It is question
of 'ordering' them *politically*, by presenting this function as corresponding to their general interest. The evolution of the objective
structures of the contemporary state – strengthening of the executive,
various committees linked to this executive – does not in itself, and as
regards the dominant fractions, betoken their direct enrolment by big
capital, but a displacement of the state's hegemonic organizing function vis-à-vis the internal contradictions of these factions onto its
regulatory function.

The hegemonic state's function of 'order' is likewise evident as
regards society as a whole. As such, it is integrated into the state's role
with regard to the dominant fractions. It equally consists in the
functions of the police, army, etc., and the norms of the *Rechtsstaat*'s
juridical system concerning 'public order', and in the extension of the
state's role as public entrepreneur in unprofitable sectors of 'general
interest' – for example, public health and hygiene, education, transport, and so on. What is referred to as the 'social order' function of
these state activities precisely consists in the fact that they render the
system as a whole more tolerable for the dominated classes. Here too,
within its objective structures, it is directly subordinated to its
regulatory function. The close relationship between the 'social state's'
regulatory and organizing functions has been clearly identified by
numerous theoreticians of the 'welfare' state, even though they have
been unable to establish the subordination of the 'social' function of
the state to its regulatory function, corresponding to the hegemonic
fraction's political interests, and thus, in the final analysis, the
subordination of the organizing function itself to these interests.
These two particular aspects of the contemporary state are in fact
regarded as being integrated into its global 'organizing' function with
respect to society as a whole.

In its current success in neo-capitalist functionalist theories, the
concept of organization contains an exemplary confusion. We can in
fact distinguish between three meanings of the term. The first is that of
'organization-as-practice' in the sense attributed it by Gramsci, when

he regards such organization as a particular aspect of intellectual practice, as performed within the ensemble of relations of a determinate mode of production conceived in accordance with the Marxist 'type' of unity. This is precisely the sense that we attribute it in its application to the state-as-practice in the context of a hegemonic class domination, and which allows us to distinguish, in such practice, between the aspect of 'regulation' and that of 'organization' *invested* in the specifically political level. The second sense is organization in the strict sociological meaning of the term, in as much as the state constitutes, for example, a social organization. The third is that of neo-capitalist theories which, in the methodological framework and with the general presuppositions of functionalist thought, refers to the articulation of the elements of an 'integrated' social whole, a society from which class struggle, as the determining factor in social relations, is absent. The confusion of neo-capitalist theories over the state-as-organizer derives precisely from the fact that they situate the organization-as-practice of the state-as-organization in the organizational site of an integrated society. To that extent, the state's organization-as-practice is not concretely considered in its relations with the structures of domination within the social relations of a class-divided social formation – an ordering subordinated to the regulation that corresponds to the political interests of the hegemonic fraction – but is grasped as an abstract function of the state-as-organizer of an already organized society. The relations between the state's regulatory and organizing functions are juxtaposed within this organizing function in general. As an example, we may cite Duverger's observations:

> Technical evolution makes government the general organizer of the community, coordinating the activity of all particular sectors in the framework of a comprehensive plan. This economic planning is only one aspect of the function of social organization in modern nations. To be more precise, the economy is only one part of overall planning. Through the plan's options concerning investment, development priorities, and so on, all aspects of national life are involved: education, culture, art, scientific progress, town and country planning, urbanism, lifestyle, and so on.[16]

In fact, the state's 'social' functions regarding the general interest are subordinate to its essential function in 'regulating' production in accordance with the interests of the hegemonic fraction. At the same time, they represent its specifically hegemonic role as regards social order, which consists in representing the real general interest of the dominant fractions of capital as a whole and presenting itself as embodying the nation's general interest:

> Health and public hygiene slow the exhaustion of labour power . . . public education cover[s] future needs for trained manpower . . . public city transportation, financed by the entire population, de-liver[s] manpower to the factories in good condition . . . nationalization of energy sources and raw materials place[s] onto the shoulders of the entire population the burden of supplying industrial needs at low cost. The expansion of public activity, in short, is welcome so long as it limits itself to publicly pre-financing the basis of monopoly expansion and accumulation . . .[17]

Thus, just as the state's class regulatory function cannot be reduced to technico-economic 'organization', so its function as guarantor of 'order' or 'well-being' cannot be reduced to social 'organization' in general. This amounts to saying that the relations between these various state functions depend on the *mode of specificity* and *articulation* assumed, within the Marxist 'type' of unity, by a social formation's various levels of structures – *a mode that precisely founds the 'peculiar' unity of this formation at a determinate stage of its transformation.* At present, these functions actually constitute 'organizational' practices on the part of the hegemonic state. The state's regulatory function, invested in its organizing function, thus endows it with a general hegemonic character of 'political organization', armour-plated by coercion, at all levels of society. This corresponds to the political interests of the hegemonic fraction. However, as in the case of its regulatory function, the state's function of order vis-à-vis society as a whole at the same time itself constitutes an aspect of its role as mediating factor in structuring the power bloc. The state's 'social' public activities correspond to the general interest of the dominant fractions which, in their entirety, benefit both from the concrete results in the production process and from the fact that these activities render the capitalist system more tolerable for the dominated classes. Considered within the political relations of domination of a class-divided society, the state's organizing practice with respect to 'society as a whole' can thus be globally related to the state's hegemonic role with respect to the dominant classes and fractions.

4

MARXIST POLITICAL THEORY
IN GREAT BRITAIN

In the last few years an important current of Marxist thought has emerged in Great Britain. The editorial committee of *New Left Review*, particularly Perry Anderson and Tom Nairn, have undertaken a political study of the structures of British society in a number of articles, which include Anderson's 'Origins of the Present Crisis'[1] and Nairn's 'The Nature of the Labour Party'[2] and 'Labour Imperialism'.[3] These articles are particularly important both for the originality of their conclusions and for their theoretical rigour. Breaking with the English empiricist tradition, which dominated Fabianism, these texts of Anderson and Nairn are written at a *critical* level, in the Marxist meaning of that term: they reveal a genuine, critical reflection on the *concepts* used in the political analysis advanced. In reply E.P. Thompson, a member of the former editorial committee of *New Left Review*, has published a long essay, 'The Peculiarities of the English'[4] which challenges the conclusions of Anderson's and Nairn's analyses with a vigour and verve characteristic of current political discussion in Great Britain. There is no point in summarizing the Anderson-Nairn articles in detail, but the need to read and re-read the articles themselves cannot be overemphasized, for they deserve to be considered *exemplary* texts of Marxist political analysis. We will simply recall their essential theses and the points attacked by Thompson, with a quotation from Anderson's central article:

> The distinctive facets of English class structure, as it has evolved
> over three centuries, can thus be summed up as follows. After a

---

* First published in French as 'La théorie politique marxiste en Grande Bretagne' in *Les Temps Modernes*, no. 238 (1966), pp. 1683–1707. This translation is taken from *New Left Review* 43 (May–June 1967), pp. 57–74.

bitter, cathartic revolution, which transformed the structure but not the superstructure of English society, a landed aristocracy under-pinned by a powerful mercantile affinal group, became the first dominant capitalist class in Britain. This dynamic agrarian capit-alism expelled the English peasantry from history. Its success was economically the 'floor' and sociologically the 'ceiling' of the rise of the industrial bourgeoisie. Undisturbed by a feudal state, terrified of the French Revolution and its own proletariat, mesmerized by the prestige and authority of the landed class, the bourgeoisie won two modest victories, lost its nerve and ended by losing its identity. The late Victorian era and the high noon of imperialism welded aris-tocracy and bourgeoisie together in a single social bloc. The work-ing class fought passionately and unaided against the advent of industrial capitalism; its extreme exhaustion after successive defeats was the measure of its efforts. Henceforward it evolved, separate but subordinate, within the apparently unshakeable structure of British capitalism, unable, despite its great numerical superiority, to transform the fundamental nature of British society.[5]

The Determinant Class

The characteristic conclusions of Anderson and Nairn follow from this short passage, which must seem strange to anyone who has been concerned with British political problems. For, in their analysis, what Marx called 'the most bourgeois of nations' presents the paradoxical situation of a capitalist formation 'typical' in its origin and evolution, within which, however, the bourgeois class has almost never taken the 'pure' role of the hegemonic or *dominant class*. Because of its 'aborted' revolution between the 15th and 18th centuries, the bourgeois class did not succeed in changing the objective structures of the feudal state, and remained *in practice* a class politically dominated until its 'absorption' within a 'power bloc' belatedly formed by the landed aristocracy.

This aristocracy, by imposing its cultural and ideological hegemony on the British social formation as a whole, remained *permanently* the determinant class within the structures of political domination of this capitalist society.[6]

The bourgeois class, having missed its vocation as the hegemonic class, did not succeed, as in France, in structuring a 'coherent' ideology of its own which could be the *dominant ideology* in this formation: the ruling ideology of English society *as a whole* was the 'aristocratic' ideology.[7]

The working class did not find a fully constituted bourgeois ideology, corresponding to the pure political domination of the bourgeois class, which it could transform into a proletarian ideology. Thus in its turn, it could not set itself up as a revolutionary hegemonic class with its own ideology: a conception of the world oriented towards a global transformation of capitalist relations.[8] *By this very fact* it was confined to a subaltern 'economic-corporative', 'trade unionist', position, and presents a 'craft-trade unionist' class consciousness. Anderson's analysis is continued in Nairn's perceptive studies of English 'Labourism' and 'Trade Unionism'.

These are the conclusions which Thompson attacks. Firstly he criticizes their conception of an *aristocratic* class in the evolution of Britain's capitalist formation; he claims that what Anderson and Nairn regard as a landed aristocracy, *a class distinct* from the bourgeoisie, was, in fact, from the beginning of the capitalist process in Great Britain, a part of the *capitalist class*. Marx described this phenomenon as the transformation of feudal revenue into capitalist surplus-value. The conception of a 'power bloc' in Britain, Thompson argues, is tendentious and erroneous, because it would only concern the several political structurations *within* the bourgeois class, which constitutes *as a whole* the dominant political class. The objective political institutions of feudalism, though they did not, as in France, undergo an obvious radical transformation to the profit of the bourgeois class, *corresponded* nevertheless to that class's political domination. Further, to this extent the bourgeois class certainly constituted an 'authentic and articulate' dominant ideology composed of the values of Protestantism as a whole, the theory of political economy of Smith, Ricardo and others, the theory of political liberalism, and the theories of the natural sciences (Darwin). Thompson proceeds, via numerous detours, to conclude that the 'Labour' movement cannot be correctly summed up if it is reduced to a corporative class consciousness, linked to the absence of a dominant bourgeois ideology, or if its strategy is conceived as purely trade unionist. In fact, Thompson argues, the working-class struggle in Britain did raise itself to a purely political struggle, manifest in the various Labour Governments.

One can see the dimensions of the discussion; one cannot pretend to resume the debate with these few remarks. It simultaneously concerns the problematic of the *dominant class* in Great Britain in the evolution of the capitalist mode of production, and that *of the strategy and organization of the working class*. In the first case Anderson and Nairn consider the 'aristocratic-feudal class' to be *consistently the hegemonic class*; this leads them to some very important practical conclusions. Thompson challenges these analyses. Nevertheless, his own analysis is primarily empirical and circumstantial, and it does not generally attain the level of critical comprehension of the concepts of Marxist political science revealed in Anderson's and Nairn's analysis. Here, we will try to reveal the *theoretical presuppositions* of the thought of these two, and to see to what extent they lead to correct or erroneous applications of these concepts. Thus we shall suggest that their scientific application allows us to account for the *definite peculiarities* in the origin and evolution of the capitalist mode of production in Britain which have been revealed by Anderson and Nairn, *even when we follow Marx and Engels, as Thompson does, in holding that since 1640 political domination in Britain has constantly been held by the 'bourgeois class'*. In the second case, on the other hand, we will allow the justness of Anderson's and Nairn's remarks on 'Labourism', but also note the risks that are entailed in the application of their theoretical presuppositions.

Historicism and Subjectivism

In effect their analysis of social classes, of political superstructures, of the hegemony of class, of the power bloc, of the dominant ideology and of class consciousness reveals a perspective which is *historicist* and *subjectivist*. Without entering into detailed analysis, we can say that, in this approach, the type of unity which characterizes a social formation is not that of an objective, complex whole with a plurality of specific levels of structure *with a 'dominant'* in the last instance, the economy.

This unity is reduced to a 'totality' of the functionalist type – circular and composed of 'equivalent' elements interacting as gestalts (the Hegelian concept of 'concrete-universal' is a good example.) In this case, the *unity* of a social formation does not consist of a *complex* organization of all the particular levels, starting from a given mode of production. It does not consist, to put it another way, in a *specific type of articulation* of these levels *determined* by the mode of production. This complex organization is rather reduced to a central 'monist' instance, the *original* donor of meaning to the unity. This instance can be represented either by the 'economic level', empirically conceived, or by a '*subject*' of history on the idealist pattern. The *succession* of the various social formations itself is reduced to the *auto-development* of this instance. History becomes the unilinear, temporal becoming of this 'subject'. The most widespread contemporary form of this historicism in Marxist thought is the concept of the 'class-subject' of history, manifested in Lukács's political theory of class consciousness. In France, Lukács's position is generally considered only in the context of his account of ideology as a 'global conception of the world'. In fact, as Lucio Magri has shown,[9] it is integrated into a *Hegelian problematic* which governs his conception of 'class'. This problematic was manifest in Kautsky's analysis of social classes, at the time of the Second International. The theoretical positions taken by Lenin and Luxemburg in their struggle against Kautsky are well-known, and these positions were ideologically used by Lukács in a return to Hegel.

Before examining the consequences of this *historicist and subjectivist* conception, let us *see* how it is introduced into the analyses of Anderson and Nairn:

> If hegemonic class can be defined as one *which imposes its own ends and its own vision on society as a whole*, a corporate class is conversely one which *pursues its own ends within a social totality whose global determination lies outside it.*[10]

In this key sentence it is clear that the 'unity' of a historically determined social formation, the global social 'totality', is referred to the social class which imposes its *'hegemonic'* structuration. Gramsci's concept of hegemony is reduced, incorrectly, to the Lukácsian notion of class consciousness and the *properly political* structuration of a class is reduced to the constitution of a 'global conception of the world', which becomes the unifying principle of a determinate social formation. This conception of a *class* which becomes the subject of society and history to the extent that it constitutes, by its conception of the world, the consciousness-will of the 'totality' of men 'who make their own history' – human praxis – thus presupposes precisely the Hegelian type of circular and unilinear totality. Here we should not forget the direct descent of Lukács from Weber, for it is this filiation which allows us to elucidate the relationship between Lukács's Hegelian 'totality' and the *functionalist* totality which in large part predominates in contemporary political science. What links Weber's theories to contemporary functionalism, as Parsons has noted, is that the global social structure is, in the last analysis, considered as the *product* of a society-subject which creates in its teleological development certain social *values* or *ends*. For functionalism these determine the formal framework for an *integration* of the various and 'equivalent' structures in the particular social 'whole'. This integration is related to an 'equilibrium' based on certain regular and recurrent processes of the *normative* elements – for example motivations – which govern social 'action'. For Weber, these social values are crystallizations of different projects of historicist 'totalization' by social 'actors', and they constitute the principles which structure his 'ideal types'. It is here that the epistemological similarity between the Weberian 'ideal type' and the Hegelian concept of the 'concrete universal, is evident.[11]

Class Consciousness

Further, the creation of these values or social ends is often related by Weber to the 'action' of a social class, subject of society and history, and these considerations are the basis both of his conception of the 'political class' and the 'spirit of capitalism' as well as of his famous analysis of bureaucracy. Thus Lukács's theory of class consciousness appears as a vulgarly Marxist version of Weber – an attempt to attribute to the social 'values' created by a class-subject the *role of 'dominant' factor* in the organization of the social 'whole'. In short, to resume the fundamental objections to the conception of class consciousness that Anderson and Nairn appear to accept: by presupposing a Hegelian 'functionalist' type of totality within which the role of 'dominant' factor in a social formation is never *in fact* required, they end by situating their 'totality' in an 'idealist' domain of class consciousness, and *in consequence* attribute the dominant factor to a 'consciousness' of the hegemonic class, subject of history.[12]

However, it is important to see why Anderson and Nairn opt for this global historicist conception. Their analyses, which are situated at the *political level proper*, show the results of the lack in Marxist thought of a systematic theory of social classes. Of course this gap can be all too easily filled at the 'economic' and 'socio-economic' level by references, often abstract, to 'pure' relations of production. But, at the political level, it takes on *such* importance, *especially with regard to the problem of delineating the 'dominant class'*, that it determines Lukács's return to the Hegelian conception of the subject of history. In short we can discern the main *constant* in the ambiguities of the analyses of Anderson and Nairn: it lies in the fact that they cannot decide *if and from what time* the 'aristocratic class', made up, according to them, of 'the landowning class as a whole' – whether this is the great landed proprietors or the small landed gentry – *forms part of the capitalist class*. This aristocracy is sometimes considered as a *class distinct* from the (mercantile) bourgeoisie, sometimes as *part* of the (industrial) bourgeoisie. Now, it is clear that Marx's analyses of

the capitalization of feudal revenues cannot constitute a master matrix
which allows us to affirm, in an actual historical situation, the
political transformation of a *'feudal class'* into a *'capitalist class'*.
The difficulties here only become greater when we remember that even
in the framework of the 'pure' and 'abstract' theoretical schema of a
mode of production characterized by the dualist opposition of two
classes, a determined *social formation* presents, according to Marx, an
overlapping of *several* modes of production, *one* of which retains the
dominant role. The elucidation of this dominance, which can – in
default of a theory of social classes – produce *simple indices* of the
politically dominant class, is particularly delicate with regard to
periods of transition. The transition from feudalism to capitalism
which preoccupies us here is just such a case. It is precisely this absence
of a rigorous theory of social classes which forces Anderson and Nairn
to seek an easy solution, yielding to what is a constant temptation for
Marxist thought – the notion of class consciousness. It is an easy
solution because they attempt to delimit the 'dominant class' by
assuming, as we shall see, that it possesses a specific and coherent
class consciousness.

Three Conclusions

However, if we take these difficulties into account, we can retain from
the analyses of this current of *New Left Review* the following
conclusions as useful for discussion, while at the same time limiting
ourselves to the criteria provided by Marx, Engels and Lenin for
assessing social classes:

> a) the specific conditions of primitive accumulation of capital in
> Britain, and the peculiar British agricultural system resulted in an
> 'aristocracy' which remained for a long time a *class distinct* from
> the bourgeoisie, and initially from the mercantile bourgeoisie;
> b) this aristocracy set out on its own process of capitalization, in
> relative independence of the mercantile bourgeoisie;
> c) within this process, from the 18th century onwards, it finally
> constituted the nucleus of an industrial bourgeoisie and *thus* it
> became, at the level *of the relations of production*, a capitalist class.

These conclusions may be accepted in spite of their historicist character. But there are two reasons why they do not solve the problem of
providing a precise delimitation of the 'hegemonic class'.

Firstly, during the period when the aristocracy formed a *class distinct* from the bourgeois class, which of the two was the hegemonic class in Britain? Secondly, when the aristocracy became a fraction of the capitalist class within a power bloc *made up of several fractions*, which of these formed the hegemonic fraction? To say that it was the bourgeois class *as a whole* which played this role – as Thompson seems to suggest – is to declare that *a crucial problem which remains open has, in fact, been solved.* In fact, all the *political* analyses of Marx, Engels and Lenin on capitalist formations are concerned with delimiting the 'hegemonic' fraction of the bourgeois class, which is the dominant class as a whole. In the British case the 'aristocratic' fraction of the capitalist class was for a long time a distinct class and consequently continued to represent *specific* interests, even as a fraction of the capitalist class. Is it then the hegemonic fraction, as Anderson and Nairn suggest, just as they claim it was the hegemonic class when it was still a distinct class from the bourgeoisie; or does this role, in fact, belong to more 'classic' fractions of the bourgeoisie, viz. the industrial and financial fractions?

In brief, then, *both before and after* its insertion into the capitalist class, is it the landed aristocracy which forms the hegemonic class or hegemonic fraction within capitalism in Britain, or is it the bourgeoisie 'proper'?

The position taken by Anderson and Nairn on this question is a logical consequence of their global historicist conception of 'class consciousness'. This is evident in their examination of the political superstructures of the state already mentioned: the historicist approach leads to a 'voluntarist' conception of the political superstructures which ultimately reduces their objective reality to the status of mere 'products' of the *class consciousness of the politically dominant class* – final, monist, determination of a social formation. In other words, a class which is socio-economically dominant (in the dominant mode of production) cannot, they claim, be 'politically' dominant as well except to the extent that the state superstructure itself is 'immediately' produced by the praxis-consciousness of this class. In this context no intrinsic *autonomy* is granted these superstructures as *specific* levels. They are implicitly considered as one of the 'homogeneous' and 'equivalent' elements in the social circular 'whole' and thus reduced to a 'function' traced out in class consciousness, the principle which both determines the whole ensemble and generates these superstructures. The reader will not need to be reminded of the general functionalist problematic of superstructural 'institutions' in which they become crystallizations of social values corresponding mechanically to the 'vital needs' of the society-subject which produces them, and thus undifferentiated elements in the circular social *integration*. Here again, the conception of class consciousness is the result of an effort to adapt the Hegelian-functionalist totality within Marxism.[13]

Thus, according to Anderson and Nairn, the state superstructure in Britain which corresponded to the peculiarities of the aristocratic class could not be *changed* by the bourgeois class. The latter could only partially establish its own political domination; it was then blocked by the survival of the feudal character of the objective political institutions which enabled the aristocracy to maintain the 'dominant' role. The subsequent development of these superstructures is therefore, according to Anderson and Nairn, to be located within a process in which hegemony over the bloc in power returns constantly to the aristocracy.

The Marxist Conception

Now, there is no doubt that the capitalist political superstructures in Britain have long had a certain 'feudal' character, *in spite of appearances*. However, this does not in itself necessarily entail a parallel political hegemony on the part of the 'aristocracy'. If we abandon a historicist-subjectivist approach, the Marxist conception of political superstructures, enables us to explain the possibility of *social formations in which there are 'disjunctions' between the class whose mode of production ultimately imposes its dominant political role on the one hand and the objective structures of the state on the other*. We must therefore relate the way these superstructures are generated to the complex set of objective factors connected with these formations and not to the class-subject; and similarly the 'transition' from one mode of production to another must be related not to the unilinear historicist evolution of the class-subject but to the articulation of specific structural levels with their own historicities. This will lead us to the following conclusion: there may be sizeable disjunctions between *the politically dominant class and the objective structures of the state*. But such disjunctions, far from making these relations unintelligible, *are the basis for understanding them*. To be more precise, the Marxist conception of these 'disjunctions' is able to take account of the autonomy of the state – which so exercised Marx and Engels in their study of the transition from feudalism to capitalism and in capitalism itself. The fact that the state has its own autonomy, correlative to the separation of state and civil society, *can give several different equations [combinatoires]*. 'Bismarckism' is one of these possibilities – i.e.

a state which is *feudal* but whose objective structures correspond during a period of transition to a class which *is not yet even the socio-economically dominant class, while the capitalist mode of production is already dominant.* This is the case of the bourgeoisie under Bismarck where the state, by its relative autonomy, *erected* this class into the socio-economically dominant class and thus into *the politically dominant class* even before its own objective structures had adapted to the bourgeois forms of political domination. Again, in the entirely different phenomenon of 'Bonapartism' we have a case of a *capitalist 'type' of state* relying on a class which is not dominant either socio-economically or politically – viz. peasant smallholders. However this 'form' of capitalist state *objectively 'corresponds' to the interest of the politically dominant bourgeois class.* The absolutist forms the state took on during the period of primitive accumulation – France before 1789 and England particularly before 1640 – caused Engels and Marx to discern a certain 'autonomy' on the part of the state due to the socio-economic 'equilibrium' of the feudal and bourgeois classes. Towards the end of these periods, this equilibrium then produced a bourgeoisie which was dominant 'socio-economically', while the feudal class remained dominant 'politically'. In France the bourgeoisie became 'politically' dominant definitively in 1789.

As to what happened in Britain after 1640, Anderson and Nairn disagree with Marx and Engels who thought that it was *the bourgeois class which established its 'hegemonic' domination* – within the context of the relative autonomy of the state. They thought that this hegemony became more firmly established with the later changes in the state. The fact that the 'aristocracy' in England appears to be in control of a state with marked feudal features (as in Bismarckism) is explained by Marx and Engels as a 'delegation of power' by the bourgeoisie to the landowning aristocracy which is 'objectively' the 'representative' of the political interests of the bourgeoisie (cf. the role of the state and the smallholders *vis-à-vis* the bourgeoisie in the case of Bonapartism).[14]

The *historicist and subjectivist* perspective of Anderson and Nairn is also evident in their analysis of the *dominant ideology* in British capitalism. As the bourgeois class was unable to hold the politically hegemonic place, it was unable to structure its own original conception of the world, as it did in France, since the dominant ideology in Britain remained that of the hegemonic aristocracy. Now, it is a well-known Marxist tenet that the *dominant ideology* in a social formation is *generally that of the dominant class.* What is the historicist-subjectivist interpretation of this position? As we have seen, as soon as the *unity* of a determinate social formation is attributed to a class-subject, and hence to its class 'consciousness', the role of *central determinant instance* of the social 'whole' must be attributed to that global world conception *which this class immediately 'produces'*. Thus the ruling ideology of a social formation is the ideology 'produced' by the politically dominant class-subject as a hegemonic class-for-itself. Lukács expresses this particularly clearly;

> A class has a vocation for dominance when, through its class interests and through its class consciousness, the whole society can be organized in conformity with these interests . . . The following question is decisive in all class struggle: which class at any given moment disposes of this capacity and class consciousness? To what extent does the class in question consciously accomplish the tasks imposed on it by history, to what extent unconsciously, or with false consciousness?[15]

We can see that Lukács here reduces the constitution of the politically dominant class not to a scientific analysis of the objective factors of a social formation, but to the thematic of its 'class consciousness' as the determinant instance of all politics: a position which Lukács tried himself to surpass by means of the ideological notion of a 'possible consciousness', a *deus ex machina* which introduces a historical 'objectivity' with claims to 'materialism' within his idealist perspective.

The Politically Dominant Ideology

Let us return to the problem of the *politically dominant ideology*. In fact, as Marx says, ideology constitutes the way in which men, agents of production, live their conditions of existence; it thus includes, as Anderson and Nairn admit, 'taste', 'fashion', and 'local colour'. In this sense, as the agents of production are the bearers of the structures of production, as 'men' are the bearers of the social structures as a whole, the *dominant ideology* in a social formation constitutes in its primordial objective function *the 'cement' in the unity of the various levels of social structure*. This ideology *necessarily* also presents its own *internal* 'unity', a feature which the Lukácsian position attributes to the 'totality' of the world conception.

But this cannot be explained by relating ideology genetically to the class consciousness of the class/subject-of-history. The dominant ideology certainly expresses *the 'totality' of a social formation*, but not to the extent that this totality is incarnated by the consciousness-will of some subject. *The internal unity of the dominant ideology derives from the fact that it 'expresses' the 'Marxist' unity of a social formation as a whole founded on a determinate mode of production.* This ideology cements the articulation of the various levels of a formation; it expresses in a coherent universe the type of articulation specifying the 'unity' of that formation. Thus, if in general the politically dominant ideology in a formation is that of the politically dominant class, this is not because it can be identified with some political will of the class-subject as if ideologies were 'political' number-plates social classes wore on their backs; it is because the dominance of this ideology is related to the set of objective co-ordinates which result in a given political domination, a given class state, and a given dominant ideology.

So the objective correspondence of the 'interests' of a politically dominant class and of the politically dominant ideology is only intelligible if the *internal* unity of this ideology is deciphered, not by means of *one* class consciousness/world-conception, but through the *unity* at the political level of the various conflicting classes. This ideology may therefore comprise a number of 'elements' which transcribe the way classes other than the hegemonic class live their conditions of existence.

The relations between the dominant ideology and the hegemonic class may well frequently be masked; the ideology, like all ideologies, hiding its own principles from itself, may in the complex constitution of the ideological level, appear closer to the way in which some class other than the hegemonic class lives its conditions of existence. Further, it is precisely these considerations which prove the truth of one of Gramsci's original theses; he tells us that the working class can deeply impregnate the *dominant ideology* of a social formation *even before the conquest of power, before it has become the politically dominant class*.

To return to the theses of Anderson and Nairn: the fact that the dominant ideology in Britain has not apparently manifested a coherent 'world conception' of the bourgeois class means neither that this ideology does not in fact correspond to its political interests, *nor because of this, that the bourgeoisie could not be in a hegemonic position*. In fact, this dominant ideology presents a number of features suggesting its relation to the bourgeoisie; we have already referred to Thompson's remarks to this effect. However, as he implicitly adopts the same problematic as Anderson and Nairn, in opposition to them, he sets out to discover the unity of the dominant ideology in Britain in the presupposed coherence of the bourgeois world conception that this ideology should, in fact, express; and among other things he refers to 'Protestantism', recalling Weber. But we may draw the following conclusions from our analysis. *Given the peculiarities of capitalist formation in Britain, the dominant ideology there is deeply impregnated with elements relating to an aristocratic 'life style', as Nairn and Anderson show. However, its internal coherence, comprehensible if related to the overall unity of the formation, corresponds to the 'political hegemony' – not to the class consciousness – of the bourgeoisie, which explains those bourgeois 'features' that Thompson insists upon.*

Further: the ruling-class/subject, producer of the dominant-ideology/world-conception of a social formation, becomes because of this for Anderson and Nairn (by frequent reference to Gramsci) the 'hegemonic' class in this formation. But it is only too obvious that this Lukácsian interpretation of Gramsci (only too popular nowadays, as the original theses of the latter are often contaminated with Labriola's historicism) prevents a rigorous understanding of his work; in fact, the concept of hegemony definitely cannot be reduced to the 'class consciousness' of one class impregnating the whole society with its particular 'world conception'; it cannot therefore be applied just in the area of ideologies interpreted in a Lukácsian sense. But it can be applied to the set of *objective co-ordinates of political domination* within this formation. *This makes it particularly useful when treating of several politically dominant classes or class fractions of which one only takes the hegemonic role, a situation typified by capitalist Britain.* But if, on the contrary, the *hegemony* of a class is seen as the Lukácsian constitution of a 'dominant class' with its own 'class consciousness', two things follow: on the one hand the concept has no utility, for we know that the dominant ideology of a formation corresponds to the interest of the 'dominant class'; on the other hand, if it is applied in a context where there is a *'plurality'* of classes or of class fractions which the facts show to be *politically dominant*, it may merely mask the complex play of the *objective relations* between their more or less contradictory interests: these classes are *declared* 'unified' by their *internalization* and *absorption* in the class consciousness thus designated as hegemonic.

Amalgamation

In fact, according to our authors, the aristocratic and bourgeois classes (the latter in practice in the position of a politically 'dominated' class until the 19th century) *fused* in the 19th century *into a single social bloc*, the bourgeoisie thus finally acceding to political domination. Certainly, this concept of a 'power bloc' is crucial for a Marxist study of political domination in a capitalist formation. However, it is essential to see how exactly its structuration is effected in the hegemony of one class or fraction.

On this point, Nairn suggests:

> . . . no 'compromise' or 'alliance' – the usual terms employed – was, in fact, possible as between contrasting civilizations. No conscious tactical arrangement, no deal lasting for a season, was conceivable between social forces of this complexity and magnitude. *Amalgamation* was the only real possibility, a *fusion* of different classes and their diverse cultures into one social order . . .[16]

Naturally, this analysis delights Thompson:

> This is not a genuine dialectical paradox, it is a dialectical trick: two forces (we are told) were so incompatible in interests and outlook that no compromise was possible between them; but, when we have turned our head we find they have *fused*.[17]

Thompson finds this all the more intriguing as Anderson and Nairn will only allow the *hegemony* of *one* of the forces present in this 'fusion' in the power bloc: the hegemonic role is taken by the aristocracy, which has, in the meantime, become a fraction of the capitalist class.

But what perhaps justifies Thompson's dismay is not the concepts of the 'power bloc' or of *the hegemony of one element of the bloc over the others*, but the tenor and application of these concepts in Anderson and Nairn; this brings out some of the consequences of their conception of 'class consciousness'. In fact, this strange bloc-fusion is *epistemologically* possible for Anderson and Nairn as for them hegemony indicates the 'class consciousness' of a politically hegemonic class-subject (the aristocracy).

Thus the constitution of this 'power bloc' is precisely related to the *internalization*, in a Hegelian sense, of the other 'dominant' classes (the bourgeois class) participating in the bloc *within* the hegemonic class. This bloc finally represents the absorption-fusion of the *objective interests* of these classes in the consciousness or world-conception (idealist agent of totalization) of the 'hegemonic' class. Further, the problem remains the same, as has already been mentioned, when it is no longer 'classes' but 'class fractions' that are at issue, for this problematic may be *globally transposed* into the context of the relations between these fractions, between a fraction with hegemonic consciousness and the other dominant fractions within the 'power bloc'.[18]

However, neither the concept of the 'power bloc' nor that of 'hegemony' are in question. Where there is a *plurality* of classes or fractions, the power bloc denotes their *contradictory unity* (i.e. the Marxist type of unity, not a fusion-totality of the Hegelian type). The domination of these classes or fractions in the 'power bloc' relates to *relatively macrochronic objective structures* – to 'phases' – of *the relations of production as a whole* (not, therefore, to tactical 'compromises' or 'alliances').[19] This *contradictory unity* is realized *under the aegis of the hegemonic fraction*; the latter constitutes precisely the *'dominant' instance* characteristic of the Marxist type of unity at the purely political level of structures of domination.

To this extent, hegemony designates the *objective* structuration of the *specific* 'interests' of a class or fraction as representative of a general *political* interest of the classes or fractions in power despite their deep contradictions; the dominant ideology is therefore only *one aspect* of this organization of the hegemonic class or fraction. However, given this interpretation of the concepts of power bloc and hegemony and the rejection of a subjectivist conception of superstructures and ideologies, it is possible to accept certain of Anderson's and Nairn's theses, but deduce different conclusions. It becomes possible to see how, in the structuration of the power bloc in Britain, as Marx and Engels showed, it was initially the merchant bourgeoisie, and later fractions more correctly designated as bourgeois (the industrial and financial bourgeoisie), which constituted the hegemonic class or fraction, despite feudal survivals in the state and in the aristocratic features of the dominant ideology. This was a bourgeois class whose specific interests were politically constituted by objectively representing those of the 'aristocracy'; the latter is merely the 'clerk' of the bourgeoisie, both in this power bloc and in relation to the state.

But, if we accept the hegemonic domination of the bourgeoisie and not of the aristocracy in the peculiar evolution of capitalism in Great Britain, several of the concrete political analyses of the group around *New Left Review* must obviously be reconsidered. We have no intention of entering on this subject here. Suffice it to say that it is their point of view on this issue which is at the origin of the divergence between their analyses and those of Miliband, one of the editors of *Socialist Register*, in his book *Parliamentary Socialism* which traces the political evolution of Britain, primarily in this century.

Labourism

Anderson's and Nairn's analyses are completed by excellent studies of *labourism* and working-class strategy in Britain; here Thompson's objections seem ill-founded. Their study of the 'trade-unionist/syndicalist' character of the working class, a class which has virtually never been able to achieve an effective form of political organization in Britain, are of an exemplary theoretical level.

But even here, the danger remains that their problematic may lead to incorrect conclusions. For example, the explanation provided by the authors of the 'trade-unionist' and 'economico-corporative' character of the working class may be queried. Anderson and Nairn argue, among other things, that this class, situated within a social formation in which the bourgeoisie ultimately occupies a 'subaltern' position, was unable to locate a coherent bourgeois ideology within it, which it could *transform* into a proletarian 'class consciousness', a revolutionary ideology.

In the last resort, this explanation presumes a *historicist* conception of the *succession* of different modes of production, a universal, supposedly Marxist schema involving the necessary and unilinear succession of slavery, feudalism, capitalism and socialism. The 'class consciousness' of different and consecutive class-subjects (the primary instance of both the unity *and* the succession of these social formations) would reveal through its Hegelian auto-development, *a process of more and more sweeping totalizations*: each class consciousness would thus *stem from* the one before, with that of the proletariat finally completing the process through a final and 'total' coincidence of concept and being, of subject and object. *This is exactly Lukács's interpretation of the relations between bourgeois and proletarian conceptions of the world.* This historicist conception is very far, as we have seen, from the original Marxist conception. Moreover, everyone knows that in the so-called 'under-developed' countries an *authentic revolutionary ideology* is often found without a preconstituted bourgeois ideology, precisely in the sense that the transition to socialism can be brought about without the anterior establishment of 'typical' capitalist relations of production. Thus, the fact that in Britain, there is no conception of the world proper to the bourgeois class, cannot be made to explain 'the trade-unionist' character of the English working class. The analyses of Anderson and Nairn concerning the absence of 'intellectuals' in the Gramscian sense from the political organization of the working class in Britain, are in this respect, much more convincing.

The dangers of the general problematic of Anderson and Nairn appear again in the application of the concept of hegemony to the strategy of the working class: if the concept is retained here in the sense of 'class consciousness', it may present *the same difficulties* as it did when it was applied to the 'power-bloc' among the dominant classes. For our authors, the constitution of the proletariat as a hegemonic class becomes its mere structuration as a 'class for itself' with its own conception of the world:

> A hegemonic class seeks to transform society in its own image, inventing afresh its economic system, its political institutions, its cultural values, its whole 'mode of insertion' into the world.[20]

However, it is only too clear, that, for Gramsci, the hegemony of the proletariat, must be inserted within a quite different perspective. Here, in fact, two problems should be distinguished if their relationship is to be kept clear. First the formation of an ideology proper to the proletariat, the transition from the 'economic struggle' to the 'truly political struggle' (the fundamental problem emphasized by Lenin). Second, the specific problem of hegemony. For Lenin's analyses cannot be reduced to the formation of some sort of proletarian 'conception of the world'.

They concern the objective co-ordinates of its political struggle as a whole, *of which the ideological formation only constitutes one aspect.* It is in this context that the concept of 'hegemony' may be a useful breakthrough, if it is related to an authentic theorization of Lenin's political practice.

In fact, to gain a clearer understanding of Gramsci's concept of hegemony, we should refer to the theoretical discussions which divided Lenin from Rosa Luxemburg and other theoreticians of the Third International. Lenin, in opposition to the latter, called for a revolutionary political strategy of the proletariat based on its 'alliance' with the dominated classes as a whole, and notably with the peasantry. This strategic 'theory' stemmed from an application of the original Marxist conception, profoundly different from that of the 'pure' and promethean proletariat-subject-agent of history: it was incorporated by Gramsci in his conception of the working class and its party as a collective 'prince', *realizing the unity of the exploited and dominated 'national' forces as a whole within the capitalist system.* However, this *relationship between the proletariat and other dominated classes,* was subsumed by Lenin under the vague term 'alliance' – a fact which has led to misinterpretations of his positions on the 'dictatorship of the proletariat' and 'socialist democracy'. It suffices to mention here the controversies on the question of the 'alliance' between Zinoviev and Stalin, echoes of which are found in Stalin's *Questions of Leninism*. Moreover these theoretical problems assume a position of capital importance within the context of the 'frontist' strategy pursued by European Communist Parties from the famous Seventh Congress of the Third International onwards.

Revolutionary Bloc

It is in this context that the concept of hegemony has genuine novelty: as in the case of the 'power-bloc', *it can be applied to what might be called a 'revolutionary bloc'* – Gramsci's 'historical bloc' having in fact, another meaning – *the contradictory unity, proper to Marxism, between dominated classes under the domination of the hegemonic proletariat*, a 'unity' which is itself related to the *set of objective co-ordinates of the capitalist social formation*. It concerns the modalities of the political struggle within these formations, and cannot simply be conceived as a tactical or provisional 'alliance', in voluntarist style, of the proletariat with these classes. On the one hand, this unity cannot reside in 'compromises'[21] which would leave forces within this bloc *intact* in their own particularity. But, on the other hand, hegemony is not at all concerned with a proletarian 'class consciousness' of a voluntarist-idealist conception. It does not designate a consciousness automatically *internalizing* in its concept the real contradictions between these dominated classes through their 'absorption-fusion' in the proletariat-subject, through their 'assimilation-amalgamation' in the proletariat by means of some sort of 'totalizing conception of the world'. *The hegemony of the proletariat denotes quite precisely the properly political constitution of the 'specific' objective interests of the working class into the real general interest of all workers, despite their particular differences*: the ideological formation of the working class forms only one aspect of this constitution.

These problems are particularly important, as Anderson himself uses this concept of the 'bloc' between the proletariat and the dominated classes. He himself emphasizes that 'this concept is radically different from that of a coalition which remains the normal type of political combination on the Left today'. Now, if this is true, as we have shown above, it is by no means clear that Anderson does not ensnare himself in the concept of a bloc-fusion or bloc-amalgamation used by Nairn in relation to the dominant class, which is achieved here by the 'class consciousness' of the proletariat.

A socialist party can only successfully pose its candidature to the direction of a society, when it is the bearer of *universal values*, recognised and experienced as such by a majority of all those whose humanity is denied and dislocated by the social order . . . the bloc is thus a synthesis of the aspirations and identities of different groups in a global project which exceeds them all. Its critique of capitalism is the truth of each particular claim . . .[22]

Is it a coincidence that a political theorist of Anderson's quality should use the term 'synthesis'? Surely only a notorious 'socialist humanism' could propose the conception of some sort of *'synthesis fusion'* of the *specific interests* of the forces composing this bloc under the objective *political* hegemony of the proletariat. Would this conception of the world, this totalizatory instance of consciousness, be 'the truth of' each specific interest? Problems as real as the 'dictatorship of the proletariat', 'socialist democracy', 'the state of all the people' or even the 'unity' of all the workers, democracy within the bloc, *cannot be discussed scientifically* from the global and historicist perspective of class consciousness.

Thus, if one wishes to understand the 'trade unionist' or 'economico-corporative' mentality of the British working class, highlighted by Anderson and Nairn, one must look for the explanation in their penetrating analyses of its political organization (structure of the Labour Party and global political strategy of this party) rather than in their references to its lack of a hegemonic class consciousness or conception of the world.

5

TOWARDS A MARXIST THEORY

Louis Althusser has just collected some of his articles published since 1960 under the title *For Marx*.[1] Scattered articles, already familiar in the international theoretical movement of Marxism, where they are the subject of discussion, their collection brings out their distinctive problematic. My aim here is to highlight their importance in several respects. In the first place, Althusser is a Communist. Loyal to his party through the crises of the workers' movement, he sets out a Marxist theoretical line of thought, prompted by the everyday political activity of a militant, which reflects the current concerns of world Communism. Secondly, Althusser's project is to establish the basic coordinates of a Marxist theory, to propose positive categories, which make it possible to account for the forms and modes of production of knowledge. Here Althusser resumes in his own right a project that Marx, as Lenin noted, was not able to carry through, and which has subsequently haunted Marxist thought, notwithstanding petty terminological disputes over the possibility and legitimacy of a Marxist 'philosophy': the project of defining the status of theory in relation to practice, of marking out the path for a definition of the concepts that lead to scientific knowledge and political action – in short, not merely establishing what is commonly referred to as the 'logic' or 'theory' of *Capital* (a mere methodology), but the general theory of scientific knowledge presupposed by that methodology:

> I shall call Theory (with a capital T), general theory, that is, the Theory of practice in general, itself elaborated on the basis of the Theory of existing theoretical practices (of the sciences), which transforms into 'knowledges' (scientific truths) the ideological product of existing 'empirical' practices (the concrete activity of

* First published in French as 'Vers une théorie marxiste' in *Les Temps Modernes*, no. 240 (1966), pp. 1952–82. Translated by Gregory Elliott.

men). This Theory is the materialist dialectic which is none other than *dialectical* materialism.[2]

Adopting a critical perspective in order to study Althusser's texts, we can identify their project of effecting, through a rediscovery of Marx, what Bachelard called an 'epistemological break' with contemporary thought. This concept of 'epistemological break', adopted by Althusser in his analysis of the transition from Hegel to Marx, indicates that in the history of thought the specific unity of a theoretical ensemble, the internal type governing the order of questions that this ensemble poses to a determinate object – its peculiar problematic – breaks, as a unitary type, with the problematic governing a different ensemble or ensembles. The latter thus become the 'theoretical pre-history' of the new scientific problematic. Before we can know whether Althusser actually effects this 'epistemological break' with contemporary thought at the level of his own thinking, we must therefore unravel the main themes around which his problematic is organized. In order to clarify these ideas, we may say that, on the basis of new meanings of the concepts of history and structure and a new sense of the relations between them, this problematic seeks to account for the originality of Marx's problematic with respect to Hegel, Feuerbach, and the 'young Marx' through a certain reading of Marx.

Indeed, Althusser tells us, the problematic that allows Marx to effect an epistemological break with Hegel is not to be found in the critique directed by the young Marx against the abstract and speculative character of the Hegelian dialectic in the works preceding *The German Ideology* and in the precise theoretical space of left Hegelianism. This critique, which appeals to the 'materialist concrete' against the 'speculative abstract', is none other than Feuerbach's. If we adopt this position, we limit ourselves to perceiving in Marx an 'inversion' of Hegel, to regarding the materialist dialectic as simply the speculative dialectic 'put back on its feet'. This conception ends up transplanting into Marx the concepts of totality and history specific to Hegelian thinking just as they are, the only difference consisting in the replacement of the 'site' of the Hegelian concept by the site of the 'economic'. This is not only inaccurate but epistemologically impossible: the Hegelian concept of totality refers to a circular type of unity comprising equivalent elements, whose mode of articulation is determined by their internalization in the concept-Idea. The Hegelian totality does not evince the particular dominance of a certain element over the others, whereas in Marx the economic possesses a dominant place that determines the type of unity governing the set of elements. Because the

Hegelian type of totality involves the simple, original unity of the concept, of which the different social realities are merely the phenomena objectified by the externalization of its own self-development, the possibility of the dominance of one of these externalizations is excluded – and this to the precise extent that their objective specificity is itself diluted. The historicist problem of the origin governs the type of unity that characterizes the Hegelian totality. For its part, Marxism attributes a quite different meaning to the concept of 'totality' by establishing the ever-pre-given complex structure of an ensemble of objective, specific levels, with their own autonomy and effectivity, of a historically determinate social formation. The complexity of the ensemble and the specificity of the various levels establish a 'Marxist' type of unity and type of 'structure': a 'structure in dominance' – in the case in point, the structure of the ensemble of a social formation under the dominance, in the last instance, of the economic. Let us allow Althusser speak for himself:

> That one contradiction dominates the others presupposes that the complexity in which it features is a structured unity, and that this structure implies the indicated domination-subordination relations between the contradictions . . . Domination is not just an indifferent *fact*, it is a fact *essential* to the complexity itself . . . So to claim that this unity is not and cannot be the unity of a simple, original and universal essence is not, as those who dream of that ideological concept foreign to Marxism, 'monism', think, to sacrifice unity on the altar of 'pluralism' – it is to claim something quite different: that the unity discussed by Marxism is *the unity of complexity itself*; that the mode of organization and articulation of the complexity is precisely what constitutes its unity. It is to claim that *the complex whole has the unity of a structure articulated in dominance.*[3]

This 'structure articulated in dominance', which defines the Marxist type of unity, is not simply characteristic of a social formation as a whole (under the dominance, in the last instance, of the economic): it also indicates the type of unity peculiar to a specific level of structures, in as much as this specificity is simply the way in which the 'dominant structure' of the ever-pre-given complex whole is reflected at that particular level.

Marx's new scientific problematic with respect to Hegel cannot therefore be construed as the 'inversion' of the speculative moment and materializes in a novel concept of structure. The same is true of the concept of history: the meaning of the latter in 'historical materialism' derives from the definition of structure by 'dialectical materialism' within the general problematic specific to Marxism. Thus, in an article not published in this collection, 'Esquisse d'un concept d'histoire' (*La Pensée*, 1965), Althusser attacks the concept of history implicitly endorsed by the contemporary social sciences in the context of a Hegelian 'historicist' problematic. This concept involves both the homogeneous continuity of 'time' and the contemporaneity of time or the category of the historical present: it precisely presupposes the type of unity characteristic of the Hegelian totality. The homogeneous continuity of time is the reflection in existence of the continuity of the dialectical development of the Idea, so that the whole problem of the science of history then consists in a simple periodization of dialectical moments-totalities within their unilinear development-evolution. But this continuous homogeneity of time assumes the legitimacy of a deciphering of the historical present such that it can, at any moment, reveal the set of elements governing the original 'whole' which commands the periodization into successive totalities. The intelligibility of the structure of a social formation thus contains a universal type of historicity and temporality in as much as, ultimately in Hegel, the historicism of the origin of the simple totality reduces the objective specificity of the different structures-moments to the self-development of the Idea. This contemporaneity indicates that:

> The structure of the historical existence [of the Hegelian social totality] is such that all the elements of the whole always co-exist in one and the same time. This means that the structure of the historical existence of the Hegelian social totality allows what I propose to call an *'essential section'* . . . When I speak of an 'essential section', I shall therefore be referring to the specific structure of the social totality that allows this section, in which all the elements of the whole are given in a co-presence, itself the immediate presence of their essences, which thus becomes immediately *legible in them*.[4]

Thus, in Hegel, such contemporaneity stems from the very type of unity that characterizes his concept of totality, which precludes the dominance of one particular element over the others. For

> [b]ecause the Hegelian whole is a 'spiritual whole' in the Leibnizian sense of a whole in which all the parts 'conspire' together, in which each part is a *pars totalis*, the unity of this double aspect of historical time (homogeneous-continuity/contemporaneity) is possible and necessary.[5]

By contrast, for Marxism, which acknowledges the type of unity formed by a 'complex whole structured in dominance', this concept of history is unacceptable. It is no longer a question of 'inverting' it, in order to replace the development of the Idea by the unilinear development of the productive forces. It is by deciphering the concrete forms taken by the structuration of a pre-given whole articulated in dominance – by deciphering the index of dominance and the 'matrix' of a formation – that we shall be able to define the different times characterizing the various levels and the process of their sequence in a differential history:

> As this concept [of history] can only be based on the complex and differentially articulated structure in dominance of the social totality that constitutes the social formation arising from a determinate mode of production, it can only be assigned a content as a function of the structure of that totality, considered either as a whole, or in its different 'levels'. In particular, it is only possible to give a content to [this] concept, [that is to say, to define the form of existence peculiar to this totality], by defining historical time as the specific form of existence of the social totality under consideration, an existence in which different structural levels of temporality interfere, because of the peculiar relations of correspondence, non-correspondence, articulation, dislocation and torsion which obtain, between the different 'levels' of the whole in accordance with its general structure.[6]

On the basis of this distinctive problematic, Althusser proceeds to the constitution of the Theory of dialectical materialism. Here we shall take up one main theme: 'overdetermination' and 'theoretical practice'.

As formulated by Althusser in his article 'Contradiction and Overdetermination', this involves the relations between different levels of social structure and practice. If it is true that Marxism has always acknowledged the relative autonomy and specific effectivity of the various levels of a social formation – schematically speaking, the action of the superstructure on the infrastructure – the theory of this action is generally constructed on the basis of an idealist problematic: it is viewed as a repercussion of the phenomenon on the essence. By contrast, if we locate this issue within the 'problematic' that Althusser uncovers in Marx, if we cease referring, in Hegelian fashion, to an original, simple contradiction-totality producing, in the course of its unilinear self-development from essence to existence, the various

moments-levels-elements in a circular equivalence, then we note that
the simple contradiction between Capital and Labour – the economic –
is never given in its actual existence and is therefore only decipherable
within a structure whose dominant is, albeit only in the last instance,
economic:

> We never deal with anything but complex processes in which a
> structure with multiple and uneven determinations intervenes pri-
> mitively, not secondarily . . . So simplicity is not original; on the
> contrary, it is the structured whole which gives its meaning to the
> simple category, or which may produce the economic existence of
> certain simple categories as the result of a long process and under
> exceptional conditions.[7]

In fact, it is precisely because the Marxist type of unity which characterizes the social formation as a whole involves such a structure that
the dominance of the economic in the last instance only exists in its
reflection within an ensemble of specific levels; one level constitutes the
condition of existence of the other levels, but they in turn constitute its
conditions of existence. This is in no way contradictory, for we are not
dealing with ontological conditions of existence of an essence, but with
the 'existing conditions' of this type of unity. This implies that:

> The 'secondary' contradictions are essential even to the existence of
> the principal contradiction . . . *reflection of the structure articu-
> lated in dominance that constitutes the unity of the complex whole
> within each contradiction*, this is the most profound characteristic
> of the Marxist dialectic, the one that I have tried recently to
> encapsulate in the concept of '*overdetermination*'.[8]

Consequently, the relations between the different specific levels of
social structures and practices cannot simply be treated as an interaction between base and superstructure, as external relations either
between levels whose specificity is cancelled by the straightforward
reduction of the one to the other, or between levels that are supposed
to be specific, but which emerge as already constituted in their
respective exteriority and heterogeneity. Overdetermination indicates
that the specificity of a level depends upon its position as a condition
of existence in the complex whole whose type of unity it reflects. Three
major consequences follow from this.
    The first is that theoretical practice is to be restored to its specificity
vis-à-vis political practice – two practices whose conflation resulted in

the formula 'bourgeois science-proletarian science'. The specificity of theoretical practice, itself regarded as a practice, consists in the fact that the raw material on which it works, in order to transform it by producing scientific knowledge, is not 'empirical facts', the 'singular real', the 'materialist concrete', and so on, but 'theoretical facts', existing ideological or pre-scientific concepts, previous 'thought' in general. The result, in Althusser, is a radical distinction between the thought-process and the real process, between the thought-concrete, which is the knowledge produced by theoretical practice on the basis of generalities-concepts, and the real-concrete that is its object – the process of production of scientific knowledge thus being located entirely within theoretical practice. It is precisely from these findings that Althusser's basic philosophical project derives: fashioning the theory of theoretical 'practice', the practice that fashions the theory of the other practices – economic, political, and so on. The epistemo-logical specificity of the 'theoretical', which is non-existent for an 'idealist' problematic, is thus connected in Althusser with the meaning of the very concepts of structure and history. As such, they must be 'theoretically' constructed, establishing, through their relationship, the specificity of the theoretical.

Second, these considerations take us to the heart of Althusser's problematic: the type of unity represented by a 'structure in dom-inance' and 'overdetermination' means that the content of this domi-nant is not always the-economic-in-last-instance, but can be some other level:

It is economism that identifies eternally in advance the determinant-contradiction-in-the-last-instance with the *role* of the dominant contradiction . . . whereas in real history determination in the last instance by the economy is exercised precisely in the permutations of the principal role between the economy, politics, theory, etc.[9]

The novelty of Althusser's problematic lies in this key distinction between the dominance of the economic in the last instance and the dominant role of a level in the ensemble of a social formation.

Third, this thematic (history, overdetermination, and theoretical practice) makes it possible to consider various problems in a new light: the existence of a supposedly universal Marxist model of a unilinear sequence of social formations (Oriental, slave, feudal, capitalist); the status of transition periods; the historicity of the various levels of a social formation; the notion of the 'backward' or 'advanced' character of certain levels with respect to the 'economic'; and so on. The process

of the 'development of forms', to which Marx referred, is characterized by a differential historical temporality, peculiar to different social
formations and their different levels, depending on the particular
'matrix' of each formation. This matrix, disclosed by theoretical
practice, defines the particular mode of structuration of the social
formation under consideration and determines the 'index of dominance' of the various specific levels within this formation. The
distinctive object of history is thus, through historical investigation,
to construct the concept of history by means of theoretical practice:

> The object of history as a theoretical discipline is the production of
> the specific determination of the variations of historical existence,
> of the specificity of the existence of the structure and process of a
> determinate social formation, pertaining to a specific mode of
> production.[10]

Following this schematic exposition of Althusser's thought, and before
proceeding to the criticisms that might be directed at it, I would like to
try to situate his problematic in the contemporary context. I would say
that this problematic is characterized by the fact that Althusser regards
the concepts of structure and history as two distinctive concepts and
seeks to establish the relations between them precisely on the basis of
their specificity. Thus, these relations cannot be boiled down to a
reduction of one concept to the other – the concept of structure
reduced to a universal type of history or, conversely, a universal type
of history included in the synchronic section of a structure. His
thinking therefore seems to presuppose that of Sartre and Lévi-Strauss
and their interpretations of Marxism. It is precisely in so far as
Althusser's reflection on Marx – his rediscovery of Marx – situates
itself in relation to Sartre and Lévi-Strauss that his deciphering of
Marxism presents the problem of the relations between structure and
history as its central theme. By the same token, this is to say that Sartre
and Lévi-Strauss have established an original interpretation of Marxism which breaks with a whole prior current of Marxism, and that this
interpretation makes Althusser's thinking theoretically possible.

Hence a second problem. Althusser's texts allow us to glimpse – for
his thinking is still at the stage where it is in search of it – the
possibility and doubtless the necessity of a new Marxist problematic
that could, at its own level, effect an 'epistemological break' with the
thought of Sartre and Lévi-Strauss – a break that makes it possible to
establish the relations between them, to account for their conclusions,
and to make a scientific assessment of their contributions to Marxism.

At this stage, can it be said that Althusser actually effects this break? Here, I shall provisionally adopt the principles set out by Althusser, in order to try to identify the perspectives opened up by his conception of 'structure in dominance' and 'differential history'. Subsequently, we shall see the objections that might be addressed to Althusser: we shall ask if he has already carried through this break or whether, at this stage in his thinking, he has established a starting-point for effecting it.

What, then, would be the basic feature of a way of thinking that effected this break? With respect to other contemporary theoretical systems, it would allow us to establish their relationship – i.e. the common problematic that governs the order of questions which they pose. Relationship does not mean resemblance or synthesis in this context. For example, in the case of Sartre and Lévi-Strauss the relationship is the following: to a certain given problematic there can only correspond two 'coherent' orders of response, two theoretical 'systems' – the thinking of Sartre and that of Lévi-Strauss; at the level at which these thinkers conceive their own thought, these two orders of response might appear to be polar opposites; and yet these systems are only the necessarily opposed expression of their common problematic, two ways – absolutely bound up with one another and yet mutually exclusive – of responding to a 'typical' order of questions.

In fact, what seems to characterize the shared problematic of Sartre and Lévi-Strauss is that they attribute related meanings – always contrary to those Althusser assigns them – to the respective concepts of history and structure, meanings that were from the outset located on a common ground – that is to say, within conceptions that identify with Marxism and which I shall define here very schematically as 'anti-speculative' and 'anti-aprioristic'. By 'anti-speculative', I refer to Sartre's position in opposition to Hegelianism; by 'anti-aprioristic', to Lévi-Strauss's in opposition to an epistemological 'formalism' whose relations with the theory of knowledge of Kantian neo-criticism have been signalled by Granger in particular.[11]

This means, in the first instance, that these two thinkers have recognized two differentiated concepts whose relation poses a 'problem' and is not immediately 'reducible' to their 'speculative' identity or their 'a priori' idealist identity. This is especially clear in Sartre. Let us take the example of Korsch or, above all, that of Lukács. From the Hegelian standpoint typical of the latter – an idealist-speculative historicist viewpoint – the relation of totality (if we want to adopt this term instead of structure) is not, and cannot be, 'problematic'. From the unvarying standpoint of a speculative identity between subject and object, where subject does not in fact have the sense of 'agent', but predominantly that of 'knowledge to which being is reduced' – a consciousness-concept-totality – history is not, strictly speaking, a totalization. It is a finalistic development in fragmentary totalities of a totality already given *in potentia* at the outset. Thus, the structure-totality ultimately has no objective site of existence, but is conceived as the objectification or externalization of the concept. It cannot be constituted by an agent since it is already given at the outset, in the original interiority of the concept. In this case, history reduces the problem of the objective specificity of structures-totalities. And it is clear that in Sartre, in so far as he refuses the Hegelian speculative problematic, in so far as the 'totalizing' *praxis*-agent is not simply said to be different from the Hegelian consciousness-concept, but is theoretically conceived as meaning-creating 'practice' in its constitutive relationship with the practico-inert, objective structures – totalizations of the 'practical' agent – and history as the constituent praxis of these structures pose the problem of a 'relationship' between two differential concepts.

Without going into detail, let us consider Lévi-Strauss's theses in *Structural Anthropology*. In opposition to Barthes and his 'formal structures-models'[12] (I offer this example by way of *mere illustration*), for whom the problem of diachrony and historicity, strictly speaking, does not exist, in so far as history is immediately reduced to transformations within an a priori, universal model of rules of intelligibility and mutation of social phenomena, and is thus already inscribed in a model of structures – in this connection, we might recall the existence of a whole current of neo-Kantian interpretation of Marxism in Austro-Marxism – Lévi-Strauss establishes valid correlations between the specifically structured, objective ensembles of a 'given society'. He thereby acknowledges the problem of a relationship between the differential terms of structure and history – hence his theme of synchrony and diachrony.

Thus, on the basis of their 'common' positions, which are respectively 'anti-speculative' and 'anti-aprioristic' – in Hegel and the young Marx, there is also an 'explicit' shared starting-point, which is not the essential thing: the 'dialectic' – Sartre and Lévi-Strauss pose a problem: the 'objective' specificity of structures and of history and, consequently, the problem of the possible and necessary relations between them. But if they pose the problem of these relations, they do not make it possible to fix one that accounts for the differential specificity of the concepts in question. Hence the consequences to which they lead: for Sartre, a primacy of history such that it appears to absorb the specificity of structures; for Lévi-Strauss, a primacy of structure such that it seems to absorb the specificity of history. The mutual exclusiveness of these two lines of thought is perhaps merely the expression of an invariant, in that they are two aspects of one and the same problematic, which can be deciphered by a theoretical grasp of their consequences on the basis of the principles stated by Althusser. This would explain the 'paradoxical' character of their relations noted by Pouillon.[13]

We might then seek to establish, in schematic fashion, the relations between Althusser on the one hand, and Sartre and Lévi-Strauss on the other, ignoring what divides the latter.

Compared with Althusser, Sartre appears to reduce history to a continuous-homogeneous-contemporaneous time and to endorse a concept of structure distinct from that of a structure articulated in dominance. In Sartre, it is the primacy of this type of historicity – even though he does not expressly define 'man' by his historicity – that determines the acceptance of a certain type of structure; and it is precisely to this extent that his thinking seems opposed to that of Lévi-Strauss. We know that, for Sartre, structures are 'those strange internal realities which are both organized and organizing . . . synthetic products of a practical totalization'.[14] As such, they presuppose a productive, practical agent; and we also know that this role is performed in Sartre by *praxis*. Now, it is true that from the anti-speculative standpoint of the *Critique of Dialectical Reason* the relationship between structures and this agent is not, strictly speaking, a speculative historical relationship, but a practical 'ontological' relationship – a condition of possibility of the intelligibility of these structures. Yet to link this problem of intelligibility to that of the presupposed practical agent constituting the object, as a condition of any 'historical' existence of the relationship between them, is the very essence of all historicism – actual history and theoretical knowledge ultimately deriving from this presupposed 'ontological' relationship. And the fact that the practical agent, conceived as creating meaning, has its original grounding in individual *praxis*, appears necessary but derivative in this specific context, for the purposes of defining Sartre's 'historicist' problematic. In fact, it is neither by directly reducing Sartre's anti-speculative problematic to a Hegelian thematic of the subject-objectification-alienation type, nor, obviously, by reducing his problematic of the individual to some 'idealism of consciousness' – in short, to a 'subjectivism of the *cogito*' – that we will be able to understand his thought, the only radical formulation of the presuppositions of any coherent historicist interpretation of Marxism. But we have to consider a priori problem concerning any historicism. Even when anti-speculative and materialist, historicism ultimately reduces – and thereby reveals that in the final analysis it remains imprisoned in the Hegelian 'problematic' – the problem of the specific type that governs the unity of objective structures and their intelligibility to that of the unilinear, continuous development of a subject, in the sense of an agent this time, whatever it happens to be: concrete individuals, social labour, social class, *praxis*, and so on. Now – and this is the central objection – the problem of the intelligibility of structures cannot be reduced to that of their ontological-historical origin. For in a thematic such as Sartre's, posing the 'problem' of the (anti-speculative) objectivity of 'structures', we can in fact (as Althusser puts it) only decipher a meaning on the basis of the ever-pre-given complex whole, which must as such, moreover, be 'theoretically' constructed. If, in contrast, we consider the objectivity of the structure starting out from the agent, from history as the genesis-origin of meaning, we cannot arrive at an adequate conception of the Marxist type of unity – the invariant 'structure in dominance'. And how in fact do things stand in Sartre as regards the structure of a social formation under the dominance, in the last instance, of the economic? The dominance of the economic is itself reduced to the historicist thematic of the agent and Sartre formulates his theory of 'scarcity', which is in fact the only consistent, possible and necessary one for any historicist interpretation of Marxism. In this context, he refers to the categories of lack, concrete labour, needs, and so on, which are thereby integrated into a thematic of the young Marx's 'concrete individual' and practice-behaviour. These categories are distinct from those of the structures of the mode of production in the mature Marx. Obviously, in Sartre, there is no question of a 'solitary' individual-subject, in short, of an idealist 'individualism'. And yet this in no way alters the problem. What matters is that it can only involve 'mediations' of historical individual-praxis and that these are situated in a general historicist thematic of the agent. 'Founded' thus, can this dominance in the last instance of the economic be translated into an invariant type of structure-in-dominance?

Since, for Sartre, this dominance in the last instance is founded on the theme of the subject-agent, the transposition of the structure-in-dominance into the decipherment of various particular levels is not carried out on the basis of an objective mode of existence of these levels as they themselves reflect this structure; at all these distinctive levels, it resorts to the same agent. As an example, I shall take Sartre's appropriate critique of the 'functionalist-gestaltist' concept of struc-

ture employed by Lefort at the political level,[15] where, in order himself
to avoid this functionalist totality, Sartre had to refer to the proletariat-party-agent of history (the dominant instance at the political level).
However, to introduce the agent-subject as the dominant instance of a
structure at all the particular levels is, by the same token, to ignore the
fact that this dominance – in the relations between levels – is only the
reflection in the complex whole of the economic itself understood as
an objective structure. It is therefore to presuppose an agent-subject
(*praxis*) 'totalizing' the various levels (specific practices); and thereby
to fall into the 'voluntarism' of an agent which is supposedly autonomous from the economic precisely to the extent, moreover, that the
dominance of the economic itself presupposes this agent. At the same
time, the danger of 'economistic mechanism' implicitly resurfaces in
the status of scarcity, the practico-inert and seriality, in as much as
anti-speculative historicism appears to be able to deconceptualize the
agent only by reducing the 'conditions' of 'original' *praxis* to a
naturalistic empiricism. The result of all this is that the autonomy
and specificity of the various levels of structures is certainly acknowledged by Sartre – no one has fought against voluntaristic idealism and
mechanistic monism more than him – but that the 'process' of
structuration and articulation of the different levels is reduced, in
the last analysis, to their ontologico-historical – i.e. continuous and
homogeneous – totalization by an agent. It thus depends on the
theoretical arbitrariness – on the 'meaning' – of the evolution of
the subject-*praxis*. There can be no doubt that, from his anti-speculative standpoint, Sartre has seen the problem very clearly and sought
to found a history without an 'author', a totalization without a
totalizing agent. Nevertheless, always brought back to his project
of grounding a type of meaning-creating intelligibility, and consequently to the thematic of the individual-*praxis* – to the individual as
essential section of history – it would not seem possible to found a
'real' history without an 'author' within his structure-history problematic.

   In Lévi-Strauss, things are clearer still. A related conception of
structure to that of Sartre – still by comparison with Althusser – and a
related conception of history, the difference being that here it is the
primacy of structure that commands the concept of history, which
explains, moreover, the differences between Sartre's totality and Lévi-
Strauss's structure. Lévi-Strauss accepts that the meaning and type of
intelligibility of structures – of the universe of culture – can only be
deciphered with respect to structures that are pre-given as such. But, in
Lévi-Strauss, the concept of structure has nothing to do with the

structure-in-dominance and, in the definition we encounter in *Structural Anthropology*, even closely resembles functionalist gestaltism. Indeed, the invariant 'structure-in-dominance', as a type of unity governing the intelligibility both of the ensemble of a social formation and of its particular levels, can only be linked to the conception of a complex whole structured under the dominance of the economic. And it is by means of this dominance – restricted by Lévi-Strauss to certain types of society, but found elsewhere through the dominance of kinship structures – that he would like, at least at the outset, to supersede the functionalist concept of structure. An alteration in a 'dominant' referential order of significations – say, the economic – does not automatically prompt an alteration in a different order, but only in so far as it is reflected – as an alteration in the dominant order – within the specific logic of that particular order. However, this does not prevent it being the case that in Lévi-Strauss the type of unity which governs each 'particular' referential order is definitely not that of a structure-in-dominance, but that of a set with equivalent elements. And this is because the various systematic levels of a social formation maintain 'external' relations of correlation, presupposing their structural heterogeneity in principle. The structure of a particular level thus does not reflect the structure-in-dominance of the 'whole'. For no 'genetic' relationship can be established between heterogeneous orders whose structures possess a historicity – rules of transformation – of their own, but which are only the transposition to each level of a continuous-homogeneous-contemporaneous history. If the specificity of the different levels of structures is acknowledged by Lévi-Strauss, it is precisely by cutting off the path to establishing the relations between them – unlike Sartre, who can suggest the possibility – in the Marxist sense, their specificity expressing for Marxism the 'systematic' reflection of their relationship within the complex whole. Indeed, these 'genetic' relations between the various particular levels are not 'genetico-historical'. Lévi-Strauss was right to criticize this 'genetico-historical' viewpoint, which, in sum, reduces the superstructures to a historicist 'product' of the 'base'. However, his problematic, close here to certain generalizations in modern linguistics, regards (to put it schematically) the various particular levels of structures as ensembles whose internal logic has first to be established, before the relations between them are established. Despite numerous Marxists' infatuation with it, this point of view is, as Althusser shows, epistemologically incorrect. The internal logic – structure-in-dominance – of a particular level is only the reflection, at this specific level, of the dominant 'matrix' of the economic, which globally defines a historically determinate social formation. The internal logic of a level, the logic of the other levels, and the logic of the relations between them involve neither 'genetico-historical' relations, nor relations of 'external correlations', but 'genetico-systematic' relations. Yet this presupposes an adequate conception of the structure-in-dominance and an adequate conception of history. In contrast, the purely external conception of the dominance of the economic leads in Lévi-Strauss both to a gestaltism of the structure of a particular level and to an empirical, pluralist conception of social formation itself as a whole, the correlations between the various referential orders being determined by the gestaltist 'type' that is the 'order of orders'. In this case, history is ultimately reduced to a universal 'a priori' model of reproduction of structures, which necessarily excludes the problem of their 'historical' relations – of the relationship between particular historicities. As Althusser puts it:

> This [ideological] conception of history and of its relation to time is still alive among us, as can be seen from the currently widespread distinction between synchrony and diachrony. This distinction is based on a conception of historical time as continuous and homogeneous and contemporaneous with itself. The synchronic is contemporaneity itself, the co-presence of the essence with its determinations, the present being readable as a structure in an 'essential section' because the present is the very existence of the essential structure. The synchronic therefore presupposes the ideological conception of a continuous-homogeneous time. It follows that the diachronic is merely the development of this present in the sequence of a temporal continuity in which the 'events' to which 'history' in the strict sense can be reduced (cf. Lévi-Strauss) are merely successive contingent presents in the time continuum.[16]

Thus, on the basis of Althusser's formulations, we can glimpse the possibility of a new problematic effecting, at its own level, the epistemological break and making it possible to identify the relations between Sartre and Lévi-Strauss. Their thinking leads to contrasting positions: the historicity of the subject-agent, reducing the problem of structures in Sartre, in the case of an essential primacy of history; a hypostasis of structures, reducing the problem of history in Lévi-Strauss, in the case of an essential primacy of structures. Thus these two systems of thought are mutually exclusive in so far as they are two aspects of one and the same invariant problematic.[17]

The task of the new problematic would therefore be to establish, by rediscovering Marx, the non-problematic character of the relations

between structure and history, without lapsing back into the ideological past that forms the background to Sartre and Lévi-Strauss – in
short, to establish the real relationship between these two concepts by
changing their content. The conceptual content of the 'structure-in-
dominance' and 'differential history', and the relations between, as
established by Althusser, appears to furnish an adequate instrument
for an epistemological break. At all events, it discloses the necessity
and possibility of such a break. However, at this stage of his thinking,
can this break be regarded as having been made by Althusser?

This is precisely where various objections might be addressed to
Althusser. In the following discussion, I shall take up the principal
theme of Althusser's book – overdetermination and theoretical practice – trying to show, very briefly, how the fundamental issues posed
by his enterprise boil down to the problem of the relations between
structure and history (this will justify the preceding references to
Sartre and Lévi-Strauss).
    However, I shall make a preliminary remark about the transition
from Hegel to Marx – a transition that does not take the form of a
simple inversion of Hegel. Althusser locates the epistemological break
from *The German Ideology* onwards. In the works prior to that,
Marx's critique of Hegel is, in its principles, nothing but the Feuerbachian critique, a

> critique of Hegelian philosophy as speculative and abstract . . . a
> critique appealing to the concrete-materialist against the abstract-
> speculative, i.e. a critique which remains a prisoner of the idealist
> problematic it hoped to free itself from.[18]

Althusser himself signals that to situate this break at the level of *The
German Ideology* has very important consequences for 'Marxist
philosophy' and the interpretation of *Capital* alike. He also refers
to the work of della Volpe and Colletti who, taking Marx's theoretical
revolution with respect to Hegel as the core of their studies, locate it at
the level of the Introduction to the *Contribution to the Critique of
Hegel's Philosophy of Right* (1843). Given the importance of the work
of della Volpe, Colletti and co., I believe it is a serious omission on
Althusser's part not at least to indicate why these authors situate the
break before *The German Ideology* – and not, in fact, in the Introduction to the *Critique of Hegel's Philosophy of Right* (the article in
the *Franco-German Yearbooks*), but in the *Critique of Hegel's Doctrine of the State*. Della Volpe has particularly drawn attention to this

confusion.[19] Unquestionably, if we restrict ourselves exclusively to the *Yearbooks* manuscript – as does Cornu, for example – we only find certain isolated 'elements', such as social class, which do not as such suffice to demonstrate the existence of a new scientific problematic. If, on the other hand, we refer to the critique carried out by Marx, in the *Critique of Hegel's Doctrine of the State*, of paragraph 262 of Hegel's philosophy of right, which according to Marx contains the whole mystery of the Hegelian dialectic, this brings out two unvarying aspects of the Hegelian dialectic: its speculative-aprioristic character and, at the same time, its empirical character. Precisely because, he tells us, the Hegelian dialectic is nothing but a speculative self-mediation of the *a priori* concept, in Hegel we observe the 'direct' emergence in the instance of the concept of the vulgarly empirical which, regarded as a 'phenomenon' of the concept, is surreptitiously harnessed by it as such, 'unmediated'. For, strange as this may seem – Lenin, I believe, registered it – Hegel also evinces a 'materialist' but empirical aspect. It is precisely this unvarying speculative apriorism/vulgar empiricism that characterizes the Hegelian dialectic according to Marx, not just its speculative character. And the theory of the della Volpean school is based precisely on these remarks. Now, it is indeed true that this critique of Hegel by Marx is still conducted in Hegelian terms, just as (according to Althusser) the epistemological break of *The German Ideology* is made in Feuerbachian terms. However, if in the *Critique of Hegel's Doctrine of the State* Marx does indeed formulate a critique both of the speculative and of the empirical, the problem that arises is whether he thereby rejects both speculative dialectics and 'vulgar materialist monism', and hence the material-concrete as such (as it presents itself, obviously, in Hegel) – in short, the idealist problematic globally. Personally, I do not believe that this suffices to establish the break at the level of the *Critique*. However, we would have to develop this point of view in order to be able to discuss it seriously and also in order to clarify Althusser's *epistemological* positions, given that at this stage we might err and be tempted to attribute to him, despite everything, the Italian standpoint of a simple critique of 'empiricism-speculation', whereas Althusser seems to go much further.

Meanwhile, the real questions posed by Althusser's work emerge in his analyses of overdetermination and theoretical practice. We have seen how the very type of structure of an 'ever-pre-given complex whole articulated in dominance' implies for Althusser the key distinction between the dominance in the last instance of the economic and the dominant role of a level in the ensemble of a social formation.

This dominant role can thus as readily be performed by the economic as by any other level. But how are we to avoid falling into a dialectical hyper-empiricism or 'eclectic pluralism' if the dominant role is displaced indifferently among the various levels? In the real process, what is the 'status' of the economic – a status known scientifically by theory – which would permit the operation of permutations of the 'dominant role' between the different levels, with the economic always retaining dominance in the last instance?

A response can be attempted by neglecting to formulate the root problem; and this is a temptation that seems fleetingly to attract Althusser (e.g., *For Marx*, pp. 193–204). What distinguishes Marxism from eclectic pluralism, Althusser seems to imply, is that for Marxism there always exists a principal contradiction, a dominant of the structure of the complex whole, whatever it might be, retrospectively, in real history. Provided that there is one, it is of little moment whether it is the economic, the political, the ideological or the theoretical. The 'structure in dominance of the economic in the last instance' and the 'dominant role' here appear to be conflated in a formalist conception of the 'structure-in-dominance', with 'dominance-in-the-last-instance' being equally capable of being exercised by any level. There is no doubt that this conclusion could lead directly to eclectic pluralism; and Althusser is well aware of it. But if the Marxist type of unity is that of a complex whole articulated in dominance, and if this type of unity is not simply one more definition of 'totality' and 'structure' – with this particularity that it is arbitrary in its acceptance of a 'dominant instance' – it is because we do not on one side have a certain 'complexity' of the process involving as such a dominant, and on the other an economic awaiting an auspicious moment to occupy this position. It is not because 'actual' complexity 'implies domination as essential to itself', but because this complexity and this dominance themselves come down to the 'dominance-in-the-last-instance-of-the-economic'. No doubt Lenin and Mao provided us with this model of 'structure-in-dominance' in the manner of 'this is how things are', 'by the nature of things', and so on; and for us it is a question, in fashioning the theory of their practice, to explain it. It nevertheless remains the case that Althusser seems to want to broach this theoretical explanation not by theoretically posing the scientific status of the economic, but by himself founding in theory the model of 'how things are', thus by founding the dominant instance of the economic in the real process by a 'theoretical' knowledge of a certain 'complexity' or 'structure-in-dominance', which as such involves dominance.

Hence Althusser's second way of posing the problem, which actually simply ends up avoiding it, by reference this time to Mao's texts and his well-known distinctions between principal contradiction and secondary contradiction, and between the principal and secondary aspects of a contradiction. Now, rather than analyzing these texts theoretically, as he proposed to do, going beyond 'how things are', Althusser in fact appears to seek a 'theoretical' solution to his 'theoretical problem' in them, taking them just as he finds them. In the mode of 'how things are', Mao observes that there is always a principal contradiction, which has the 'dominant role', and that this might globally not pertain to the economic-political contradictions, for example. The problem that Althusser should have resolved, on the basis of his distinction between the real process and the thought-process, is how the economic continues to be dominant in the last instance without, in this case, being the 'principal contradiction', without playing the dominant role, and without even being an aspect of this contradiction – that is to say, without this contradiction lying, for example, between the economic and the political. However, it is in this connection that he refers to the 'aspect' of a contradiction, suggesting that the distinction between the 'dominance-in-the-last-instance-of-the-economic' and 'dominant role' is due to a simple differentiation between 'aspects' of a contradiction:

> It is economism that identifies eternally in advance the determinant-contradiction-in-the-last-instance with the *role* of the dominant contradiction [even the principal contradiction; and everything is fine up to this point – except that it needs to be explained: NP], which for ever assimilates such and such an 'aspect' (forces of production, economy, practice) to the principal role, and such and such another 'aspect' (relations of production, politics, ideology, theory) to the secondary *role* – whereas in real history determination in the last instance by the economy is exercised precisely in the permutations of the principal role between the economy, politics, theory, etc.[20]

In the final passage of this quotation, it is evident that the displacement of the dominant role is not attributed, as it is in Mao, to the global displacement (which would require explanation) of the principal contradiction itself to the different levels (economic, political, theoretical, etc.), but to a permutation of 'aspects' of one contradiction, the dominant role thus being attributed to the principal 'aspect' – whatever it might be – of a contradiction: something that

Mao does not say. Indeed, Althusser appears to explain the problem of the 'dominant role' by implicitly accepting that if the principal contradiction might not be globally situated at the economic level, between the forces and relations of production, it nevertheless always exists and in any event exists 'between' the economic and another level – politics, theory – so that the economic is always one of the 'aspects' of the principal contradiction. The 'dominant role' can thus be allocated to the other – political or theoretical – 'aspect'. Besides, what else could the application of the concept of 'dominant role' to one of the aspects of the contradiction mean? Yet it is precisely here that Mao breaks new ground by not simply saying that; and this innovation needs to be explained. Or again, notwithstanding appearances, even though Althusser's texts are clear, does he mean that the 'dominant role' is ultimately held by the principal aspect of the principal contradiction which, globally displaced to a level other than the economic, possesses the dominant role? But in that case, where is the theoretical explanation of the problem posed by Mao of the dominance in the last instance of the economy, which is not the principal contradiction or one of its aspects?

But there is more and I come back here to the problem of empirical pluralism. For, by not clearly posing the problem of the status of the economic, and by seeking to explain the global displacement of the principal contradiction to a level other than the economic, while maintaining that the economic is always one of the aspects of this contradiction, we risk arriving at the following result: making the principal aspect and the secondary aspect attributes of the new concept represented by the 'role'. If the complex whole presents 'such and such' an aspect, it is because the dominant-principal role is displaced 'functionally' to all the levels, in a new functionalist gestaltism, and in the form of 'how things are', comprising a 'structure-in-dominance' severed from the determination in the last instance of the economic. The latter is given no status here, unless it is identified with an aspect of the principal contradiction – which is precisely what Mao does not do. If Mao's novelty is explained by Althusser's interpretation of it, we end up with a principal level-contradiction (in its globality) other than the economic, which is the dominant aspect-role of nothing, like the mirror reflection of an 'absentee'. I am not discussing the correctness of Mao's theses, adopted by Althusser. I am simply saying that to attempt to fashion the theory of Mao's practice – a vital project – while avoiding a clear, radical formulation of the problem of the scientific status of an economic whose determination in the last instance operates by displacement of the dominant role, is to risk lapsing into an inverted gestaltism.

I would certainly not have stressed these points, which at first glance seem 'scholastic', if they did not seem to me to entail important practical consequences. The scientific status of the economic has been, and remains, the touchstone of any interpretation of Marxism – Sartre's, for example. To the question of the status of the economic, he offers the response of 'scarcity', from the distinctive standpoint of the subject-agent. From his perspective, Althusser would have to establish a scientific status of the economic that would allow him to account for his personal, and genuinely novel, distinction between 'dominance-in-the-last-instance' and 'dominant role'. We might be tempted to formulate Althusser's position, which is still implicit in this respect, by reference to the specific science of psychoanalysis, from which he borrows a series of distinctive concepts – overdetermination, decentring, displacement, condensation, and so on – but without adopting a clear position on it and mentioning it only in a few lines in a note on p. 206. However, we would not be able to get a clear idea from this, since in his transposition Althusser introduces a specific problematic that should lead to a new interpretation of psychoanalysis. For Althusser, does the economic correspond to the unconscious, which would seem to be a 'way' of founding its status of dominance in the last instance, translatable by a necessary reflection of the dominant role in the various levels of particular structures? Thus, in this sense, and in the real process, is the economic the great absentee, never given as such, permanently concealed by the sets of significations of other levels, never captured in its own site but always reflected in the ensemble of the complex whole, its dominance in the last instance essentially conveyed by a necessary, invariable displacement, an asymptotic decentring, of the dominant role onto the other levels? But in this context, playing on the notion of the unconscious and the 'unconscious laws' of the economy – and also on that of the 'unconscious rules' governing the set of levels of a social formation – what is the precise meaning (if we are referring to psychoanalysis) of a distinction between 'dominance in the last instance' and 'dominant role'? Moreover, in this framework, could the economic, always dominant in the last instance, ever also occupy the dominant role, given that its status constitutes it, in the real process itself, as absent, as always present at a level other than its own?

This is only a hypothesis and it is for Althusser to clarify his own thinking. I shall, however, take advantage of my last question to observe that the absence of a clear scientific status of the economic in

Althusser has important consequences for the scientific status of the political. All of Althusser's concrete analyses pertain to the Marxist-Leninist political thematic of the struggle against the invariant couple voluntarism-economism implied by a monist viewpoint. Thus Althusser recalls Engels and Lenin's critique of opportunistic economism. Quite correctly in this context, he 'tells' us that the dominant role can fall to the economic, but also to the political and the theoretical. Now, in the event that the economic, along with its permanent dominance in the last instance, also occupies the dominant role, we are faced with the trade-union (Lenin) or economic-corporate (Gramsci) level, the level of an 'economic struggle' which is expressly and radically distinct from the 'political struggle' in the classics of the Third International. However, what we notice in Althusser's analyses is that everything seems to unfold as if the economic, always dominant in the last instance, can never 'in addition' occupy the dominant role – he provides no example of such an eventuality – as if the economic did not, strictly speaking, possess its own level of existence in the real process. Thus, according to Althusser, every 'class struggle' is necessarily a 'political class struggle'. The concept of 'economic struggle' is devoid of meaning; in the real process, the economic is necessarily reflected in a class struggle that has no site of constitution other than the political level. By its very essence, the dominant role thus cannot fall to the economic itself. Otherwise, '[h]ow is it possible, theoretically, to sustain the validity of this basic Marxist proposition: "*the class struggle is the motor of history*"?[21]

Here we should signal two problems that are not clarified in Althusser: on the one hand, the particular problem posed by the status of the economic; on the other, that of the respective domains of the economic and the political. These two domains, and hence the relations between them, cannot be grasped by generic references, but only through a concrete investigation of their specificity within the 'matrix' of a historically determinate social formation. This is precisely the conclusion to be drawn from Althusser's premises. In this respect, we can see that capitalist formations are characterized, as Marx clearly showed, by an autonomization of the economic and the political, of economic struggle and political struggle. In this sense, if it is true that for Marx the political struggle is the 'motor of history', it is by no means true that for him every class struggle is a political struggle in the case of capitalist formations.[22] In order to be able to grasp the autonomization of the economic struggle and the political struggle in capitalist formations theoretically – and hence the possibility of a dominant role for the economic and economic struggle – one should not have been led first, as this appears

[. . .]23

between 'economic struggle' and 'political struggle'. If, in the complex whole of the capitalist formation, every reflection of the economic was translated at the political level, the creation of the Third International would simply have answered to a question of technique and effectiveness. Moreover, economism-trade unionism-anarcho-syndicalism (spontaneism), and so on, would not exist in the specificity – dominant role of the economic struggle – attributed to it by Marxist-Leninist thought vis-à-vis the political level, in the 'scientific' and 'rigorous' sense of the term. In short, in what specific 'site' is economic struggle – the level of socio-economic 'interests', which are not luminous absences in real history but so very present – situated? Alternatively put, to what extent can the economic be 'overdetermined' in the real process, while retaining its specificity? Furthermore, how can it be overdetermined in its very specificity?

[. . .]24

be the case for Althusser, to epistemological 'aporiae' that lead to assigning a necessarily dominant role to the political in general in any possible social formation. We must therefore assign the economic, as opposed to the political, a 'general' status such that it can explain why, for Marxism, it is always dominance-in-the-last-instance, and yet can also exercise the dominant role, depending on its *specific* place in a determinate formation. For, unlike the political, which does not always have the dominant role, the economic is always – in every formation – dominant in the last instance. To return to the problem of economic struggle in capitalist formations, we know that Lenin, Luxemburg, Gramsci, and so on had as the central theme of their struggle, their lives, and their prisons, an expressly formulated distinction

[. . .]25

What scientific status is to be attributed to the 'mode' and 'relations' of production conceived as objective 'structures', making it possible to situate a 'practice' that delimits economic struggle without placing ourselves in Sartre's problematic – an agent that is perfectly capable of situating economic struggle by distinguishing it from political struggle as the 'socio-economic interests' of the series and group organization – but also without arriving at the apparent conclusions, at least at this stage in Althusser's thinking, of overdetermination? In any event, is it fortuitous that Althusser, having recalled that Lenin referred to economic, political and ideological practices, and having also indicated that he himself construes practice as 'struggle', subsequently mentions only political practice and theoretical practice, and never economic practice (struggle)?

Once again, here it is a question of defining the precise relations between the real process and the thought-process. The fact that scientific theory reveals the economic – unconscious laws – as always 'lived' in the capitalist system in an 'ideological' form, as always 'absent', as 'present' at a level other than its own, and 'concealed' under the significations of that level, does not entail that in the real process the economic always exists 'elsewhere', has no level of 'existence' of its own, and therefore cannot occupy, in the framework of the *theoretically* decipherable index of effectivity of a formation, the 'dominant role'. This does not mean, as Althusser would seem to imply, that the political is in some sense the 'mode of existence' of human beings in the real process – their 'concrete activity', to adopt his expression.

The 'danger' of lapsing back into a gestaltist functionalism, through a distinction between dominance in the last instance and dominant role that is not based on a scientific status for the economic, is real. For, by not clearly posing the problem of this status, attempts will doubtless be made to avoid gestaltism while ending up, theoretically, in an over-politicization – a result that would be just as contrary to Althusser's premises as economism, since he proposes to underscore the respective specificity of the economic, the political, and the theoretical. Moreover, this result risks reviving the historicist problematic.

Indeed, Althusser defines the political as a practice whose specific 'object' is not a particular level of structures, but the 'current situation' constituted by the reflection of various contradictions in 'their paradoxical unity, all of which are the very existence of that "current situation" which political action [is] to transform'.[26] The political is thus the privileged 'situation' reflecting the unity of the complex whole, and on the basis of which the unity of a social formation in its entirety can be deciphered. Precisely here, with the political assuming this status by virtue of the fact that the economic does not appear capable of assuming the dominant role in Althusser, we arrive at the over-politicization signalled above.[27]

This becomes clearer if we compare the positions of Althusser and Gramsci. As readers may know, Gramsci, this quasi-unique Marxist 'philosopher', sometimes arrived, precisely under the influence of Croce and Labriola's historicism, at an ambiguous conception of the political as a 'moment-level' similar to Althusser's – a conception that necessarily involves an over-politicization of theory:

> In a philosophy of praxis, the distinction will certainly not be between the moments of the absolute Spirit, but between the levels of the superstructure. The problem will therefore be that of establishing the dialectical position of political activity (and of the corresponding science) as a particular level of the superstructure. One might say, as a first schematic approximation, that political activity is precisely the first moment or first level; the moment in which the superstructure is still in the unmediated phase of mere wishful affirmation, confused and still at an elementary stage. In what sense can one identify politics with history, and hence all of life with politics? How then could the whole system of superstructures be understood as distinctions within politics, and the introduction of the concept of distinction into a philosophy hence be justified?[28]

In my opinion, this is rather surprising. Level-degree on the one hand, moment on the other – are we not still situated in the 'structure' and 'history' thematic here, this time as regards the status of the political? Does Althusser not in fact risk reintroducing, via the political as moment, a historicist conception of history, in as much as the historically 'overdetermining' political is merely a surreptitious reflection, within the structure-in-dominance of the ensemble of a social formation, of the 'current situation' – materialization of a unilinear time, of a historicist 'diachrony'? And this in so far as the complex whole structured in dominance is simply the requisite invariable dominance – the sole means of avoiding gestaltism – of the role of the political as a moment of simple unilinear development. Do we thereby end up with an over-politicization that ultimately involves the same – 'monist' – problematic as economism? Are we therefore obliged to say that, in excluding the possibility of a dominant role being exercised by the economic, it is its dominance-in-the-last-instance that risks being called into question and, with it, the structure of the complex whole articulated in dominance – the outcome being an over-politicization, an 'over-dominance' of the political, a historicism of the political as conscious agent of the economic (unconscious laws): in short, ultimately a standpoint of 'class consciousness'?[29]

If the 'structure-in-dominance' of the complex whole does indeed
characterize the Marxist type of unity, it is also in so far as it is
expressed, as an invariant, within each particular level of structure and
practice. In this context, I indicated how Sartre, in order to rediscover
the structure-in-dominance of the political level, appealed to the
proletariat-agent, in so far as the dominance in the last instance of
the economic boiled down to the thematic of the agent in his work. In
Althusser, by contrast, this structure-in-dominance seems to disappear
as soon as we are confronted with the political, whose dominance is
ever-pre-given. When, he tells us, the various contradictions governed
by overdetermination 'fuse', following their displacement or condensation, in a determinate political moment, then we are in the presence
of a situation of revolutionary 'rupture' that cannot be explained by
the development of the simple contradiction between Capital and
Labour. The various contradictory circumstances and currents 'fuse'
when

> they produce the result of the immense majority of the popular
> masses *grouped* in an assault on a regime . . . How else [i.e. without
> this fusion presupposing overdetermination – NP] could the class-
> divided popular masses (proletarians, peasants, petty bourgeois)
> throw themselves *together*, consciously or unconsciously, into a
> general assault on the existing regime?[30]

Now, the kinship between the terms 'fusion', 'group', 'together' –
terms emphasized by Althusser himself – is not fortuitous. The
concept of 'fusion', indicating here the mode of existence of the
political as a situation of various contradictions within the overdetermination of the complex whole, results in the disappearance of
the structure-in-dominance – a disappearance indicated by the itali-
cized terms 'grouped' and 'together'. How do the popular masses
group themselves together? In short, precisely how is this fusion
translated at the political level? In his problematic, Sartre will tell
us that it is through the proletariat-party-agent, representing the
dominant instance of the political structure and the constitutive factor
in the political structure-'group' – a group that transcends 'trade-
union' seriality. As for Althusser, he tells us literally nothing. The
'grouping together' thus risks seeming to occur in him in the same way
that mechanistic economism treats it or, theoretically, Lefort's gestaltism. And one might even ultimately ask what role the party can have in
all this 'interplay', for, just as an economistic monism oscillates
between voluntarism and economism, so a monism of the political

risks oscillating between historicism – ultimately, 'class consciousness' – and gestaltist mechanism transposed to the political.

Althusser's work demonstrates the necessity and the possibility of establishing, on the basis of his principles, a new Marxist problematic which, through a rediscovery of Marx, effects an epistemological break at its own level with contemporary thought. The objections that might be made to it are directed at an as yet insufficient degree of explanation. However, the ambiguities we have signalled risk giving rise to misinterpretations that it is important to eliminate. They possibly also stem from the fact that Althusser seeks the means to found a new problematic where he finds them, that he in some sense gets by as best he can. But he has defined principles that cannot be ignored and which it remains to set to work in the domains of particular sciences. It will then be possible to demonstrate the fertility of the new problematic and its capacity to induce this 'epistemological break'.

However that might be, together with Sartre's *oeuvre*, which pertains to a different interpretation of Marxism, and alongside the works of the Italian theoreticians, Althusser's enterprise is of capital importance. It marks a milestone in the history of Marxist theory; it is already an essential instrument of work for every Marxist researcher.

6

THE POLITICAL FORMS OF
THE MILITARY COUP D'ÉTAT

While these lines are being written, the problem of the political forms that the military coup in Greece is assuming and will assume, if it is finally stabilized, has not as yet been crystallized. The political transformations that we witness can be subject to many interpretations and can give rise to different forecasts depending on our assessment of the character of the coup.[1]

These measures are still at the stage of the generalities that characterize a regime that represents the foreign and domestic forces of reaction abolition of parliamentarism and of the fundamental articles of the Constitution, overt repression, suspension of individual and trade-union freedoms, 'anti-communism', suppression of the parties and of the political organizations of the Left, etc. However, these measures will, sooner or later, be specified in certain political forms. In this connection we must note that these forms will develop within the relatively broad limits set by the balance of forces. We must also note that, with the exception of a few texts by Gramsci and Dimitrov, Marxist analysis has not sufficiently focused on the problem of the differentiation between such forms. For instance, the concepts *dictatorship of the bourgeoisie, fascist state, police state, military state*, etc., have often been employed in an interchangeable manner. In the final analysis, to say that there is a dictatorship in Greece is to simply describe and not to explain. Is it a 'fascist dictatorship', a 'Bonapartist dictatorship', a 'paternalistic dictatorship', or what?

An observation is apposite before we tackle the essence of the problem: the relationship of the military coup in Greece with the

* First published in Greek in *Poreia*, no. 2 (June 1967), the journal of the association of Greek students in Paris. This translation is based on the reprint published in the journal *Politis*, no. 29 (October 1979). Translated and annotated by Grigoris Ananiadis.

current aggressive phase of American imperialism, as well as the relationship of Greece with Europe, do not provide us with an automatic response to the problem of the political forms that the coup will assume. It is obvious that these two factors make room for a whole range of differentiations. It is the internal situation and the balance of forces in Greece that are here of decisive significance. And not only in this respect, but also in relation to the question of the coup's survival or overthrow. On its own, the international situation can neither definitively impose the coup, nor indeed overthrow it.

From this remark, which is absolutely essential, we can pass to our analysis by posing a first question that refers to certain political forms of bourgeois dictatorship already experienced by the workers' movement in Europe. Is the coup d'état in Greece in reality a fascist coup? On the answer to this question depends the answer to the question whether the coup will assume forms of a *fascist state*.

I think that the answer should be that we are not dealing with a fascist coup. Now, we must not forget that the word 'fascism' has been charged with a very broad significance in socialist and communist ideology. Scientifically, however, the concept 'fascism' refers to certain characteristics of political forms that were imposed in Europe, especially in Germany and Italy, and, to a different degree, in Spain. What are the basic characteristics of fascism?

In the first place it represents the interests of monopoly capital which, however, is in the final analysis a characteristic of all right-wing governments in the stage of imperialism. Second, it is a form of dictatorship. But we are still not advancing enough. In reality the specific characteristic of fascism is that it manifests an *undoubted popular basis* forged by the function of the ruling ideology in historically determinate conditions. Its popular basis consists of: sections of the peasantry, a part of the petty bourgeoisie, and also, as pointed out by Dimitrov in his report at the VII Congress of the Third International and by Gramsci, of sections of the working class. This is demonstrated by the fact that the fascist regimes in Europe were established through peculiar *fascist parties*.

At this point I am not posing the question of the balance of forces in the class struggle that resulted in that situation. As it *appears* in this moment, such a popular basis does not obtain in Greece. I say 'as it appears' fully conscious of the significance of the word, even if this is to annoy some of the readers. For the question is this: is it certain that the Greek coup does not have forms of support – the characteristic apathy included – among sections of the popular classes? Those who think that we can escape the complexity of the problem by merely declaring our wishes about the 'general outcry' against the coup I refer back to the above-mentioned Congress of the Third International. For instance, what is the exact attitude of the peasantry that principally consists of smallholding peasants, who, in the case of France, provided the support for Bonapartisms, and, in the case of Greece, until four years ago voted in their majority for Karamanlis and not only because of the 'violence and fraud'.[2]

Personally I do not think that the coup does *already* have a popular basis, although the problem must be given serious consideration. In that sense we cannot presently characterize the coup as a fascist one. This is of significance with respect to the political forms that it will assume. It is most important that it appears very unlikely that the coup will be successful in creating broad party organizations that might enable it to last without taking recourse to other forms of political 'openings'.

A second problem. Are we dealing in Greece with a form of 'Bonapartist dictatorship'? A clarification is due here which is also pertinent in the case of the fascist dictatorship. By Bonapartist form we mean the political forms that correspond, at the level of the configuration of forces, to a 'balance' between the political forces which are crossed through by the fundamental class contradiction. In a situation of this kind, the ruling class responds with a dictatorship and with a state-form whose function is to prevent a transformation of power that might favour the dominated classes: in that case the state is characterized by a relative framework of autonomy and, appearing as the agent of the 'general interest', uses alternately one side against the other, serving, of course, in the long run the interests of the dominant class, although it appears as an 'arbiter' of the class struggle. There are here certain differences in relation to the fascist dictatorship. The latter, as Gramsci demonstrated in his texts on fascism, seems to correspond not to a simple balance of forces but to a 'catastrophic' one. That is to say, to a balance of forces where either one of the sides has already lost and the other has not as yet won the capacity to rule, or the prolongation of the struggle in the given forms seems to be leading to the mutual destruction of both sides, without there being an immediate possibility of a definitive imposition of the one over the other.[3] In the case of a Bonapartist dictatorship, the state does not need a serious popular support to the extent a fascist one does, because its function is to serve in the long run the interests of the dominant class by playing upon the dynamic of the fundamental contradiction itself. Thus it allows for the existence of legal political struggle which it favours and directs accordingly. It is the case, as Engels characterized it, of a 'demi-dictatorship'. The fascist dictatorship, though, is different.

Now, with respect to the Greek internal situation. I do not think that we can talk about a balance of the political forces – simple or catastrophic – crossed through by the fundamental class contradiction, that is to say, the peasantry in its greatest part, the working class, the petty bourgeoisie, and the middle bourgeoisie on the one hand, and monopoly capital, on the other. The supremacy of the latter was obvious, among other indications, also from its connections within the Centre Union itself.[4] I leave open the problem of the 'national bourgeoisie', as its insertion in the schema of the balance of forces does not drastically alter this configuration in Greece. Conclusion: contrary to what is implied by the somewhat diffused position that the granting of a constitution by the junta will result in a certain opening that might create an exploitable margin, we are not dealing with a form of Bonapartism which could be expected to grant certain forms of legal and to some degree essential forms of class struggle in a parliamentary framework, in the absence of any real form of resistance, under merely external pressures.

Finally the political forms of the coup cannot develop in a way similar to certain forms of dictatorship that emerge in the so-called 'under-developed countries', more specifically, in countries where the feudal class or the big capitalist landowners play a decisive role, with all that this might entail, as, for instance, the important weight of the religious ideology – dictatorships that are usually characterized as 'paternalistic'. Greece is not an 'under-developed' country in this sense.

Let us now consider the real situation in Greece. The coup, in an economy engaged in a process of development dependent on foreign imperialist capital, corresponds to an international strategy of American imperialism as specified in a particular zone, and to an internal situation marked by a serious intensification of the struggles of the popular masses – although they have not reached a point of balance with the ruling bloc – as well as to the internal contradictions of the ruling bloc (foreign imperialist capital, domestic monopoly capital). In this conjuncture, if we accept that the coup lacks a popular basis, an important function in the development of its specific political forms will be performed by certain factors which, precisely in this conjuncture, assume a relative autonomy.

(a) *The military*: it is said, for instance, that the actual coup is not exactly coincidental with the one that was being prepared by the official IDEA.[5] We must study more thoroughly the social origins and

the general political role of the middle and superior officers as
constituting a 'social category'. We must examine to what extent a
purely military dictatorship could possibly be secured today in Greece
that would be based on the support of middle and upper military
strata, and that would serve the foreign monopolies as well as its own
corporatist interests. A particular problem in this connection is the
role of the security forces and their relationship with the military (one
caste 'excludes' the other, etc.).

(b) *The general state apparatus*: we already know that Greece is
characterized by an *immense parasitism*, a typical phenomenon in a
country with a pauperized peasantry consisting of smallholding
peasants, with a voluminous and *especially parasitic petty bourgeoisie*,
and with many residual *déclassés* elements (e.g. the lumpenproletariat)
that stem from the peculiar co-existence in Greece of many modes of
production, a big part of the country being covered by small commodity production. We must consider the possibility that this huge
state parasitism, along with the military, might function for the coup
as a substitute for the popular basis that it presently lacks.

(c) *The political personnel*: by this we refer to the personages that
performed a basic political function within the framework of parliamentarism, viz. deputies, higher party functionaries, 'men of politics',
etc. As far as the Greek political personnel is concerned, its character
reflects the internal structure of the parties: with the exception of
EDA,[6] we were basically dealing not with *programmatic parties* – I am
employing here terms of political sociology – but with *parties of
electoral clienteles*, a fact with roots in the political under-development of the ruling classes and of other social strata in our country. We
are familiar, from the consequence, with the low quality of a great
section of the political personnel, viz. their embezzlement, their
considering of the political function as a 'profession', the childish
level of their ideology, etc. In such conditions the co-optation of
political personages – as individuals – by the regime is highly possible,
the necessary façade of a potential pseudo-political 'opening' as a
substitute for popular support, with all the misunderstandings that
such a move might give rise to because of the political past of those
personages.

After these very schematic considerations, we may conclude the
following: the coup can be secured without necessarily having acquired a 'popular basis', contrary to this opinion according to which it
would be impossible for it to last long without such a basis and that a
mere 'passive resistance', that is to say, a withholding of popular
support, would suffice for its collapse. On the other hand, the

conception of 'modern' technico-military coups without any popular basis is equally mistaken; a position that had already been developed by Malaparte in his *The Technique of the Coup d'État*. We know that the 'technical' factor is always overdetermined by the socio-political ones. The 'support' can perhaps be found in the castes of the military and those of the state apparatus, as well as in the political personnel, social categories which, as Lenin remarked, can, in historically determinate conditions, be transformed into relatively autonomous 'social forces'.

The political forms that the dictatorship in Greece will assume, as indeed the forms of the resistance against it, will depend on all these factors. I mention a simple, albeit especially 'inflammable', example: if we are dealing with a *fascist* coup with a popular basis, and if it is successful in establishing mass organizations, then the question that is posed is whether these fascist organizations should be 'boycotted' or whether they should be *used* as instruments through the participation of resistance-militants in them. According to Dimitrov's report, for instance, such organizations *must* be used – as was the case in Germany and Italy – for a revolutionary should be *wherever the masses are*. And Dimitrov pours endless ridicule on the 'revolutionaries' who pose the question at the level of individual 'honesty'. On the other hand, if, as I believe is the case, we are not dealing with a fascist coup, and certainly not with a stabilized one, then the line must be the absolute boycotting of the organizations that the regime might create to attract the masses, so that its isolation be maintained. More specifically, the line of the EDA with respect to the workers' union movement had previously been against the formation of an autonomous workers' centre outside the GSEE,[7] although the latter was in the hands of a co-opted leadership, because many workers' mass organizations were part of it. What is to be done now? Should the GSEE, whose leadership was quick in welcoming the coup, be boycotted or not?

In the end, of course, the political forms of the coup will depend on the *popular resistance*. A hope: that the resistance will not only affect its forms, but will also overthrow it. A more extensive discussion of this theme would require a serious and well-documented study of all the parameters, and not a mere exposition of 'rough impressions'.

THE PROBLEM OF
THE CAPITALIST STATE

Ralph Miliband's recently published work, *The State in Capitalist Society*,[1] is in many respects of capital importance. The book is extremely substantial, and cannot decently be summarized in a few pages: I cannot recommend its reading too highly. I will limit myself here to a few critical comments, in the belief that only criticism can advance Marxist theory. For the specificity of this theory compared with other theoretical problematics lies in the extent to which Marxist theory provides itself, in the very act of its foundation, with the means of its own internal criticism. I should state at the outset that my critique will not be 'innocent': having myself written on the question of the state in my book *Pouvoir politique et classes sociales*,[2] these comments will derive from epistemological positions presented there which differ from those of Miliband.

First of all, some words on the fundamental merits of Miliband's book. The theory of the state and of political power has, with rare exceptions such as Gramsci, been neglected by Marxist thought. This neglect has a number of different causes, related to different phases of the working-class movement. In Marx himself this neglect, more apparent than real, is above all due to the fact that his principal theoretical object was the capitalist mode of production, within which the economy not only holds the role of determinant in the last instance, but also the dominant role – while for example in the feudal mode of production, Marx indicates that if the economy still has the role of determinant in the last instance, it is ideology in its religious form that holds the dominant role. Marx thus concentrated on the economic level of the capitalist mode of production, and did not deal specifically with the other levels such as the state: he dealt only with these levels

* First published in *New Left Review* 58 (1969), pp. 67–78.

through their *effects* on the economy (for example, in the passages of *Capital* on factory legislation). In Lenin, the reasons are different: involved in direct political practice, he dealt with the question of the state only in essentially polemical works, such as *State and Revolution*, which do not have the theoretical status of certain of his texts such as *The Development of Capitalism in Russia*.

How, by contrast, is the neglect of theoretical study of the state in the Second International, and in the Third International after Lenin, to be explained? Here I would advance, with all necessary precautions, the following thesis: the absence of a study of the state derived from the fact that the dominant conception of these Internationals was a deviation, *economism*, which is generally accompanied by an absence of revolutionary strategy and objectives – even when it takes a 'leftist' or Luxemburgist form. In effect, economism considers that other levels of social reality, including the state, are simple epiphenomena reducible to the economic 'base'. Thereby a specific study of the state becomes superfluous. Parallel with this, economism considers that every change in the social system happens first of all in the economy and that political action should have the economy as its principal objective. Once again, a specific study of the state is redundant. Thus economism leads either to reformism and trade-unionism, or to forms of 'leftism' such as syndicalism. For, as Lenin showed, the principal objective of revolutionary action is *state power* and the necessary precondition of any socialist revolution is the destruction of the bourgeois state apparatus.

Economism and the absence of revolutionary strategy are manifest in the Second International. They are less obvious in the Third International, yet in my view what fundamentally determined the theory and practice of 'Stalinist' policy, dominant in the Comintern probably from 1928, was nevertheless the same economism and absence of a revolutionary strategy. This is true both of the 'leftist' period of the Comintern until 1935, and of the revisionist-reformist period after 1935. This economism determined the absence of a theory of the state in the Third International, and this *relation* (economism/absence of a theory of the state) is perhaps nowhere more evident than in its analyses of fascism – precisely where the Comintern had most need of such a theory of the state. Considerations of a concrete order both confirm and explain this.

Since the *principal symptoms* of Stalinist politics were located in the relations between the state apparatus and the Communist Party in the USSR, symptoms visible in the famous Stalin Constitution of 1936, it is very comprehensible that study of the state remained a forbidden topic *par excellence*.

It is in this context that Miliband's work helps to overcome a major lacuna. As is always the case when a scientific theory is lacking, bourgeois conceptions of the state and of political power have pre-empted the terrain of political theory, almost unchallenged. Miliband's work is here truly *cathartic*: he methodically attacks these conceptions. Rigorously deploying a formidable mass of empirical material in his examination of the concrete social formations of the USA, England, France, Germany or Japan, he not only radically demolishes bourgeois ideologies of the state, but provides us with a positive knowledge that these ideologies have never been able to produce.

However, the procedure chosen by Miliband – a *direct* reply to bourgeois ideologies by the immediate examination of concrete fact – is also to my mind the source of the faults of his book. Not that I am against the study of the 'concrete': on the contrary, having myself relatively neglected this aspect of the question in my own work (with its somewhat different aim and object), I am only the more conscious of the necessity for concrete analyses. I simply mean that a precondition of any scientific approach to the 'concrete' is to make explicit the epistemological principles of its own treatment of it. Now it is important to note that Miliband nowhere deals with the Marxist theory of the state as such, although it is constantly implicit in his work. He takes it as a sort of 'given' in order to reply to bourgeois ideologies by examining the facts in its light. Here I strongly believe that Miliband is wrong, for the absence of explicit presentation of principles in the order of exposition of a scientific discourse is not innocuous: above all in a domain like the theory of the state, where a Marxist theory, as we have seen, has yet to be constituted. In effect, one has the impression that this absence often leads Miliband to attack bourgeois ideologies of the state whilst placing himself on their own terrain. Instead of *displacing* the epistemological terrain and submitting these ideologies to the critique of Marxist science by demonstrating their inadequacy to the real (as Marx does, notably in the *Theories of Surplus-Value*), Miliband appears to omit this first step. Yet the analyses of modern epistemology show that it is never possible simply to oppose 'concrete facts' to concepts, but that these must be attacked by other parallel concepts situated in a different problematic. For it is only by means of these new concepts that the old notions can be confronted with 'concrete reality'.

Let us take a simple example. Attacking the prevailing notion of 'plural elites', whose ideological function is to deny the existence of a ruling class, Miliband's reply, which he supports by 'facts', is that this plurality of *elites* does not exclude the existence of a ruling *class*, for it is precisely these elites that constitute this class:[3] this is close to Bottomore's response to the question. Now, I maintain that in replying to the adversary in this way, one places oneself on his ground and thereby risks floundering in the swamp of his ideological imagination, thus missing a scientific explanation of the 'facts'. What Miliband avoids is the necessary preliminary of a *critique of the ideological notion of elite* in the light of the scientific concepts of Marxist theory. Had this critique been made, it would have been evident that the 'concrete reality' concealed by the notion of 'plural elites' – the ruling class, the fractions of this class, the hegemonic class, the governing class, the state apparatus – can only be grasped if the very notion of elite is rejected. For concepts and notions are never innocent, and by employing the notions of the adversary to reply to him, one legitimizes them and permits their persistence. Every notion or concept only has meaning within a whole theoretical problematic that founds it: extracted from this problematic and imported 'uncritically' into Marxism, they have absolutely uncontrollable effects. They always surface when least expected, and constantly risk clouding scientific analysis. In the extreme case, one can be unconsciously and surreptitiously contaminated by the very epistemological principles of the adversary, that is to say the problematic that founds the concepts which have not been theoretically criticized, believing them simply refuted by the facts. This is more serious: for it is then no longer a question merely of external notions 'imported' into Marxism, but of principles that risk vitiating the use made of Marxist concepts themselves.

Is this the case with Miliband? I do not believe that the consequences of his procedure have gone so far. It nevertheless remains true that, as I see it, Miliband sometimes allows himself to be unduly influenced by the methodological principles of the adversary. How is this manifested? Very briefly, I would say that it is visible in the difficulties that Miliband has in comprehending social classes and the state as *objective structures*, and their relations as an *objective system of regular connections*, a structure and a system whose agents, 'men', are in the words of Marx, 'bearers' of it – *Träger*. Miliband constantly gives the impression that for him social classes or 'groups' are in some way reducible to *inter-personal relations*, that the state is reducible to inter-personal relations of the members of the diverse 'groups' that constitute the state apparatus, and finally that the relation between social classes and the state is itself reducible to inter-personal relations of 'individuals' composing social groups and 'individuals' composing the state apparatus.

I have indicated, in an earlier article in *New Left Review*, that this conception seems to me to derive from a *problematic of the subject* which has had constant repercussions in the history of Marxist thought.[4] According to this problematic, the agents of a social formation, 'men', are not considered as the 'bearers' of objective instances (as they are for Marx), but as the genetic principle of the levels of the social whole. This is a problematic of *social actors*, of individuals as the origin of *social action*: sociological research thus leads finally, not to the study of the objective co-ordinates that determine the distribution of agents into social classes and the contradictions between these classes, but to the search for *finalist* explanations founded on the *motivations of conduct* of the individual actors. This is notoriously one of the aspects of the problematic both of Weber and of contemporary functionalism. To transpose this problematic of the subject into Marxism is in the end to admit the epistemological principles of the adversary and to risk vitiating one's own analyses.

Let us now consider some of the concrete themes of Miliband's book in the light of this preamble.

The False Problem of Managerialism

The first problem which Miliband discusses, very correctly, is that of the *ruling class*, by way of reply to the current bourgeois ideologies of *managerialism*. According to these ideologies, the contemporary separation of private ownership and control has transferred economic power from entrepreneurs to managers. The latter have no interest as owners in the strict sense, and hence do not seek profit as their aim – in other words, profit is not a motivation of their conduct, but growth, or development. Since the ruling class is here defined by the quest for profit, and this quest no longer characterizes the directors of the economy, the ruling class itself no longer exists: we are now confronted with a 'plurality of elites', of which the managers are one. What is Miliband's response to this?[5] He takes these ideologies literally and turns their own arguments against them: in fact, managers do seek profit as the goal of their actions, for this is how the capitalist system works. Seeking private profit, they also make up part of the ruling class, for the contradiction of the capitalist system according to Marx, Miliband tells us, is 'the contradiction between its ever more social character and its enduringly private purpose'.[6] While not excluding the existence of some managerial goals relatively different from those of owners, Miliband considers managers as one among the distinct economic elites composing the ruling class.

I consider this a mistaken way of presenting the problem. To start with, the distinctive criterion for membership of the capitalist class for Marx *is in no way* a motivation of conduct, that is to say the search for profit as the 'aim of action'. For there may well exist capitalists who are not motivated by profit, just as there are non-capitalists (the petty bourgeoisie in small-scale production, for instance) who by contrast have just such a motivation. Marx's criterion is the objective place in production and the ownership of the means of production. It should be remembered that even Max Weber had to admit that what defined the capitalist was not 'the lure of gain'. For Marx, profit is not a motivation of conduct — even one 'imposed' by the system — it is an objective category that designates a part of realized surplus-value. In the same way, the fundamental contradiction of the capitalist system, according to Marx, is not at all a contradiction between its social character and its 'private purpose', but a contradiction between the socialization of productive forces and their *private appropriation*. Thus the characterization of the existing social system as capitalist in no way depends on the motivations of the conduct of managers. Furthermore: to characterize the class position of managers, one need not refer to the motivations of their conduct, but only to their place in production and their relationship to the ownership of the means of production. Here, both Bettelheim and myself have noted that it is necessary to distinguish, in the term 'property' used by Marx, formal legal property, which may not belong to the 'individual' capitalist, and *economic property or real appropriation*, which is the only genuine *economic power*.[7] This economic property, which is what matters as far as distribution into classes is concerned, still belongs well and truly to *capital*. The manager exercises only a functional delegation of it.

From this point of view, the managers as such do not constitute a distinct fraction of the capitalist class. Miliband, basing himself on the non-pertinent distinction of motivations of conduct, is led to consider the managers a distinct 'economic elite'. By doing so, he not only attributes to them an importance they do not possess, but he is prevented from seeing what is important. For in effect, what matters is not the differences and relations between 'economic elites' based on diverging aims, but something of which Miliband says virtually nothing, *the differences and relations between fractions of capital*. The problem is not that of a plurality of 'economic elites' but of fractions of the capitalist class. Can a Marxist pass over in silence the existent differences and relations, under imperialism, between comprador monopoly capital, national monopoly capital, non-monopoly capital, industrial capital, or financial capital?

The Question of Bureaucracy

The next problem that Miliband selects for discussion, again correctly, is that of the relation between the ruling class and the state. Here too, Miliband's approach to the question is to provide a direct rebuttal of bourgeois ideologies. These ideologies affirm the *neutrality* of the state, representing the general interest, in relation to the divergent interests of 'civil society'. Some of them (Aron, for example) claim that the capitalist class has never truly *governed* in capitalist societies, in the sense that its members have rarely participated directly in the government; others claim that the members of the state apparatus, the 'civil servants', are neutral with respect to the interests of social groups. What is the general line of Miliband's response to these ideologies? Here too, he is led to take up the reverse position to these ideologies, to turn their argument against them. He does so in two ways. First of all he establishes that the members of the capitalist class have in fact often directly participated in the state apparatus and in the government.[8] Then, having established the relation between members of the state apparatus and the ruling class, he shows (a) that the *social origin* of members of the 'summit' of the state apparatus is that of the ruling class, and (b) that *personal ties* of influence, status, and milieu are established between the members of the ruling class and those of the state apparatus.[9]

I have no intention of contesting the value of Miliband's analyses, which on the contrary appear to me to have a capital *demystifying* importance. Yet, however exact in itself, the way chosen by Miliband does not seem to me to be the most significant one. Firstly, because the *direct* participation of members of the capitalist class in the state apparatus and in the government, even where it exists, is not the important side of the matter. The relation between the bourgeois class and the state is an *objective relation*. This means that if the *function* of the state in a determinate social formation and the *interests* of the dominant class in this formation *coincide*, it is by reason of the system itself: the direct participation of members of the ruling class in the state apparatus is not the *cause* but the *effect*, and moreover a chance and contingent one, of this objective coincidence.

In order to establish this coincidence, it would have been necessary to make explicit the role of the state as a specific instance, a regional structure, of the social whole. Miliband, however, seems to reduce the role of the state to the conduct and 'behaviour' of the members of the state apparatus.[10] If Miliband had first established that the state is precisely *the factor of cohesion of a social formation and the factor of reproduction of the conditions of production of a system* that itself determines the domination of one class over the others, he would have seen clearly that the participation, whether direct or indirect, of this class in government *in no way changes things*. Indeed, in the case of the capitalist state, one can go further: it can be said that the capitalist state best serves the interests of the capitalist class only when the members of this class do not participate directly in the state apparatus, that is to say when the *ruling class* is not the *politically governing class*. This is the exact meaning of Marx's analyses of 19th-century England and Bismarckian Germany, to say nothing of Bonapartism is France. It is also what Miliband himself seems to suggest in his analyses of social-democratic governments.[11]

We come now to the problem of the *members of the state apparatus*, that is to say the army, the police, the judiciary and the administrative bureaucracy. Miliband's main line of argument is to try to establish the relation between the conduct of the members of the state apparatus and the interests of the ruling class, by demonstrating either that the social origin of the 'top servants of the state' is that of the ruling class, or that the members of the state apparatus end up united to this class by personal ties.[12] This approach, without being false, remains descriptive. More importantly, I believe that it prevents us from studying the specific problem that the state apparatus presents; *the problem of 'bureaucracy'*. According to Marx, Engels and Lenin, the members of the state apparatus, which it is convenient to call the 'bureaucracy' in the general sense, constitute a specific *social category* – not a class. This means that, although the members of the state apparatus belong, by their class origin, to different classes, they function according to a specific internal unity. Their class origin – *class situation* – recedes into the background in relation to that which unifies them – their *class position*: that is to say, the fact that they belong precisely to the state apparatus and that they have as their *objective function* the actualization of the role of the state. This in its turn means that the bureaucracy, as a specific and relatively 'unified' social category, is the 'servant' of the ruling class, not by reason of its class origins, which are divergent, or by reason of its personal relations with the ruling class, but by reason of the fact that its internal unity derives from its actualization of the objective role of the state. The totality of this role itself coincides with the interests of the ruling class.

Important consequences follow for the celebrated problem of the *relative autonomy* of the state with respect to the ruling class, and thus for the equally celebrated question of the relative autonomy of the bureaucracy as a specific social category, with respect to that class. A long Marxist tradition has considered that the state is only a simple tool or instrument manipulated at will by the ruling class. I do not mean to say that Miliband falls into this trap, which makes it impossible to account for the complex mechanisms of the state in its relation to class struggle. However, if one locates the relationship between the state and the ruling class in the social origin of the members of the state apparatus and their inter-personal relations with the members of this class, so that the bourgeoisie almost physically 'corners' the state apparatus, one cannot account for the relative autonomy of the state with respect to this class. When Marx designated Bonapartism as the 'religion of the bourgeoisie', in other words as characteristic of *all* forms of the capitalist state, he showed that this state can only truly serve the ruling class in so far as it is relatively autonomous from the diverse fractions of this class, precisely in order to be able to organize the hegemony of the whole of this class. It is not by chance that Miliband finally admits this autonomy only in the extreme case of fascism.[13] The question posed is whether the situation today has changed in this respect: I do not think so, and will return to this.

The Branches of the State Apparatus

Miliband's approach thus to a certain extent prevents him from following through a rigorous analysis of the state apparatus itself and of the relations between different 'branches' or 'parts' of this apparatus. Miliband securely establishes that the state apparatus is not only constituted by the government, but also by special branches such as the army, the police, the judiciary, and the civil administration. Yet what is it that governs the *relations* between these branches, the respective importance and the relative predominance of these different branches among themselves, for example the relation between parliament and the executive, or the role of the army or of the administration in a particular form of state? Miliband's response seems to be the following:[14] the fact that one of these branches predominates over the others is in some way directly related to the 'exterior' factors noted above. That is to say, it is either the branch whose members are, by their class origin or connections, nearest to the ruling class, or the branch whose predominance over the others is due to its immediate 'economic' role. An example of the latter case would be the present growth of the role of the army, related to the current importance of military expenditures.[15]

Here too, I cannot completely agree with Miliband's interpretation. As I see it, the state apparatus forms an *objective system* of special 'branches' whose relation presents a *specific internal unity* and obeys, to a large extent, *its own logic*. Each particular form of capitalist state is thus characterized by a particular form of relations among its branches, and by the predominance of one or of certain of its branches over the others: liberal state, interventionist state, Bonapartism, military dictatorship or fascism. But each particular form of capitalist state must be referred back, *in its unity*, to important modifications of the relations of production and to important stages of class struggle: competitive capitalism, imperialism, state capitalism. Only *after* having established the relation of a form of state as a unity, *that is as a specific form of the system of state apparatus as a whole*, with the 'exterior', can the respective role and the mutual internal relation of the 'branches' of the state apparatus be established. A *significant* shift in the predominant branch in the state apparatus, or of the relation between these branches, cannot be *directly* established by the immediate exterior role of this branch, but is determined *by the modification of the whole system of the state apparatus and of its form of internal unity as such*: a modification which is itself due to changes in the relations of production and to developments in the class struggle.

Let us take as an example the present case of the *army* in the advanced capitalist countries. I do not think that the 'immediate' facts of the growth of military expenditure and increasing inter-personal ties between industrialists and the military are sufficient to speak of a *significant* shift of the role of the army in the present state apparatus: besides, in spite of everything, Miliband himself is very reserved in this matter. In order for such a shift to occur, there would have to be an important modification of the form of state as a whole – without this necessarily having to take the form of 'military dictatorship' – a modification which would not be due *simply* to the growing importance of military expenditure, but to profound modifications of the relations of production and the class struggle, of which the growth of military expenditures is finally only the *effect*. One could thus establish the relation of the army not simply with the dominant class, but with the totality of social classes – a complex relation that would explain its role by means of a shift in the state as a whole. I believe that there is no more striking evidence of this thesis, in another context, than present developments in Latin America.

The Present Form of the Capitalist State

Can we then speak in the present stage of capitalism of a modification of the form of the state? I would answer here in the affirmative, although I do not believe that this modification is necessarily in the direction of a preponderant role of the army. Miliband also seems to give an affirmative reply to the question. How does he situate this present modification of the form of state?[16] If the relation between the state and the ruling class is principally constituted by the 'interpersonal' relations between the members of the state apparatus and those of the ruling class, the only approach that seems open is to argue that these relations are now becoming increasingly intense and rigid, that the two are practically interchangeable. In effect, this is just the approach which Miliband adopts. The argument seems to me, however, merely descriptive. Indeed, it converges with the orthodox Communist thesis of *state monopoly capitalism*, according to which the present form of the state is specified by increasingly close interpersonal relations between the monopolies and the members of the state apparatus, by the 'fusion of state and monopolies into a single mechanism'.[17] I have shown elsewhere why and how this thesis, in appearance ultra-leftist, leads in fact to the most vapid revisionism and reformism.[18] In fact, the present modification of the form of state must mainly be sought and studied not in its simple effects, which are besides disputable, but in profound shifts of the articulation of economy and polity. This modification does not seem to me to alter the relative autonomy of the state which at present, as J.M. Vincent has recently noted in connection with Gaullism,[19] only assumes different forms. In brief, the designation of any existent state as the pure and simple agent of big capital seems to me, *taken literally*, to give rise to many misinterpretations – as much now as in the past.

The Ideological Apparatuses

Finally there is one last problem which seems to me very important, and which will provide me with the occasion to go further than I have done in my own work cited above. I wonder in effect if Miliband and myself have not stopped half-way on one critical question. This is the role of *ideology* in the functioning of the State apparatus, a question which has become especially topical since the events of May–June 1968 in France. The classical Marxist tradition of the theory of the state is principally concerned to show *the repressive role of the state*, in the strong sense of organized physical repression. There is only one notable exception, Gramsci, with his problematic of hegemony. Now Miliband very correctly insists in long and excellent analyses (*The process of legitimization*, I, II, pp. 179–264) on the role played by ideology in the functioning of the state and in the process of political domination: which I have tried to do from another point of view in my own work.

I think however that, for different reasons, we have both stopped half-way: which was not the case with Gramsci. That is to say, we have ended by considering that ideology only exists in ideas, customs or morals without seeing that ideology can be embodied, in the strong sense, in *institutions*: institutions which then, by the very process of institutionalization, belong to the system of the state whilst depending principally on the ideological level. Following the Marxist tradition, we gave the concept of the state a *restricted* meaning, considering the principally repressive institutions as forming part of the 'state', and rejecting institutions with a principally ideological role as 'outside of' the state, in a place that Miliband designates as the 'political system', distinguishing it from the state.[20]

Here is the thesis I would like to propose: the system of the state is composed of *several apparatuses or institutions* of which certain have a principally repressive role, in the strong sense, and others a principally ideological role. The former constitute the repressive apparatus of the state, that is to say the state apparatus in the classical Marxist sense of the term (government, army, police, tribunals and administration). The latter constitute the *ideological apparatuses of the state*, such as the Church, the political parties, the unions (with the exception, of course, of the *revolutionary* party or trade union organizations), the schools, the mass media (newspapers, radio, television), and, from a certain point of view, the family. This is so whether they are *public* or *private* – the distinction having a purely juridical, that is, largely ideological character, which changes nothing fundamental. This position is in a certain sense that of Gramsci himself, although one he did not sufficiently found and develop.

Why should one speak in the plural of the state ideological apparatuses, whilst speaking in the singular of the state repressive apparatus? Because the state repressive apparatus, the state in the classical Marxist sense of the term, possesses a very rigorous internal unity which directly governs the relation between the diverse branches of the apparatus. Whilst the state ideological apparatuses, by their principal function – ideological inculcation and transmission – possess a greater and more important autonomy: their inter-connections and relations with the state repressive apparatus appear, by relation to the mutual connections of the branches of the state repressive apparatus, vested with a greater independence.

Why should one speak of *state* ideological apparatuses; why should these apparatuses be considered as composing part of the state? I will mention four principal reasons:

1. If the state is defined as the instance that maintains the cohesion of a social formation and which reproduces the conditions of production of a social system by maintaining class domination, it is obvious that the institutions in question – the state ideological apparatuses – fill exactly the same function.

2. The condition of possibility of the existence and functioning of these institutions or ideological apparatuses, under a certain form, is the state repressive apparatus itself. If it is true that their role is principally ideological and that the state repressive apparatus does not in general intervene *directly* in their functioning, it remains no less true that this repressive apparatus is always present behind them, that it defends them and sanctions them, and finally, that their action is *determined* by the action of the state repressive apparatus itself. The student movement, in France and elsewhere, can testify to this for schools and universities today.

3. Although these ideological apparatuses possess a notable autonomy, among themselves and in relation to the state repressive apparatus, it remains no less true that they belong to the same system as this repressive apparatus. Every important modification of the form of the state has repercussions not only on the mutual relations of the state repressive apparatus, but also on the mutual relations of the state ideological apparatuses and of the relations between these apparatuses and the state repressive apparatus. There is no need to take the extreme case of fascism to prove this thesis: one need only mention the modifications of the role and relations of the Church, the parties, the unions, the schools, the media, the family, both among themselves and with the state repressive apparatus, in the diverse 'normal' forms through which the capitalist state had evolved.

4. Finally, for one last reason: according to Marxist-Leninist theory, a socialist revolution does not signify only a shift in *state power*, but it must equally '*break*', that is to say radically change, the state apparatus. Now, if one includes ideological apparatuses in the concept of the state, it is evident why the classics of Marxism have – if often only in implicit fashion – considered it necessary to apply the thesis of the 'destruction' of the state not only to the state repressive apparatus, but *also to the state ideological apparatuses*: Church, parties, unions, school, media, family. Certainly, given the autonomy of the state

ideological apparatuses, this does not mean that they must all be 'broken' in homologous fashion, that is, *in the same way* or at *the same time* as the state repressive apparatus, or that any one of them must be. It means that the 'destruction' of the ideological apparatuses has *its precondition* in the 'destruction' of the state repressive apparatus which maintains it. Hence the illusory error of a certain contemporary thesis, which considers it possible to pass here and now, to the 'destruction' of the university in capitalist societies, for instance. But it also means that the advent of socialist society cannot be achieved by 'breaking' only the state repressive apparatus whilst maintaining the state ideological apparatuses intact, taking them in hand as they are and merely changing their function.

This question evidently brings us closer to the problem of the *dictatorship of the proletariat* and of the *cultural revolution*: but I have the feeling that it takes us farther from Miliband. I do not however, want to enter here into the problem of the political conclusions of Miliband's book, in which he shows himself very – too – discreet: the question remains open. I will end by recalling what I said at the beginning: if the tone of this article is critical, this is above all proof of the interest that the absorbing analyses of Miliband's work have aroused in me.

8

ON SOCIAL CLASSES

What are social classes in Marxist theory? They are groups of social agents, of men defined *principally* but not exclusively by their place in the *production process*, i.e. by their place in the economic sphere. The economic place of the social agents has a *principal* role in determining social classes. But from that we cannot conclude that this economic place is sufficient to determine social classes. Marxism states that the economic does indeed have the determinant role in a mode of production or a social formation; but the political and the ideological (the superstructure) also have an important role. For whenever Marx, Engels, Lenin and Mao analyze social classes, far from limiting themselves to the economic criteria alone, they make explicit reference to political and ideological criteria. We can thus say that a social class is defined by its *place* in the ensemble of social practices, i.e. by its place in the ensemble of the division of labour which includes political and ideological relations. This place corresponds to *the structural determination* of classes, i.e. the manner in which determination by the structure (relations of production, politico-ideological domination/subordination) operates on class practices – for classes have existence only in the class struggle.[1] This takes the form of the effect of the structure on the social division of labour. But it should be pointed out here that this determination of classes, which has existence only in the class struggle, must be clearly distinguished from *class position* in the *conjuncture*. In stressing the importance of political and ideological relations in the determination of classes and the fact that social classes have existence only in the class struggle, we should not be led into the 'voluntarist' error of reducing class determination to class position. From that error flow extremely important political consequences, which will be mentioned in the sections dealing with technicians,

* First published in French as 'Les classes sociales' in *L'Homme et la Société* 24/25 (1972). This translation is taken from *New Left Review* 78 (1973), pp. 27–54.

engineers and the labour aristocracy. Yet the economic criterion remains determinant. But how are we to understand the terms 'economic' and 'economic criterion' in the Marxist conception?

Social Classes and Relations of Production

The 'economic' sphere is determined by *the production process* and the place of the agents, i.e. by their distribution into social classes by *the relations of production*: in the unit consisting of production/consumption/division of the social product, it is production which has the determinant role. The distinction between the classes at this level is not, e.g. a distinction based on relative sizes of income (a distinction between 'rich' and 'poor'), as was believed by a long pre-Marxist tradition and as is still believed today by a whole series of sociologists. The undoubted distinction between relative levels of income is itself only a consequence of the relations of production.

What then are the production process and the relations of production which compose it? In the production process, we find first of all *the labour process*: it is that which in general designates man's relation to nature. But the labour process always appears in an historically determined social form. It exists only in its unity with relations of production. In a society divided into classes, the relations of production consist of a double relation which encompasses men's relations to nature in material production. These two relations are relations first between men and other men – class relations, and secondly between the agents of production and the object and means of labour – the productive forces. These two relations thus concern the relation of the non-worker (the owner) to the object and means of labour and the relation of the immediate producer (direct worker) to the object and means of labour. These relations involve two aspects: (a) Economic ownership: by this is meant the real economic control of the means of production, i.e. the power to assign the means of production to given uses and so to dispose of the products obtained. (b) Possession: by this is meant the capacity to put the means of production into operation.

The owners and the means of production

In every society divided into classes, the first relation (owners/means of production) always coincides with the first aspect: it is the owners who have real control of the means of production and thus exploit the direct workers by extorting surplus-value from them in various forms. But this ownership is to be understood as real economic ownership, control of the means of production, to be distinguished from *juridical* ownership, which is sanctioned by the law and belongs to the super-structure. Certainly, the law generally ratifies economic ownership, but it is possible for the forms of juridical ownership not to coincide with real economic ownership.

We can illustrate this by two examples, beginning with the case of *the big farmers* in the division of classes in the countryside. According to Lenin, they belong to the rich peasantry, even though they do not have formal, juridical ownership of the land, which belongs to the rentier capitalist. These big farmers belong to the rich peasantry not because of their high incomes, but because they have real control of the land and the means of labour, of which they are thus the effective economic owners. I mention this case merely as an example. Space does not permit a detailed analysis of the class divisions of the peasantry, which does not in itself constitute a single class. It should, however, be pointed out that we can divide the countryside into big landowners, rich, medium and poor peasants, such that each class encompasses groups arising from different forms of ownership and exploitation, only if we make a rigorous distinction between formal, juridical ownership and real, economic ownership.

The case of the USSR and the 'socialist' countries is a second example. This is highly controversial, but it should not be omitted here. In these countries, formal, juridical ownership of the means of production belongs to the state, which is held to be 'the people's state'; but real control (economic ownership) certainly does not belong to the workers themselves – as we can see from the extinction of the soviets and the workers' councils – but to the directors of enterprises and to the members of the party apparatus. It can therefore be argued that the form of collective juridical ownership conceals a new form of economic 'private' ownership; and hence that one should speak of a new 'bourgeoisie' in the USSR. In reality, the abolition of class exploitation cannot be equated simply with the abolition of juridical private ownership, but with the abolition of real economic ownership – i.e. control of the means of production by the workers themselves.

These considerations have a bearing on the question of the transition to socialism. By keeping in mind the all-important theoretical and real distinction between economic and formal, juridical, ownership, we can see that the mere *nationalization* of enterprises is not a solution. This is not only because nationalizations are adapted by the bourgeoisie to their own interests. It is because even when they are accompanied by a change in state power, a nationalization or a take-over of the economy by the state only changes the form of juridical ownership. In the last resort, the one thing which can fundamentally modify economic ownership and thus lead to the abolition of classes is the control of production by the workers themselves.

The exploited class and the means of labour

Let us return to our second relation – that of the direct producers (the workers) to the means and object of labour. This relation defines *the exploited class*. It can take various forms, according to the various modes of production in which it occurs. In pre-capitalist modes of production, the direct producers (the workers) were not entirely separated from the object and means of labour. In the case of the feudal mode of production, for instance, even though the lord had both juridical and economic *ownership* of the land, the serf had *possession* of his parcel of land, which was protected by custom. He could not be purely and simply dispossessed by the lord. In that mode of production, exploitation was by *direct extraction of surplus labour*, in the form of *corvée* payable in labour or in kind. In other words, economic ownership and possession were distinct in that they did not both depend on the same relation between owners and means of production. By contrast, in the capitalist mode of production, the direct producers (the working class) are completely dispossessed of their means of work, of which the capitalists have the actual possession: Marx called this the phenomenon of the 'naked worker'. The worker possesses only his labour-power, which he sells as a *commodity*, and this fact determines the generalization of the commodity form. Thus the capitalist extracts surplus labour not in a direct way, but rather through the medium of labour embodied in the commodity – by amassing *surplus-value*.

Important consequences follow from this. The *production process* is defined not by technological factors, but by relations between men and the means of production; it is defined therefore by the unity of the labour process and the relations of production. In societies divided into classes, there is no such thing as 'productive labour' as such, understood as a neutral term. In every mode of production divided into classes, productive labour is labour corresponding to the relations of production of that mode: it is that labour which gives rise to a specific form of *exploitation*. In such societies, production always stands for division, exploitation and struggle between classes. Thus in the capitalist mode of production, productive labour is that which (always on the basis of use-value) produces exchange-value in the form of *commodities*, and so *surplus-value*. It is precisely in this way that the *working class* is economically defined in the capitalist mode of production: productive labour relates directly to the division between classes in the relations of production.

Productive and unproductive labour

This formulation allows us to solve certain problems, while it also poses new ones. The working class is not defined by its *wages*, since wages are a juridical form in which the product is divided up according to the contract governing the buying and selling of labour-power. While every worker is a wage-earner, not every wage-earner is a worker, since not every wage-earner is necessarily a productive worker, i.e. one who produces surplus-value (commodities). Marx provides some explicit analyses on this point: he considers, for example, that transport workers (railwaymen, etc) are productive workers, belonging to the working class. This is because a commodity does not exist until it appears on the market: and in the definition of productive labour, the important factor is the commodity (surplus-value); whereas wage-earners in commerce, banks, advertising agencies, service industries, etc., are not included among productive workers. This is because some of them belong to the sphere of circulation, while the rest do not produce surplus-value, but merely contribute to its realization.

The problem is yet more complicated with respect to the technicians and engineers working within and on the periphery of material production in enterprises: a group which includes those who are often (incorrectly) called 'bearers of science'. There is no coherent or explicit account of this problem to be found in Marx, who, in confining himself to the economic plane, in fact produces two more or less contradictory responses. In *Theories of Surplus-Value* and the *Grundrisse*, Marx uses the notion of *collective worker*. In view of (a) the progressive socialization of the productive forces and the labour process, and (b) the increasing interpenetration of the various tasks contributing to commodity production, Marx argues that science tends to become part of the productive forces and that technicians, through the medium of the collective worker, should be considered part of the working class. This leads to the notion that they form a labour aristocracy – which Lenin considered to be a stratum of the working class itself. But, in *Capital*, Marx clearly considers that this category of agents is not part of the working class, since science is not a direct productive force, as only its applications enter into the production process. Moreover these applications contribute only to the increase and realization of surplus-value, not to its direct production. So technical agents do not form part of the working class. What is the significance of this? We must first point out the limitations of certain 'economic' criteria (understood in a 'technicist' manner) which cannot provide an answer. First there is a division between 'manual' and 'intellectual' labour, understood in a technicist manner, i.e. as a division dependent on the technical division of labour. Now, even at the level of the production process alone, that division is not in itself a sufficient condition for the division into classes. The productive worker, producing surplus-value, is not in any way reducible to the manual worker alone. On the other hand, we can see how important this division between manual and intellectual labour is when we consider how it characterizes the ensemble of places in the social division of labour, determining social classes, where authority and direction of labour are linked in the enterprise to intellectual labour and the 'secret of knowledge'. The division between manual and intellectual labour becomes important in the determination of classes only when it is situated within political and ideological relations. Secondly, there is the distinction between the collective worker and the productive worker, as claimed in the French Communist Party's recent publication *Le capitalisme monopoliste, Traité d'économie marxiste*.[2]

This work is based almost exclusively on technico-economic criteria. The problem is of such importance that it is worth dwelling on it. In Volume I, pp. 211 ff., the authors attempt to define '*collective worker*' as 'those who contribute "technically" to the production of surplus-value, as distinct from the stricter notion of "productive worker", defined as those who directly produce surplus-value (the working class)'. These notions embody a whole series of bastard categories, of agents who are considered not to be workers, but yet to be part of the 'collective worker', i.e. 'quasi-workers'.

These notions constitute an *economistic deformation*, harnessed to a specific political objective. It is an economistic *deformation*, in that when Marx uses the notion of *collective worker*, he in fact identifies it with an extension of the working class itself, of the productive worker. He never makes any distinction between collective worker and productive worker; instead he uses the term 'collective worker' to designate transformations *of the working class itself*. On the other hand, it is true that, in *Capital*, Marx uses only economic criteria to define the collective worker, and it is for that reason that the term remains fluid and ambiguous in that work.

We should put forward the following proposition: the collective worker is none other than the working class, though the term 'collective worker' has different connotations in that it introduces ideological and political criteria into the delimitation of the working class. This is its fundamental significance, to which we shall return later. The erroneous view which distinguishes between the collective worker and the working class by inventing strata 'quasi-workers' all but adopts the myth of the 'wage-earning class', the myth which identifies *wage-earners* and *working class*.

From this issue, we can move to an important problem. We stated above that the production process consists of the *unity* between the labour process and the relations of production. We can now put forward an additional proposition: within this unity it is not the labour process (including 'technology' and the 'technical process') which has the dominant role: *rather it is the relations of production which have primacy over the labour process and the 'productive forces'*. This has an important bearing on the question of social classes. The determination of classes depends on the relations of production, which relate directly to the social division of labour and the politico-ideological superstructure, not to the data of any 'technical process' as such. *The technical division of labour is dominated by the social division.* So we do not define productive labour as consisting of those who take part in production understood in a technical sense, but as consisting of those who produce surplus-value and who are thus exploited as a class in a determinate manner, i.e. those who occupy a determinate place in the social division of labour.

Mode of Production and Social Formation

Before we go on to the political and ideological criteria necessary for delimiting social classes, we should pause to consider the classes in a concrete mode of production and social formation or 'society'. In talking of a *mode of production* or of a form of production, we are placing ourselves at a general and abstract level, e.g. the slave, feudal and capitalist modes of production. We are, as it were, 'isolating' these modes and forms of production in social reality, in order to examine them theoretically. But as Lenin demonstrated in *The Development of Capitalism in Russia*, a concrete society at a given moment of time (*a social formation*) is composed of several modes and forms of production which coexist in it in combination. For example, capitalist societies at the start of the 20th century were composed of (i) elements of the feudal mode of production, (ii) the form of simple commodity production and manufacture (the form of the transition from feudalism to capitalism) and (iii) the capitalist mode of production in its competitive and monopoly forms. Yet these societies were certainly capitalist societies: this means that the capitalist mode of production was *dominant* in them. In fact, in every social order, we find the dominance of one mode of production, which produces complex effects of *dissolution* or *conservation* on the other modes of production and which gives these societies their character (feudal, capitalist, etc.). The one exception is the case of societies in transition, which are, on the contrary, characterized by an *equilibrium* between the various modes of production.

To return to social classes: if we confine ourselves to modes of production alone, examining them in a pure and abstract fashion, we find that each of them involves two classes – the exploiting class, which is politically and ideologically dominant, and the exploited class, which is politically and ideologically dominated: masters and slaves in the slave mode of production, lords and serfs in the feudal mode of production, bourgeois and workers in the capitalist mode of production. But a concrete society (a social formation) *involves more than two classes*, in so far as it is composed of various modes and forms of production. No social formation involves only two classes: but the two fundamental classes of any social formation are those of the dominant mode of production in that formation. Thus in contemporary France, for example, the two fundamental classes are the bourgeoisie and the proletariat. But we also find there the traditional petty bourgeoisie (craftsmen, small traders), dependent on the form of simple commodity production, the 'new' petty bourgeoisie composed of non-productive wage-earners, dependent on the monopoly form of capitalism and several social classes in the countryside, where vestiges of feudalism are still to be found in a transformed state (e.g. forms of share-cropping).

These considerations have an important bearing on the question of *alliances* between the working class and the other popular classes. The petty bourgeoisie and the popular classes in the countryside (agricultural labourers, poor peasants, middle peasants) are in fact *classes* which differ from the working class. Now, in so far as the two fundamental classes are the bourgeoisie and the working class, it is true that in the course of their expanded reproduction the other classes *tend to polarize* around the working class. But this does not mean that as classes they dissolve into an undifferentiated mass: they are still *classes* with their own specific interests. In other words, the concepts of 'class' and 'people' are not coextensive: *according to the conjuncture*, a class may or may not form part of the 'people', without this affecting its class nature.

It is here that the problem of alliances arises. On the one hand, the working class must accept responsibility in its alliances for the *specific interests of the classes* which make up the 'people' or the 'popular masses' along with it, as for instance in the worker-peasant alliance advocated by Lenin. On the other hand, it must not lose sight of the fact that − as in every alliance − contradictions do exist between the specific interests of the working class, *qua* class and, the other popular classes. By recognizing these facts, we provide ourselves with the means of giving a just solution to the contradictions 'among the people'.

This is important since there are two other interpretations of the phenomenon, both equally mistaken. According to the first interpretation, upheld by many sociologists, the transformations which capitalist societies are currently undergoing are supposed to have given rise to a vast 'intermediate class' which comprises all social groups except the bourgeoisie and proletariat and which, by virtue of its numerical weight, provides the real pillar upholding modern societies. As has been noted, we are here faced with several classes: there is no justification at present for claiming that these intermediate classes are fused into a single class. The second mistaken interpretation is currently set out in the Communist Party's recent *Le capitalisme monopoliste,* mentioned above (vol. I, pp. 204 ff.). According to this interpretation, under 'monopoly state capitalism', a polarization is now taking place which is *effectively dissolving all the other classes of society except the bourgeoisie and the proletariat*: the other social classes (the peasantry, the various fractions of the petty bourgeoisie) no longer have any existence as classes, but only as *intermediate strata.* This deserves to be stressed, since it is the first time that such a gross misinterpretation has been explicitly formulated in an authorized manner. It should moreover be related to the interpretation of the concept of 'collective worker': according to this, there exist on the one hand the working class (productive worker) and on the other hand 'quasi-workers' (collective worker) with more or less identical interests to those of the working class; and in addition, various intermediate *strata* which, lacking any specific class interests, are automatically grouped around the working class. This interpretation obviously opens the way to *an unprincipled alliance*, which can have dangerous consequences. Those who begin by denying that there are any differences between the members of the popular alliance end up (once contradictions emerge which they have made no attempt to resolve − e.g. those between the proletariat and peasantry in the USSR under Stalin) by repressing these contradictions with police action:

they simply proclaim that the real interest of the other members of the alliance is automatically identical, at any moment of time, with that of the working class.

Political and Ideological Criteria

It is now time to develop the other side of the thesis, outlined in the introduction, that purely economic criteria are not sufficient to determine and locate social classes. This becomes particularly obvious when we consider a concrete social formation. Here it becomes absolutely necessary to refer to positions within the ideological and political relations of the social division of labour; and this becomes even clearer when we examine the question of the *reproduction* of social classes.

We shall begin with those problems which relate to definitions of the working class. In the course of this investigation, we shall attempt to solve the problem, indicated above, of the technicians and engineers. While economic criteria alone are sufficient to exclude wage-earners in commerce, banks, etc., from the working class, they provide us with no answer to our question concerning the technicians and engineers. For that, we have to refer to the social division of labour as a whole. When we do this, we see that the ensemble of technicians and engineers occupies a *contradictory* position: from the economico-technical point of view it increasingly contributes to the production of surplus-value; but at the same time it is entrusted with a special authority in overseeing the labour process and its despotic organization. It is thus placed 'alongside' (see above) intellectual labour in its maintenance of the monopoly of knowledge. It can be suggested that, up to now at least, this latter aspect of its situation outweighs the former in determining its class: so that as a *whole*, engineers and technicians cannot be considered as belonging to the working class.

In thus referring to ideological-political criteria, we are still talking of the *structural determination* of the technician class, i.e. their *place* in political and ideological relations. This place is not reducible to their *class position* in the conjuncture. Because of their contradictory class determination, they may, in strikes for example, sometimes take the side of the employers and sometimes that of the workers. If in referring to ideologico-political criteria, we were merely alluding to class position, we should have to say that this ensemble is part of the working class whenever it takes the working-class's side, and that it is not part of it whenever it takes the opposing side. But this would undermine the *objective* definition of classes made by Marxism. The point to remember is that even when engineers and technicians take the working class's side, they are not workers: and this has an important bearing on a correct policy of alliances.

Distinguishing strata: the problem of the labour aristocracy

It is also necessary to refer to political and ideological criteria in differentiating the various *strata* in the working class itself. Many authors, especially Alain Touraine, have tried to reduce the ideologico-political differences within the working class to technico-economic differences in the organization of labour, or even to differences in the size of wages. These are differences which are directly classifiable – manual labourers, semi-skilled labourers, skilled (qualified) labourers, etc. The basic criterion is that of 'skills' conceived in a 'technicist' fashion. These differentiations can be used as the basis of contradictory generalizations: either to maintain that unskilled labourers, etc., have a higher class consciousness and revolutionary potential than the rest of the working class, or to attribute the same thing to skilled workers. But current inquiries, historical experience and sociological analyses show that these generalizations based on purely technico-economic criteria are arbitrary. Differentiations within the working class do not purely and simply *coincide* with positions in the organization of labour. They depend rather on political and ideological criteria, on forms of struggle and of combative organization and on tradition; and these criteria have their *own autonomy*. To take just the example of anarcho-syndicalism in France: how, on simple 'technico-economic' criteria, can we explain an ideological form which took root *par excellence* both amongst unskilled labourers in big enterprises and amongst skilled workers in small manufacturing plants?

A further example is that of the famous *labour aristocracy*. This, according to Lenin, *is a stratum of the working class which is the basis of social democracy*. According to the 'economistic' version of the conception (advocated notably by the Third International), this stratum consists of *the most skilled and best paid* workers in the imperialist countries, receiving the crumbs of surplus profits drawn from the colonies, crumbs distributed to them by the imperialist bourgeoisies: it is these workers who form the basis of reformism and social democracy. The first difficulty is, of course, the fact that the interpenetration and fusion of capitals at the stage of imperialism make it virtually impossible rigorously to distinguish those parts of the working class paid by imperialist surplus profits and those paid by domestic capital. But quite apart from that, the economistic version seems to be disproved by rigorous historical and sociological studies of the class basis of those who supported and voted for the communist and socialist parties (mainly between the wars) in various capitalist countries. Their most important finding is that the two groups consisting of (a) the best paid and most skilled workers and (b) the unskilled labourers and poor workers were divided *roughly equally* between the communist party and communist trade unions and the socialist party and socialist trade unions. If there are national variations, they are far from conclusive. This does not mean that the notion of a labour aristocracy is false, only that in defining it we must refer to positions in the ensemble of the social division of labour: positions relating to the division between manual and intellectual labour reproduced in the very heart of the working class. It may well be applicable to certain agents within 'bureaucratic' trade-union organizations devoted to class collaboration.

The last problem in this context is that of *wage differentials* within the working class. While it is true that common class interest and effective class solidarity are dominant within the proletariat, mainly grouped around class organizations, it still remains true that wage differentials present a real problem. They do not, in fact, correspond to simple economic data. Marx defines *wages* as a juridical form of division of the social product, and so political elements intervene in determining the form. Considered as an ensemble in a society, from the viewpoint of abstract analysis, wages correspond to the costs of reproducing labour-power. But labour-power is here being considered in a 'general', 'abstract' fashion. It does not follow from such an analysis that every *concrete* wage differential within the working class corresponds to 'technical' necessities, i.e. to the fact that the labour-power of a group of relatively better-paid workers necessarily costs more (or as much more as the wage differential) than that of a group of lower-paid workers.

In fact, all historical and economic analyses tend to show that wage differentials coincide to an important extent with political data – the most important being *the bourgeoisie's policy of maintaining the division of the working class*. This does not, of course, mean that the bourgeoisie must effectively *succeed* in its policy of creating political differences within the working class, and that 'better paid' workers should be considered suspect. But it does demonstrate the futility of a trade-union policy of defending the wage hierarchy at all costs, on the pretext that wage differentials are simple economic necessities dependent purely and simply on the costs of reproducing labour-power. Indeed, a certain policy of defending the wage hierarchy at all costs is only one step away from the myth of the 'wage-earning class'.

Two kinds of petty bourgeoisie

The need to refer to political and ideological criteria in defining classes is particularly clear when we deal with the *petty bourgeoisie*, or the question of whether there is such a thing as a petty bourgeois *class*, and what ensembles of agents are part of it. In general it is thought that two large groups of agents with quite different positions in production are part of the petty bourgeoisie. The first is the 'traditional' petty bourgeoisie, which is tending to decline in size: these are the small-scale producers and small traders (small property). They include forms of artisanal work and small family businesses in which one and the same agent is both owner of the means of production and of labour and is the direct worker. Here there is no economic exploitation in the strict sense, inasmuch as these forms do not employ paid workers (or only very rarely do so). Labour is principally provided by the real owner or the members of his family, who are not remunerated in the form of wages. Small-scale producers derive profit from the sale of their goods and from participating in the total redistribution of surplus-value, but they do not extort surplus value directly. Secondly there is the 'new' petty bourgeoisie, which tends to increase under monopoly capitalism. It consists of the *non-productive wage-earning workers* mentioned above; we should add to it civil servants employed by the state and its various apparatuses. These workers do not produce surplus-value. Like others, they sell their labour-power and their wage is determined by the price of reproducing their labour-power, but they are exploited by the direct extortion of surplus labour, not by the production of surplus-value.

Now, these two large groups occupy different and utterly dissimilar positions in production. Can they then be considered to constitute a *class*, the petty bourgeoisie? To this there are two possible replies. The first admits the intervention of political and ideological criteria. It can be held that these different positions in production and the economic sphere do, in fact, have *the same effects* at the political and ideological level. Both smallholders and those wage-earners who live out their exploitation in the form of 'wages' and 'competition' far removed from production present the same political and ideological character-istics for different economic reasons: petty bourgeois individualism; attraction to the *status quo* and fear of revolution; the myth of 'social advancement' and aspirations to bourgeois status; belief in the 'neutral state' above classes; political instability and a tendency to support 'strong states' and Bonapartist regimes; revolts taking the form of 'petty bourgeois' *jacqueries*. If this is correct, then these *common* ideologico-political characteristics provide sufficient ground for considering that these two ensembles with different places in the economy constitute a relatively unified class, the petty bourgeoisie.

Yet, even in this case, nothing prevents us from distinguishing between *fractions of one and the same class*. As we shall see later in the case of the bourgeoisie, Marxism establishes distinctions *between fractions* of a class. Fractions are distinct from simple strata since they coincide with important economic differentiations and, as such, can even take on an important role as social forces, a role relatively distinct from that of the other fractions of their class. It might thus be possible to establish that the petty bourgeois fraction of non-productive wage-earners is closer to the working class than the fraction comprising the traditional petty bourgeoisie. In talking of fractions, it should also be possible to introduce the element of *the conjuncture*: to establish that one or other of the fractions is nearer or further from the working class according to the conjuncture. (See especially the currently important process of the proletarianization of artisanal production.) It should also be possible to introduce differentiations between *strata* of the petty bourgeoisie, with particular reference to ideologico-political divergences over and beyond the ideologico-political position basically common to the petty bourgeoisie as a whole: these divergences depend on the particular situation of the various petty bourgeois ensembles, particularly with respect to their *reproduction*. But it should not be forgotten that we are still basically concerned with a single class and that our attitude towards these fractions and strata, whether we are discussing alliances with them or predicting their political behaviour (especially their instability), should be framed accordingly. This position seems to be the more correct.

A second position has two versions: (a) The term 'petty bourgeoisie' can be reserved for the traditional petty bourgeoisie and the non-productive wage-earners be described as a new social class. But this poses difficult problems in theory and practice. Unless we consider that the capitalist mode of production has been superseded and that we are now in some kind of 'post-industrial' or 'technocratic' society which produces this new class, how can we maintain that capitalism itself produces *a new class* in the course of its development? This thesis is possible for the ideologists of the 'managerial class' and the 'technostructure', but it is unthinkable for Marxist theory. (b) Following the Communist Party, the non-productive wage-earners can be assigned not to the petty bourgeoisie but to the 'intermediate strata'. We have already considered one reason why this view is false. Another is that while Marxism uses the terms *strata, fractions and categories* to designate particular ensembles, it yet remains true that these strata, fractions and categories *always belong to a class*. The labour aristocracy is certainly a specific stratum, but a stratum *of* the working class. The 'intellectuals' or the 'bureaucracy' are, as we shall see, certainly particular *social* categories, but *they belong to the bourgeois or petty bourgeois class*. This is one of the features which distinguishes Marxism from various American conceptions of social stratification. By defining social groups in an entirely fanciful fashion, these conceptions dilute and eliminate social classes. Marxism on the other hand introduces differentiations in a rigorous fashion *within class divisions*. Fractions, strata and categories are not 'outside' or 'alongside' social classes: they form part of them.

Comprador bourgeoisie and national bourgeoisie

Reference to political and ideological criteria is also important in defining fractions of *the bourgeoisie*. Some of its fractions are to be located already at the economic level of the constitution and reproduction of capital: industrial, commercial and financial capital, big and medium capital at the stage of monopoly capitalism (imperialism). But precisely at the imperialist stage, a distinction arises which is not to be located at the economic level alone – the distinction between the '*comprador*' bourgeoisie and the *national bourgeoisie*. The comprador bourgeoisie is that fraction of the class whose interests are constitutively linked to foreign imperialist capital (capital belonging to the principal foreign imperialist power) and which is thus completely bound politically and ideologically to foreign capital. The national bourgeoisie is that fraction of the bourgeoisie whose interests are linked to the nation's economic development and which comes into relative contradiction with the interests of big foreign capital. Although this distinction only holds for certain colonial countries, it is an important one: according to the steps of the process, it is possible to envisage forms of alliance between the working class and the national bourgeoisie against foreign imperialism and for national independence, as in the case of China.

The distinction between comprador bourgeoisie and national bourgeoisie does not entirely coincide with economic position. Because of the marked interpenetration of capitals under imperialism, the distinction between capitals tied to foreign imperialism and national capitals becomes extremely vague and questionable. Moreover, the distinction does not coincide with that between big and medium capital: it is possible for big national monopolies to exist whose interests are in relative contradiction with those of foreign monopolies, just as it is possible for medium enterprises to exist which are bound by a series of sub-contracts to foreign imperialism. But with respect to developed capitalist countries, in the present phase when social relations are becoming *world-wide*, it hardly seems possible to talk of a national bourgeoisie, i.e. one which is in practice opposed to American imperialism. This is due to the increasing *internationalization* of capital, to the massive dominance of American capital, to the political and economic decadence of the bourgeois class and to the increasing tendency towards an *asymmetrical* relation of *dependence* between the old centres of imperialism (notably in Europe) and the USA: this does not mean that we cannot talk of an *internal bourgeoisie* in these countries. In particular, it is extremely doubtful whether the Gaullist policy of national independence (anyway more imaginary than real) corresponded to any kind of French 'national bourgeoisie'. What was really at stake was a divergence (purely dependent on the conjuncture) between American and French capitals, an internal problem of decolonization and neocolonization, and a plebiscitary politics in search of mass support.

Social Categories

In addition to class fractions and strata, Marxism asserts that there are *social categories*. The feature which distinguishes social categories from fractions and strata is the following: while political and ideological criteria can intervene in a more or less important fashion in determining fractions and strata, in the determination of social categories they have the *dominant role*. So the term social category designates an ensemble of agents whose principal role is its functioning in *the state apparatuses and in ideology*. This is the case, for example, with the administrative *bureaucracy* which is composed in part of groups of state functionaries (civil servants). The same is true of the group designated by the common term *intellectuals*, whose principal role is the inculcation of ideology. But it is necessary to repeat a remark made above: *social categories themselves belong to classes*: they are not groups 'outside' or 'alongside' classes, any more than they are, as categories, social classes themselves. Social categories do not, in fact, belong to one single class: their members generally belong to

various social classes. Thus, in their way of life, political role, etc., the
senior personnel, the top of the administrative bureaucracy, generally
belong to the bourgeoisie, while the intermediate and lower echelons
may belong either to the bourgeoisie or to the petty bourgeoisie. These
social categories belong to classes and do not in themselves constitute
classes: they have no specific role of their own in production. This
must be pointed out, since many sociologists and 'political scientists'
have claimed that social categories are effective classes: as in the case
of the bureaucracy, which has often been considered to be a class.

It should be noted that, although Trotsky himself attributed to the
Soviet bureaucracy an important role in the explanation of the USSR's
development, he never considered that the bureaucracy could constitute a class. But many contemporary sociologists do hold that the
intellectuals constitute a distinct class; this view is generally based on
fanciful ideas concerning the role of science as a productive force and
the intellectuals as bearers of science. The ideological function of these
conceptions is clear: they are invariably combined either with the
denial of the role of the class struggle (bourgeoisie/proletariat) as the
principal motor of the historical process (in the case of the conception
of the bureaucracy as a class) or with the denial of the working class's
fundamental role as vanguard (in the case of the conception of the
intellectuals as a class, the latter take over the role of vanguard).

Conjunctural unity and class alliances

If social categories are not classes but themselves belong to a class,
what is the point in trying to identify them? The reason is that social
categories may, because of their relation to the state apparatuses and
ideology, present a *unity of their own*, despite the fact that they belong
to various classes; and what is more, in their political functioning, they
can present a relative autonomy *vis-à-vis* the classes to which their
members belong. Thus, in the case of the administrative bureaucracy,
the internal hierarchy of delegated authority characteristic of the state
apparatuses, the particular status attributed to functionaries, the
specific internal ideology circulating within the state apparatuses
(the 'neutral state' as an arbitrator above classes, 'service to the
nation', 'general interest', etc.) allow the bureaucracy to present a
unity of its own in certain conjunctures, welding together the ensemble
consisting of members of the bourgeoisie and the petty bourgeoisie. In
this way, the bureaucracy as a whole can serve class interests different
from the interests of the classes to which its members belong,
according to relations of state power. For example, Marx stressed

that in England the 'top' of the bureaucracy belonged to the *aristocracy*, while the ensemble of the bureaucracy served the interests of the bourgeoisie. The petty bourgeois members of the bureaucracy can frequently serve 'state' interests which are contrary to their own interests. The result of all this, as Lenin recognized, is that these social categories can at times function as effective *social forces*; i.e. they have an *important* political role *of their own* in a given conjuncture. This role is not reducible to the fact of being 'in tow' behind the social classes to which their members belong or even behind the fundamental social forces, the bourgeoisie and the proletariat. The political behaviour of the ensemble of the bureaucracy under Bonapartism and fascism exemplifies this.

This analysis is important because it has two consequences bearing on the question of the working class's alliances. In its indispensable alliance with the 'intellectuals' and the intermediate and subordinate strata of the civil service, the working class must relate to them in a specific fashion. They often have particular interests which cannot be reduced to – for example – the general interests of the petty bourgeoisie to which they belong. For example: guarantees of freedom of intellectual, scientific and artistic production, of freedom of expression, of circulation of information are important to the intellectuals. But on the other hand, we must never lose sight of the relation between social categories and social classes. For social categories belong to social classes; and despite their internal unity, the *breaks and contradictions* which show themselves within social categories often coincide with the different class membership of their various members. In the administrative apparatus, these breaks take the form of contradictions between upper echelons (bourgeois) and lower echelons (petty bourgeois). In the case of the intellectuals, the breaks are sometimes due to the different ideologies fashioned and transmitted by them, as for instance the sharp contradictions which have recently appeared within the French teaching profession.

We must also remember that during these alliances, the members of the state apparatus or intellectuals swinging over to the working class's side still remain petty bourgeois, considered both overall and from the point of view of their *class membership* (as opposed to their *class origin*). This should certainly not lead to sectarianism: there are frequent cases of intellectuals who side politically and ideologically with the working class, are active militants in its class organizations and for whom the criterion of class membership becomes blurred and even disappears. But this is a different problem and relates to the question of the working class's organization. The fact remains that in the alliance with the intellectuals, they are, considered overall, still petty bourgeois. They often show the fundamental characteristics of the petty bourgeoisie: political instability and leftist extremism coupled with rightist opportunism, etc.

There are therefore two equally false and dangerous extremes against which we must guard, in dealing with the question of social categories. *Overestimating* the importance of their class membership is the first: this leads to pronouncing a once-and-for-all sentence on an intellectual as a 'son of a bourgeois or petty bourgeois', whilst neglecting the importance of his practical conduct and his political and ideological choices. The second is *underestimating* the importance of their class membership: treating them as homogeneous units along- side and outside classes. It is possible simultaneously to adopt both these false courses, as do the positions currently adopted by the Communist Party and the CGT and the direction now being taken by SNESUP.[3] Overestimating the importance of the 'intellectual' class membership leads to slogans like 'students/sons of bourgeois/leftists = Marcellin'.[4]

Despite verbal caveats, social categories are here treated as unified entities, alongside and outside classes: the class divisions which appear within them are neglected. Thus appeals are made to the state administrative corps as a whole, from the technocratic heights to the subordinate echelons. It is as if this was a unified social category apart from the direct representatives of big capital (Pompidou = banker) – even though the upper personnel's 'technocratic ideology' is alluded to, while their bourgeois class membership is glossed over. This position is even clearer so far as the 'teaching body' is concerned: it is held to be an irreducible unity which represents all teachers from full professors to assistants with short-term contracts and which, bearing the general label 'intellectuals', is thought to have the same claim as others to be a possible ally of the working class.

The class character of intellectuals

Social categories are also included in the notorious *intermediate strata*, which have already been discussed. As one of the intermediate strata, the category of intellectuals is considered to be alongside and outside classes. The problem raised by their class membership is conjured away and the policy adopted towards them is no more than a demagogic appeal to a broad and indiscriminate alliance between the working class and the intellectuals: this is despite the fact that the term 'petty bourgeois' is automatically applied to any intellectual siding with the working class who diverges in the slightest from the CP leadership. This is meant to be an irrefutable demonstration of the source of such divergences.

That being said, the question of the alliance between the working class and the intellectuals is now arising in a particularly sharp form in advanced capitalist societies. This has happened partly because of the considerable enlargement of the category of intellectuals (in the broad sense of the term), but above all, because of the *ideological crisis* preceding or accompanying the political crisis of contemporary imperialism. More and more intellectuals are breaking free from the grip of bourgeois ideology and are thus capable of being enlisted to the working class's cause. The traditional form of proletarian/intellectual alliance, based exclusively on the intellectuals' class membership and reducible to a working-class/petty bourgeoisie alliance disregarding the intellectuals' status as a social category, is now probably inadequate for the solution of the problem.

Different solutions have been proposed, from Garaudy's conception of an historical bloc (going back to Gramsci's analyses) to the theses recently published by the Italian *Manifesto* group. These solutions have points in common and present a series of common problems. In general, the alliance between the working class and the intellectuals (in the broad sense) is considered by them to take priority over the traditional alliance between the working class and the poor and medium peasantry (but this goes equally for the CP's current position). Certainly, the two objectives do not exclude each other, but this position represents a kind of readaptation of the Third International's old schema: first, a workers' front (within the working class) and then, based on it, a popular front (alliance between the working class and the other classes). But, in this case, the alliance constituting the basic bloc is that between the workers and the intellectuals; and it is on that basis that the alliance between the bloc and the peasants is built. This is a questionable position, even if we take into account the exodus from the countryside and the peasantry's drop in numbers. It also helps to propagate a series of ideologies of intellectuals as quasi-workers (science = a productive force). It should be noted by the way that in Gramsci's conception of the 'historical bloc', the fundamental relation was that between workers and peasants. A second problem is that the importance of the term 'historical bloc' (uniting workers and peasants) is that it is distinct from a simple alliance. While 'alliance' implies that the members, with their specific interests and their own organizations, are distinct and autonomous, 'historical bloc' means that the members have interests which are in the long term identical and that they are bound by an organic link. There is nothing, however, to prove that the intellectual petty bourgeoisie is now seeing its own interests dissolving into those of the working class, despite the fact that it is increasingly capable of taking its stand alongside the working class. Although this solution is intended to overcome the distinction between workers and intellectuals as reproduced within political organizations, it remains an entirely verbal one. The real debate concerning the forms of working-class organization remains open.

The Dominant Classes

It is essential to analyze the dominant classes, in particular the bourgeoisie. The important problem here concerns the division of the bourgeoisie into industrial, commercial and financial fractions. Under monopoly capitalism, the division into big and medium capital is superimposed on the former division without entirely abolishing it. In talking of the bourgeoisie as the dominant class, it must not be forgotten that we are really dealing with an alliance between several dominant fractions of the bourgeoisie sharing in political domination. Moreover, at the start of capitalism, this power alliance, which may be called the power bloc, often encompassed several other classes, notably the landed aristocracy. This alliance between several classes and fractions *which are all dominant* can only function regularly under the *leadership* of one of those classes and fractions. This is the *hegemonic fraction* which unifies the power alliance under its leadership. The hegemonic fraction is the one which guarantees the general interest of the alliance and whose specific interests are particularly guaranteed by the state.

While the dominant fractions' internal contradictions and their internal struggle to occupy the hegemonic place have a secondary role *vis-à-vis* the principal contradiction (bourgeois/proletariat), their role is still important. In fact, as Marx observed in the *Eighteenth Brumaire*, the various forms of state and forms of regime are marked by the changes in hegemony between the various bourgeois fractions. Still less can *economic domination* and *political hegemony* be identified in a necessary and mechanical fashion. It is possible for a fraction of the bourgeoisie to have the dominant role in the economy without thereby having political hegemony. An important instance of this was the lengthy economic domination of big monopoly capital while political hegemony belonged to one or other fraction of medium capital. We can see the importance of these remarks for an examination, for example, of Gaullism. The important point to stress is that the power alliance between dominant classes and fractions under the leadership of a hegemonic fraction (to whose interests the state apparatus in particular corresponds) is *always a function of the form of bourgeois domination*. In particular, when we speak of the hegemonic fraction, we must remember that it is not the only dominant force, but simply the hegemonic force in an ensemble of fractions which are all equally dominant. For example, when Marx said that under Louis Bonaparte the industrial bourgeoisie was the economic fraction, he never meant that the other fractions of the bourgeoisie were excluded from political domination. The same also holds in particular for the relation between big and medium capital in contemporary capitalist countries. In them, big capital is the hegemonic fraction, but this does not mean that medium capital is excluded from political power: as a dominant fraction it shares in political power under the hegemony of big capital. The contradictions between big and medium capital are simply the contemporary form of the contradictions between dominant bourgeois fractions.

Certain contemporary analyses of 'state monopoly capitalism' and the 'anti-monopoly alliance' make it necessary to emphasize this point. These analyses are nearly always restricted to the hegemonic fraction, big capital, and fail to mention the other dominant bourgeois fractions. The failure to distinguish between the hegemonic fraction and the dominant fractions has led to the following result: it is held that big capital alone occupies the place of political domination, from which the other bourgeois fractions are henceforth excluded. The question is of importance because of the political consequences which can be seen to flow from it: namely, advocacy of a broad 'anti-monopoly alliance' 'liberal bourgeoisie', 'sincere democrats', etc., for the occasion, in order to expel the '200 families' (considered to be the dominant fraction) from power. The working class's strategic alliances (an entirely different thing from tactical compromises) are thereby extended as far as dominant bourgeois fractions – medium capital. This, broadly speaking, is the path of 'advanced democracy' advocated by the western CPs.

Certainly, things are not presented in quite such a crude fashion, but they are still clear enough in the *Traité d'économie marxiste*, mentioned above. In this, whenever political domination is discussed, only the big monopolies are mentioned. In contrast, whenever capital other than big capital is discussed, it is always small capital with which an alliance is expressly sought. But we must establish agreement on terms. If by small capital we mean the *petty bourgeoisie* of crafts, manufacture and commerce, it is correct to seek an alliance with it since the petty bourgeoisie *does not belong to the bourgeoisie as such*, i.e. to the fractions of the bourgeoisie. But, in fact, the term small capital is here used for quite another purpose. In speaking only of big monopolies and small capital (i.e. conjuring away medium capital), it is implied that everything which does not belong to the big monopolies (the one dominant fraction) is automatically part of small capital and is capable of allying with the working class: medium capital being thus included in small capital. On the rare occasions when the *Traité* talks of medium capital (Vol. I, p. 223), it explicitly locates it *on the same side* as small capital, supposedly sharing with it a contradiction with big capital.

Hegemonic class distinct from reigning class

There are difficult problems involved in locating the hegemonic fraction of the power bloc with precision, especially as the hegemonic class or fraction may be distinct from the *reigning* class or fraction. By reigning class or fraction is meant that one from which the upper personnel of the state apparatuses is recruited, i.e. its political personnel in the broad sense. This class or fraction may be distinct from the hegemonic class or fraction. Marx gives us a prime example in the case of Britain at the end of the last century. There, the hegemonic class fraction was the financial (banking) bourgeoisie, while the upper personnel in the administration, army, diplomatic corps, etc., was recruited from within the aristocracy, which thus occupied the position of reigning class. The same case can also arise under the hegemony of big monopoly capital, where the upper personnel often continues to be recruited from within medium capital, from the medium bourgeoisie. In exceptional cases, it is even possible for the political personnel to be recruited from within a class which is not itself part of the power bloc. An important example of this was fascism, where, under the hegemony of big capital, it was the petty bourgeoisie (the reigning class) which provided the upper cadres of the state apparatuses through the medium of the fascist party.

The distinction between hegemonic class or fraction and reigning class or fraction, which depends ultimately on the strategy of alliance and compromises necessary for the establishment of hegemony, is important. Its neglect leads to two consequences. It becomes impossible to reveal the real hegemony lying beneath the appearances of the political arena, the conclusion being that that class which occupies the top of the state apparatus is the hegemonic class or fraction. For example, in the case of fascism, several social-democratic authors and politicians have been led to consider it as the dictatorship of the petty bourgeoisie. Misled by the fact that the petty bourgeoisie occupied the place of reigning class, they identify it with the position of real hegemony, occupied by big capital. But there are other forms of state too in which the position of the reigning fraction, occupied by the petty bourgeoisie, has often masked the political hegemony of big capital coexisting with the petty bourgeoisie's reign: the most obvious example is Roosevelt's New Deal.

A second consequence of neglecting the hegemonic/reigning distinction is that the overriding aim becomes to discover political hegemony in the automatic recruitment of the top of the state apparatuses from within the hegemonic fraction itself. This tendency shows itself today in formulations concerning 'state monopoly capitalism', which is held to represent 'the fusion of the state and the monopolies into a single mechanism'. The scientific proofs put forward consist of hidden relations of kinship and background between members of the big monopolies and the tops of the state apparatus and political organizations. This type of argument proceeds from theorems like 'Pompidou = Rothschild's banker'. It cannot be denied that a tendency is underway in which the top of the apparatus is increasingly occupied by the actual members of big monopolies. But this is far from being a general or even a predominant tendency. Counter-examples are provided by the political hegemony of big monopolies which is often nowadays realized under social-democratic governments (Austria, Germany, Sweden, Britain under Wilson), i.e. under a political personnel originating mainly from the medium or even petty bourgeoisie, to say nothing of the labour aristocracy. Even in France, because of the particular way in which the bureaucracy and the state corps are constituted and because of the Jacobin type of compromise between the bourgeoisie and petty bourgeoisie, the top of the state apparatus is still to a large extent occupied by persons originating from the medium or even petty bourgeoisie.

But though this is an important and undeniable fact, it does not prevent the establishment of political hegemony by big capital. If we deny it and consider that political hegemony must be identified with the position of the reigning class or fraction, we open ourselves to attacks which are both unjust and unnecessary. The correspondence between the interests of the hegemonic fraction (in this case the big monopolies) and state policy is not, in fact, based on any personal ties. It depends fundamentally on a series of *objective coordinates* concerning the ensemble of the organization of the economy and society, under the sway of the big monopolies, and the state's objective role with regard to it. The state is not a simple instrument which the hegemonic fraction has to hold physically, in a personal way, in its hands, if it is to adapt it to its interests. The problem of the possible differentiation between reigning and hegemonic class and fraction is connected with the question of the relative autonomy of social categories, such as the administrative bureaucracy, *vis-à-vis* the classes and fractions to which their members belong. Because of the objective role of the state, these categories thus serve hegemonic interests which often contradict their own class or fractional interests.

This, of course, does not mean that the fact that the upper state personnel belongs to one or another class or fraction is unimportant. For example, it is not without reason that there is now a growing interpenetration between the members and direct agents of the monopolies and the state personnel: it facilitates the monopolies' grip on the state. But it must be noted that this is not the most important question. A 'popular government', for instance, could not limit itself simply to modifying the upper ranks of the state personnel, thinking that good political intentions are enough to get things changed. The real task is to change the very structures of the state and of society. On the other hand, it is also obvious that these transformations cannot be carried through while the state apparatus and personnel are left intact. For structural transformations may remain completely ineffective, so long as they run up against reaction on the part of the state personnel. The importance of these questions emerges from a re-reading of Lenin's texts concerning the employment of bourgeois experts in the apparatus of the workers' state.

The ideological apparatuses of the state

Some observations are necessary on the form in which the contradictions between dominant, hegemonic and reigning classes and fractions are expressed within the *state apparatus*. The important point to bear in mind is that the state is composed of *several apparatuses*: broadly, the *repressive apparatus* and the *ideological apparatuses*, the principal role of the former being repression, that of the latter being the elaboration and incubation of ideology. The ideological apparatuses include the churches, the educational system, the bourgeois and petty bourgeois political parties, the press, radio, television, publishing, etc. These apparatuses belong to the state system because of their objective function of elaborating and inculcating ideology, irrespective of their formal juridical status as nationalized (public) or private. The repressive apparatus contains several specialized branches – army, police, administration, judiciary, etc. It has already been stated that the terrain of political domination is not occupied by the hegemonic class or fraction alone but by an ensemble of dominant classes or fractions. Because of this, the contradictory relations between these classes and fractions are expressed in the form of *power relations* within the apparatuses and their branches. These latter therefore do not all crystallize the power of the hegemonic class or fraction, but may express the power and interests of other dominant classes or fractions. It is in this sense that we can talk of a relative autonomy (a) of the various apparatuses and branches *vis-à-vis* each other within the state system and (b) of the ensemble of the state *vis-à-vis* the hegemonic class or fraction.

In the case of an alliance or compromise between the bourgeoisie and landed aristocracy in early capitalism, the bourgeoisie had its seat of power in the central bureaucratic organization, while the landed aristocracy had its in the Church (in particular the Catholic Church). Such dislocations can also appear between the actual branches of the repressive apparatus: for example, before the arrival of Nazism in Germany between the two World Wars, the big landowners had their seat of power in the army, big capital in the judiciary, while the administration was shared between big and medium capital. In the case of the transition towards the hegemony of big capital, the administration and the army often constitute the seat of power (the 'military-industrial complex'), while Parliament continues to constitute medium capital's seat of power: that is one of the reasons for the decline of Parliament under monopoly capitalism. Because of their function, the ideological apparatuses in particular possess a greater relative autonomy than the repressive apparatus and they can sometimes provide seats of power for classes other than the dominant classes. This is sometimes true of the *petty bourgeoisie*, because of the alliances and compromises made between it and the dominant bloc. In France especially, these compromises have taken on a great importance for historical reasons, and the *educational system* has for a long time constituted a state apparatus, as it were, 'made over' to the petty bourgeoisie. The petty bourgeoisie has thus for a long time been set up as a *class supporting* the system.

None of this means that the capitalist state is an ensemble of separate parts, expressing a 'share-out' of political power among the various classes and fractions. On the contrary, over and beyond the contradictions within the apparatuses, the capitalist state always expresses a *specific internal unity, the unity of the power of the hegemonic class or fraction*. But this happens in a complex fashion.

The functioning of the state system is assured by the *dominance* of certain apparatuses or branches over others: and the branch or apparatus which is dominant is generally that one which constitutes the seat of power of the hegemonic class or fraction. Thus, when hegemony is modified, modifications and displacements also occur in the dominance of certain apparatuses and branches *vis-à-vis* others. It is moreover these displacements which determine the changes in forms of state and forms of regime.

Thus every concrete analysis of a concrete situation must evidently take into account both relations of class struggle and real power relations within the state apparatuses, the latter being generally concealed beneath formal institutional appearances. Precise analysis of power relations within the apparatuses can help us to locate the hegemonic fraction with accuracy. For example, by noting the dominance of one apparatus or branch over others and by also noting the specific interests served by that apparatus in a dominant fashion, we can draw some conclusions concerning the hegemonic fraction. But this must be a *dialectical* method: it is possible to start from the other side, by locating the hegemonic fraction, with its privileged relations to an apparatus or branch, within the ensemble of relations of a society; and in this way to solve the question of which is the dominant apparatus in the state, i.e. the apparatus by means of which the hegemonic fraction holds *the real controlling levers* of the state. *But it is also clear that in the complex relation between class struggle and apparatuses*, it is the class struggle which has the principal role. Institutional modifications do not lead to social movements, as a whole series of institutionalist sociologists believe: it is the class struggle which determines how the apparatuses are modified.

Expanded Reproduction of Social Classes

The enormous importance of this last remark will become clear if we consider it from the point of view of the expanded reproduction of social classes. Social classes have existence only in the class struggle, which has an historical, dynamic dimension. It is only possible to constitute and even delimit classes, fractions, strata and categories by considering them in the historical perspective of the class struggle. This immediately raises the problematic of their reproduction. For some time now, a certain number of us have been analyzing the important question of the reproduction of social relations. *As the reader will realize, this question, with all its implications, could be correctly grasped only within the problematic of social classes and the class struggle set out above.* Parallel to our analysis of state power, we emphasized one of the decisive roles of the state apparatuses (in particular, of the state ideological apparatuses) – namely, the role they play in the reproduction of social classes. So in these final remarks, I do not intend to go over this question in general again. I shall try rather to elucidate some aspects of it and give a warning against certain misinterpretations which may arise. I shall take as my example the role of the educational apparatus in the reproduction of social classes (an example which has recently been subject to Marxist analysis).

The state apparatuses including the school *qua* ideological apparatus, do not create class division but they contribute to it and so contribute also to its expanded reproduction. It is necessary to bring out *all* the implications of this proposition: not only are the state apparatuses determined by the relations of production, but furthermore they do not command the class struggle, as the whole institutionalist tradition claims: *it is rather the class struggle at all its levels which is in command of the apparatuses.* The exact role of the ideological apparatuses in the reproduction of social relations (including relations of social production) is, in fact, of supreme importance: for it is their reproduction which dominates the process of reproduction as a whole, particularly the reproduction of the labour force and means of labour. This is a consequence of the fact that it is the *relations of production,* themselves constitutively linked to the relations of politico-ideological domination/subordination, which dominate the *labour process* within the production process.

Reproduction of positions, reproduction of agents

The expanded reproduction of social classes (of social relations) involves *two aspects which cannot exist in isolation from one another.* First, there is the expanded reproduction of the positions occupied by the agents. These positions mark out the *structural determination* of classes, i.e. the manner in which determination by the structure (relations of production, politico-ideological domination/subordination) operates in class practices. The way in which classes are determined also governs the way in which they are reproduced: in other words, as Marx himself emphasized, the very existence of a mode of production involving bourgeoisie and proletariat entails the expanded reproduction of these classes. Secondly there is the reproduction and distribution of the *agents* themselves to these positions. This aspect of reproduction, which involves the questions of who occupies a given position, i.e. who is or becomes a bourgeois, proletarian, petty bourgeois, poor peasant, etc., and how and when he does, *is subordinate to the first aspect* – the reproduction of the actual positions occupied by the social classes: i.e. it is subordinate to the fact that in its expanded reproduction, capitalism is reproducing the bourgeoisie, proletariat and petty bourgeoisie in a new form in its current monopoly phase or to the fact that it is tending to eliminate certain classes and class fractions within the social formations where its expanded reproduction is taking place (e.g. the small-holding peasantry, petty bourgeoisie, etc.). In other words, while it is true that the agents themselves must be reproduced – 'trained' and 'subjected' – in order to occupy certain places, it is equally true that the distribution of agents does not depend on their choices or aspirations but on the very reproduction of these positions. It is important to emphasize that the distinction between the two *aspects* of reproduction (reproduction of positions and of agents) *does not coincide* with the distinction between reproduction of social relations and reproduction of labour-power. These two aspects are features of the ensemble of reproduction, inside which the reproduction of the social relations under discussion is dominant. But in the ensemble of reproduction, including the reproduction of social relations, the reproduction of places constitutes the *principal aspect*.

The state apparatuses, including the school *qua* ideological apparatus, have different roles relative to these two aspects of reproduction. The structural determination of classes is not restricted to places in the production process alone (to the economic situation of 'classes-in-themselves') but extends to all levels of the social division of labour: so the apparatuses enter into the process of determining classes as the *embodiment* of ideologico-political relations (of ideologico-political domination). It is in this way that, through their role of reproducing ideologico-political relations, they enter into the reproduction of the *positions* which define social classes. It should therefore be mentioned that the superstructure's role is not, as is sometimes maintained, limited to reproduction alone, any more than the base's role is limited to the production and reproduction of the means and products of labour: in fact, it extends to the reproduction of social relations. As in all cases of reproduction, the role of the apparatuses in reproduction is explicable only by reference to its role in the actual constitution of a mode of production and of its relations of production, i.e. its role in the actual production of social relations.

So the state ideological apparatuses enter actively into the reproduction of the positions occupied by the social classes. But if we are not to fall into an idealist, institutionalist view of social relations according to which social classes and the class struggle are the product of the apparatuses, we must recognize that this aspect of reproduction goes beyond the apparatuses, generally escapes their control and in fact assigns them their limits. We can say that there is a *primary, fundamental* reproduction of the social classes in and by the class struggle, in which the expanded reproduction of the structure (including the production relations) operates and which governs the functioning and the role of the apparatuses. To take an intentionally schematic example: it is not the existence of a school forming proletarians and new petty bourgeois which determines the existence and reproduction (increase, decrease, certain forms of categorization, etc.) of the working class and the new petty bourgeoisie; on the contrary, it is the action of the production relations, of complex forms of economic ownership and possession on the labour process, i.e. the production process articulated with respect to political and ideological relations, and thus the economic, political and ideological class struggle, which has the school as its effect. This explains why the process of reproduction by means of the apparatuses is marked by internal struggles, contradictions and frictions. It is in this way that we can understand the other side of the question: just as the expanded reproduction of social relations depends on the class struggle, so also does their revolutionary transformation.

Thus the fundamental reproduction of social classes does not concern only positions in the relations of production, i.e. social relations of production. It is no 'economic self-reproduction' of classes over and against an ideological and political reproduction by means of the apparatuses. It is no less than a process of *primary reproduction* in and by *the class struggle at all stages* of the social division of labour. This reproduction of the social classes (like their structural determination) is also concerned with the (social) political and (social) ideological relations of the social division of labour: these latter have a decisive role in their relation to the social relations of production. The reason is that the very social division of labour is not only concerned with political and ideological relations but also with the social relations of production within which it has dominance over the technical division of labour. This is a consequence of the fact that the production relations have dominance over the labour process within the production process.

To say that the primary reproduction of social classes depends on the class struggle also means that its concrete forms depend on the *history* of the *social formation*. Any given reproduction of the bourgeoisie, of the working class, of the peasant classes, of the old and new petty bourgeoisie depends on the class struggle in that formation. For example, the specific form and pace of the reproduction of the traditional petty bourgeoisie and smallholding peasantry under capitalism in France depends on the specific forms of their long-standing alliance with the bourgeoisie. It is therefore only possible to locate the apparatuses in this reproduction by referring to the class struggle: the particular role of the school in France can only be located by referring to the alliance between bourgeoisie and petty bourgeoisie which has for so long been a mark of the French social formation. Moreover, while the expanded reproduction of the *positions* occupied by the social classes 'invokes' the state ideological apparatuses (especially in the ideologico-political sphere), it is not limited to them.

Let us return to the case of the division between manual and intellectual labour mentioned above. That division, which has a role in determining positions in the social division of labour, is by no means limited to the economic domain. In that domain, it should be noted, it has no role of its own to play in class division, since productive workers (the proletariat) who produce surplus-value/commodities are not to be identified with manual workers alone. The division between manual and intellectual labour can be grasped only when it is extended to the *political and ideological relations* of (a) the social division of labour within enterprises, where authority and direction of labour are linked to intellectual labour and the secrecy of knowledge, and (b) the ensemble of the social division of labour – relations which contribute to defining the positions occupied by the social classes. But clearly it is neither the school nor any other ideological apparatus which create this division; nor are they the sole or primary factors in reproducing it, even though they do enter into its reproduction where (in their capitalist form) they appear as the effect of this division and its reproduction in and by the class struggle. In other words, the reason why the school reproduces the division between manual and intellectual labour *within itself* is this: because of its capitalist nature, the school is already situated in a global setting relative to a division (and a reproduction of the division) between manual and intellectual labour; and the reproduction of the school as an apparatus is functionally determined by that division. It is a division which goes beyond the school and assigns it its role: the separation of the school from production is linked to the direct producer's separation from and dispossession of the means of production.

In talking of state apparatuses, we must recognize that these apparatuses neither create ideology nor are they even the sole or primary factors in reproducing relations of ideological domination/

subordination. Ideological apparatuses only serve to fashion and inculcate the dominant ideology. Thus, Max Weber was wrong in claiming that the Church creates and perpetuates religion: rather it is religion which creates and perpetuates the Church. In the case of capitalist ideological relations, when Marx analyzes the fetishism of commodities as relating directly to the process of valorization of capital, he offers us an excellent example of the reproduction of a dominant ideology which goes beyond the apparatuses: this was noted by Marx in his frequent references to a 'correspondence' (implying a distinction) between 'institutions' and 'forms of social consciousness'. So the role of ideology and of the political in the expanded reproduction of the positions occupied by the social classes here directly corresponds to the class struggle which governs the apparatuses. It follows from what has been said above that the reproduction of positions in the relations of ideologico-political domination does indeed invoke the apparatuses, but it also invokes apparatuses *other* than the state ideological apparatuses – most importantly *the economic apparatus itself*. As a unit of production in its capitalist form, an enterprise is also an apparatus, in the sense that, *by means of the social division of labour within it* (the despotic organization of labour), the enterprise itself reproduces *political and ideological relations* concerning the places of the social classes. In other words, the reproduction of the all-important ideological relations is not the concern of the ideological apparatuses alone: just as not everything that goes on in 'production' is reserved for the 'economic', so the ideological apparatuses have no monopoly over reproducing the relations of ideological domination.

Let us now turn to the second aspect of reproduction, the reproduction of *agents*. It encompasses (as two moments of one and the same process) *the qualification/subjection* of agents to enable them to occupy positions, and *the distribution* of agents to the positions. It is especially necessary to grasp exactly how the two aspects of reproduction (of positions and agents) are articulated, if we are to see the inanity of the bourgeois problematic of *social mobility*. In this respect, the state ideological apparatuses, in particular the school, have a decisive function.

The reproduction of agents, in particular the notorious 'qualification' of the agents of actual production, is no simple technical division of labour (technical education) but rather an effective qualification/subjection which extends into politico-ideological relations. The expanded reproduction of agents in fact corresponds here to an aspect of the reproduction of social relations which impresses its mark on the reproduction of the labour force. While this does entail a particular role for the school, we must remember that it is not just an on-the-spot technical education, but the very process of qualification/subjection as such, which goes on within *the economic apparatus* as well, since the enterprise is more than a simple production unit. And this entails a particular role for the enterprise as precisely that apparatus which distributes agents within itself. In the case of *immigrant workers*, the economic apparatus actually has the dominant role: but it is not limited to them. If we forget the role of the economic apparatus and consider that agents have already been completely distributed in school, *prior* to the economic apparatus, we shall fall into the same type of one-way regressive explanation which considers that this complete distribution has already occurred in the family, *prior* to the school. Capitalist classes are not educational castes any more than they are hereditary castes. This regressive explanation does not hold for the relation between family and school because the family remains an active force during schooling; and similarly it does not hold for the relation between school and the economic apparatus because the school remains an active force in agents' economic activity.

It is important to see that the second aspect of reproduction is subordinate and indissolubly linked to the first. This is because a given type of reproduction and distribution of agents to positions depends on the expanded reproduction of those positions. It should not be forgotten that it is the labour market (as the expression of the expanded reproduction of production relations) which has the dominant role in distributing agents in the ensemble of the social formation. This is the case even when there is not, strictly speaking, a unified labour market, i.e. when the labour market's demands are directed to a sphere which is already compartmentalized – due partly to the specific action of the state ideological apparatuses (e.g. an unemployed graduate will not fill a place vacated by a semi-skilled worker). The reason is that, underlying the distribution aspect as well, there is a constitutive relation between distributive apparatuses and labour relations. Amongst other things, this constitutive relation imposes *limits* to the action of the state ideological apparatuses in compartmentalizing the labour market. For example, it is not the school which brings it about that *peasants* are the principal occupants of the spare places in the working class. On the contrary, it is *the exodus from the countryside*, i.e. the elimination of places in the countryside, plus the expanded reproduction of the working class, which governs the school's role in this respect.

Finally, in the case of *expanded* reproduction, in so far as the second aspect of reproduction is subordinate to the first, *we must define the direct effects which the actual places have on the agents: this comes down to locating the primacy of the class struggle over the apparatuses.* Strictly speaking, we do not find agents who are in origin (in a world 'before' or 'outside' school) 'free' and 'mobile', who circulate among the places following the orders of the ideological apparatuses, the ideological inculcation and the education which they receive. It is true that in the capitalist mode of production and in a capitalist social formation, social classes are not castes, that agents are not tied by their origin to determinate places and that the school and the other apparatuses have an important role of their own in distributing agents to the places. But it is also true that the effects of distribution show themselves in the fact that by means of the ideological apparatuses, the vast majority of bourgeois (and their children after them) remain bourgeois and the vast majority of proletarians (and their children after them) remain proletarians. This shows that the school is not the sole or principal reason for distribution taking this form. It is caused rather by the effects which the positions themselves have on the agents, effects which go beyond the school and *beyond the family itself.* We are not, as some current debates suggest, trying to decide which comes first − family or school − in a causal sequence. We are not even considering the 'pair' family/school as the basis of these effects of distribution. We are faced rather with a *series of relations* between apparatuses, whose roots are deep in the class struggle. In other words, the primary distribution of agents is tied to the primary reproduction of the positions occupied by the social classes. According to the stages and phases of the social formation, that primary distribution assigns to a given apparatus or series of apparatuses its own proper role which it is to play in distributing agents.

9

INTERNATIONALIZATION OF CAPITALIST RELATIONS AND THE NATION-STATE

The new phase of imperialism and the rise in the class struggle in the imperialist metropoles have raised a series of key questions for revolutionary strategy: what are the new relations between one imperialist metropolis and another and what are their effects on the state apparatuses? Can one at the present time speak of a *national state* in the imperialist metropoles? What are the relations between these states and the 'internationalization of capital' or the 'multinational firms'? Do new superstate institutional forms tend to be substituted for the national states or, again, what are the modifications of these states which permit them to fulfil the new functions required by the extended reproduction of capital on the international scale?

These questions are, as we know, particularly acute in the light of the problem of the EEC and the 'political future' of Europe. They are of decisive importance, as it is clear that the existing state, now more than ever the centre of revolutionary strategy, can only be studied in relation to the current phase of imperialism and its effects actually within the zone of the metropoles. But it is just as well known that Marxist research has been less concerned with these questions than with questions about the relations between centre and periphery and about peripheral social formations. Not least among the reasons for this are political positions and the 'Third World' ideology. So, whilst the effects of current imperialist domination within the dominated and

* First published in French as 'L'Internationalisation des rapports capitalistes et l'État-Nation' in *Les Temps Modernes*, no. 319 (February 1973). This translation is taken from *Economy and Society*, vol. 3 (1974), pp. 145–79. Translated by Elizabeth Hindess.

dependent social formations are beginning to be seen clearly, its effects within the imperialist metropoles are studied much less.

Even so, two main tendencies can be detected, albeit schematically, in the positions taken with respect to this last question.

1. The first represents what might be called the current left version of Kautskyite 'ultra-imperialism'. Various forms of this position are associated with authors such as Sweezy,[1] Magdoff, Nicolaus, Jalée,[2] etc. They have in one way contributed greatly to the clarification of the currently dominant role of the United States among the capitalist countries but they underestimate the interimperialist contradictions based on uneven development and their only line of demarcation within the imperialist chain is between 'centre' and 'periphery.' The analyses of the relations between the imperialist metropoles depend on the principle of pacification and integration under the uncontested domination and exploitation of American capital. This domination is itself conceived *in the same analogical mode* as the relation between imperialist metropoles and dominated and dependent countries. It is thus allied to the type of 'neo-colonization' that has the relations between the United States and Canada both as a borderline case and as its exemplar. On this view we are witnessing the rapid destruction, not to say the quasi-disappearance, of the powers of the national states of the imperialist metropoles, be it under the domination of the American superstate or under the domination of large American capital or of 'international' capital liberated from the shackles of the states.[3]

2. In the second case, on the other hand, there are two theses in which the analyses often diverge, but in this case at least they are dependent on a common foundation. We can therefore discuss them together here *without any intention of amalgamating them.*

Firstly, there are authors such as Mandel,[4] Kidron, Warren, Rowthorn, and Valier[5] in France. Their thought is in no danger of misrepresentation if it is said that for them the current phase of imperialism is in no way marked by a change in the structure of the relations between the imperialist metropoles. Here again, the sole line of structural cleavage allowed in the imperialist chain is the one between the centre and the periphery, and this cleavage is itself understood in a uniform manner throughout the history of imperialism. The interimperialist contradictions actually within the centre have the same meaning at the present time as in the past and are placed in a context of states and 'autonomous' and 'independent' bourgeoisies struggling for hegemony. It would thus be a matter of 'national bourgeoisies' and of 'national states' with purely external relations, with a tendency towards internationalization only affecting *at its limit* relations of exchange alone. The dominance of the United States over the imperialist metropoles is seen as the essence of the matter, in the same analogical manner as was Great Britain's in the past. Even now, on this view, we are once again witnessing a radical challenge to this hegemony in the emergence of equivalent 'anti-imperialisms', those of the European Common Market and of Japan. The enlarged EEC in particular is considered to be a 'cooperation' and an 'internationalization' of European capitals leading to a European supranational state for the elimination of the supremacy of American capital, a thesis in fair contradiction with the thesis of 'autonomous national states'.

Then there are the analyses of the western Communist parties, in this case the French CP.[6] The existing relations within the centre are thought to be founded not on modifications of the imperialist chain but on modifications of the capitalist mode of production (CMP) into national 'state monopoly capitalisms' which are juxtaposed and added on; at its limit the process of internationalization is here thought to reach only the notorious 'productive forces'. The relations are thus understood essentially as reciprocal external 'pressures' between bourgeoisies and autonomous and independent national states elsewhere. The EEC and 'United Europe' are considered the manifestation of an increased domination of American capital. This domination, however, is conceived in some sense under the form of 'grafts' of cosmopolitan foreign bodies onto the European national state monopoly capitalisms, and the role of the national state towards the profit of American or cosmopolitan capital is conceived under the form of functions 'superadded' to the 'national' functions of these states.

We shall have occasion later to discuss the more precise positions within these modes and their political implications. Let it be said now, however, that they do not succeed in identifying either the existing modifications in the imperialist chain or their effects on the relations between metropoles and in particular on the national states. We shall restrict ourselves here to the case of the European metropoles, both because of its political importance for us here and now and because of certain important particularities which are present in the case of Japan, even though tendentially they do not appear as exceptions to the rule at all.

Given the existing state of research, an adequate analysis of the current phase of imperialism demands that the problems be studied from scratch and that a series of questions be opened up which may seem intractable or difficult. The reader is asked to excuse us and to grant that it is the only way to clarify the political debate.

The Current phase of Imperialism and the Domination the United States

Periodization

In its extended reproduction the CMP is characterized by a *double* tendency: its reproduction within a social formation where it 'takes root' and establishes its dominance, and its extension to the exterior of this formation, the two aspects of this tendency acting *at the same time*. Because of its characteristic limits the CMP can exist only by extending its relations of production and by extending its limits in this way. If this double tendency characterizes the CMP from its beginning, it takes on a very particular importance in the imperialist stage. This stage, which accentuates the tendency towards a decline in the rate of profit, is characterized by the pre-eminence, in the extension to the exterior of the CMP, of *the export of capitals* over the simple export of commodities. The imperialist stage, corresponding to monopoly capitalism, is marked by the displacement of dominance from the economic to the political (the state) both in the social formation and in the imperialist chain.

The imperialist chain is itself marked by *uneven development*. In each link the chain is reflected in a specificity of each social formation. This specificity depends on the forms taken by the dominance of the CMP on an international scale over the other modes and forms of production within each social formation. Indeed, the reproduction of the CMP in its double tendency bears witness to the fact that the CMP can exist only by suppressing the other modes and forms of production and by appropriating their elements (labour-power, means of labour). It is the articulation, in its reproduction, of the CMP and of the modes and forms of production it encounters in the social formations that produces the uneven development.

This dominance of the CMP has complex effects of *dissolution/conservation* (since it is a matter of a class struggle) on the other modes and the forms of production which it dominates.[7] The differential forms taken by these effects on an international scale mark the *phases* of the imperialist stage; they thus correspond to precise forms of accumulation of capital, that is, to precise forms of world relations of production and of international imperialist division of labour.

From the beginning of imperialism, therefore, the imperialist chain has been marked by a fundamental cleavage between on the one hand *the imperialist metropoles* and on the other hand *the dominated and dependent social formations*. This cleavage, which is founded on the very structure of the imperialist chain, is radically different from the relation of the colonial type at the beginning of capitalism and later the capitalist/commercial type of relation, principally through the constitution of the world market and of the export of commodities. It is no longer a matter of the economic juxtaposition of social formations in relatively external relations. The process of imperialist domination and dependence now appears as the reproduction, actually within the dominated social formations and under specific forms for each of them, of the *relation* of domination which links them to the imperialist centre.

This position is of maximum relevance to our project and we can now try to state it more precisely. A social formation is dominated and dependent when the articulation of its own economic, political and ideological structure expresses constitutive and asymmetrical relations with one or more social formations in a position of power in relation to that social formation.[8] The organization of class relations and state apparatuses in the dominated and dependent formation reproduces within itself the structure of the relation of domination and thus expresses in a specific manner the forms of domination characterizing the class(es) in power in the dominant social formation(s). This domination corresponds to both indirect (through the position of the dominated formation in the imperialist chain) and direct (through direct investments) forms of *exploitation* of the popular masses of the dominated formations by the classes in power in the dominant formations. This exploitation is articulated with the exploitation they suffer at the hands of their own classes in power. Each phase of imperialism is marked by different forms of realization of this domination and dependence.

By taking these elements into account, we can determine the periodization of the imperialist stage into phases. Let it be made clear immediately that this is not a matter of a periodization in the sense of a necessary 'succession' following a scheme of chronological linear 'incrementalism'. These phases, which we shall try to discern in the fundamental traits of the *extended reproduction* of the CMP, are the historical effects of the class struggle.

On the other hand, we want to raise a supplementary problem which is posed by the periodization of imperialism when imperialism is itself a particular stage of the CMP. The periodization into phases of imperialism *itself* is legitimate to the extent that the CMP presents a certain particularity with respect to the 'pre-capitalist' modes, namely, being marked by *two stages* which are distinguishable by a different articulation of its structure. But that indicates that the periodization of imperialism in the enlarged reproduction of the CMP must be discerned in the relations between imperialism (monopoly capitalism) and *both* the pre-capitalist modes and forms of production *and* the 'pre-imperialist' stage of the CMP (which for convenience will be designated 'competitive capitalism').

We can thus distinguish the following phases of imperialism. *The phase of transition* – from the competitive capitalist stage to the imperialist stage. This phase extends from the end of the nineteenth century to the inter-war period; in the metropoles of imperialism, it covers the period of *unstable equilibrium* between competitive capitalism and monopoly capitalism. In the extension of the CMP towards the 'exterior' and the establishment of the imperialist chain, this phase covers relative equilibrium between the form of commercial-capitalist domination of the dominated formations by means of the export of commodities and domination by means of the export of capitals. During this period, both the imperialist metropoles and the relations metropoles/dominated formations are marked by an unstable equilibrium between the dominance of the economic and the dominance of the political, of the state.

The phase of consolidation of the imperialist stage – initiated between the two wars, in particular after the crisis of 1930, the stabilization or initiation of the fascisms, and Roosevelt's New Deal. Within the metropoles, monopoly capitalism establishes its dominance over competitive capitalism, connoting the dominance of the political, of the state, within these formations. But in the contradictory effects of dissolution/conservation which monopoly capitalism imposes, be it on the pre-capitalist forms (simple market form of production, traditional petty bourgeoisie, etc.) or on competitive capitalism (non-monopoly capital), the effects of conservation still override those of dissolution. In the imperialist chain it is the export of capitals that overrides the export of commodities, and it is the political that prevails in the relations metropoles/dominated and dependent formations.

It must be pointed out, however, that during these phases and to unequal degrees the CMP characterizing the imperialist chain dominates the dependent formations principally by means of their insertion in that chain. The imperialist centre/periphery social division of labour is essentially between town (industry) and country (agriculture). This permits, precisely, a domination by the CMP of formations in the interior of which modes of production other than the CMP can often predominate. It is under this predominance (for example, feudal predominance i.e. the domination of the great 'feudal' landowners) that there intervenes the reproduction in the dependent formation of the relation of domination linking it to the centre.

As for the relation between the imperialist metropoles during these phases, it is a matter of interimperialist contradictions often giving way to the alternating predominance of one of the metropoles over the others: Great Britain, Germany, USA. But this predominance is *essentially* founded both on the type of dominance and exploitation which the metropolis imposes on its own empire of dominated formations and on the rhythm of development of capitalism within the metropolis. The sole line of polarized demarcation relating to the structure of the imperialist chain is that between metropoles and dominated formations.

The current phase of imperialism – established progressively after the end of the Second World War and itself marked by various stages of class struggle. It is during this phase that within the imperialist metropoles the domination of monopoly capital is exercised over the pre-capitalist forms and over competitive capitalism, though this is to unequal degrees, through the effects of dissolution which override those of conservation. This does not, however, mean that the CMP in its monopoly form tends to become 'exclusive' in the metropoles. The forms in question continue to exist but henceforth in the form of 'elements' (traditional petty bourgeoisie, peasant proprietorship of land parcels, medium capital) that are restructured and directly subsumed under the reproduction of monopoly capitalism.

This phase corresponds to modifications of the relation metropoles/ dominated formations. Henceforth the CMP dominates these formations not simply from the 'exterior' and by means of the reproduction of the *relation* of dependence *but establishes its direct domination within them. The mode of production of the metropoles is reproduced in a specific form in the very interior of the dominated and dependent formations.* This presents no obstacle to the ability of the effects of conservation, to unequal degrees and counter to what happens in the metropoles, to override those of dissolution in the double tendency imposed by the internal domination of the CMP over the other modes and forms of production in these formations. What further characterizes this phase is that this induced reproduction of the CMP within these formations extends in a decisive manner to the sphere of their state apparatuses and their ideological forms.

The current forms of this dependence (the development of under-development, peripheral industrialization and blockages in the economy, internal disarticulation of social relations, etc.) have been widely studied in the last few years.[9] Less attention has been paid to the modifications of the imperialist chain in the relations between the metropoles. In fact, as we shall see shortly, the forms of accumulation of capital and of international division of labour that are at the base of this extended reproduction of capitalism in the relation metropoles/dominated formations introduce here, in this phase, a crucial modification. At the very time when the line of demarcation and cleavage between metropoles and dominated formations is becoming accentuated and is getting deeper, we are witnessing the establishment of a new line of demarcation in the metropoles' camp between the USA on the one hand and the other metropoles of imperialism, in particular Europe, on the other. The structure of domination and dependence of the imperialist chain organizes the relations of even the formations of the centre. In fact, this hegemony of the USA is neither analogous to the hegemony of one metropolis over the others in the preceding phases nor does it differ from it only from a purely quantitative point of view; it appears in the establishment of relations of production characterizing American monopoly capitalism and its domination in *the very interior* of the other metropoles, and in the reproduction within the other metropoles of this new relation of dependence. It is this *induced reproduction* of American monopoly capitalism within the other metropoles and its effects on their modes and forms of production (pre-capitalist, competitive capitalist) that characterizes the current phase and that equally implies the extended reproduction within them of the political and ideological conditions of the development of American imperialism.

But it nonetheless remains a matter of the lines of demarcation being asymmetrically divided into two. This new dependence is not identical to the dependence that characterizes the relations metropoles/periphery, precisely to the extent that these metropoles continue to constitute real centres of capital accumulation and to dominate the peripheral formations

With respect to these characteristics, this current phase of imperialism, taking various turnings, is marked by a prodigious rise in the struggles of the popular masses on the world front, *both* in the peripheral formations *and* in the imperialist metropoles, particularly in Europe. It is the accumulation of these struggles that, at *determinate conjunctures* of this phase, confers the character of *crisis* on the entire system.

The signs of the domination of American capital

If it is seen in this light, it is advisable first to establish the characteristics of this situation before going on to analyze it in greater depth.

(a) The first striking fact is the regular *proportionate* increase after Second World War in the global volume of capital investments abroad by American capital. In 1960, the foreign investments of the USA already counted for 60 per cent of the world total whereas in 1930 they reached only 35 per cent. Although it has a much less spectacular rhythm this tendency has been confirmed, and the gulf separating the USA from the other metropoles became deeper still in the period 1960–68, the dates for which we have comparative statistical data.[10]

But even more important are certain new characteristics of these investments.

(b) From now on it is no longer the peripheral formations but the European metropoles that in a massively increasing manner are becoming the privileged place of American direct investments; these quadrupled in the years 1957–67 in Europe, whereas they not quite doubled in Canada and hardly increased at all in Latin America. This, moreover, corresponds to the general tendency of the capitals of the countries in the centre to be invested in the interior of that zone.

(c) Considerable differences occur in a parallel way with respect to the forms of investment of these capitals. It is a matter of the growing predominance of *direct investments* over *investments in securities*. Although this distinction is in fact relative, it is important as an index since it corresponds directly to modifications in the relations of production. By direct investments we mean both investments in fixed capital and investments which involve, or in the short or long term tend towards, *taking control* of the firms and enterprises; although the percentages vary according to the statistics and the different institutions, investment in excess of 25 per cent of the shares of a company is in general regarded as direct investment. Investments in securities, however, concern ordinary purchases of bonds or short-term Stock Exchange and financial transactions. Currently, direct investments, constitute approximately 75 per cent of the exports of private capitals of the main industrial countries, as against only 10 per cent before 1914.[11]

Now, whilst the total *flux* of global investments from Europe to the USA is more or less in equilibrium with the flux from the USA towards Europe (the argument favoured by Mandel, Rowthorn, etc.), approximately 70 per cent of the American investments in Europe are direct investments, as against only a third of the European investments in the USA.[12] This also indicates that American capital in Europe is in fact geared down by the reinvestment of profits on the spot. As a matter of fact, contrary to what happens in the peripheral formations, a considerable part (approximately 40 per cent) of the profits is here reinvested on the spot or in the same zone.

(d) A progressively increasing part of foreign investments by the developed countries reverts to the processing industries (manufactured products) in comparison with the extraction industries (primary materials) and the 'services' sector, commerce, etc. This is especially *processing industries*, the proportionate growth of American capital in Europe in relation to the global export of American capital in this sector is even more striking. Whereas in 1950 Europe received only 24.3 per cent of American capital in this sector, it received 40.3 per cent in 1966. In a parallel manner, whereas the overwhelming part of American direct investments in Europe is concerned with the processing industries, *hence directly productive capital*, a minor part (approximately a third) of the direct European investments in the USA is concerned with directly productive capital, the greater part going towards the 'services' sector, insurance, etc.[13]

(e) These American investments in Europe are linked to the concentration and centralization of capital. They come from the most concentrated branches and sectors in the USA.[14] In Europe they head for the sectors and branches with a strong concentration and contribute, furthermore, to the acceleration of the rhythm of concentration; the European subsidiaries of American companies are in the majority of cases situated in very concentrated branches where the subsidiary most often occupies a dominant position.[15] Finally, the sectors and branches in which investments are made are the ones that experience fastest expansion and offer the most advanced technology. They are, that is, the ones with the highest productivity of labour and the dominant characteristics of intensive exploitation of labour by means of the rise in the organic composition of capital; 85 per cent of the American investments in the sphere of processing industries are concerned with metallurgy and mechanical industries, chemistry and synthetic products, the electrical industry, electronics, etc. The rhythm of expansion and of growth of these capitals is between 8 per cent and 10 per cent per annum, that is, approximately double the growth of the European GNP. Further, if one examines the directions in which these capitals develop, it is clear that in the majority of cases they seem to be taking over concessions of licences and patents from the European firms whilst engaging in the direct exploitation of these technological advantages.

(f) The export of capitals and the hegemony of American capital are just as concerned with *the centralization of money capital*, the large banks and properly financial holdings. From this situation as a whole, moreover, there derives the role that the dollar played for a long time in the monetary sphere and that is currently being replaced by the Eurodollar market.

It must be noted, however, that the tendency towards the 'fusion' of industrial and banking capital into finance capital in the monopoly capitalism stage does not eliminate the distinction, in the cycle of extended reproduction of capital, between the *concentration of productive capital* and the *centralization of money capital*. The accumulation of capital and the rate of profit in the cycle as a whole *are determined by the cycle of productive capital*, capital which produces surplus-value. This is contrary to a fairly widespread conception which, through a terminological confusion, identifies 'finance' capital with dominance of 'banking' capital. Finance capital designates the *process* of reproduction in 'fusion' of fractions of capital and the mode of their functioning in this 'fusion'. This implies the distinction between monopoly capital with industrial dominance and monopoly capital with banking dominance. Further, this determinant role of productive capital does not prevent the process of finance capital from taking place *historically* under the economic aegis and under political hegemony, be it of industrial capital itself (as in the case of the USA) or of banking capital (as in the classic case of Germany). It is therefore in the cycle of productive capital that the modifications of the current phase of imperialism are precisely readable, which explains the privileged position we have accorded it here.

Finally these modifications have repercussions to a certain extent on the current organization of world foreign commerce with regard to *the export of commodities*, a tendency which is inherent in capitalism in its tension of the market and which in spite of being dominated by the export of capitals in the imperialist stage does not weaken. In world commerce the proportion of internal commerce between 'developed countries' is increasing in relation to the proportion of commerce *between* these countries and the countries of the periphery. The proportion of internal transfers in the centre went from 46 per cent of world commerce in 1950 to 62 per cent in 1965 and is increasing very much faster than commerce between centre and periphery (+17.5 per cent in 1969). Corresponding to this evolution, moreover, is the growing proportion of *manufactured products* in world commerce. These represented approximately 66 per cent of world commerce in 1969 as against less than 50 per cent before 1963.[16]

We must, however, make an incidental comment here. It is true that in the imperialist countries we are witnessing a proportionate increase in the export of commodities on the part of the other imperialist countries, in particular Europe, compared with the USA. Here, then, is the *principal argument* of the Mandel tendency to doubt the supremacy of American capital. We shall say a few words on the significance of this phenomenon in our conclusion but let it be pointed out at once: (a) that the decisive role in imperialism reverts to the export of capitals; (b) that, on the one hand, Mandel's analyses do not take into consideration the commodities directly produced in Europe by firms under American control and which are thus 'substituted' for American exports and that on the other hand his analyses count as 'European' exports the exports of firms under American control in the countries of Europe. The full importance of this becomes clear if one takes account of the fact that huge amounts of the American investments in Europe are in the sectors that are themselves geared towards export, even including exports in the form of re-exporting to the USA under a European label. Dunning thus estimates that a third of the growth in European exports in advanced technology products between 1955 and 1964 comes from enterprises controlled by American capital and that in 1980 approximately a quarter of all British exports may come from these enterprises.

Returning to the question of the export of American capitals, the facts outlined above are important only as signs of modifications currently affecting, in the cycle of social capital, the international concentration of capital (relations of production) and the imperialist social division of labour on the world front (the labour process). In this perspective the facts can be estimated at their proper value.

Their significance absolutely cannot, therefore, be reduced to the notorious question of the 'percentage' of the rise in American direct investments in the European countries in relation to the global rise of investments, including autochthonous investments, in these countries, a form of argument dear to the Mandel tendency and also to the various bourgeois specialists on the subject. If this percentage is truly an index of the fact that the European countries are not mere 'colonies' of the USA it is in no way indicative of the new process of dependence if it is considered in isolation. But consider it in this way for a moment. According to the official statistics this percentage seems relatively insubstantial, being placed somewhere around 6.5 per cent (1964 figures). There is, however, every reason to think that the basis of these data is considerably skewed, to the point where it has limited meaning.

To begin with, these data more often than not, though this depends on the countries, only take account of American investments coming either from the flux of new capitals from the USA or from reinvestments through the auto-financing of American subsidiaries in Europe. They thus disregard the fact that American capital has recourse to the *European market of capitals* (the issue of bonds) and to the Eurodollar market. This currently accounts for two thirds of the rise in American real investments in Europe. Next, these data generally treat as direct investments those in excess of 25 per cent of the assets of a firm, whereas in the existing context of concentration of capital and of socialization of the labour process a lot less than that is often enough to guarantee control by American capital. Again, these figures relate to direct investments throughout the economy, whereas if one considers only the industrial sector (productive capital) the percentage is considerably higher. *Finally, and most importantly,* these figures do not take account of the American investments made in Europe under cover of firms which are legally 'European' but which are under American control and economic property. This is particularly true in the case of Switzerland and her investments in the EEC countries. The importance of this will be understood if one takes into consideration the fact that from 1961 to 1967 the proportion of American investments in the foreign direct investments in France was 30 per cent but Switzerland's investments took up 29 per cent. Braun, the Director of the EEC Commission, adds these two together to arrive at the figure of 59 per cent of USA direct investments.[17] It is also known that this phenomenon takes on considerable proportions with the entry of Great Britain into the EEC.

But this, to repeat, is a different question from that of percentage. We must therefore come to the current modifications in the international concentration of capital and in the imperialist social division of labour. It is the action of the new forms of world relations of production on the labour process that currently marks the changes in the imperialist chain and in the relations USA/Europe.

The international socialization of labour processes
and the internationalization of capital

(i) The new forms of international imperialist division of labour correspond to the direction which the current concentration of capital impresses on the socialization of the labour process and productive forces on a world scale. The concentration of capital on an international scale and the constitution of financial empires date in fact from the beginning of the imperialist era. As was also true in the case of the process of concentration in the interior of a social formation, they imply a distinction between formal legal property and real economic property (joint-stock companies) which has been understood in the ideological form of a 'separation of private property and control'. This distinction still continues today. The important modifications have a bearing on the current articulation of *economic property* and of *possession*, namely, on the forms of the relations of production themselves.

In fact, the form of production which prevailed at the time of the progressive extinction of the entrepreneurial capitalist was either that of cartels and international financial *holdings* or that of a capital having at its disposal one determinate *unit of production* (a centre for the appropriation of nature) in one external country or several 'separate' units of production in different countries. This consequently massively dominant form implies a *relative distinction and off-centring* between the relations of possession (management and control of a determinate labour process) and economic property (power to affect the means of production and to allocate resources and profits for this or that utilization) this economic property concentrating several *separate* units of production (and possessions) under a single control. What characterizes this process in the current phase of imperialism, on the other hand, is the constitution under a single economic property of effective *complex units of production*[18] *with closely articulated and integrated labour processes (integrated production) with its various establishments spread over several countries.* This integrated production presents no obstacles – quite the contrary – to the diversification of finished products and is not limited to one branch. Even exchanges between the different establishments are not fixed on the basis of the market price but constitute exchanges 'internal' to the units (transfer price). In other words, we see the reabsorption of the distance between economic property and possession under a different form. However, this does not prevent the *plurality of powers* required by these relations from being distantiated in new ways and their exercise by different supports and agents.

The reabsorption of the distance between economic property and possession must be understood at the level of the whole process, that is, branches, industries, inter-branches, *and* primary materials and commercialization, the upstream and downstream of production. Further, and as we shall see, this reabsorption has, on the one hand, the general consequence of *extending* (and sometimes shattering) *the traditional limits* of the 'enterprises' on the international front, and, on the other hand, a particular *effect*, namely, the constitution of *multinational industrial firms*. This is only one effect, however, for these firms only partially cover the *process* of unifying complex units of production by means of branches and industries. But these firms constitute an excellent example of the current integration of the labour process. It is to these modifications in particular that the pre-eminence of direct investment over investment in securities corresponds.

The integration of the labour processes in the interior of a firm on an international scale can take several forms. It can be a matter of vertical integration, with each subsidiary in a country committed to one stage of production, to one series of component parts of a product, or to one group of products. IBM is the classic case. It can just as well be a matter of horizontal integration, with each establishment or subsidiary specializing from end to end in the production of products which they exchange among themselves. Ford is a case in point. This integrated production, furthermore, is often partly realized *over several branches* in the current forms of *conglomerate*. Whether vertical or horizontal integration, these forms of socialization of the labour processes constitute in any case the most marked tendency,[19] even if they do not yet dominate the international concentration of capital. In fact they form part of a much wider process of international socialization of labour.

(ii) This socialization of labour on the international scale is therefore not principally due to factors of the 'technical' order – the 'technological revolution' – but operates under the sign of important modifications in world relations of production. Consequently, it can be seen in the full extent of the imperialist social division of labour only through the existing forms of *internationalization of capital*, although it is important to be very careful here, because of the different ideologies which gravitate around the interpretations of multinational firms. What are the particular characteristics of this internationalization in the current phase when these firms are only one of its effects?

(a) The development of the bases of exploitation of a particular capital (or of several capitals in combination) *in several nations*.

(b) The marked tendency towards the combination under a single economic property *of capitals coming from several different countries*.

But it must be added immediately that, in the overwhelming majority of cases where this legal and economic participation of capitals from several nations is found, this internationalization is achieved under the decisive dominance of the capital coming from a determinate country. It is this capital that concentrates in its grasp the single economic property. Witness the fact that the 'joint ventures' which are supposed to represent an 'egalitarian fusion' of the property of the capitals of different countries are still, in their legal appearances, quite exceptional; for example, Royal Dutch/Shell, Dunlop/Pirelli, Agfa/Gevaert.

This is owing to the very nature of capitalist relations of production as expressed in the current process of concentration, capital being not a 'thing' but a relation of production. It is the *place* circumscribed by the relations of economic property and possession that determines the different powers stemming from it. The occupation of this place by different capitals reproduced in the interior and in the exterior of a social formation is in no way an 'association' but depends on a *relation of force*. Contradictions and competition between the components of a concentrated capital continue, the more so as the narrow correspondence currently being established between economic property and possession and which is the counterpart of the current process of international concentration works precisely towards a unified control and a central directing instance under a determinate capital.

(c) The internationalization of capital described above *is effected under the decisive dominance of American capital*.

In the case of productive industrial capital, in 1968, 55 per cent of the assets of multinational firms in the exterior of their countries of origin belong to American capital, 20 per cent to British capital, the rest being shared among European and Japanese capitals. Contrary to Mandel's argument, this is accompanied by the massive tendency of an *extrapolated fusion* of the European capitals *with* American capital, in preference to a fusion of these capitals with themselves, and the EEC has merely accentuated this tendency. Further, note that even in the case of a combination of European capitals it is rarely a matter of a fusion, more rarely still a matter of integrated production, but more often than not a matter of various 'ententes', Fiat/Citroën for example, between limited companies and securities transactions, whereas the exact opposite is the case when it is a matter of concentrations under the aegis of American capital.[20]

The imperialist social division of labour
and the accumulation of capital

These are the modifications that mark the new forms of imperialist social division of labour and the relations between imperialist metropoles. They correspond to new forms of accumulation of capital on a

world scale. In fact, by requiring that the centre-periphery line of
demarcation be split in two by the new line of demarcation crossing
the very metropoles of imperialism, and by displacing the bases of
exploitation and accumulation towards the zone of the centre, these
modifications take place in response to the *existing conditions* of the
tendency for the rate of average property to fall. Whereas exports of
capitals previously appeared to be linked principally to the control of
primary materials and to the extension of markets, *in essence they are
currently responding to the necessity of the development of imperialist
monopoly capital by taking part in every relative advantage from the
direct exploitation of labour.* (This is not to deny the presence of the
necessity of the extension of markets, as, for example, in the case of the
investment of American capital in Europe.) *All the modifications*
which have been under discussion here as implying the dominance
of American capital over the other metropoles *tend towards a single
goal*, namely, a rise in the rate of exploitation so as to counteract the
tendency towards a fall in the rate of profit. It is here in particular that
we find the underlying cause both of the interiorization of the
reproduction of the dominant capital actually within the 'external'
bases of exploitation and of the new forms of articulation: economic
property/possession which correspond to the existing forms of domination of monopoly capital over the other modes and forms of
production on the international scale and to the new forms of
exploitation.

In fact, this rise in the rate of exploitation is the result *both of the
level of wages and of the productivity of labour*, comprising the degree
of technological development, the qualification of labour tied to the
degree of development of the productive forces, etc. The level of wages
and the productivity of labour are, *in the long term*, tied. In other
words, the rate of exploitation and of surplus-value is not just
measurable by the level of wages but also *by the intensive exploitation
of labour* (new technical processes, diversification of products, intensification of labour and work rhythms). In a different context of the
development of productive forces, a higher wage in real and nominal
value can correspond to a weaker proportion of the value produced
and, thus, to a greater exploitation compared with a lower wage in the
context of a lesser productivity of labour.

Now we know that if the wages of the peripheral zone are lower
than those of the countries in the centre, the productivity of labour is
considerably higher in the centre than in the periphery. But this still
does not explain the displacement of the bases of exploitation of
capital towards the metropoles. This is explained by *the displacement*

of the weight of exploitation towards the intensive exploitation of labour in the current phase of imperialism and at the level of world accumulation. This displacement is itself a function of the main characteristic of monopoly concentration, namely, *the rise in the organic composition of capital* which consists in the increase of constant capital in relation to variable capital (wages costs) and in the diminution of living labour in relation to 'dead labour' (incorporated in the means of labour). This rise in the organic composition of capital being in inverse proportion to the rate of profit, it is here that the current tendency towards technological innovations is inscribed. But labour is still the basis of surplus-value, and it is this that explains the current tendency of an increase in the rate of surplus-value principally by means of an intensive exploitation of labour which is directly tied to the productivity of labour (relative surplus-value).

The new forms of world relations of production and of international socialization of labour, running concurrently with this intensive exploitation of labour on the world front, are thus concentrated in the new forms of the *imperialist social division of labour*. In the order of exploitation, this division no longer goes through the traditional line of demarcation: 'town-industry-metropolis/country-agriculture-periphery'. It is doubled by a division actually within the *industrial sector of productive capital* (with the process of 'industrialization' of agriculture on the international front also taken into account). It is here that the displacement of the exports of capitals towards direct investments and towards processing industries is inscribed, together with the importance of manufactured products in external commerce.

This new imperialist social division of labour certainly concerns the relations centre/periphery. It corresponds to the 'development of under-development' and to peripheral industrialization, and it produces in the peripheral formations dislocations and deformations of a new type, namely, the general sectioning off of the formations with capital investments in forms of light industry (principally concerned with consumer goods) and with inferior technology, the maintenance of weak qualification of labour power, that is exploitation of labour principally by means of low wages, and also the existence of isolated centres with a high concentration of capital and productivity of labour. *But the new division of labour is mainly concerned with the new demarcation between the USA on the one hand and the other imperialist metropoles on the other*. It has important effects, firstly, on the disparities in and the hierarchies of wages in these formations (the disparities in wages between the USA and Europe here playing a peculiar role), secondly, on the level of qualification and the disparities in the qualification/disqualification process of labour within the metropoles, thirdly, on technological disparities, fourthly, on the disparities between the forms of unemployment and the role of immigrant labour, etc.

The new division of labour and the displacement of the dominant towards the intensive exploitation of labour thus expresses itself under different forms of exploitation following the two lines of demarcation. Whereas the exploitation of the popular masses of the peripheral formations by the dominant classes of the metropoles is effected principally in an indirect manner (through the place of the formations in the imperialist chain and its polarization) and secondarily in a direct manner (exploitation of the labourers of these countries by foreign capital directly invested there), exploitation by American capital of the popular masses in Europe is effected principally in a direct manner and secondarily in an indirect manner.

The forms of European dependence

It is not, however, the analysis of the different aspects of this division of labour actually within the imperialist metropoles that is our objective here but the illustration of the dependence implied by these aspects. By taking account precisely of the new division of labour, it is clear that the domination of American capital cannot be evaluated according to the percentage of means of production which it formally controls within each European nation, nor can it be done according to the individual role of multinational firms under American control. These firms are only one of the effects of the existing process and reflect this domination *only very partially*. This can be shown with just a few examples.

First of all, the American direct investments in Europe take on a quite other meaning if one considers international concentration according to *branches*, and if one takes account of the fact that they are principally centred on certain branches which they have a tendency to control on a massive scale.[21] But this control is not simply to be measured in the importance of American firms in Europe in these branches, and the new division of labour cannot be reduced to the division of labour 'in the interior' of the multinational firms and their establishments in different countries. In fact, these branches are in general the ones where the process of socialization of labour and the international concentration of capital are the most advanced. In this context, as is patently the case for the mechanical and electrical industries in particular, a *standardization of base materials* (which does not exclude their variation and diversification in the finished products) is often seen *on a world scale*. This standardization is far from corresponding to mere 'technical' necessities; more often than not, it is imposed by the American industry dominant in these branches. A 'European' firm which would like to be competitive in this sphere has to 'restructure' its production and its labour processes in the light of this standardization and on the basis of the internationalization of the branch. But it is very often here that the firm becomes enmeshed in its insertion into the process of dependence and is forced into multiple forms of subcontracting in the face of American capital, even if it has not been legally absorbed by an American firm. In the same context, dependence extends to the fact that, in the branches and sectors where American capital leaves its mark on the entire labour process, European capital engages in the purchase of patents and licences which have been carefully selected by American capital.

This process is even more important if one takes account of the fact that the existing socialization of labour processes and of concentration of capital are not simply measurable within a single branch but extend to different industrial branches, with American capital succeeding in establishing its dominance over different branches by means of its dominance in a single branch. This is patently the case in the sphere of the electrical industry. Janco has recently shown that on the current scale the use of computers by European industry, a sphere in which the pre-eminence of American capital is known, is far from corresponding to technical needs; in fact, their use often verges on the superfluous or even the uneconomical.[22] Their use corresponds to the control of certain labour processes by American capital and serves only to accentuate this domination; further, this domination is not limited to the single sphere of computers but extends by these means to certain sectors where these computers are used on a massive scale.

With the international imperialist division of labour thus reflected in the highest degree in the *social division and organization* of the entirety of the labour processes (as the analyses of Gorz have amply shown, this social division dominates the 'technical division'),[23] we can see how the existing division in favour of American capital is not limited to a division 'within' the American multinational firms. In fact there is every reason to think that with the new forms of social division currently extending, through certain of their features, to

sectors and branches of 'European industry', in particular the reproduction under new forms of the division intellectual labour/
manual labour (forms of qualification/disqualification of labour,
and the place of engineers and technicians in relation to a particular
application of technology), the new forms of authority and of division
of the tasks of decision and execution in the 'advanced' European
enterprises (the notorious problem of their *modernization*) correspond to and reinforce the control of the labour processes in their
entirety by American capital.

Finally, in the framework of the concentration of capital, it is only
necessary to point to the fact that in certain branches and sectors,
electro-mechanics for example, the internationalization of the cycle of
productive capital is expressed by the process, and its forms, that
American productive capital (Westinghouse, General Electric, etc.)
imposes on the concentration of European productive capital, namely,
the movement of 'internal' restructuration of European capital in
accordance with the enlarged reproduction of American capital, which
must lead in the end to its inclusion in it. Further, this illustrates the
illusory character of the considerations according to which an increased 'interior' accumulation of a European country, or even of
European capitals, would be the best means of resisting American
penetration; such a flight forward often serves only to precipitate them
into the grasp of American capital.

We could multiply examples, but it is clear that the process can only
appear in its full extent if we also take account of the international
centralization of money-capital and of the role of the big American
banks. We can, however, summarize by saying that apart from
displacements of the relation of economic property towards American
capital under cover of the maintenance of an 'autonomous' European
legal property (minority control), the following displacements are
often to be seen at the present time.

(a) Displacements towards American capital of the (or certain of
the) powers stemming from economic property under cover of the
maintenance of 'autonomous' European property, as in the case of
multiple and complex subcontracting. Sometimes this goes so far as to
overlay the effective *actual expropriations* which are not yet visible
and whose effects will only be felt gradually.

(b) Displacements towards American capital of the (or certain of
the) powers stemming from the relation of possession (control and
management of the labour process), even in the cases of 'autonomous'
European economic property. Owing to the current tendency for the
space between economic property and possession to be reabsorbed,

this leads in the long term to a displacement towards American capital of economic property.

The process can, therefore, be understood only by taking account of the retreat, the shattering even, of the traditional frontiers between 'firms' and 'enterprises' on the international front.

The coordinates relating to the enlarged reproduction of the dominant imperialism actually within the other imperialist metropoles are not, however, solely concerned with the relations of production. They imply the extension of the *ideological conditions* of this reproduction in the interior of these metropoles. In order to understand this process it is absolutely necessary to see that ideology is not concerned solely with 'ideas', the articulated ideological units, but is concretely embodied in a whole series of practices, know-how, modes and rituals to do with the economic sphere as well.

This is a doubly important point in that it relates equally to differences between on the one hand, the ideological dependence of the peripheral formations with respect to the centre and, on the other hand, the ideological dependence of the metropoles with respect to the United States. In the case of the peripheral formations, it is because of their original dependence with respect to the centre and because of the ideological under-determination of their own bourgeoisies that the extension within the peripheral formations themselves of the ideological forms of the centre provokes a profound disarticulation of the ideological sectors in their entirety which has been understood in the false image of 'dualist society'.

In the case of the relation between the imperialist metropoles and the United States, the extension is mainly concerned with the practices, rituals and know-how articulated on production. One has only to mention the notorious problems of 'know-how' ('savoir-faire' could hardly express it better!), *management*, techniques of 'organization', the mass of rituals gravitating around information-processing − it would be a long list. These practices do not in fact correspond to some sort of 'technological' rationality. It is often a matter of ideological forms which, in their above-mentioned effects on the social division of labour, overlay the complex dependence of the metropoles on the dominant imperialism.

The National State

After the previous remarks, it is now possible to deal with the question of the national state in the imperialist metropoles and to see in which respects the various positions on this subject outlined at the beginning of this article are erroneous.

The state and the question of the national bourgeoisie

Once again it is necessary to denounce myths living on even in the framework of Marxist analyses. Even the customary formulations of the problem, typified by questions such as, 'What can, or can't, the state do *in the face of* the large multinational firms?' and 'What is the degree or form of destruction of the state's powers in the face of the possibilities of international giants?' (formulas favoured by Servan-Schreiber), *are fundamentally false, so true is it that the institutions or the apparatuses do not 'possess' 'power' proper but do nothing but express and crystallize class powers*. So the question is displaced and becomes, in the first place, the question of the relations between the European bourgeoisies and American capital. And to ask exactly which bourgeoisies are involved here is to pose the question of the *national bourgeoisie*.

To begin with, notice that the national bourgeoisie is to be distinguished from the *comprador bourgeoisie* in more ways than on the purely economic front. It is impossible to delimit the national bourgeoisie without referring to the political and ideological criteria of its structural class determination. The national bourgeoisie cannot just be understood as an 'autochthonous' capital radically distinct from 'foreign' imperialist capital, nor by reference to the solely economic relations separating them. In fact the imperialist stage from its very beginning shows a tendency towards the international interpenetration of capitals. And the distinction between national and comprador bourgeoisie is not, as is often thought, coextensive with the distinction between industrial and commercial capital. What is more, the national bourgeoisie cannot be understood just by reference to the criteria of the market, that is, as the autochthonous bourgeoisie which operates on the 'interior' national market. It is possible at one and the same time to find sectors of the industrial bourgeoisie and of this commercial bourgeoisie which are entirely held in fee by foreign capital, in the same way that it is possible, as is shown in certain Latin American countries, to find landowning bourgeoisies which export monoculture products, such as coffee, but which have assumed the characteristics of national bourgeoisies. Finally, and even more significantly, the distinction between national and comprador bourgeoisie certainly is not coextensive with the distinction between monopoly capital (large capital) and non-monopoly capital (medium capital). It is possible to find large monopolies functioning like national bourgeoisies and sectors of medium capital which are themselves entirely held in fee by foreign capital.

These remarks do not mean that the economic contradictions between foreign and autochthonous capital do not play a determinant role in the delimitation of the national bourgeoisie but they do mean that this is not sufficient. In fact, by *national bourgeoisie* is understood the autochthonous fraction of the bourgeoisie that, starting from a certain type and degree of contradictions with foreign imperialist capital, occupies a relatively autonomous position in the ideological and political structure, and thus presents a proper unity. This position of the national bourgeoisie, relevant to its structural class determination, does not reduce to its class position but has effects on it. In determinate conjunctures of anti-imperialist struggle and national liberation the national bourgeoisie is susceptible to the adoption of class positions which include it in the *people* and it is therefore prone to a certain type of alliance with the popular masses.

On the other hand, by *comprador bourgeoisie* is traditionally understood the bourgeois fraction that does not have its own base of capital accumulation, that operates in some sort as a simple 'intermediary' of foreign imperialist capital (which is why the 'bureaucratic bourgeoisie' is sometimes included in the comprador bourgeoisie), and that from the simultaneously economic, political and ideological point of view is entirely held in fee by foreign capital.

It can be seen clearly, therefore, that these two concepts are insufficient for the analysis of the bourgeoisies of the imperialist metropoles in the face of American capital in the current phase of imperialism. In fact, sticking to a single distinction in this case is fatally conducive to an economist reduction of the case and to false conclusions as follows.

(a) Either economic contradictions of interest are affirmed between sectors of the autochthonous bourgeoisie and foreign imperialist capital, owing above all to the fact that the autochthonous bourgeoisie offers an industrial foundation and its own bases for the accumulation of capital in both the interior and the exterior of the formation, and the peremptory conclusion is that it is a matter of *effective national bourgeoisies* (as we shall see, this is the case in the Mandel/CP mode), or,

(b) on the contrary, it is affirmed that the bourgeoisies of the centre are such that they can no longer adopt class positions which lead them to take sides with the people. But the immediate conclusion is then that it is a matter of comprador bourgeoisies *only*, in the sense that they

would be just the simple 'intermediaries' between the national economy and foreign capital (this is the case in the 'super-imperialism'
mode).

It will, therefore, be necessary to introduce a new concept permitting the analysis of at the very least the concrete situation of the
bourgeoisies of the imperialist metropoles in their relations with
American capital. *Interior bourgeoisie* is that concept. This bourgeoisie coexists with properly comprador sectors but no longer possesses
the structural characteristics of the national bourgeoisie in the different imperialist formations, though this is to unequal degrees. Because
of the reproduction of American capital within these formations, this
bourgeoisie is imbricated, by multiple links of dependence, with the
processes of international division of labour and international concentration of capital under the domination of American capital, and
this can even take the form of a transfer of part of the surplus-value to
this capital's profit. In addition, because of the induced reproduction
of the political and ideological conditions of that dependence, this
bourgeoisie is affected by the effects of the dissolution of its politico-
ideological autonomy in the face of American capital.

From another angle, however, this is not a matter of a simple
comprador bourgeoisie. The interior bourgeoisie possesses its own
economic base and its own base of accumulation of capital both in the
interior of its formation, since the dominance of American capital does
not affect the economies of the other metropoles in the same way as
the economies of the peripheral formations, and in the exterior of its
formation. Even at the politico-ideological level, it continues to
present its own specificities, deriving both from its present situation
and from its past as 'auto-centred' imperialist capital. It is this latter
that distinguishes it from the bourgeoisies of the peripheral formations. Important contradictions thus exist between it and American
capital; they are without the power to lead it forward to the adoption
of positions of effective 'autonomy' or 'independence' in the face of
this capital but they do have effects on the state apparatuses of these
formations in their relations with the American state.

It is precisely by taking account of the existing forms of alliance, and
of the contradictions, between imperialist bourgeoisies and American
capital that it is possible to pose the question of the *national states*.
The current internationalization of capital neither suppresses nor
short-circuits the national states, neither in the sense of a peaceable
integration of capitals 'over' the states, with every process of internationalization working under the dominance of a determinate country, nor in the sense of their extinction under the American super-state,

as if American capital purely and simply swallowed up the other imperialist bourgeoisies. But, from another angle, this internationalization does have a profound effect on the political and on the institutional forms of these states by their inclusion in a system of interconnections which is in no way limited to the interplay of 'exterior' and 'reciprocal' pressures between states and juxtaposed capitals. *The states themselves assume responsibility for the interests of the dominant imperialist capital in its extended development actually within the 'national' formation, that is, in its complex interiorization in the interior bourgeoisie which it dominates.* This system of interconnections does not tend towards the constitution of 'supra-national' and 'super-state' institutional forms or instances. This might be the case if it were a matter of an internationalization in a context of juxtaposed states with external relations that had to be superseded. Rather the system is founded on an induced reproduction of the form of imperialist power dominant in each national formation *and its own state.*

To begin with, the states engage in assuming responsibility for the interests of the dominant capital in a direct manner. In its investment within the formation, American capital is often given support of the same type as that accorded to the autochthonous capital, public subsidies for example, but also support necessary to American capital in its extension further in the chain to the exterior of the formation, thereby acting as a *relay* in the chain. Further, this support can even reach the point where it assists American capital in the circumvention of certain aspects of the American state itself (in the case of anti-trust legislation, for example). The international reproduction of capital under the domination of American capital is supported by those same vectors that are the national states, with each state trying to fasten on itself a 'moment' of this process. Consequently, support for American capital is also given in an indirect manner. The industrial politics of each state with respect to the autochthonous capital aims at the international concentration and expansion of that capital.

It is true that important contradictions exist over a whole series of points between the interior bourgeoisies of the imperialist metropoles and American capital and that each state takes on these contradictions more often than not by lending its support to its interior bourgeoisie. This, moreover, is *one* of the aspects of the EEC. But here the matter must be taken further *by pointing out that these contradictions are not currently the principal contradiction within the imperialist dominant classes.* The currently dominant form of interimperialist contradiction is not that between 'international capital' and 'national capital', nor that between the imperialist bourgeoisies understood as juxtaposed *entities*.

To understand that, it is absolutely necessary to see that the dependence of the autochthonous capital in relation to American capital *cuts across the different fractions* of the autochthonous capital. This precisely provokes its *internal disarticulation*, with the contradictions between American capital and autochthonous capital as the principal constituents of the complex form of reproduction within autochthonous capital of the contradictions peculiar to American capital. In other words, the contradictions of autochthonous capital are, by complex mediations, extrapolated in terms of American capital, and the interior bourgeoisie is currently composed of heterogeneous and *conjunctural* elements. Even less today than in the past, in the case of the national bourgeoisie, the distinction between interior bourgeoisie and comprador bourgeoisie is coextensive neither with the distinction between large monopoly capital and non-monopoly capital, nor with that between productive (industrial) capital and banking capital, nor, finally, with that between a limited bourgeoisie with an interior market and a bourgeoisie with a strategy of international expansion. Rather the distinction cuts across them in a direction which depends on the conjuncture. (Witness the vicissitudes of de Gaulle's politics.)

In its role as the promoter of hegemony, therefore, the national state intervenes in an 'interior' field already crossed by 'interimperialist contradictions' and where the contradictions among the dominant fractions within its social formation *are already internationalized*. The interventions of the state in favour of certain large autochthonous monopolies and against others, in favour of large monopolies or sectors of autochthonous medium capital and against others, in favour of certain fractions of 'European' capital and against others, these interventions are often only indirect interventions in favour of certain fractions and sectors of American capital and against others of this same capital, and the different fractions and sectors of autochthonous capital and European capital depend on these interventions. According to the conjuncture, the principal contradiction passes in this way to within the contradictions of the dominant imperialist capital and of the internationalization it imposes or to within even the interior bourgeoisie and its internal struggles, but it is rarely displaced between the interior bourgeoisie *as such* and American capital.

Furthermore, it is this disarticulation and heterogeneity of the interior bourgeoisie, this conjunctural constellation, that compels the various spasms of the feeble resistance of the European states in the face of American capital. The different and new *real* means of 'pressure' on the European states by American multinational firms – tax evasions, speculation against currencies, diversion of tariff walls – are only a secondary element of the affair, contrary to what underlies the dominant ideological mode which poses the problem: national state versus multinational firms.

We have noted, then, the distance separating us both from the conceptions of super-imperialism and from the conceptions of the mode of Mandel and western CPs. As for the two components of this last mode, it can be said that they both accept the existence of a national bourgeoisie in the European countries but that they do not delimit it in the same way. To each his national bourgeoisie!

For Mandel the national bourgeoisie is constituted by the 'European' *great monopolies*, contrary to what happens with medium European capital.

> The era of national big capital and of the nation state has not yet been superseded in Western Europe . . . the growing desire to resist American competition, manifest not only in 'autonomous state capitalism' but also clearly expressed by the great European concerns, the increasing consolidation of the EEC, and the growing force of supranational state organs within it, are all parallel processes.[24]

> The frailest companies, those whose branch of industry is not expanding, and stagnant family businesses usually prefer to take the easy way out and to allow themselves to be bought up or taken over by American companies. The wealthier, more dynamic European businesses generally have a wider choice and prefer to take the path of European cooperation and capital interpenetration.[25]

That is all there is to say. It is not surprising that after these claims, which are contradicted by the facts, Mandel goes along with all the current bourgeois propaganda about the 'united Europe'. Furthermore, Mandel is not thereby prevented from noting two pages later what he calls a paradox.

> Extra stimulus to do this [sc. 'to counteract the relapses in European economic integration (*sic!*) caused by the indecision of national governments'] is provided by the fact that when European capital interpenetration is lacking, US concerns stand, paradoxically, to

profit more from the Common Market than those of Western Europe.[26]

Now, if the analyses given above are applied to the European front it becomes clear that it is not at all a matter of a paradox due to technical incompetences or incompatibilities of temperament. In fact, if the European bourgeoisies do not cooperate and do not cordon themselves off *in the face of* American capital it is because of the tendential effects on them of the new structure of dependence in relation to American capital. The *relations between these bourgeoisies* are off-centred relations, that is, they function by means of their own interiorization of American capital. Each European state assumes responsibility for the interests of the other European bourgeoisies, taking account, moreover, of their competition with its own interior bourgeoisie but thus assuming their state of dependence in relation to American capital.

By contrast, the analyses of the European CPs, and in particular the analyses of the French CP and its researchers, insist on the inter-penetration of the great monopolies and on the dominance of American capital. As Herzog says,

> These remarks show that we are careful not to characterize the new stage as a struggle between 'national' capital and trans- or multi-national capital. Currently the great national monopolies and the foreign capitals have common interests, and 'resistance', like 'competition', loses its 'national' character. It is groups with partially linked interests, or groups about to become cosmopolitan, that confront each other.[27]

But, in fact, the problem lies elsewhere. The CP does indeed have its national bourgeoisie and it is non-monopoly capital or medium capital. This is not the place to go into the details but that much is clear from the fact that the CP analyses consider that the *sole fraction* currently dominant is that of the globally 'cosmopolitan' great monopolies, *to the exclusion* of medium capital. Medium capital is included in national 'small capital' (that is, the petty bourgeoisie) and democrats and sincere patriots seek its alliance for purposes of the establishment of an 'advanced democracy' to face American capital.[28] Among other things, this ignores the effects of the socialization of the labour process and of concentration on the existing dependence of medium capital in relation to large capital.

The state and the nation

If the existing state of the imperialist metropoles is modified whilst retaining its nature as a national state, that is likewise owing to the fact *that the state is not a mere tool or instrument* of the dominant classes, to be manipulated at will, with the entire stage of the internationalization of capital automatically provoking a 'supranationalization' of states. The state, the apparatus of cohesion, the apparatus of the unity of a formation and of reproduction of its social relations, concentrates and epitomizes the class contradictions of *the social formation as a whole*, by sanctioning and legitimizing the interests of the dominant classes and fractions in the face of *the other classes* of the formation, at the same time as assuming world class contradictions. It follows that the problem we are concerned with does not, moreover, reduce to a simple contradiction of mechanistic composition between the base (internationalization of production) and a superstructural envelope no longer 'corresponding' to it. The superstructural transformations depend on the forms which *the class struggle* assumes in an imperialist chain marked by the uneven development of its links.

Now, we have just seen in the first place that the internationalization of capital does not give rise to an effective 'trans-national fusion' of capitals. But this is only one aspect of the problem. What happens as regards the working classes of the European countries? In fact, whilst the struggles of the popular masses are developing more than ever on a world *foundation* determining concrete conjunctures, and whilst the establishment of world relations of production and the socialization of labour *objectively* reinforce the international solidarity of workers, it is the national form that prevails in their essentially international struggle. This is, in part, owing to the uneven development and to the concrete specificities of each social formation, and thus to the characteristics of the very nature of capitalism, but, in the particularities which these forms currently assume, it is also owing to the organizations (parties, unions) preponderant in the European working classes.

It is, furthermore, just as necessary to attach the greatest importance, on the one hand, to the petty bourgeoisie (which is currently being reproduced in new forms) and to the peasant classes whose indispensable support is sought by these states and whose class situation has a quite particular 'nationalism' as an effect, and, on the other hand, to the *social categories* of the state apparatuses (administrative bureaucracies, personnel of the political parties, etc.) for whom the state remains a source of privileges.

The problem of the permanence of the nation is therefore discovered through the effects it produces on the 'national forms' of the class struggles. But, for all that, the question of the *relation* between state and nation posed by the 'national state' remains unsolved. In fact, if the nation is constitutively tied to the existence of capitalism, including its imperialist stage, then Marxism-Leninism has never confused *state* and *nation*, having simply maintained in this respect the emergence of the 'national state' and of the 'national social formation' under capitalism. The problem is thus reposed under a different perspective. If the current internationalization of production and the world relations of production do not after all eliminate the national entity (uneven development), do they not modify the *space* of the social formation to the point where the 'national social formation' is shattered and the links between state and nation – supranational state – are broken?

There is nothing in that at all, in fact, to the extent that neither the nation nor the relation state/nation reduce to simple economic links. In all the *complexity of its determination* – an economic, territorial, linguistic, symbolico-ideological unit linked with 'tradition' – the nation retains *its own existence* with respect to the 'national forms' of the class struggle, and by this means the relation state/nation is maintained. In the imperialist metropoles at least, the existing modifications only affect certain elements of this determination (and this in an unequal manner). They are thus crystallized as modifications of a state which remains a national state to the core. But these modifications nonetheless remain considerable, making an issue of the legal conception of national sovereignty, the role assumed by each state in the international repression of the class struggle (NATO, etc.). The existing modifications also include the exteriorized nature of the functions and interventions of each state as they extend to exterior formations where its autochthonous capital is developed, and they include modifications of even the internal legal systems of each state so as to cover the internationalization of its interventions, etc.

That said, in the case of the imperialist metropoles we are concerned with, certain *distensions* are currently manifested between the state and the nation, but not in the sense generally meant by the 'supranationalization' of the state. It is not the emergence of a new state over the nations that we are witnessing but rather ruptures in the national unity underlying the existing national states. It is the very important current phenomenon of regionalism, expressed through the resurgence of nationalities, which shows that the internationalization of capital brings about splits in the nation as historically constituted more than it brings about the supranationalization of the state. Now, this phenomenon is even more characteristic in that, far from an alleged supranational co-operation of European capitals against American capital, it corresponds to the enlarged reproduction of international capital under the dominance of American capital within the European countries and to the new structure of dependence. This brings about a tendency to the internal disarticulation of the European social formations and of their economies which can go so far as the real phenomena of *interior colonization* under the various labels of the parcelling out of the territory. It is on this disarticulation that the disintegration of capitalist national unity takes root.

Internationalization and the economic role of the state

It can therefore be seen that the current internationalization of capital and the emergence of 'multinational giants' in their relations with the state cannot be posed in terms of two entities 'possessing' a 'power' and redistributing it. To maintain in particular that the more 'economic strength' increases and is concentrated the more it detracts from state 'power' is to fail to recognize not only that the state does not possess 'power' proper but also that it intervenes in this concentration in a decisive manner. The current process in no way undermines *the dominant role of the state* in the monopoly capital stage.

This dominance of the state corresponds to the considerable increase in the economic functions of the state that are absolutely indispensable to the extended reproduction of large capital. But this deals with only a part of the problem and in particular does not explain why these economic interventions continue to have, and this is the essential aspect, the national states as their *supports*. Might we not allow, with Murray,[29] that these economic interventions, whilst remaining essential, change their support and that the national state is currently dispossessed of a large part of these interventions to the profit of superstate institutions or of an embryonic supranational state?

Now, there is no doubt that the forms of co-ordination of the economic politics of the different states are currently proving necessary (various international institutions, the EEC). But these institutional forms do not in fact constitute apparatuses either supplanting the national states or superimposed on them. And this is for a reason which is supplementary to those already indicated and which it will be useful to mention. These economic interventions of the state are not, as one firmly established tradition would have it thought, 'technical' and 'neutral' functions imposed by necessities of the 'production' that is itself thought of in the same neutral manner. These economic functions of the state are in fact expressions of its political role as a whole in exploitation and class domination. They are articulated in the field of the class struggle of a social formation, which brings us back precisely to the preceding remarks. It is therefore impossible to separate the different interventions, and their aspects, of the state, in envisaging the possibility of *effective transfer* of the 'economic functions' to the supra-national or superstate apparatuses, with the national state maintaining only a repressive or ideological role. At most it is a matter, sometimes, of *delegation* in the exercise of these functions.

In fact, by straining in that direction, one loses sight of the *real tendencies, namely, the interiorized transformations of the national state itself with a view to assuming responsibility for the internationalization of public functions with respect to capital.* In that way one ends up with a line of defence for one's 'own' national state against the 'cosmopolitan institutions'. In fact these international institutional forms are not, moreover, 'superadded' (the expression favoured by the French CP[30]) to these national states but they are precisely the expression of their interiorized transformations. These transformations are not concerned solely with the economic inter-relations of the national state but also with the repressive and ideological aspects of the state by means of which these interventions are realized.

Notice, furthermore, that the conception of the neutral and technical economic functions of the existing state is the conception of the western CPs and in particular the French CP ('state as organic factor of production', the 'state forming part of the base'[31]) in the theorization of 'state monopoly capitalism'. These functions, neutral *per se*, are supposed to be currently 'diverted' to the profit of the large monopolies alone and could be utilized to the profit of the popular masses by means of a simple change in the power of the state without shattering the state apparatus. These analyses, it might be said, would have had to make the French CP fall into the conception of the supranational state in the context of an internationalization of production. If that is not the case, it is because the analyses are situated in a conception of the imperialist chain as the juxtaposition and addition of national state monopoly capitalisms. The fact is therefore stressed that 'international capital' is inserted in each national social formation 'whilst adopting and submitting to the specificities of its state monopoly capitalism', whereas in fact it is the very structure of each social formation that is reorganized in relation to the internationalization of capital. The functions of the national state itself with respect to the internationalization of capital are not, in the French CP version, supposed to transform and modify this state profoundly but are quite simply supposed to be *superadded* to its 'national' functions. It follows that by means of a defence of the national state, which is supported by the 'national bourgeoisie/medium capital' against 'cosmopolitan' capital, these functions could be utilized for an effective 'international co-operation' imposed by the necessities of 'production' *without shattering the state apparatus.*

To return to our problem, the capital that transgresses these national limits does indeed have recourse to the national states, *not only to its own state of origin* but also to other states. This produces a complex distribution of the role of the states in the international reproduction of capital under the dominance of American capital. This distribution can have as effects off-centrings and displacements in the exercise of these functions *among their supports*, which remain essentially the national states. Depending on the conjuncture, it comes about that it is to this or that national state of the metropoles that the responsibility reverts for this or that intervention of international scope concerning this reproduction and the maintenance of the system in its entirety.

The state in the international reproduction of social classes

The different functions of the state at issue until now are all concentrated towards the extended reproduction of the CMP, and the determinant 'moment' of this reproduction concerns the extended reproduction of social classes, of social relations. But the state has here a peculiar and specific role, intervening, on the one hand, in the reproduction of the places of the social classes and, on the other hand, in the qualification/subjugation of the agents in such a way that they can occupy these places, and thus in the distribution of these agents among these places. In this respect, may we simply mention here the role of the school mechanism.

Now if it is indeed to the national state that this role currently always reverts, and if this role in turn depends on the specificity of the social formation and its class struggles, it is nothing less than that this role is currently placed more and more under the mark of the imperialist social division of labour and of a capitalist reproduction of social classes on the world front. The role of the European national states in this respect (the school mechanism, further education) consists among other things in the reproduction of new forms of division of labour established between the United States and Europe. The forms of, for example, extended reproduction of the working class, of its qualification and of its composition (skilled and unskilled labourers, etc.), the forms and rhythms of reproduction of the new petty bourgeoisie (technicians, engineers, etc.), of exodus from the country or of immigrant labour in Europe, and the role of the European national states in this respect, all these are closely dependent on the division of labour: United States/Europe. This division of labour is characterized by technological discrepancies, discrepancies in the levels and hierarchies of wages, forms of socialization of labour in integrated production (with the aspect of disqualification of labour which currently accompanies its aspect of high qualification having a tendency to be localized in the exterior of the United States, with Europe being sectioned up, moreover, into relatively inferior forms of 'technology').

These examples only indicate the problem, but they do lead to a more general thesis, in that they show the limitations of a currently most widespread conception (Sweezy and Baran are a case in point) which sees the United States as the *model* or *the foreshadowed image* of the future towards which Europe is tending ineluctably and in an unequivocal manner. This conception has only analogical value, for it neglects the new cleavages of dependence which have been inserted there. To take only the notorious example, which has caused a lot of ink to flow, of the 'inflation of the tertiary [sc. industries]' in the United States, it is clear that the rhythms and the forms of this development, which are in fact quite different in the United States and in Europe, are due to the place which the United States currently holds as the world administrative centre and not to a mere 'delay' that Europe is ineluctably making up for. This is to say that an examination of the social classes and the state apparatuses in the metropoles cannot rest content with an analysis of the United States which deals with this formation in the same 'exemplary' manner as Marx dealt with Great Britain in his time. The other imperialist metropoles, Europe in particular, constitute a specific field and object.

Finally, considering its extent and importance, we must just mention one last question. The modifications of the role of the European national states in order to assume responsibility for the international reproduction of capital under the domination of American capital and the political and ideological conditions of this reproduction *bring about decisive transformations of these state apparatuses.* There is no doubt that the particular forms of 'strong state' (authoritarian/police) one sees being established more or less everywhere in Europe on the one hand and the accumulation of the conditions of the eventual processes of fascization on the other hand are the expression both of the class struggle in these formations and of their place in the new structure of dependence.

Conclusion

A few final remarks are necessary.

1. The first concerns the *historical* establishment of this dependence. Dating from the end of the Second World War, it has adopted the concrete characteristics of the period. It follows that American hegemony, which was established in a period of the destruction of the European economies, has shown certain particular traits as nearing elimination. This often creates the illusion of the 'end' of American hegemony and, gives rise to the judgements in the Mandel mode that are of the genre 'the American bourgeoisie still maintains its absolute domination but is in relative decline', this decline being considered tendentially as the end of this hegemony. In fact, what is currently *in retreat* are certain forms of this hegemony (in particular the role of the dollar), with Europe occupying the position of dependent or satellite imperialism which reverts to it in the current process and its contradictions. But if one refers to the essential traits of the domination and dependence, American hegemony has not ceased to be affirmed. Considering the extent of the question, furthermore, one has only to mention here the prodigious economic agreements recently concluded between the USA and the USSR which indicate only the intensification of this hegemony.

2. The second point concerns the current *crisis* of imperialism and is thereby connected with the first remark. In fact, what is undergoing a crisis is not American hegemony under the effect of the rise in equivalent contra-imperialisms but the whole of imperialism under the effect of world class struggles which are today reaching even the zone of the centre. This crisis of imperialism does not objectively make an issue of the actual domination of American imperialism over the other metropoles but reaches *the whole* of the centre and is thus manifested *both at its head and in the reactivation of interimperialist contradictions.* In other words, it is not the domination of American

imperialism which is undergoing crisis but the whole of the imperialism of the centre under that domination.

It follows that it is no solution in the face of this crisis for the European bourgeoisies to adopt the tactic of again making an issue of the domination of American capital, *and the European bourgeoisies are perfectly well aware of this*. The question for them, and the vicissitudes of the EEC – witness the last meeting of the nine in Paris – make this perfectly clear, is actually to maintain imperialism under the domination they recognize even if it involves secondary changes affecting the entire system. It is on this, of course, that the sharing of the cake depends. And this brings us to the second claim. The route taken by this crisis (for there are crises which have a long life) will depend on the struggle of the popular masses. In the midst of this struggle, in the current phase of imperialism, and in the present conjuncture, the struggle of the popular masses in Europe has a fundamental role.

We thus come to the question concerning the revolutionary possibilities and strategy in a European country in the current phase of internationalization. The principal question in this respect is not the one concerning the possibility or otherwise of a revolutionary *process* (the notorious question of *one single country*), in so far as it is true that the different metropoles of imperialism are always marked by an uneven development and by the specificity of the concrete situation. The essential problem concerns the very forms of the process in these social formations. What stands out in the preceding analyses is that, in this uninterrupted revolutionary process, there cannot be an individual stage of 'national liberation' or of 'new democracy' based on forms of alliance with a 'national bourgeoisie' against 'foreign' imperialism and its 'agents'. And this is not because it is not a matter of dependent social formations; quite the contrary.

In fact, in the current phase of internationalization, the rupture of the imperialist chain in one of its links becomes terribly difficult, and in particular for the metropoles, it can only begin by means of radical socialist measures which are the sole means of anti-imperialist struggle. The means at the disposal of the dominant imperialism are considerable. To cite only one known example, we know that the large monetary fluctuations and speculative movements of capital in recent years have been principally due to the possibilities of action of the multinational firms, in the face of which the classic means of control of exchange transactions seem pretty derisory. But there is more, of course. It emerges from the above analyses that in the current context of the domination of American capital, it is possible to break *the simple imperialist dependence* only by making a direct attack on, among other things, the labour process itself and on the forms of social division of labour in the process of production. As for the question of the state apparatuses, we have seen that it is indeed a matter, of the first importance, of fighting the assumption of responsibility for the dominant imperialism by the interiorized modifications of the national states themselves. Now more than ever, and *as an elementary anti-imperialist measure*, this cannot proceed without radically shattering these state apparatuses.

10

ON THE POPULAR
IMPACT OF FASCISM

One of the most important problems posed by the study of fascism, both because of the real dimension of the phenomenon and because it has served as the basis of an entire mythology, is that of its popular impact. I will limit myself in these few lines to examining the general aspects and refer the reader to my book *Fascism and Dictatorship* where this problem is treated in detail.

I will say, then, that the popular impact of fascism is a real phenomenon. Moreover, it concerns one of the essential, distinctive characteristics of fascism in relation to other exceptional regimes of the capitalist state in open war against the popular masses (military dictatorships, Bonapartisms, etc.). In effect, fascism succeeded in activating specific state apparatuses for the mobilization of the masses (parties, unions, etc.), a phenomenon one does not come across generally, at least not to the same extent and under the same institutional form (conditioning the very form of the state), in the other exceptional regimes. This implies precisely that fascism had a basis among the popular masses, which I will provisionally designate by the descriptive and neutral term, *impact*, since, in fact, it is the very nature of the phenomenon that must be studied.

This poses two, linked questions: 1. What was the extent and the exact nature of the phenomenon? 2. What were its causes?

Now, we currently come across two tendencies in studying this phenomenon, *both* of which are mistaken on the first and second questions. Regarding the first question, these two tendencies commonly demonstrate that they examine seriously neither the meaning of

* First published in French as 'A propos de l'impact populaire du fascisme' in M. Macciochi (ed.), *Éléments pour une analyse du fascisme*, Paris 1976, pp. 88–107. Translated by James Martin.

that *impact* nor the meaning of its *popular* character. They accept as a brute and incontestable fact that, on the one hand, the fascisms would, throughout their existence and to the same degree, have earned an active popular support and, on the other, by means of a totally idealist use of the terms *masses* and *people*, that this support would have been uniform for all the *atoms* of this *mass* without any other distinction between the *class fractions* and *social categories* that constitute the popular masses. Regarding the second question, they give explanations for the phenomenon that are either entirely mistaken or mistaken in their very partiality. In fact, one suspects, it is the ideological principles governing their explanations which leads them to define the real phenomenon as a so-called uniform and undifferentiated popular support by the 'masses' for fascism.

a) The first tendency – all-in-all quite dated but one which we currently find, among others, in the numerous texts of the journal *Tel Quel* – is that of an attempt at a falsely *psychoanalytic* explanation of fascism. The fact to be explained will be *why the masses desired fascism*. Properly understood, grasping the phenomenon under this formulation is itself dependent on all the current ideological verbiage on *desire* and is supportive of a certain conception of the relationship between Marxism and psychoanalysis which *Freudo-Marxism* – a jarring term by virtue of its implied *conjunction* – has already given us an initial taste. That tendency – somehow presuming, with feigned confidence, to have resolved the problem, which is only beginning to be put in its proper place, of the relation between *ideology* and the *unconscious* – can in fact only supply the explanation to the false question 'why did the masses desire fascism' by implicit reference to the (absurd) notion of the *collective unconscious*; a notion that magically establishes a relation between the *individuals* who supposedly desire fascism – we are not dealing here with classes – and the *masses* made up by these individuals. Masses: just as Marxism requires, but classes are always absent; masses are themselves presumed to have adhered to fascism, uniformly and indistinctly. This is a conception of the individual-masses relationship that, through the comings and goings it implies between *individual psychology* and *collective unconscious* (*Les Psychologie des foules* by G. Le Bon is not very far away), likewise, entirely misses the problem of the relation between ideology and the unconscious.

b) The second tendency in explaining the phenomenon, always defined in the same way, that is, as the undifferentiated and uniform support for fascism by the masses – classes are always absent – privileges, if not refers itself exclusively to, the *language* employed by fascism in relation to the *people*. This is a tendency that we currently find, amongst others, in J.P. Faye's book *Les langages totalitaires*, which I have criticized elsewhere. All things considered, this explanation participates in the old idealist utopia according to which it is ideas that make history. Moreover, it renders impossible the examination of a real problem, that of the precise functioning of *fascist ideology* in the popular impact of fascism. In effect – we will return to this issue – such an examination presumes a reference to the *class functioning* of that ideology (with respect to the diverse classes and to their ideological sub-ensembles). So, for that tendency, ideas can make history if and only if, in place of the class functioning of ideology, a word was *transmitted* by a – or some – subject, indistinctly addressed to and perceived by some individuals-subjects who are pure, undifferentiated *receivers* of this Word-Idea. This conception, likewise, commands the manner in which the phenomenon of fascism's popular impact is defined. If for the first tendency the question will be how and why 'the masses had desired fascism', here it will be how 'fascism had talked to the masses', which explains why it would have been understood by these *masses*, assumed to be globally and indistinctly subjugated by fascist language – and classes remain absent as ever.

For my part, I will first attempt to delimit more closely this phenomenon of fascism's popular impact (German Nazism and Italian Fascism) before making two remarks regarding its causes. But I will say at the outset that the preceding remarks must not lead us to an arbitrary simplification of the problem, nor to its reduction to the well-known general phenomenon of certain reactionary ideologues, in specific circumstances, striking a chord among the popular classes, of which the particularly *enthusiastic adhesion* of the popular masses in France and Germany to the inter-imperialist war of 1914–18, *at its beginning*, offers us the characteristic example. The popular impact of fascism, entirely in keeping with this phenomenon, presents some unique aspects.

To begin with, concerning the real facts:
   1. *One must distinguish between the social classes that comprise the popular masses.*
   a) In the first place, *the working class* – which still fails to distinguish between its layers – was much less contaminated by

fascism than we are led to believe, and in all ways less than the other popular classes. It was always considerably under-represented in the fascist apparatuses (parties, unions) in relation to its importance in the overall population of Germany and Italy. Even from the electoral point of view, precise and serious studies of the results of the last, relatively free elections in these countries show that, as a whole, the working class remained faithful to its traditional organizations: the communist and socialist parties.

But, in the case of the working class, there is more: throughout Nazism and Fascism, there was important resistance by the working class which, even if it rarely took the form of an open and armed insurrection (the Italian resistance), it manifested itself no less through surreptitious forms of *spontaneous workers' resistance*; a fact, of course, that those who declare, on behalf of the working class, that it had 'desired' fascism totally ignore. Sabotage and the lowering of production levels, massive absenteeism, unofficial strikes, etc., created considerable problems for the fascist leaders, as the permanent measures taken to remedy them prove. These were forms of resistance that, considering the character of the fascist state, constituted well and truly *political* modes of opposition to the regime.

b) *The popular classes in the countryside*, for we know that the peasantry is itself divided into classes. If German Nazism, in particular, succeeded in finding a popular impact among certain of the popular classes of the countryside in the regions of the East, in Eastern Prussia, where the feudal relations showed a remarkable persistence; if the fascisms still sometimes struck a chord, although in a very unequal way, among certain sectors of the rural petty bourgeoisie, the famous *paysans parcellaires*, on the other hand, the great mass of the poor peasantry with, at its head, the agricultural workers, remained impermeable to fascism. The poor peasantry, too, remained under-represented in the fascist apparatuses and never constituted the marching wing of fascism. Moreover, *rural fascism in Germany and Italy closely resembles the traditional phenomenon of the 'white terror' of the great property owners against the popular classes of the countryside* who, in their majority, would have been quite surprised to hear that they 'desired' fascism.

c) *The petty bourgeoisie, both traditional* (small tradesmen and artisans) *and new* (employees, civil servants): it effectively, massively and quite openly swung towards fascism. It was considerably over-represented in the fascist apparatuses and constituted its marching wing. In all, the *specificity* of the phenomenon of the popular impact of fascism, of the *fascism-masses relation*, is reduced in essence to the problem of the relation between fascism and the petty bourgeoisie; a relation marked by numerous ambiguities, as we shall see.

2. Because of the current importance of these questions, it is still necessary to distinguish – and I point this out although in my view it is, ultimately, a secondary element – among the different *social categories* that make up the popular classes. In particular, it is certain that fascism encountered its most marked popular impact among *young people*, but also among the *female population*. This is due, amongst other things, to the dominant institutional forms of the *family* and the *school*, and the ideological sub-system which ruled in these apparatuses at the time in Germany and Italy.

3. Regarding its popular impact, *fascism itself must be periodized, including both the process of fascistization and established fascism*. Indeed, if, among other things, because of the complex, politico-ideological ambiguity of the origins of fascism, bearing in mind the remarks just formulated, its impact appeared clearly throughout the process of fascistization, we may note no less clearly a *process of disaffection* regarding first-stage and established fascism as, increasingly, it openly demonstrates its anti-popular face (a face marked moreover by massive and bloody expulsions from its own ranks – the classic episode being the 'Night of the Long Knives' in Germany). This is a process of disaffection that translates into the growing role of systematic repression but which, whilst it remains uninterrupted and culminates in the Second World War, *presents ups and downs*. In particular, we see a renewed popularity for Nazism during the *Anschluss* (the annexation of Austria) and for Italian Fascism during the Libyan war, both of which are due to complex, national reasons. If we do not take account of this process of disaffection we will understand nothing, for example, of the phenomenon of the *suddenly* and massively anti-fascist Italy during and following the collapse of Mussolini. We will then attempt to attribute this, unconvincingly, to the *versatility* or the *opportunism* of the Italian *people*.

4. *From what has just preceded, we end up in fact having to question the very term popular 'impact' in relation to fascism.* Effectively, wherever there has been an 'impact' this is constituted by a whole *diversified range*, from active and almost unconditional adhesion to circumstantial support and to passive resignation. Which is to say nothing of forced neutralization as repression increases enormously. Although, certainly, repression far from explains everything, never-

theless it was necessary to indicate it at those particular times when the Jews, too, were surprised to learn through Liliana Cavani in her film, *Portier de nuit*, that they were not far from having *desired* fascism.

Let us be more serious: we could respond that the existence of this diversified range in the popular *impact* of fascism has no real political meaning and that passive resignation does not differ so much from active adhesion as regards its repercussions for established fascism. But this is entirely false because, precisely in so far as it is a mass phenomenon – that is to say, for an important mass of the population – resignation in fact came close to a permanent mass resistance, which progressively provoked the isolation of established fascism from the classes and class fractions where it had acquired support. Isolation, in its turn, considerably accentuated the internal contradictions of fascism, expressed in a series of mistakes (false military manoeuvres, compromises) which contributed to precipitating its collapse.

Now we come to the second facet of the problem, that of the causes of the popular impact of fascism, the nature and extent of which we have defined. Here, too, I will simply mention some scattered points which to me seem particularly important:

1. *Economic policy during the first period of established fascism.* If this policy consisted in the considerably increased exploitation of the popular masses, that exploitation was, on the one hand, for certain classes and popular class fractions, mainly relative (in view of the considerable increase in profits) and not absolute (real purchasing power was maintained for a time for certain popular classes); on the other hand, it was managed according to a diversified strategy, which consisted in *dividing* those classes and fractions and having the one profit on the back of the others. But the most important reason was the *success* of fascism (Italian, during the crisis of 1920; German, during the crisis of 1930) *in spectacularly absorbing unemployment*, which formed an important part of the process of fascistization in those countries. This relative *overcoming* of the economic crisis by fascism was, of course, led, in that period of transition from competitive capitalism towards monopoly capitalism, not only by a policy in the service of monopolistic concentration and by the worsening exploitation of the popular masses, but also by a frenzied policy of economic expansion and arming which led to the Second World War. It does not prevent, at the time and for a while, the absorption of unemployment playing an important role in the popular impact of fascism.

2. *The real coordinates of the national question and their exploitation through fascism.* This is a decisive question, the importance of which was underestimated by Marxism for a long time and which, in Germany and Italy, took on a particular form distinct from that taken in the other imperialist countries. This is so in two respects:

First, *national unity* proper to capitalism, given that the process of bourgeois democratic revolution in these two countries (revolution from above by Bismarck in Germany, Risorgimento *manqué* in Italy) was far from being accomplished, at the moment of accession to power by Nazism and Fascism, to the same degree as in the other developed capitalist countries. In one sense, Nazism and Fascism *completed* the process of capitalist national unity in these countries; achieved, certainly, with the internal unevenness of development proper to all similar processes, but which permits them nevertheless to pose as champions of national unity and to fully play upon the ambiguities of this nationalism among certain popular classes (notably the popular classes of the countryside and the petty bourgeoisie). It is therefore important to see that the fascisms did not simply play the card of aggressive, expansionist imperialist nationalism but, equally, that otherwise more ambiguous and complex card of national unity (Mussolini, *successor* to Garibaldi, Hitler to Bismarck), which formed a considerable part of their popular impact.

Next, it is necessary to indicate the real consequences, at the conjuncture of the national question, of the place of Germany and of Italy in the imperialist chain after the First World War.[1] In the case of Germany, the fact, with incalculable repercussions, of the Treaty of Versailles, characterized by Lenin as the most monstrous act of brigandage in history. In the case of Italy, the fact that, having come late in the process of the establishment and reproduction of capitalism, she suffered the real consequences of the exploitation of her popular masses on the part of imperialist capital – massively implanted in Italy well before the accession of Fascism to power – which, moreover, wanted it to be treated as the poor relation at the feast of the victors of the 1914–18 war (during the war Mussolini, the *socialist*, was the representative of the tendency of *left interventionism*, supporting the intervention of Italy in the war). On the basis of these real facts, fascists were able to exploit the ideological theme of *proletarian nations*, a theme that in Germany had even assumed among certain sectors of the said *national-socialist left* strictly anti-imperialist connotations. Gregor Strasser – who, incidentally was executed, not by chance, during the Night of the Long Knives – wrote:

To see German industry and the German economy in the hands of international finance capital, is the end of any possibility of social liberation, the end of any dream of a socialist Germany . . . we national-socialist revolutionaries, will engage in the struggle against capitalism and imperialism incarnated in the Peace of Versailles . . . We national-socialists have recognized that there is a link between the national freedom of our people and the economic liberation of the German working class. German socialism will be possible and durable only when Germany is free.

In short, here, too, is fascism's *corrupted reiteration*, though based on real facts, of an *anti-imperialist* nationalism deeply anchored in the masses, which partly explains their popular impact – as opposed to their official, openly imperialist, aggressive and expansionist nationalism.

3. *Fascist ideology and its institutional materialization in the fascist state apparatuses.*

To grasp this vital question, it is necessary, indeed, to clarify the *class functioning* of that ideology and abandon once and for all the conception of a unified and uniform fascist *discourse* or *language* addressed indistinctly to the *masses*. As Togliatti correctly reported at the time, there is nothing more false than to consider fascist ideology a unified and univocal 'system': 'Fascist ideology contains a series of heterogeneous elements . . . Beware the tendency to consider fascist ideology as something solidly constituted, finished, homogeneous . . .'. In fact, the role of fascist ideology among the masses nowhere involves the slightest repetition of an identical discourse, a vehicle for the techniques of propaganda in the face of atomized and undifferentiated *masses* (as, in my view, a recent film, *El fascista*, lets it be understood, despite being anti-fascist and animated by the best intentions). *Quite to the contrary*, this role is such that these ideologies and that discourse *present themselves in a considerably differentiated way, such that they are incarnated in diverse fascist politico-ideological apparatuses according to the different classes, class fractions and social categories to which they are addressed*, which permitted them precisely to exploit the material conditions of existence of those classes and fractions. Fascist ideological discourse is, in fact, considerably different depending on whether it is addressed to the working class and is incarnated in the apparatuses especially intended for it (fascist unions), to the popular classes of the countryside or to the petty bourgeoisie (fascist party). This is nothing but the functioning of the same theme, that of *corporatism* which, under the appearance of a pure and simple repetition of the same, in fact reveals a considerably different meaning depending on whether it is addressed to the working class, the poor peasantry or the petty bourgeoisie.

It is precisely from this point that fascism (and this is a particular trait of its ideological functioning) *was able in its ideological discourse to recapture, by corrupting them, a series of deep-seated popular aspirations*, often specific to each of the classes, class fractions and social categories concerned. This was the case with the themes of *self-management* and workers' control of production, formulations of *socialization* against private property, the power of monopolies, imperialist capital, etc., advanced in the relations of fascism and the working class, and present notably amongst the national-socialist *left* in Germany and amongst the anarcho-syndicalist wing of Italian Fascism. It was the case with the themes of peasant unity and of the bonds *of blood and soil* against the exploitation of the countryside by the cities, founded on the real industry-agriculture contradiction, advanced in the relations of fascism and the popular classes of the countryside. It was, finally, equally the case for the numerous themes advanced in the fascist discourse specifically addressed to the petty bourgeoisie.

But in order fully to grasp the real (class) functioning of these differentiated fascist ideologies, it is necessary to give greatest attention to the institutional structures within which this ideology is materialized, and not to stop at the simple analysis of fascist *discourse* supposedly circulating between the transmitter-leader and the masses-receivers. Besides, this will permit us precisely to grasp the intense *class struggle* which permanently traverses the fascist apparatuses, and to clarify further the meaning of the popular impact of fascism.

Here, too, instead of witnessing a pure and simple, univocal uniformization of the different apparatuses of the fascist state, we see in fact, parallel to their centralization 'at the summit', an effective dislocation and decentring of these apparatuses according to the classes, class fractions and social categories which are principally addressed. From the *family* to the *school, youth organizations, cultural apparatuses* and to the *Church*, from *parties* to *fascist unions*, from the *administration* (bureaucratic apparatus of the state) to the *army*, from the *SA* to the *SS* (Nazism) and to the *political police* (militia), in actual fact we discover, under the unifying shadow of discourse and of the 'rule' of the leader, the prodigiously contradictory entanglement of several regional ideological sub-ensembles. This has as its effect the constant winning back and alignment of the apparatuses, networks and transmission-belts of power, and gives rise to the internal contradictions of fascism. In short, it is also this precise system of management and mobilization of the masses – inside of which classes, class fractions, and social categories think power is suited either to one of the specific apparatuses or to their utilization to assert, or impose, their own interests – that in part explains the popular impact of fascism.

But this focus on the state apparatuses which materialize fascist ideology permits us, precisely, to understand the class struggle that permanently traverses them; a class struggle that disappears in the conception of a univocal and disembodied discourse addressed to the *masses*. We can also see better the entire ambiguity of the popular impact of fascism. In fact, where there has been an *impact*, and for the classes and fractions concerned and actively involved in the fascist apparatuses, this constantly borders on *resistance* to fascism. Except that resistance does not in this case take an open form but is often given, owing to this differentiation of the apparatuses, in the form of a claim on behalf of those masses to *true fascism*, a fantasy through which they invest their popular aspirations (these were the constant demands for a *second, anticapitalist revolution* in Germany and Italy). To take a descriptive example: an anarcho-syndicalist worker, an unapologetic member of the fascist union who leads (we come across this in numerous cases in Italian Fascism) a fierce struggle against the bureaucrats in the party and the militia in the name of his corporatist dream – against the power of capital – and considers this *pure and authentic fascism*. Does he adhere to fascism or, rather, does he resist it; that is to say, does he adhere to its true nature and class function? In any case, for him fascism has not been a mistake, which we see in the purifications, eliminations and constant reforging that he makes in his own apparatuses. In short, I repeat, the popular 'impact' of fascism, manifest in the adhesion of popular class fractions to fascist apparatuses, constantly went hand in hand with an intense class struggle by the same fractions against fascism across those very apparatuses. Dimitrov understood this perfectly when, at the Seventh Congress of the International, he urgently recommended that Communists participate in the fascist unions in order to lead the struggle against fascism.

4. *The policy of the Communist International and the Italian and German Communist parties at the time of the advent of fascism and thereabouts up until the Seventh Congress (1935) of the International.*

The problem is too important for me to deal with in a few lines. Here I will touch only on two points concerning not the question of the responsibility for that policy during the advent of fascism, that is to say, its failure to prevent that accession of fascism to power in the two countries, but the question of its effects on fascism's popular impact, which constitutes a relatively different question.

I will say immediately that if that policy had direct consequences in failing to block the accession of fascism to power, it could not avoid having *indirect* effects on the popular impact of fascism. By this I mean that that impact consisted not so much in noticeably tipping certain classes and popular class fractions towards fascism by the *fear of communism* or *Bolshevism*, even though this element, of course, forms one part of that impact and, moreover, constitutes an essential element of the ideology of the fascist regimes. What is otherwise more important to see is, in fact, that some of the popular classes which swung towards fascism, *did so because of the failure of the Italian and German Communist parties to accomplish revolutionary objectives; and, in the face of this deficiency, in order to initiate a process of transition to socialism, those fractions considered, in fact, that fascism would be more able to meet those objectives.* For a while, large collections of these fractions switched their revolutionary aspirations to fascism. It is here that the colossal ambiguity of the initial relation of the masses to fascism resides, and we understand nothing of the popular impact of fascism if we assimilate everything, purely and simply, at least amongst the urban masses, to a 'white-guard-ism' of armed bands of capital. This is probably one of the penetrating aspects of the analysis Clara Zetkin made of fascism at the Third Plenum (1923) of the Communist International:

> Fascism is quite different from Horthy's dictatorship in Hungary . . . Fascism is decidedly not the bourgeoisie's vengeance against a militant uprising of the proletariat. Historically and objectively, fascism is more of a punishment of the proletariat for not taking the revolutionary road.

From this point of view, the fault of the policy of the Italian Communist Party – by contrast with the period of the establishment of fascism and the policy of the International under the aegis of Lenin – and of the German Communist Party under the direct instigation of the International was not to have *diverted* the masses from revolutionary objectives and to have provoked in them some reactionary reflexes, but, essentially, to have left those masses *disoriented* and *disarmed* in the face of fascism's *corrupted ideological recuperation* of deep-seated popular aspirations, and also to have let them, unknowingly, sweep in a policy in the service of big capital. This amounts to saying that, for a long time, these parties did not know how to lead an effective *ideological-political* struggle against fascism. But it is quite evident that I cannot, in this short paper, touch upon the complex reasons for this situation, reasons which I have dealt with at length elsewhere.

11

THE CAPITALIST STATE:
A REPLY TO MILIBAND AND LACLAU

Six years ago, the publication of Ralph Miliband's *The State in Capitalist Society* gave rise to a debate between the author and myself in the columns of *New Left Review*.[1] I reviewed the book and Miliband responded, presenting in the process a critique of my own *Pouvoir politique et classes sociales*.[2] I did not reply to this critique at the time; nor did I do so when Miliband subsequently published a full-length review of my book, on the occasion of its appearance in English.[3] However, now that English-speaking readers are in a position to refer to both my second book, *Fascism and Dictatorship*, and my more recent *Classes in Contemporary Capitalism*, I feel that the moment has come to continue the debate.[4] For if discussion is to be useful and not run in circles, it should draw its strength from new evidence; this new evidence in my case being the writings I have published since *Political Power*.

Before entering into the discussion proper, I feel I should make a number of preliminary remarks. Although the discussion involves primarily Miliband and myself, it does not stop there. A good many others, in Europe, the United States, Latin America and elsewhere, have joined in, in articles and books. I cannot hope to take into consideration all these contributions to the discussion. I shall attempt, however, to show that the way in which the differences between Miliband and myself have sometimes been perceived, especially in England and in the United States, as a controversy between 'instrumentalism' and 'structuralism', is an utterly mistaken way of situating the discussion, at least with respect to the application of the latter term to *Political Power*. Moreover, I shall be taking into consideration one

* First published in *New Left Review* 95 (1976), pp. 63–83. Translated by Rupert Swyer.

of the more recent contributions to the debate, namely Ernesto Laclau's 'The Specificity of the Political: Around the Poulantzas-Miliband Debate'.[5] Though far from sharing all of Laclau's views, I believe his article helps to place the debate on its true terrain, and especially it touches upon some of the real questions to which *Political Power* gave rise.

The following text will thus be more of a contribution to the general discussion than a reply to Miliband's articles, for two fundamental reasons. In the first place, one can only hope to carry on a far-reaching debate with the aid of a precise language, and one that is also, necessarily, situated on a specific theoretical terrain, in the sense that the participants in this debate manage, from within their respective problematics, to attach precise definitions to the concepts, terms or notions they are using. Miliband's writings, however, are marked by the absence of any theoretical problematic. It is this absence above all that lies behind his repeated criticisms of my work for its lack of 'concrete analyses'. This reference to concrete analyses is *certainly valid*, but only when made from within another theoretical problematic, one showing that it is capable of providing a better explanation of historical facts. Thus I do not at all say that Miliband is wrong to discuss 'facts' with me or to quote them against me. All I am saying is that one can only begin to counter a theory by citing the 'proof' of facts, the proof of 'practice', when this approach – which is a perfectly valid one – can be said to flow from a different theoretical position. This is an elementary principle of epistemology. Such a position is lacking in Miliband's writings. As a result, as Laclau has correctly observed, our respective texts are situated on disparate terrains, i.e. they often deal with different matters. Furthermore, this means that the critical terms Miliband uses with reference to me, such as 'abstractionism', 'structuralism' or 'superdeterminism', remain extremely vague and imprecise in his usage.

In the second place, on the subject of Miliband's own work, I have nothing to add to what I wrote in my original review of his book. And while I do have something to say about the evolution of my own positions and analyses since the publication of *Political Power*, in particular concerning a series of rectifications I have felt it necessary to make (I embarked on this process in *Fascism and Dictatorship*, and the rectifications have now crystallized in *Classes in Contemporary Society*), this aspect of the present article can in no way be seen as a reply to Miliband. For Miliband has failed to see the real problems, the real lacunae, ambiguities and debatable points in my first book – the shortcomings which have in fact led me to make the rectifications in question. A large part of the following text is, therefore, a reply to Laclau and a clarification of the criticisms I myself am now in a position to make concerning *Political Power*, rather than a reply to Miliband.

On the Question of Abstractionism

I shall nevertheless begin by returning to the above-mentioned reproach, made repeatedly by Miliband, concerning the characteristic absence in my writings of concrete analyses or reference to concrete historical and empirical facts. This is the chief meaning, as I understand it, of the term 'abstractionism' which he employs when writing about my work.

First of all, I do not think this reproach is in any way justified. Constant and precise references to the state of the class struggle and to the historical transformations of the state are abundantly present in *Political Power*, ranging from analyses of the absolutist state to others which concern the historical models of the bourgeois revolution, the transformations of blocs in power and of the bourgeoisie, the forms of the capitalist state and of capitalist regimes, etc. I could easily go on citing examples. But I doubt whether this would be worthwhile, for I think that the real reason why Miliband makes this criticism of my work lies in the difference in our respective approaches to 'concrete facts'. For me, as against any empiricist or neo-positivist approach such as that of Miliband, these facts can only be rigorously – that is, demonstrably – comprehended if they are explicitly analyzed with the aid of a theoretical apparatus constantly employed throughout the length of the text. This presupposes, as Durkheim already pointed out in his time, that one resolutely eschews the demagogy of the 'palpitating fact', of 'common sense' and the 'illusions of the evident'. Failing this, one can pile up as many concrete analyses as one likes, they will prove nothing whatsoever. I fear that Miliband has confused my eschewal of the illusion of the evident with what he calls 'total lack' of concrete analyses in my work. Miliband himself certainly does not reject, as I have already shown in my first article, the demagogy of common sense – in which, moreover, he is assisted by the dominant 'Anglo-Saxon culture' as a whole. As Perry Anderson clearly demonstrated some time ago, this dominant Anglo-Saxon culture is constitutively imbued, and not by accident, with a prodigious degree of empiricism.[6]

That said, I nonetheless think that the first criticism one can make of *Political Power* concerns not the absence of concrete analyses, but the way they operate within the text, involving a certain *theoreticism*. To some extent this is attributable to an over-rigid epistemological position, one that I shared with Althusser at the time. By concentrating the main weight of our attack against empiricism and neo-positivism, whose condensates, in the Marxist tradition, are economism and historicism, we rightly insisted on the specificity of the theoretical process, that of the production of knowledge which, with its own specific structures, occurs in the thought process. In our view, the 'real fact' or 'practice' was situated both *prior* to the engaging of the thought process (*prior* to Generalities I, which already constituted a 'thought fact', upon which Generalities II would get to work, the latter being concepts which in turn produced 'concrete knowledge', General-ities III) and *after* the conclusion of the thought process, i.e. General-ities III, at which point the question of 'experimentation' and of the adequacy of the theory to the facts and of theory to practice would arise.[7] In Althusser's case, this even created the highly dubious impression that the theoretical process, or 'discourse', would itself contain the criteria for its own validation or 'scientificity': this much is clear in the term he used, with Balibar, and which he has since abandoned, namely *theoretical practice*. This term conjured away the problem of the 'theory-practice' relation by situating this relation entirely *within theory* itself. What we failed to see at the time was that, while firmly upholding the specificity of the theoretical process in relation to the 'concrete real', we should have perceived the particular way in which this 'real' intervenes, and the way in which the theory-practice relation functions throughout the entire theoretical process.

Most of us have since rectified this state of affairs. I must say, for my own part, that I was highly critical of the more extreme forms of this epistemological schema right from the beginning. One can see this in the various warnings I gave in my Introduction to *Political Power*, and in the fact that the term 'theoretical practice' is virtually non-existent in my book. Even so, in the form it took at the time, this epistemological schema had certain specific consequences upon my thinking.

A Necessary Distinction

In the first place, it led to an excessively sharp differentiation between what I called the 'order of exposition' and the 'order of research' (the famous problem of the *Darstellung*). Let me make myself clear: in view of the specificity of the theoretical process, we need to establish a distinction between the order of exposition of a theoretical text, which is supposed to take into account the specific way in which concepts link up, and the order of research, which by dealing with real facts gives rise to the creation of these concepts. As we can see with Marx's *Capital*, the exposition of a theoretical text is more than just a retracing of the steps taken by the underlying research or an account of the history of its production (see the difference, among others, between the *Grundrisse* . . . and *Capital*). I have to admit, however, that by making this distinction rather too sharply in *Political Power* I frequently found myself, in the *order of exposition*, presenting concrete analyses as mere examples or illustrations of the theoretical process. This gave rise to a certain amount of confusion on Miliband's part, for which I am partly responsible: having utterly neglected the distinction between the order of exposition and the order of research (which I had nevertheless analyzed in the Introduction to my book) in his own empirical and neo-positivist approach, Miliband thinks that because the concrete analyses contained in my book were *expounded* in this way, my research itself was not founded upon these concrete-real analyses but merely grew out of abstract concepts. Because I frequently expounded these concrete analyses as examples or illustrations of my theory, Miliband hastily – and naïvely – concluded that that was how I had thought of them within the context of my research, which itself thus became 'abstract'. To convince him of the contrary, I would have had to make a laughing stock of myself by publishing my drafts and notes for *Political Power*!

Formalism

Nonetheless, this theoreticism not only led me to a relatively 'improper' presentation of concrete analyses but also, as Laclau has correctly noted (and I shall be coming back to this), to a second fault: a certain formalism in my research itself – and ultimately a certain neglect of concrete analyses. But I think I can say that I have made the necessary corrections on all these points, both in *Fascism and Dictatorship*, which is a detailed historical analysis of German and Italian fascism, and in *Classes in Contemporary Capitalism*, which deals very concretely with contemporary capitalist society, explicitly referring to a whole range of so-called 'empirical' material. In both these books, however, I naturally maintain my essential difference with Miliband, one that is irreducible, namely the absolute necessity, in my view, of handling 'concrete facts' theoretically. For, to stretch my point further still, this is the only way to conduct genuinely concrete analyses in the full sense of the term, the 'concrete' being, as Marx pointed out, 'the unity of a multiplicity of determinations'. Indeed, one consequence of the absence of any theoretical problematic in Miliband's writings is that, in spite of all appearances, it is hard to find any concrete analyses in his texts. What we find, mainly, are narrative descriptions, along the lines of 'that is the way it is', recalling powerfully to mind the kind of 'abstractionist empiricism' that Wright Mills spoke of. One cannot emphasize too heavily the fact that in neglecting theory one ends up failing to notice the concrete.

But before I say any more about the consequences of this theoreticism in my work, I feel I ought to say a few words in order to help the reader to grasp this phenomenon more clearly. To begin with, one should bear in mind that this can only be understood as a reaction against a certain theoretico-political situation – leaving aside a few exceptions – of Marxism (at least European Marxism) prior to 1968, this situation being characterized by a neo-positivist mechanism and empiricism, and by a pronounced economism. This was of particular importance for me, as I was dealing with problems of the state, a sphere in which the poverty of Marxist thought (for a number of complex reasons, of which Stalinism is not the least) is only too well-known. In my reaction to this state of affairs, I certainly 'bent the stick too far in the other direction', as Lenin would have put it. Nor should it be forgotten, moreover, that the nature of the 'concrete analyses' in *Political Power* stemmed also (aside from my own 'individual' problem) from a precise situation obtaining in the European workers' movement prior to 1968; at that time, it will be recalled, in the absence of a massive development of the movement, the prevailing analyses of the day were those of Gorz and Mallet on 'structural reforms', with all their reformist potential. Many of us in France and elsewhere, taking our cue from various advance signs of the growing popular movement (*Political Power* was published in France in May 1968), criticized these analyses. But there were relatively few significant facts available concerning the class struggle that would have enabled us to base our thinking upon constructive concrete analyses. I think a good many European comrades, of various tendencies, would have little difficulty agreeing with this observation. Confining myself to my own personal case, evidently (and how could it have been otherwise?) the development of class struggles in Europe since 1968 has not been without influence upon my changes in position and rectifications mentioned earlier. In Miliband's case, however, to judge from his published work, what has happened since 1968 has had no effect at all. But this is only an apparent paradox for a fervent advocate of the palpitating real; for in fact nothing could be more academic than the demagogy of the 'empirical real'. Real history can only have an impact upon theoretical positions (and not only upon mine). It can never do so upon positivist empirical positions because, for the latter, facts 'signify' nothing very much: they prove nothing, for the simple reason that they can be reinterpreted *ad infinitum* in any way one chooses. It is this noisy illusion of the evident that gives rise to immutable dogmas.

Difficult Language

Finally, to return to *Political Power*, the theoreticism of which I have spoken undoubtedly led me also to fall prey to a third failing. It led me to employ a sometimes needlessly difficult language, which I have tried to remedy in my subsequent writings. However, in the first place, there is no royal road in science, and the theoretical handling of my object itself called, to some extent, for a language that breaks with customary descriptive discourse. Secondly, my text requires a certain sensitivity to the political problems of the class struggle on the part of the reader, since it is entirely determined by the theoretico-political conjuncture. It is above all to a lack of this political sensitivity, in other words to academism, that I am obliged to attribute Miliband's failure to comprehend some of the analyses in my book. I shall quote only one symptomatic example of this.

> 'A class', Poulantzas says, 'can be considered as a distinct and autonomous class, as a social force, inside a social formation, only when its connection with the relations of production, its economic existence, is reflected on the other levels by a specific presence' . . . One must ask what is a 'specific presence'? The answer is that 'this presence exists when the relation to the relations of production, the place in the process of production, is reflected on the other levels by *pertinent effects*'. What then are 'pertinent effects'? The answer is that 'we shall designate by 'pertinent effects' the fact that the reflection of the place in the process of production on the other levels constitutes a *new element* which cannot be inserted in the typical framework which these levels would present without these elements'. This might be interpreted to mean that a class assumes major significance when it makes a major impact upon affairs – which can hardly be said to get us very far. But Poulantzas does not mean even that. For he also tells us, 'the dominance of the economic struggle' (i.e. 'economism' as a form of working-class struggle – RM) does *not* mean 'an absence of '*pertinent effects*' at the level of the political struggle' – it only means 'a certain form of political

struggle, which Lenin criticizes by considering it as *ineffectual*'. So, at one moment a class can only be considered as distinctive and autonomous if it exercises 'pertinent effects', i.e. a decisive impact; next moment, the 'pertinent effects' may be ineffectual. Poulantzas never ceases to insist on the need for 'rigorous' and 'scientific' analysis. But what kind of 'rigorous' and 'scientific' analysis is this? Indeed, what kind of analysis at all?[8]

What kind of analysis? Miliband seems to have some difficulty understanding so I shall explain right away. My analysis, which incidentally offered the relation between the peasantry and Bonapartism as a concrete example of 'pertinent effects', was chiefly concerned with the nonfundamental classes in a capitalist society (peasantry, petty bourgeoisie), in which cases its usefulness strikes me as evident.[9] But, in the remainder of the text, it also concerned the working class and had two precise political objectives. The first was to attack directly those conceptions according to which the working class has become either integrated or dissolved in contemporary capitalism ('neo-capitalism'); English readers will certainly have heard of these conceptions. My aim was to show that even when the working class has no revolutionary political organization and ideology (the famous 'class consciousness' of the historicists), it still continues to exist as an autonomous and distinct class, since even in this case its 'existence' has pertinent effects on the politico-ideological plane. What effects? Well, we know that social democracy and reformism have often amounted to quite considerable ones, and I should have thought it evident that one cannot analyze the state structures of a good many European countries (including England), without taking into account social democracy in all its forms. But even in these cases, the working class is neither integrated nor diluted in the 'system'. It continues to exist as a distinct class, which is precisely what social democracy demonstrates (pertinent effects), since it too is a working-class phenomenon (as Lenin knew only too well), with its own special links with the working class. Were this not the case, we would be hard put to explain why the bourgeoisie should feel the need to rely upon social democracy (which, after all, is not just any institution) from time to time. So the working class continues to be a distinct class, which also (and chiefly) means we can reasonably hope that it will not eternally continue – where it still does – to be social-democratic and that socialism's prospects therefore remain intact in Europe.

However, this brings us to my second objective. For if – and here I refer directly to Lenin – I have insisted upon the fact that economism/

reformism does not amount to a political absence of the working class, and that this economism/reformism therefore does have pertinent effects on the political and ideological plane in the capitalist system, I have also said that this economist/reformist policy is ineffectual from the point of view of the long-term strategic interests of the working class, from the class viewpoint of the working class: in other words, that this policy cannot lead to socialism. At the same time, no analysis of the capitalist system should ever, as Marx himself said, neglect the class viewpoint of the working class. Miliband has failed to understand this. For him, it is just a quibble over words, or a question of pure 'scientificity'. This would not matter greatly if Miliband at least agreed with me about the fundamental questions. However, I am inclined to doubt this in view of the highly academic style of political discretion which he observes in his own book, for which I reproached him in my article triggering off this controversy.

On the Question of Structuralism

I come now to Miliband's second fundamental criticism of my book, concerning its 'structuralism' ('structural super-determinism' in his first article, 'structural abstractionism' in the second). But what is this structuralism of mine as seen by Miliband? I confess, in all simplicity, that I can find no precise definition of the term in his reviews. Consequently, I feel I ought to attempt a definition myself in order to be able to reply.

One meaning we can attribute to this term falls within the humanist and historicist problematic, indeed within a traditional problematic of bourgeois subjectivist idealism such as has frequently influenced Marxism, namely the problematic of the subject. In this view, I am a Marxist structuralist because I do not grant sufficient importance to the role of concrete individuals and creative persons; to human freedom and action; to free will and to Man's capacity for choice; to the 'project' as against 'necessity' (hence Miliband's term, 'super-determinism'); and so on and so forth. I would like to state quite clearly that I have no intention of replying to this. I consider that everything there is to say on this subject has already been said, and that all those who have not yet understood, or who have yet to be convinced, that we are not here concerned with any genuine alternative of humanist Marxism against structuralist Marxism, but simply with an alternative of idealism against materialism – including as this crops up even within Marxism itself, due to the force of the dominant ideology – are certainly not going to be convinced by the few lines I could possibly add here on this subject. I shall, therefore, merely repeat that the term structuralism applied in this sense to *Political Power* is nothing more, in the final analysis, than a reiteration in modern terms of the kind of objections that bourgeois idealism has always opposed to Marxism of whatever stripe. I may be exaggerating in attributing, even partially, this use of the term structuralism to Miliband; nevertheless, in view of the astonishing vagueness of the term as he employs it, it is essential to clear up this ambiguity.

There is a second, far more serious, meaning of the term structuralism. We may, descriptively (conforming with fashion, but how are we to do otherwise?), designate as structuralism a theoretical conception that neglects the importance and the weight of the class struggle in history, i.e. in the production, reproduction and transformation of 'forms', as Marx put it. Certainly, this is a very summary and negative-diacritical definition; but it is the only one, aside from the first given above, that I can discover in Miliband's use of the term. This meaning cannot be identified with the former one, for one may very well be against humanism and historicism and still fall, or not fall, into structuralism in the second sense. As I have said, this is a far more serious sense of the term structuralism; but as applied to *Political Power*, it is utterly inappropriate. To show this more concretely, I shall deal briefly with the three cases Miliband cites to justify this last use of the term structuralism with references to my book.

The Relative Autonomy of the State

Case One: according to Miliband, my structuralism – in the sense of the absence of reference to the class struggle in my book – prevents me from understanding and analyzing the relative autonomy of the state.

Now, when I examined the relative autonomy of the capitalist state, I established its foundations in two directions, which in fact were merely two aspects of a single approach. The first lay in the precise type of 'separation' between the economic and the political, between the relations of production-consumption-circulation and the state which, according to Marx, define the capitalist mode of production.[10] The second direction lay in the specificity of the constitution of classes and of the class struggle in the capitalist mode of production and social formations. I am thinking here of all my analyses on the specificity of classes in capitalism, on the power bloc and the different fractions of the bourgeoisie, on hegemony within the power bloc, on supporting classes, on the forms of struggle adopted by the working class, etc. All these being reasons that attribute to the capitalist state a precise role as

political organizer and unifier, and as a factor for the establishment of
the 'unstable equilibrium of compromises', which role is constitutively
connected with its relative autonomy.[11]

Two directions that are nothing more than two aspects of a single
approach. The separation of the economic and the political provides
the general framework, depending upon the different stages and
phases of capitalism (this separation is itself liable to transformation),
for an examination of the relative autonomy of the capitalist state –
with the concrete form taken by this autonomy depending upon the
precise conjuncture of the class struggle at any one time. For this
separation of the economic and the political is itself nothing more than
the form taken by the constitution of the classes, and hence it too is a
consequence of their struggles under capitalism.

The fact that certain readers, including Miliband, have chiefly
fastened upon the first direction followed in my book and have
neglected the second is, if I may say so, primarily the outcome of
the 'structuralist' way in which they have read it; it is the outcome of
the structuralism lingering in their own minds. Let us now return,
following this elucidation, to Miliband's shock-question concerning
the relative autonomy of the state, to which my own text is allegedly
incapable of replying because of its structuralism: 'How relative is this
autonomy?'

All I can say here is that, indeed, I cannot reply to this question,
since in this form it is utterly absurd. I could only have answered this
question, couched in these general terms, if I really had been guilty of
structuralism. I can give no *general answer* – not, as Miliband believes,
because I take no account of concrete individuals or of the role of
social classes, but precisely because the term 'relative' in the expression
'relative autonomy' of the state (relative in relation to what or to
whom?) *here* refers to the relationship between state and dominant
classes (i.e. relatively autonomous in relation to the dominant classes).
In other words, it refers to the class struggle within each social
formation and to its corresponding state forms. True, the very
principles of the Marxist theory of the state lay down the general
negative limits of this autonomy. The (capitalist) state, in the long run,
can only correspond to the political interests of the dominant class or
classes. But I do not think that this can be the reply which Miliband
expects of me. For since he is not some incorrigible Fabian, he of
course knows this already. Yet, within these limits, the degree, the
extent, the forms, etc. (*how* relative, and *how is it* relative) of the
relative autonomy of the state can only be examined (as I constantly
underline throughout my book) with reference to a given capitalist

state, and to the precise *conjuncture* of the corresponding class struggle (the specific configuration of the power bloc, the degree of hegemony within this bloc, the relations between the bourgeoisie and its different fractions on the one hand and the working classes and supporting classes on the other, etc.). I cannot, therefore, answer this question in its general form precisely on account of the conjuncture of the class struggle. That said, both in *Political Power* and in my subsequent writings I have amply examined the relative autonomy of precise state forms (absolutist state, Bismarckism, Bonapartism, forms of state under competitive capitalism, the German and Italian fascisms, forms of state in the present phase of monopoly capitalism and, finally, in *La Crise des dictatures*,[12] the military dictatorships in Greece, Portugal and Spain).

Class Power or State Power?

Case Two: Miliband appears to have been particularly shocked[13] by the fact that I have distinguished between *state power* and *state apparatus* and that I have refused to apply the concept of power to the state and to its specific structures. What I have tried to do is to establish that by state power one can only mean the power of certain classes to whose interests the state corresponds. Miliband thinks that, by refusing to speak of the power *of* the state, one cannot, *inter alia*, establish its relative autonomy: only 'something' that possesses power can be relatively autonomous. Here too, the appeal to common sense is blatant.

I think Miliband's incomprehension on this point is highly significant. For he explicitly contradicts himself as regards my 'structuralism', and my analyses on this point (which he rejects) would in fact suffice, if that were necessary, to wipe out all suspicion of structuralism on my part. According to an old and persistent conception of bourgeois social science and politics – 'institutionalism-functionalism', of which true structuralism is merely a variant, and which harks back to Max Weber (though if we scrape off a few more layers, it is always Hegel that we find at the bottom) – it is the structures/institutions which hold/wield power, with the relations of power between 'social groups' flowing from this institutional power. One sees this tendency currently not only in the theory of the state, but also in a range of other spheres: in the present trend of the sociology of work, which grants pride of place to the business enterprise/institution/power as against classes (cf. Lockwood, Goldthorpe); in the present, highly fashionable, trend of the sociology of organizations (including Galbraith); and so on. What disappears, when one acritically allows this tendency to contaminate Marxism, is the primordial role of classes and the class struggle by comparison with structures – institutions and organs, including the state organs. To attribute specific power to the state, or to designate structures/institutions as the field of application of the concept of power, would be to fall into structuralism, by attributing the principal role in the reproduction/ transformation of social formations to these organs. Conversely, by comprehending the relations of power as class relations, I have attempted to break definitely with structuralism, which is the modern form of this bourgeois idealism.

Does this mean that by not applying the concept of power to the state apparatus we prevent ourselves from situating its relative autonomy? Not at all – provided, of course, that we break with a certain naturalist/positivist, or even psycho-sociological conception of power ('A brings pressure to bear on B to make the latter do something he would not have done without pressure from A'). All this means is that the relative autonomy of the capitalist state stems precisely from the contradictory relations of power between the different social classes. That it is, in the final analysis, a 'resultant' of the relations of power between classes within a capitalist formation – it being perfectly clear that the capitalist state has its own institutional specificity (separation of the political and the economic) which renders it irreducible to an immediate and direct expression of the strict 'economic-corporate' interests (Gramsci) of this or that class or fraction of the power bloc, and that it must represent the political unity of this bloc under the hegemony of a class or fraction of a class. But it does not end there. By refusing to apply the concept of power to the state apparatus and to its institutions, one also refuses to account for the relative autonomy of the state in terms of the group made up of the agents of the state and in terms of the specific power of this group, as those conceptions which apply the concept of power to the state invariably do: the bureaucratic class (from Hegel via Weber to Rizzi and Burnham); the political élites (this is Miliband's conception, as I pointed out in my review of his book); the techno-structure (power of the 'business machine' and the state apparatus, etc.

The problem is not a simple one, and this is not the place in which to go into it at length. I should point out that, since *Political Power*, I have had occasion to modify and rectify certain of my analyses, not in the direction of Miliband but, on the contrary, in the opposite direction, i.e. in the direction already inherent in *Political Power*. I am inclined to think, in effect, that I did not sufficiently emphasize the primacy of the class struggle as compared with the state apparatus. I was thus led to refine my conceptions, in *Classes in Contemporary Capitalism*, by examining the form and the role of the state in the current phase of capitalism/imperialism, and its specifically relative autonomy, depending on the existing social formations. Still taking the separation of the political and the economic under capitalism, even in its present phase, as our point of departure, the state should be seen (as should capital, according to Marx) as a relation, or more precisely as the condensate of a relation of power between struggling classes. In this way we escape the false dilemma entailed by the present discussion on the state, between the state comprehended as a thing/instrument and the state comprehended as subject. As a thing: this refers to the instrumentalist conception of the state, as a passive tool in the hands of a class or fraction, in which case the state is seen as having no autonomy whatever. As subject: the autonomy of the state, conceived here in terms of its specific power, ends up by being considered as absolute, by being reduced to its 'own will', in the form of the rationalizing instance of civil society (cf. Keynes), and is incarnated in the power of the group that concretely represents this rationality/power (bureaucracy, élites).

In either case (the state as thing or as subject), the relation state/social classes is comprehended as a relation of externality: either the social classes, subdue the state (thing) to themselves through the interplay of 'influences' and 'pressure groups', or else the state (subject) subdues or controls the classes. In this relation of externality, the state and the dominant classes are thus seen as two entities confronting each other, with the one possessing the power the other does not have, according to the traditional conception of 'zero-sum power'. Either the dominant classes absorb the state by emptying it of its own specific power (the state as thing in the thesis of the merger of the state and the monopolies upheld in the orthodox Communist conception of 'state monopoly capitalism'); or else the state 'resists', and deprives the dominant class of power to its own advantage (the state as subject and 'referee' between the contending classes, a conception dear to social democracy).

But, I repeat, the relative autonomy of the state, founded on the separation (constantly being transformed) of the economic and the political, is inherent in its very structure (the state is a relation) in so far as it is the resultant of contradictions and of the class struggle as expressed, always in their own specific manner, within the state itself – this state which is both shot through and constituted with and by these class contradictions. It is precisely this that enables us exactly to

pinpoint the specific role of the bureaucracy which, although it
constitutes a specific social category, is not a group standing above,
outside or to one side of classes: an élite, but one whose members also
have a class situation or membership. To my mind, the implications of
this analysis are of great importance. Starting from this analysis, I have
attempted to examine the precise role of existing state machines in the
reproduction of capitalism/imperialism (*Classes in Contemporary
Capitalism*), and to examine certain state forms, such as the Greek,
Portuguese and Spanish military dictatorships (*La Crise des dictatures*).

I cannot pursue this analysis here, but suffice it to say that, in my
view, this is the approach that will enable us to establish theoretically,
and to examine concretely, the way in which the relative autonomy of
the capitalist state develops and functions with respect to the particular economic-corporate interests of this or that fraction of the power
bloc, in such a way that the state always guards the general political
interests of this bloc – which certainly does not occur merely as a result
of the state's and the bureaucracy's own 'rationalizing will'. Indeed,
conceiving of the capitalist state as a *relation*, as being structurally
shot through and constituted with and by class contradictions, means
firmly grasping the fact that an institution (the state) that is destined to
reproduce class divisions cannot really be a monolithic, fissureless
bloc, but is itself, by virtue of its very structure (the state is a relation),
divided. The various organs and branches of the state (ministries and
government offices, executive and parliament, central administration
and local and regional authorities, army, judiciary, etc.) reveal major
contradictions among themselves, each of them frequently constituting
the seat and the representative – in short, the crystallization – of this or
that fraction of the power bloc, this or that specific and competing
interest. In this context, the process whereby the general political
interest of the power bloc is established, and whereby the state
intervenes to ensure the reproduction of the overall system, may well,
at a certain level, appear chaotic and contradictory, as a 'resultant' of
these inter-organ and inter-branch contradictions. What is involved is
a process of structural selectivity by one of the organs from the
information provided and measures taken by the others: a contradictory process of decision and also of partial non-decision (consider
the problems surrounding capitalist planning); of structural determination of priorities and counter-priorities (with one organ obstructing
and short-circuiting the others); of immediate and mutually conflicting
'compensating' institutional reactions in the face of the falling rate of
profit; of 'filtering' by each organ of the measures taken by other
organs, etc. In short, the relative autonomy of the state with respect to

this or that fraction of the power bloc, which is essential to its role as political unifier of this bloc under the hegemony of a class or fraction (at present the monopoly capitalist fraction), thus appears, in the process of constitution and functioning of the state, as a resultant of inter-organ and inter-branch contradictions (the state being divided). These inter-organ contradictions, moreover, are themselves inherent in the very structure of the capitalist state seen as the condensate of a class relation, founded on the separation of the political and the economic. This is a fundamental theoretical approach, as can be seen not only in my own work, but also in that of a number of other researchers, notably M. Castells in France and J. Hirsch in Germany.[14]

Fascisms and Parliamentary-Democratic State

Case Three: According to Miliband, my abstractionist or super-determinist structuralism prevents me from situating precisely the differences between different forms of bourgeois state. In particular, it leads me, as happened with the Comintern in its notorious Third Period (1928–35), to more or less identify fascist forms with the parliamentary-democratic forms of the capitalist state. However, this charge is pure mythology. It is simply not true in so far as *Political Power* is concerned; in attacking the concept of totalitarianism, I precisely pointed to the direction that an analysis of the differences between the fascist state and the parliamentary-democratic forms of the bourgeois state would have to take. In *Fascism and Dictatorship* I then applied and further defined this direction, attempting to establish the specificity of the capitalist state in its exceptional form, and within this exceptional capitalist state the specificity of fascism as compared with Bonapartism, military dictatorship etc. I did so by attacking the theoretico-political principles that had led the Comintern to those identifications which Miliband rightly points to – the very principles which I had already passed under critical review in *Political Power*. What is amazing is that Miliband makes the above criticism of me not only in his first article in 1970, at a time when *Fascism and Dictatorship* had not yet appeared, but again in his latest article, in 1973. Such methods make any constructive dialogue impossible.

Now that these points have all been examined, does there remain any serious substance in Miliband's charge of structuralism? None, I think. All that remains is a polemical catch-phrase pure and simple, masking a factual and empirical critique – which itself turns out to be inconsistent – of my positions. The reason why I am labouring this point a little is that certain authors, especially in the United States, have perceived the debate between Miliband and myself as a supposed debate between instrumentalism and structuralism, thus posing a false dilemma, or even an ideological alternative, from which some thought it would be possible to escape by inventing a 'third way' which like all third ways would be the true one and which like all truths would lie somewhere 'in between'.[15] Doubtless the academic and ideologico-political conjuncture in the United States is substantially responsible for this, but that is beside the point. I have tried to show why it is that the second term of this debate, as conceived here, is wrong, and why it thus resulted in a false dilemma.

Does this mean I have no criticisms to make of *Political Power* other than those I have already made? Or that my writings have not evolved in any way other than the ones I have already mentioned? By no means. But if we are to make real progress, the impasse represented by Miliband's positions will not help us. Let us now, therefore, try out a detour via Laclau.

On the Question of Formalism

While I am far from agreeing with all of Laclau's criticisms of *Political Power*, he does nevertheless raise several crucial questions to which my position gave rise at the time. Very briefly, I shall try to summarize what I believe to be the most interesting aspect of Laclau's criticism of this position as 'formalist'.

Laclau starts by criticizing our (the Althusserians') conception of 'instances' (economic, political, ideological) which are both specific and autonomous with respect to each other, and whose interaction produces the mode of production – determined by the economic in the last resort, but in which another instance may play the dominant role. But, Laclau says, this inevitably leads to formalism and taxinomism in establishing the relations between the various instances, the content of their concepts and the construction of their object. For we begin by assuming, *a priori*, that these 'elements/instances' are quasi-Aristote-lian notions existing as such in the various modes of production, these modes themselves being merely the outcome of the *a posteriori* combination of these elements. Laclau further charges that we treat the economic instance as unequivocal, in other words as having the same meaning and the same content in all modes of production; and furthermore that the relative autonomy of these different instances (economic, political, ideological) with respect to each other does not, as our formalism had led us to believe, characterize other modes of production, but is specific to capitalism.

I think that, to some extent, Laclau is right in his criticisms.[16] However, it is incorrect to hold that these criticisms concern all of us to the same degree. For, although the writings of a whole number of us were perceived, and in many ways functioned, as if they all arose from an identical problematic, in fact essential differences existed among certain of these writings right from the outset. In the field of historical materialism, for example, there were already essential differences between *Political Power* (as well as Bettelheim's writings, but here I shall speak only for myself), on the one hand, and Balibar's essay 'The Basic Concepts of Historical Materialism' in *Reading 'Capital'*, on the other. These differences have now come out into the open, with Balibar publishing a self-criticism which is correct on certain points.[17] Laclau, however, does not take these differences into account in his article.

Briefly, then, I would say that Balibar's essay was characterized not only by a pronounced formalism, but also by economism and by an almost systematic underestimation of the role of the class struggle, the two latter elements being in fact the principal causes of the former. For, in the first place, as Balibar himself now recognizes, his writings did contain the idea of an economic instance in-itself, made up of elements that remained invariant in all modes of production. This entailed a self-reproducible and self-regulating economic instance, serving as the basis of the historical process. It was precisely this that led him to try to construct a general theory of 'modes of economic production'. It should be pointed out here that, in Balibar's view, the concept of the mode of production was limited exclusively to the economic sphere. This conception then led him to comprehend, by analogy, the other instances (political, ideological) in the same way, i.e. as made up of elements which do not vary from one mode of production to another and which only combine *afterwards*: all these instances were seen as autonomous in relation to each other by virtue of their essence, by virtue of their pre-existing intrinsic nature as predetermined elements. As with the economic, the political and ideology were seen as having the same meaning in all the various modes of production.

In the second place, all this went hand in hand with a considerable underestimation in Balibar's essay of the role of the class struggle. This can be seen in the fact that nowhere did he make the rigorous distinction between mode of production and social formation that would have enabled him to grasp the precise role, in the reproduction/transformation of social relations, of the class struggle – that class struggle which, in point of fact, operates within concrete social formations. As Balibar himself admits, he 'did not conceive of the *two* concepts, social formation, on the one hand, and mode of production on the other, as distinct from each other'.[18] The same underestimation can be seen in the absence, in Balibar's essay, of the concept of historical conjuncture, the strategic condensation point of the class struggle: '[My analyses] applied what should have served to deal with the historical conjuncture to a comparison of modes of production'.[19]

On all these points, and on others, there were already a number of essential differences between Balibar's text and *Political Power*. First, on the fundamental and decisive concept of the mode of production. For Balibar, in *Reading 'Capital'*: 'The terms production and mode of production will be taken in their restricted sense, that which defines, within any social complex, the partial object of political economy, that is, in the sense of the economic practice of production.'[20] In *Political Power*, on the other hand:

> By *mode of production* we shall designate not what is generally marked out as the economic (i.e. relations of production in the strict sense), but a specific combination of various structures and practices (economic, political, ideological) which, in combination, appear as so many instances or levels . . . of this mode.[21]

In any case, Balibar has now criticized himself on this point:

> And this is why, as against all economism, the concept of the mode of production designates, for Marx, even on an abstract level, the complex unity of determinations arising out of both the base and the superstucture.[22]

The difference is fundamental. Concerning the crucial, nodal concept of the mode of production, it clearly shows that I was trying to break with the conception of a self-regulating and inherently unchangeable economic level/instance whose intrinsic nature remains the same in any given mode of production, and that I attributed the highest importance to the class struggle. Furthermore, I need hardly remind the reader of the central rôle played in *Political Power* both by the difference between mode of production and social formation,[23] and by the concept of conjuncture, whose absence from Balibar's work I expressly criticized.[24] That said, I nevertheless think that *Political Power* did suffer from this formalism to some degree. This can be seen more concretely if we return to Laclau's criticisms.

'General Theory'

1. As compared with Balibar's concept of the mode of production, mine had the advantage of considering the relation between the various instances, their unity, as primary, i.e. as defining their specificity itself: it was the mode of production (whichever it might be) that determined, in my view, the specificity, the dimensions and the specific structure of each instance, and hence of the political, in each mode. As a result, I was able to avoid conceiving of the different instances (in particular the political, the state) as being by nature immutable and pre-existing, in essence, their meeting together within a precise mode of production. In particular, this helped me to avoid trying to elaborate a 'general theory' of the political/state through the various modes of production, as Balibar tried to do for the economic. In *Political Power* I constantly repeat that the only theory I shall be attempting to construct is that of the capitalist state, and that the very meaning of the state under capitalism is different from the meanings it can take on in other – pre-capitalist – modes of production. In addition, my distinction between mode of production and social formation, the role that I attributed to the concept of conjuncture, and hence the attention I paid to the class struggle, more often than not helped me to avoid confining myself to a taxinomic typology of the different forms of the capitalist state itself – i.e. a conception that sees these forms as simple differential 'combinatory concretizations' of some essence/nature of the capitalist state as such, in itself.

But this formalism nonetheless had its effects upon my own analyses. For example, while stating that all I intended was to construct a theory of the capitalist state, I also said: 'In the circumstances, it seems to me particularly illusory and dangerous (theoretically of course) to proceed further towards systematizing the political in the general theory, inasmuch as we do not yet have enough systematic regional theories of the political in the different modes of production, nor enough systematic theories of the different modes of production.'[25] Which shows that, even if I did not attempt the same undertaking on behalf of the political/state as Balibar had for the economic, I did nevertheless consider this undertaking to be both possible and legitimate. The reason why I did not, in fact, set about constructing this general theory of the political was not, as I thought and suggested, because of any shortage of information, but because, apart from a few indications given by Marx and Engels, by Lenin in *State and Revolution* and by Gramsci, this theory is impossible to construct. The dimensions, the extent and the content of the very concept of the political/state, as indeed those of the economic, and the form taken by their relation (the relation between the economic and the extra-economic, as Laclau puts it), differ considerably from one mode of production to another. I have explained this in somewhat greater detail in *Classes in Contemporary Capitalism*, and indeed have also attempted to show the transformations of the respective spaces of the political/state and the economic in the different stages and phases of capitalism itself – particularly its current phase.

2. Despite my clear differentiation between mode of production and social formation, and the fact that I focused my analyses upon social formations, this formalism nevertheless on occasion led me to consider social formations as being the 'concretization/spatialization' of modes of production existing and reproducing themselves as such, in the abstract; hence sometimes to see the concrete forms of the capitalist state as the concretization/spatialization of elements of the type of capitalist state existing in the abstract. This, as Perry Anderson correctly noted in his recent major work, emerges clearly in my analyses of the absolutist state.[26] I have corrected this point of view in *Fascism and Dictatorship* and, above all, in *Classes in Contemporary Capitalism*, where I consider social formations, wherever the class struggle is at work, as the effective locus of the existence and reproduction of modes of production; hence the concrete forms of the capitalist state as the effective locus of the existence, reproduction and transformation of the specific characteristics of the capitalist state.

3. Let us now turn to the 'relative autonomy' of the instances (economic, political, ideological) of which I spoke earlier. In Balibar's writings, but also sometimes with Althusser himself, this was seen as an invariable characteristic related to the intrinsic nature or essence of each instance and cutting across the different modes of production. In Althusser's writings, this can be seen in certain formulations concerning the 'ideological instance', and even in his article 'Ideology and Ideological State Apparatuses', which I criticized on this point in *Fascism and Dictatorship*.[27]

   The problem was entirely different in my case. I was dealing with a precise and crucial problem, that of the separation of the political and the economic which, according to Marx, defines the capitalist mode of production underlying the relative autonomy of the capitalist state. At no time does Balibar deal with this phenomenon as such, for in his view this capitalist 'separation' was nothing more than the form assumed, under capitalism, by an autonomy – in nature and essence

– of instances in all modes of production. My own mistake here was of a completely different order. It was, as Laclau correctly observes, that I rather hurriedly (after all, this was not my problem) suggested that this separation/autonomy specific to capitalism might also make its appearance, though in different forms, in pre-capitalist modes of production. This was a classic error of historical hindsight. Emmanuel Terray, in *Marxism and Primitive Society*,[28] Laclau in his various articles and others too have since put matters straight on this point.

4. The formalism from which *Political Power* suffers led me to convey, within the separation of the political and the economic specific to capitalism, a certain view of instances as being to some extent partitioned from and impermeable to each other. Even though, unlike Balibar (for whom the economic is a self-reproducing and self-regulating instance in itself), I substantially analyzed the decisive role of the political/state as compared with the economic in the reproduction of capitalism, I did not manage to situate with precision the status and functioning of economic 'interventions' by the state, implying that under capitalism the instances might well be 'external' to each other, their relations being defined precisely by the ambiguity of the term 'intervention'. One of the most important and difficult problems I tried to resolve in *Classes in Contemporary Capitalism* – one already outlined in *Fascism and Dictatorship* and which is crucial in the current phase of monopoly capitalism, given the specific economic role which the state assumes in this phase – is that of comprehending the capitalist separation of the political/state and the economic as the form taken by a specific presence of the political 'within' the economic's reproductive space under capitalism. In other words, this problem was one of grasping the precise status and functioning of the current economic role of the state, without at the same time abandoning the separation of the political and the economic (as do the 'state monopoly capitalism' theoreticians in the final analysis, for whom this separation has been abolished in the present state monopoly phase). This, moreover, is one of the fundamental questions now dominating Marxist work on the state in Germany, where Marxist discussion of the economic role of the state is probably the most advanced in Europe. These considerations also led me, in my last book, to develop and elaborate a concrete basis for the analyses in *Political Power* according to which social classes cannot be determined solely on the economic level. I showed, in particular, that politico-ideological class determinations are also present 'within' economic class determinations right at the heart of the relations of production.

5. One last point should be made, which brings us back to something I mentioned earlier concerning my supposed 'structuralism'. In *Political Power*, I made a distinction between structures and practices, or rather between structures and class practices, with the concept of social classes covering the entire 'field' of practices.[29] This distinction has sometimes been criticized as containing a structuralist deviation. In fact, however, the purpose of this distinction was the very opposite; in other words, my objectives were patently anti-structuralist. The fact is, this distinction enabled me, while still retaining the class foundation and objective class determination (structures) – which are simply Marxist materialism – to advance a fundamental proposition with considerable political implications. I argued that social classes, although objectively determined (structures), are not ontological and nominalist entities, but only exist within and through the class struggle (practices). The class division of society necessarily means class struggle, for we cannot speak of classes without speaking of the class struggle. This runs counter to official modern sociology, which is prepared to speak about classes, but never about the class struggle.

Even so, this distinction was marked by a certain degree of formalism. Through my own fault, for example, certain readers may have been led to think that structures and practices constituted, as it were, two ontologically distinct domains. A distinction designed to demonstrate the importance of the class struggle in the very process of the definition of classes (which can also be seen in the fact, mentioned above, that I refused to apply the concept of power to the state/structure/institution) was perceived as according pride of place to 'structures' that were said to be external to or outside the class struggle. Consequently, in *Classes in Contemporary Capitalism*, and particularly in the Introduction, I seek to rectify this position. With respect to social classes, I speak only of class practices, as a single field covering the entire range of the social division of labour, but within which I distinguish between structural class determination and class position in a given conjuncture. This makes it possible to retain all that was positive in *Political Power* while dispelling its ambiguities. One simple example will show what I mean. As against historicist conceptions of the 'class consciousness' type, even if the working-class aristocracy has a bourgeois class position in the present conjuncture: 1. it remains, in its structural class determination, a part of the working class – a 'layer' of the working class, as Lenin put it; 2. this structural class determination of the working-class aristocracy is necessarily reflected in working-class practices ('class instinct' as Lenin used to say) – practices that can always be discerned beneath its bourgeois 'discourse', etc. This conception, moreover, also has considerable implications for the analysis of the petty bourgeoisie put forward in the same book.

I have already taken up a good deal of space, but I would like to make one last remark before concluding. While discussions such as this one do help to elucidate problems, they suffer from a twin disadvantage. In the first place, any debate of this kind necessarily entails, on both sides, a high degree of schematization, whereas in reality things are often a good deal more complex. In the second place, such a debate is only too easily personalized (Poulantzas versus Miliband and vice versa), even though it is quite clear that if the discussion has been fruitful, as I happen to think it has, this is because a lot of people have become involved in it and helped to propel it forward. Their comments have often been very useful to me, and have contributed to the evolution of my positions mentioned above. I especially want to draw attention to this point, even though it has not been possible here to refer to all these comments directly.

=== 12 ===

THE POLITICAL CRISIS AND THE CRISIS OF THE STATE

In this essay, I will clarify certain methodological points that are essential to understand before both the transformations and the crisis of the capitalist state in the current situation of monopoly capitalism can be analyzed. I will pose certain problems facing this analysis and sketch some directions for further research.

Thus announcing my plan I immediately face a problem in establishing a theoretical line for the research: the transformations that affect the state apparatuses in the developed capitalist countries and that permit us to speak of new forms of the capitalist state are not reducible to specific characteristics. Certain transformations suggest general characteristics that come from the current crisis of capitalism and that concern the reproduction of capitalism; in other words, even if the crisis of capitalism and the crisis of the state were eventually reabsorbed, these profound modifications of the state apparatus would nonetheless persist. This also means, on the other hand, that this crisis is articulated to the more general transformation relevant to the form of the state in the current phase of monopoly capitalism and that the characteristics of the crisis of the state that effect these states are part of these more general transformations.

On the Concept of Crisis

The distinction between the reproduction phase of capitalism and the crisis of capitalism, and thus the distinction between the transformations of the state relevant to this phase and those relevant to the crisis

* First published in French as 'Les transformations actuelles de l'état, la crise politique, et la crise de l'état' in Nicos Poulantzas (ed.), *La Crise de l'état*, Presses Universitaires de France, Paris 1976, pp. 19-58. This translation is taken from J.W. Freiburg (ed.), *Critical Sociology: European Perspectives*, New York 1979, pp. 373–93. Translated by J.W. Freiburg. [Translation modified by the editor.]

of the state, require a more precise definition of 'crisis.' This definition is necessary because of the current overuse of the term, which embraces economic crisis, political crisis, ideological crisis, and the relationships among these. Proceeding from this profusion, let us ask ourselves about the different types of crises of capitalism, particularly, about the precise characteristics and modes of the current political crisis and the crisis of the state.

1. One can delimit the concept of crisis already at the level which is called economic crisis by realizing that it is necessary to do so to avoid a double danger:

(a) The economic and bourgeois-sociological conception of crisis, now so popular, which views crisis as a dysfunctional moment that ruptures an otherwise harmonious functioning of the 'system,' a moment that will pass when equilibrium is re-established. This narrow conception excludes the contradictions and class struggles that are inherent in the reproduction of capitalism. Now, because historically the average rate of profit tends to fall insofar as the relations of capitalist production conflict with the exploited class, we know for a fact that economic crises are not only inherent to the fundamental capital-labour contradiction but also fulfil an organic role; these crises function as periodic and savage purges of capitalism to counter the tendency for the average rate of profit to fall. Massive devaluations and permanently increased productivity and rates of exploitation work to elevate the average rate of profit. This means, on the one hand, that economic crisis, far from being moments of disarticulation, (dysfunctions of the economic 'system') are necessary to the survival and the reproduction of capitalism. It follows that not just any economic crisis can automatically bring down capitalism, but only those that translate themselves into *political crises*, for then the issue *can be* the overthrowing of capitalism. On the other hand, it also means that crises are not accidental explosions of anomic or hetero-geneous elements in the otherwise normally functioning, equilibrated, and harmonious system, but that the generic elements of crises (due to class struggle) are always at work in the reproduction of capitalism.

(b) The mechanistic, evolutionistic and economistic conception of the crisis, dominant in the Communist International between the two world wars, still makes itself felt in its repercussions and made the way for an economistic catastrophe (its political implications also were very se-vere). This conception, starting from the point that the reproduction of capitalist relations, particularly in the imperialist-monopoly capitalist stage, because of the new contradictions, would accentuate the tendency of the rate of profit to fall, included in an organic and intensified fashion some elements of crisis and concluded that crisis was constantly present. The conception thus stretched the concept of crisis to the point where it covered a stage or phase of the reproduction of capitalism; the Third International viewed this state of monopoly capitalism as one of constantly present crisis, a conception that in fact led to the notion of 'the general crisis of capitalism' and to the use to which this was put. In its contemporary form, this conception considers the current reproduction of monopoly capitalism as a phase of 'general crisis' continuing to the end of capitalism, that is, as a permanent crisis of capitalism. Economism pictures capitalism insofar as it reproduces itself, to automatically accentuate its own 'rotting' and to be presently in its last phase of reproduction (which is always, as if by chance, the one in which the analyst finds himself), and that this coincides with a permanent crisis. In one fashion or another, it always comes out the same: this time (a 'this time' that is beginning to get a bit repetitive) the crisis is the real general crisis, the final and apocalyptic crisis. It should be evident that capitalism can always (although depending on class struggles this could be *cannot*) reabsorb these crises and prolong its reproduction. What is important to remember here is that this conception dissolves the specificity of the concept of crisis because, in this sense, capitalism was always in crisis.

We can, with these precautions, situate the first problem underlying the makeup of the concept of crisis: if it is indeed true that the generic elements of crisis are present and permanently at work in the reproduction of capitalist relations, more particularly in its current phase, it would nevertheless be necessary to limit this concept to a particular situation of a condensation of contradictions. This means that the elements of the crisis permanently existing in the reproduction of capitalism must be grasped in their function as real transformations in the state and phase that cut across capitalism but that also point to the situation of a condensation of contradictions that can be called 'crises.' These crises therefore carry the marks of the period that occur throughout capitalism without so much as watering it down; and this is also true for the current crisis. In brief, all teleological concepts of crisis must be mistrusted: the end of capitalism does not depend on any crisis whatsoever but on the issue of the class struggles that manifest themselves therein.

2. What has just been said for the economic crisis also is true, *mutatis mutandis*, for political crises, of which the crisis of the state is a constituent element.

In effect, here, we also find the two dangers I spoke of earlier:

(a) The bourgeois-sociological and political science conceptions of political crisis and the crisis of the state. This crisis is considered as a 'dysfunctional' moment rudely breaking the naturally equilibrated 'political system' that otherwise functions in a harmonious and internally self-regulating fashion. From traditional functionalism to the currently popular 'systems' approach, in the end it is always the same story: the underlying vision ignores class struggle when conceptualizing an integrated pluralist society of 'powers' and 'counter-powers,' the 'institutionalization of social conflicts,' and so forth. This not only makes it impossible to realize the proper place of the political crises but also, precisely to the extent that they reduce socio-political 'conflicts' to those of ideas and opinions, to speak of political crises in terms other than 'crises of values' or crises of 'legitimization'. So, in fact: first, the generic elements of political crisis, due to class struggle, are inherent in the reproduction of institutionalized political power; and second, the political crisis and crisis of the state although slackening in certain aspects, play an organic role in the reproduction of class domination because, unless the struggle leads to the transition to socialism, this crisis can establish the way (sometimes the only way) for the restoration of an unsteady class hegemony and the way (sometimes the only way) for a transformation-adaptation of the capitalist state to the new realities of class conflict.

(b) The prevailing conception, at the end of a certain period of the Communist International (post-Leninist, to simplify), the effects of which are still felt, leads, when applied to the political crisis and the crisis of the state, to the same experiences as when it is applied to the economic crisis. Starting with the point that the political domain, particularly in the imperialist stage, carried permanent generic elements of political crisis because of the class struggle, the analysis concluded with the conception of this stage as that of a constantly present political crisis with a conception of the state as being in permanent open crisis. This also has dissolved the specificity of the concept of political crisis, which has had some serious effects: as far as the political crisis is concerned, because of the impossibility of a theoretical elaboration of the concept of crisis in this context, the identification of all political crisis with 'revolutionary situations', which was almost constantly declared until the Seventh Congress (1935) of the International, opened the way to the Popular Fronts. As far as the state is concerned this conception had some effects, in particular from 1928 to 1935, when it culminated in the conception of the transformations of the capitalist states relevant to this stage and phase of the reproduction of capitalism as a crisis of these states – the fascistization of these states made during the supposed permanent 'revolutionary crisis'. Thus, the democratic-parliamentary forms under which certain of these transformations took place were identified with the fascist form of state and were dependent on a political crisis of specific characteristics.

We can, therefore, delimit the problems posed by the concept of political crisis: although the political domain, including that of the state apparatus, carries permanently within it, particularly under capitalism in its current phase, generic elements of crisis, we must reserve the concept of political crisis for the field of a particular situation of the condensation of contradictions even if the crises appear in general and permanent contexts, of instability that are thoroughly singular. In brief, political crisis consists of a series of particular traits, resulting in this condensation of contradictions in their political struggles with the state apparatus.

3. This elucidation of political crisis in its turn poses a series of new problems: to begin with, that of the relations between the economic crisis and the political crisis. In effect, contradicting the 'economist' conception, an economic crisis does not automatically translate itself into a political crisis or a crisis of the state because the political is not a simple reflection of the economic; the capitalist state is marked by a relative 'separation' from the relations of production, the accumulation of capital, and the extraction of surplus-value, a separation that constitutes in a specific field a proper organizational structure. The political conflict of social classes over power and the state apparatus is, moreover, not reducible to the economic conflict; it also is inscribed in a specific field. From this it follows that:

(a) The political crisis, accompanying the political conflict of classes and the state apparatus, has a series of particular traits that can only be grasped in specific frames of reference; this means that an economic crisis does not necessarily translate itself into a political crisis.

(b) We can witness political crises that are in tune with the fundamental coordinates of the reproduction of the relations of production and the conflicts over exploitation but that are not related to any economic crisis whatsoever; nothing is more false than to believe that a political crisis, an intensification of class conflict at the political level, can only 'result' from an economic crisis.

(c) An economic crisis *can* translate itself into a political crisis, and this is precisely what is currently happening in certain capitalist countries. In order to designate these crises that envelop the ensemble of the social relations, we will reserve a particular term: the crisis of hegemony, following Gramsci, or structural crisis, following a current term. In effect, the structural character of the current crisis does not reside only in its peculiarities as an economic crisis but also in its repercussions as a political crisis and a crisis of the state. It is still necessary to discuss any ambiguity that the term of 'structural crisis' risks gliding over. We must not take 'structural' in the usual sense that designates 'structure' according to the degree of its permanence as opposed to 'conjuncture', meaning that which is secondary and ephemeral, because we risk succumbing to the danger I already have mentioned, that is, understanding by structural crisis a permanent trait of capitalism in its current phase, seeing in this the final crisis of capitalism, and thus diluting the specificity of the concept of crisis. We can only continue to use this term if we reserve it to the field of a particular conjunction and by precisely designating how the crisis affects the ensemble of social relations (economic crisis and political crisis) and manifests itself in a conjuncture of a situation that reveals and condenses the inherent contradictions in the social structure. In other words, we must make the very notion of structural crisis relative: if the current economic crisis distinguishes itself from the simple cyclical economic crises of capitalism, it does not constitute a structural crisis or a crisis of hegemony except for certain capitalist countries where it translates itself into a political-ideological crisis in the proper sense of the term.

(d) Economic crisis, then, can translate itself into political crisis. But this does not imply a chronological concordance, that is, a simultaneity of the two crises and their own processes. Because of the specificity of the political field, we often find displacements between the two crises, each with its own rhythm. The political crisis and the crisis of the state can come later than the economic crises, that is, wait until it culminates, occur when it is losing its intensity (this was the case for the political crisis in Germany, which led in 1933 to the accession of Nazism, and for the political crisis in France, which led to the accession of the Popular Front in 1936), or even after it has been reabsorbed. It is important to note that where the signs of economic 'recovery' are doubted is indeed a situation of political crises. But political crisis also can precede economic crisis, articulating it (always according to its divergences) as in the case of the prolonged and current effects in France of May 1968, a time when the economic crisis, even supposing that it had actually begun, was still far from producing any massive effects. Finally, political crisis can precede economic crisis and can even constitute a principal factor of it (as was the case in Chile under Allende).

4. Finally, it is necessary to mention some supplementary points concerning political crisis.

(a) We can determine the general characteristics of a political crisis and a crisis of the state, that is, grasp the general sense of the concept. But proceeding from this conceptualization of the political crisis, we can specify some particular species of this crisis: political crises, for example, can be identified neither with a revolutionary situation nor with a crisis of fascistization; these, while indeed containing general characteristics of political crisis, constitute particular types specified by their own traits. This is currently quite important insofar as we sometimes have the tendency to identify the political crisis–crisis of the state with a process of fascistization.

(b) A political crisis, while being a precise conjunctural situation, cannot be reduced to an instantaneous conflagration but instead constitutes a real process with its own rhythm, to its own strong times and weak times, highs and lows, and that often can spread itself over a long period: it is this very process that consists of a particular conjunctural situation of condensation of contradictions.

(c) The political crisis contains, as one of its own elements, the crisis of the state, but it is not reducible to this which is contrary to all current 'institutionalist-functionalist'-'system' analyses of bourgeois sociology and political science, which see in the political crisis an aspect of the crisis of institutions or the 'political system'. The political crisis consists principally in substantial modifications of the relations of force of class conflict, modifications which themselves specifically determine the exact elements of crisis at the heart of the state apparatus. These elements are formed by the contradictions between the classes in conflict, the configurations of class alliances of the power bloc and of the exploited-dominated classes, the emergence of new social forces, the relations between the organizational forms and the representation of classes, and the new contradictions between the power bloc and certain of the dominated classes, that support the power bloc, and so forth.

Now, these traits that constitute the political crisis in class struggle determine the crisis at the centre of the state apparatus, but because of the relative autonomy of the capitalist state in relation to the power bloc and because of its own organizational framework that tends specifically to separate it from the economic space, this determination is neither direct nor one-directional. The political crisis in class relations always expresses itself at the centre of the state in a specific manner and by a series of mediations.

(d) I have up to now spoken only of political crisis in its relation with economic crisis. It is now necessary to face the question of ideological crisis, and advance the following proposition: the political crisis always articulates an ideological crisis that is itself a constituent element of the political crisis.

First of all, the relations of ideological domination-subordination are themselves directly present not only in the reproduction but also in the constitution of social classes, whose position at the heart of the social division of labour does not reduce to the relations of production, although these play a determining role. This role of ideology is all the more important in the constitution of the classes into social forces, that is, in the position of the classes in the heart of a given conjuncture of their conflict, a conjuncture that is the proper place of a political crisis: ideological relations are directly part of the relations of force among the classes, in the configuration of alliances, in the forms of organization-representation that these classes use, in the relations between the power bloc and the dominated classes, and so forth.

Furthermore, the ideological relations, notably the dominant ideology, are organically present in the very constitution of the state apparatus, which reproduces the dominant ideology in its relations to other ideologies, or sub-ensembles of the dominated classes. In effect, ideology does not consist only of ideas; it is incarnated (Gramsci) in the material practices, the morals, the customs, the way of life of social formation. As such, and insofar as the ideological relations themselves constitute relations of power that are absolutely essential to class domination, the dominant ideology materializes and incarnates itself in the state apparatus.

On the one hand, the dominant classes cannot dominate the exploited classes by the monopolistic use of violence; dominance must always be represented as legitimate by state manipulation of the dominant ideology, which provokes a certain consensus on the part of certain classes and factions of dominated classes. On the other hand, from the perspective of the power bloc, the state has a role of organizing, unifying and installing its own political interests in light of the struggles of dominated classes: from the perspective of the dominated classes themselves, who make direct appeal to the dominant ideology, the state has a role of unification-representation. Finally, in the form of functioning-inculcation that it uses in the interior and even at the very heart of the state apparatus, the dominant ideology constitutes an indispensable 'cement' unifying the personnel of the diverse state apparatuses, enabling it to function 'in the service' of the dominant classes.

Therefore, political crisis, both in modifying the relations of force in class conflict and in the internal ruptures that it provokes at the centre of the state apparatus, necessarily articulates crisis of legitimization: notably, the political crisis articulates a crisis of dominant ideology, as this materializes itself not only in the ideological state apparatuses (church, mass media, cultural apparatus, educational apparatus, etc.) but also in the state apparatus of economic intervention and its repressive apparatuses (army, police, justice, etc.).

The State and the Economy

Having examined the political crisis in its aspects of crisis of the state, it is now necessary to clarify certain supplementary points concerning the capitalist state, particularly in its current phase of monopoly capitalism.

1. First of all, let us consider the relations between the state and the economy. We must stress here that the space of the relations of production, exploitation, and extraction of surplus work (that of reproduction and of the accumulation of capital and the extraction of surplus-value in the capitalist mode of production) has never constituted, neither in other modes of production (pre-capitalist) nor in the capitalist mode of production, a hermetic and partitioned level, that is, self-producible and in possession of its own laws of internal functioning. It is necessary, in effect, to move away from an economist-formalist conception, which views the economy as composed of invariant elements throughout the diverse modes of production, a self-producible, internally self-regulated space. In addition to eliminating the role of class struggle, which is at the very heart of the relations of production, this conception considers the space or the field of the economy (and, conversely, that of the state) as immutable, possessing intrinsic limits traced by the process of its alleged self-reproduction across all modes of production. When the relations between the state and the economy are considered as essentially external, this can be presented under different forms: (a) under the form of traditional economism, attached to a descriptive and topological representation of relations between the 'base' and the superstructure, which considers the state as a simple appendage-reflection of the economy: the relation between the state and the economy would consist, at best, in the famous 'action and reaction' of the state on an economic base

essentially considered as self-sufficient; (b) under the more subtle form, the social ensemble is represented in 'instances' or 'levels' by nature or by essence 'autonomous,' intrinsic spaces that cut across the diverse modes of production, the essence of these instances being a presupposition for putting them at the centre of a mode of production.

To move on from this conception, I want to advance certain propositions:

(a) The political-state (although it is equally true for ideology) was always, even if under different forms for different modes of production, constitutively 'present' in the relations of production and, thus, in their reproduction, including the pre-monopolist stage of capitalism. This is true in spite of a series of illusions that deemed that the 'liberal state' did not intervene in the economy except to maintain the 'exterior conditions' of production. Although the place of the state in relation to the economy is certainly modified according to the diverse modes of production, this place is always the modality of a presence and specific action of the state and is at the very heart of the relations of production and of their reproduction.

(b) It follows that the space, the object, and thus the concepts of economy and state do not and cannot have either the same extension or the same field in the diverse modes of production. Even at an abstract level, the several modes of production do not constitute purely economic forms; instead, they constitute different combinations of 'economic' elements, in themselves invariant but moving in a closed space with intrinsic limits; moreover, they do not constitute combinations between these elements and invariant elements of other instances (ideology, the state) which are themselves considered to be in immutable spaces. It is the mode of production, the unity of the ensemble of economic, political, and ideological determinations that delimits these spaces, designates their field, and defines their respective elements: they are defined by their internal relations.

(c) However, in respect to the relations between the state and the economy, the capitalist mode of production presents a characteristic specificity that is different from the perspective of the pre-capitalist modes of production; that is, a relative separation exists between the state and the economy, in the capitalist sense of these terms. This separation is linked to the relations of capitalist production, specifically to the depossession of the workers from the objects and means of their labour; it also is linked to the constitution of the classes and to their conflict under capitalism. This separation begins with the 'narrow overlapping' (Marx) of the state and the economy in the pre-capitalist modes of production, which is at the base of the institutional framework of the capitalist state because it traces its new spaces and respective fields from the economy and the state.

In considering these remarks, however, we realize that this separation is capitalist not only because of its autonomous nature but also because there is no effective externality of the state and the economy, with the state only intervening in the economy from the outside. This separation pervades the history of capitalism; it does not impede it, however. Even at the pre-monopolist stage of capitalism, the constitutive role of the state in the relations of capitalist production was only the precise form that recovers, under capitalism, the specific and constitutive presence of the state in the relations of production and, therefore, in their reproduction.

(d) Now it is necessary to propose a supplementary proposition: this separation of the state and the economy transforms itself, without being abolished, in accordance with the stages and phases of capitalism. In effect, the space, the object, and thus the content of the concepts of politics and of economy change not only under diverse modes of production but also in the stages and phases of capitalism itself.

It is in the 'transformed form' of this separation and in the changes in these enlarged spaces (due to the changes in the relations of capitalist production) *that the decisive role of the state is inscribed in the very cycle of reproduction and accumulation of capital in the current phase of monopoly capitalism*, a role qualitatively different than what it fulfilled in earlier capitalism. Therefore, to the extent that a series of domains (qualification of the work force, urbanism, transportation, health, environment, etc.) becomes integrated in the growth of the very space of the accumulation of capital, and insofar as entire economic sectors of capital (public and nationalized) become integrated in the growth of the space of the state, the relations between the two and the functions of the state in relation to the economy become modified. But these changes do not obliterate the relative separation of the state and the economy. Notably, this separation marks the structural limits of the 'intervention' of the state in the economy.

(e) This is the only way to situate the meaning of the current interventions of the state in the economy and their limits (*who* intervenes; *where*, and *how*?) and also to perceive the current relations between the economic crisis and the political crisis–crisis of the state. I have already mentioned several important elements from this perspective.

First, insofar as the respective spaces of the state and the economy are currently changing, and insofar as state intervention in the economy is different than it was in the past, the repercussions of the economic crisis in the political crisis change in the sense that, on the one hand, the economic crisis translates itself into political crisis in a more direct and organic way than in the past and, on the other hand, the interventions of the state in the economy themselves become productive factors of economic crisis; second, however, insofar as the separation of the state and the economy is maintained, even though it is transformed, the interventions of the state in the economy, including efforts to overcome an economic crisis, always present limits that correspond to the reproduction-accumulation of capital, which in turn corresponds to the very structure of the state. This explains the impossibility of current 'organized-planned' capitalism, which attempts to succeed in avoiding, mastering, or 'managing' the crises by the skewing of the state interventions. Furthermore, the political crisis–crisis of the state is always situated in a specific field in relation to an economic crisis: the current economic crisis, although different from cyclical crises of capitalism, does not necessarily translate itself into a political crisis–crisis of the state.

2. (a) The transformations of the relations between the state and the economy, the new economic role of the state, and thus the new relations between economic crisis and political crisis lead back to substantial modifications of the capitalist relations of production on both the world and the national levels; these modifications underlie such processes as the concentration of capital. Focusing research on the capitalist relations of production and their transformations leads us to break with the economist conception of these relations, particularly insofar as, in exactly situating the content of these two forms, we must grasp the pre-existence of the relations of production over the 'productive forces' pre-existing because the process of producing is the effect. As far as the relations of production are concerned, we are led to consider them as the social division of labour, not as the simple crystallization of a process of the productive forces as such: this is precisely what allows us to grasp the capitalist separation of the state and the economy as a specific presence of politics (and of ideology) in the relations of production and the social division of labour in capitalism. In other words, the current modifications of the role of the state in the recovering economy amount to the biasing of changes in the relations of production, in substantial changes in the reproduction of labour-power and of the division of labour (understanding as part of this the new forms of the division manual intellectual–intellectual intellectual). This appears elsewhere as the priority of

the production of production and the relations of production over the relations of circulation of capital in the cycle of the ensemble of reproduction of social capital (production-consumption-distribution of the social product). The economic crisis and the relations between this and the political crisis–crisis of the state are constantly spreading out over the whole of the cycle of reproduction of social capital, situating themselves in the first place in the new relations of the state, on the one hand, and in the relations of production and the division of labour, on the other, contrary to a current tendency to see the crisis only in the single space of circulation and to see the crisis of the state as simply a crisis of legitimacy.

(b) Therefore, examining this new relation of the state and the economy, of the political crisis and the economic crisis, takes us directly to the tendency of the rate of profit to fall and therefore to directly consider the particular conditions of the functioning of this tendency in the current phase of capitalism. In the first place, the current crisis of the state must be situated in the efforts taken by the state to counter this tendency. In relation to the dominant counter-tendency, the role of the state raises the rate of exploitation and surplus-value which returns us to the very heart of class conflict about exploitation (the dominant displacement towards the intensive ex-ploitation of work and relative surplus-value, technological innova-tions, and industrial restructurations, the process of qualification-dequalification of the labour force, the extension and modification of the very space of reproduction and the 'management' of the labour force, etc.). The role of the state in this counter-tendency also consists of devaluing part of the over-accumulated capital (public and natio-nalized) in order to raise the average rate of profit and produces considerable transfers of surplus-value from fractions of capital to others and leads back to intense class struggles within the dominant class. Furthermore, the current functioning of this tendency thus explains the fact that the elements of the crisis are accentuated in the current phase of capitalism, the crisis itself being situated in a context of particular instability characterizing the ensemble of this phase.

(c) I will not go any further on this subject, for what I have said is enough to show one decisive point for the study of the political crisis–crisis of the state in its relations to the economy and the crisis of the economy: these relations cannot be taken as relations between the state and some unconscious 'laws' of the economy; instead, they lead back directly to the class struggles lodged in the very heart of the relations of production and exploitation. To understand the crisis of the state in its relation to the economy and to the economic crisis means, in the final analysis, understanding the relations between the economic struggle (economic crisis) and the political struggles of classes (political crisis) *and to understand the manner in which class contradictions have repercussions in the very heart of the state apparatus.*

The State and Class Relations

Now, in order to understand how class contradictions (economic crisis and political-ideological crisis) have repercussions in the heart of the state (state crisis), it is necessary to make some supplementary remarks on the very nature of the state and its relations to social classes, in particular, in the current phase of monopoly capitalism.

1. (a) The capitalist state must represent the long-term political interests of the whole of bourgeoisie (the idea of the capitalist collective) under the hegemony of one of its factions, currently, monopoly capital. This implies that, first, the bourgeoisie is always presented as divided in class fractions: monopoly capital and non-monopoly capital; (monopoly capital is not an integrated entity but designates a contradictory and unequal process of 'fusion' between diverse fractions of capital). Second, taken as a whole, these fractions of the bourgeoisie, which are to a certain degree increasingly unequal, enjoy a political domination as part of the power bloc; third, the capitalist state must be a given fraction of the power bloc in order to assume its role as political organizer of the general interest of the bourgeoisie (from 'the unstable equilibrium of compromise' between these fractions, said Gramsci) under the hegemony of one of its fractions; and fourth, the current forms of the process of monopolization and hegemony particular to monopoly capital over the whole of the bourgeoisie restrict the limits of the relative autonomy of the state in relation to monopoly capital and to the field of the compromises it makes with other fractions of the bourgeoisie.

Now, how can we prove that state politics act in favour of the power bloc? This is only another way of asking how class contradictions echo at the centre of the state, a question that is at the heart of the problem of the crisis of the state. To understand this question, the state must not be considered as an intrinsic entity, but, as is also true for 'capital' itself, it must be considered as a *relation*, more exactly, as a material condensation (apparatus) of a relation of force between classes and fractions of classes as they are expressed in a specific manner (the relative separation of the state and the economy giving

way to the very institutions of the capitalist state) at the very heart of
the state. Understanding the state as a relation avoids the impasses of
the pseudo-dilemma between the state conceived as a thing and the
state conceived as a subject. The state as a thing is the old instrumentalist conception that views the state as a passive, if not a neutral,
tool totally manipulated by a single fraction, in which case the state
has no autonomy. The state as a subject: the state has absolute
autonomy and functions of its own will. This conception started
with Hegel; was revitalized by Weber; is the dominant current of
bourgeois political sociology (the 'institutionalist-functionalist' current); and carries this autonomy to the power itself, which is supposed
to restrain the state, those in power, and the state bureaucracy or
political élites. In effect, this tendency endows the institutions-appa-
ratuses with power, when in fact the state apparatuses possess no
power, because state power cannot be understood only in terms of the
power of certain classes and fractions of classes to whose interest the
state corresponds.

What is more important here is to see that in both cases (state
conceived as thing and as subject) the relation of state to social classes
and, in particular, state to classes and dominant fractions is understood as a relation of externality: either the dominant classes submit
the state (thing) to itself by a game of 'influences' and 'pressure groups'
or the state (subject) submits the dominant classes to itself. In this
relation of externality, state and dominant classes are considered as
two intrinsic entities, one 'confronting' the other, one having 'power'
while the other does not. Either the dominant class 'absorbs' the state
by emptying it of its own power (state as thing) or the state 'resists' the
dominant class and takes power for its own purposes (state as subject).

Let us now postulate that the state is a relation; so saying, we return
to our original problem: the state's relative autonomy and its role in
establishing the general interests of the bourgeoisie and the hegemony
of one fraction (currently monopoly capital), in brief the political
direction [*politique*] of the state, cannot be explained by its own power
or by its rationalizing will. A political direction is established because
of class contradictions that are inscribed in the very structure of the
state – the state, therefore, is a relation. In effect, when we understand
that the state is a material condensation of a relation of forces between
classes and fractions of class, it becomes obvious that class contradictions thoroughly constitute and permeate the state. In other words,
the state, destined to reproduce class divisions, is not and cannot be
state-thing or state-subject, a monolithic bloc without fissures; because of its very structure, it is divided. But in what specific forms are

these class contradictions found, particularly, those between fractions of the power bloc that constitute the state? They manifest themselves in the form of internal contradictions between the diverse branches and apparatuses of the state, while having a privileged representative of a particular interest of the power bloc: executive and parliament, army, justice, regional-municipal and central apparatuses, various ideological apparatuses, and so forth.

In this framework, the state establishes the general and long-term interests of the power bloc (the unstable equilibrium of compromises) under the hegemony of a given fraction of monopoly capitalism. The concrete functioning of its autonomy, which is limited in the face of monopoly capitalism, seems to be a process whereby these intrastate contradictions interact, a process that, at least for the short term, seems prodigiously incoherent and chaotic. However, what is really at work is a process of structural selectivity: a contradictory process of decisions and of 'non-decision', of priorities and counterpriorities, each branch and apparatus often short-circuiting the others. The politics of the state are therefore established by a process of interstate contradictions insofar as they constitute class contradictions.

All this is thus translated into considerable divisions and internal contradictions that accrue in the state personnel and that question the state's own unity, but that, here also, take a specific form. They occur in the organizational framework of the state apparatus, but following the line of its relative autonomy, they do not correspond exactly to the divisions in class conflict. Notably, these divisions often take the form of 'quarrels' among members of various apparatuses and branches of the state. In this context, this poses the problem of the *unity* of the power of the state, that is, the problem of its global political direction in favour of monopoly capital. This unity is not established by a simple physical seizure of the state by the magnates of monopoly capital and their coherent will. Instead, this contradictory process implicates the state in institutional transformations that cannot, by their nature, be favourable to other than monopoly interests. These transformations can take several shapes: a complex domination of an apparatus or branch of the state (a ministry that, for example, crystallizes monopoly interests over other branches and state apparatuses, centres of resistance of other fractions of the power bloc); a *trans-state* network that covers and short-circuits the various apparatuses and branches of the state, a web that crystallizes, by its very nature, the monopoly interests; finally, the circuits of formation and functioning of the body – special detachments of high state functionaries endowed with a high degree of mobility not only within the state but also between the state and monopoly concerns (École Polytechni-que, École Nationale d'Administration,[1] which, by constant bias of important institutional transformations, are charged with (and led to) implementing policies in favour of monopoly capital.

(b) The nature of the capitalist state, particularly as it manifests itself in the current phase of monopoly capitalism, must be grasped before the translation of political crisis into a crisis of the state can be understood. In effect, on the side of the power bloc, the political crisis accentuates the internal contradictions among its constituent frac-tions, politicizes these contradictions, challenges the hegemony of one fraction by other fractions, and often modifies the relations of force between the various parts of this bloc. This concomitantly involves an ideological crisis leading to a rupture of the representatives-repre-sented link between the classes and the class fractions of the power bloc among not only their political parties but also among certain other state apparatuses that represent them. The role of the state as organizer of the power bloc is then challenged. These contradictions, specific to a political crisis of the power bloc, have certain repercus-sions at the heart of the state in the form of accrued internal contra-dictions between branches and apparatuses of the state: complex displacements of dominance and functions from one branch and apparatus to others; breaks between centres of real power and those of formal power; increased ideological role of representative appara-tuses accompanying the expanded use of state violence; deterioration of the organizational role of the state, from certain apparatuses particularly destined to this role (notably political parties) to others (the administration, the army); the passing and short-circuiting of 'official' state apparatuses by a series of parallel networks; substantial overturning of the laws, which, among other things, limits the field of action of the state apparatuses and regulates their relations; and important changes in the personnel of the state. These cannot be reduced to a simple crisis of the political scene; they are manifested by an incoherency that characterizes the politics of state that maintains its relative autonomy and restores a toppling class hegemony.

2. (a) These characteristics of the crisis of the state can only be studied from the perspective of the dominated classes. In effect, in exercising repression and physical violence, the state apparatuses conserve and reproduce class domination; they also organize class hegemony by allowing for provisional compromises between the power bloc and certain dominated classes and by installing an ideological 'consensus' of the dominant class. By permanently disorganizing-dividing the

dominated classes, by polarizing them toward the power bloc, and by short-circuiting their own political organization, the state apparatuses organize-unify the power bloc. The relative autonomy of the capitalist state is essential in order for the hegemony of power to be organized over the dominated classes.

This also is inscribed in the organizational framework of the capitalist state as a relation: the state concentrates the relation of force not only between fractions of the power bloc *but also between the power bloc and the dominated classes*. Of course, this latter relation does not crystallize in the state apparatuses in the same way as the former relations; due to the unity of state power, as the power of class domination, the dominated classes do not exist in the state because of the bias of the apparatuses that concentrate the real power of these classes. However, this does not mean that the struggles of the dominated classes are 'exterior' to the state and that the contradictions between the dominant classes and the dominated classes remain contradictions between the state, on the one hand, and the dominated classes 'outside' the state, on the other. In fact, the struggle between the dominant and the dominated classes cuts across the state apparatuses insofar as these apparatuses materialize and concentrate the power from the dominant classes and class fractions in their contradictions with the dominated classes.

Thus, the precise configuration of the ensemble of the state apparatuses – the relation of dominance-subordination between the branches and apparatuses of the state, the ideological or repressive role of a given apparatus, the exact structure of each apparatus or branch of the state (army, justice, administration, school, church, etc.) – depends not only on the internal relations of force in the power bloc but also on the role they fulfil in respect to the dominated classes. If, for example, a given apparatus plays the dominant role at the heart of the state (political party, administration, army), it generally is not only because it concentrates the power of the hegemonic fraction of the power bloc but also because, simultaneously, it concentrates in itself the political-ideological role of the state with respect to the dominated classes. Moreover, the more important the role of the state in class hegemony, in the division and disorganization of the popular masses, the more that role consists of organizing compromises between the power bloc and the dominated classes (particularly the petty bourgeoisie and the rural popular classes) in order to set them up as *supporting classes* of the power bloc and to short-circuit their alliance with the working class. This is expressed in the very organizational framework of a given state apparatus, which exactly fulfils this function; for example, in France, the educational apparatus does this for the petty bourgeoisie, while the army does it for the rural popular classes.

Finally, the contradictions between the power bloc and the dominated classes directly intervenes in the contradictions between the dominant classes and the fractions of which it is composed: for example, the tendency of the falling rate of profit, a primordial element of division at the centre of the power bloc, ultimately is only an expression of the struggles of the dominated classes against exploitation. It follows not only that the various fractions of the power bloc (monopoly capital, non-monopoly capital, industrial capital, commercial capital, etc.) have different contradictions with the popular masses but also that their strategies with respect to them are different, A given policy of the state results from a process of contradictions not only between fractions of the power bloc but also between it and the dominated classes.

(b) We return to the political crisis. For the dominated classes this manifests itself (here again, it is necessary to distinguish between various sorts of political crisis) in a considerable intensification of their struggles: these struggles are politicized and the relations of force between the power bloc and dominated classes are modified; the relations of the power bloc and supporting classes are broken and emerge as effective social forces; ideological crisis enables the dominated classes to challenge the 'consensus' of the dominant classes and their representation-regimentation biased by the state apparatuses (which accentuates the objective possibilities of alliance and union of the popular masses); their autonomous political organization and the accrued weight of their own class organizations are accentuated, as well as the articulation of the political crisis and the economic crisis that restrains the objective possibilities of compromise between the power bloc and the dominated classes and accentuates the divisions at the heart of the power bloc with respect to strategies toward the dominated classes. This series of contradictions expresses itself at the very heart of the state (the state is a relation) and is a factor in determining the characteristics of the state crisis: accrued internal contradictions between branches and apparatuses of the state, complex displacement of dominance between apparatuses, permutations of function, accentuations of the ideological role of a given apparatus accompanying the reinforcement in the use of state violence, and so forth. These all bear witness to efforts of the state to restore a toppling class hegemony.

The State Personnel

I have so far stressed the aspect of the state crisis that affects its institutions and apparatuses and that is fundamental to this crisis. This state crisis also is manifested in another aspect, a crisis of the state personnel (politicians, functionaries, judges, military men, police, teachers, etc.), in brief, a crisis of the state bureaucracy. In effect, the political crisis is translated to the very heart of the state personnel in several manners: (1) insofar as it is an institutional crisis of the state, that is, precisely insofar as the ensemble of the state apparatuses is reorganized; (2) insofar as there is an accentuation of the class struggles and contradictions as expressed at the heart of the state personnel; and (3) insofar as there are increased demands and struggles of the state personnel.

To understand this, we must first see clearly that the state personnel themselves hold a class position (they are not a separate social group) and they are divided because of this. The higher spheres of personnel of the state apparatuses have membership in the bourgeois class; the intermediates and subordinates, in the petty bourgeoisie. These positions must be distinguished from the class origins of this personnel, that is, the classes from which this personnel come. But this personnel nevertheless constitutes a specific social category, possessing, across its class divisions, its own unity, because of the organizational framework of the capitalist state apparatus (separation of the state and the economy) and because of its relative autonomy from the dominant classes, which goes back to the very role of this personnel in elaborating and implementing the policies of the state.

Thus, the characteristics of the political crisis, that is, of the class struggles that correspond to it, necessarily impregnate the state personnel because of their class membership, the intensification of the divisions and contradictions at the heart of the power bloc, the politicization of these contradictions, the ruptured links of representation between the classes and dominant fractions and their political representatives, the conflicting diversification of the strategies and tactics of the dominated classes, and the particularly contradictory characteristics of the policies of the state which have repercussions at the heart of the higher spheres of state personnel, just as the characteristics of the political crisis of the dominated classes, notably the petty bourgeoisie (recalling its role as a supporting class of the power bloc) have repercussions at the heart of the intermediate and subordinate ranks of this personnel.

All this is therefore translated into considerable divisions and internal contradictions that accrue in the state personnel and that question the state's own unity, but that, here also, take a specific form. They occur in the organizational framework of the state apparatus, but following the line of its relative autonomy, they do not correspond exactly to the divisions in class conflict. Notably, these divisions often take the form of 'quarrels' among members of various apparatuses and branches of the states that result from fissures and reorganizations arising from the institutional crisis of the state. Or they take the form of quarrels between 'leagues', 'factions', 'great bodies of the state' at the very centre of each branch and apparatus. Even when class positions have repercussions at the heart of the state personnel, more precisely, when there is politicization of this personnel, one part leaning, let us say, 'to the left,' another 'to the right,' this follows specific paths: notably, those of ideological crisis. In effect, the dominant ideology, which the state reproduces and inculcates, also functions to constitute the internal cement of the state apparatuses and of the unity of their personnel, a personnel that (Gramsci saw this clearly), because of the general role of organization, representation, and hegemony of the state, make up, in its ensemble, part of the 'intellectuals'. This ideology, the internal cement of the state personnel, is precisely that of the neutral state representing the interest of the general will, arbitrating among the conflicting classes: the administration or judiciary as above the classes, the army, pillar of the 'nation,' the police, the 'order of the Republic,' the 'freedom' of the 'citizens,' the administration as the motor of 'efficacy' and of the general 'well-being' and so on. The ideological crisis, in its relations to the political crisis, places a veil over the real nature of the state and as such is experienced at the very heart of the state personnel. To this we must add, of course, the particular effects of the ideological crisis on the personnel of the ideological apparatuses (schools, church, mass media, cultural apparatus, etc.) that rupture the links between the power bloc and its 'organic intellectuals'.

The divisions and contradictions at the heart of the state personnel, repercussions of their positions in class conflict, do not therefore follow a simple line of cleavage between the intermediate and subordinate levels, on the one hand, and the higher personnel spheres, on the other; the cleavage is indeed more important, but these divisions cut vertically through the state hierarchy. These contradictions are further articulated in a complex fashion in the demands of 'corporatist' struggles of the state personnel, struggles that intensify in the general context of the political crisis.

Imperialism and the Nation-State

Finally, an important problem for the analysis of both the political crisis and the current crisis of the state involves the imperialist context, and, therefore, the current phase of imperialism (which is only the other face of the current phase of monopoly capitalism) and its repercussions on the very form of the nation-state. The current phase of imperialism is characterized, more and more, by the internationalization of capital and work processes, therefore by the dominant imperialist relations of production (notably in the United States) as they reproduce themselves at the very heart of other social formations, by an induced reproduction of these relations. This tendency also manifests itself in the relations between the dominant imperialism, that of the United States, and the other imperialist countries, notably Europe, by producing a specific *dependency* of these countries on the dominant imperialism. This internalization also works for the imperialist relations of the foreign capital within the power blocs of these social formations and affects their state, a state that intervenes in the reproduction of the dominant imperialist relations at the heart of its own social formation.

Thus, the nation-state and its formations undergo important modifications in order to take charge of this internationalization of capital. On the other hand, the current phase of imperialism and this internationalization do not detract from the importance of the nation-state in this process. This does not mean that there is a process of internationalization that takes place 'above' the states and that either replaces the role of nation-states by that of 'economic powers' (multinational corporations) or implies the birth of an effective supernational state (United Europe or the American superstate). Indeed, the more there is class struggle between the dominant class and the dominated class, of which the state condenses the relations of force, the more this struggle is essentially situated in the frame of the national space and takes a national form.

I return to the current crisis in order to make one last far-reaching remark. It is, on the one hand, evident that the current crisis concerns the whole of capitalism-imperialism; this means that 'external factors,' in the sense of external contradictions, intervene at the very centre of the various social formations, where the reproduction of capitalism and the existence of the imperialist chain actually occur. But in the economic crisis, and more particularly in the political crisis, where the economic crisis is translated into political crisis, *the internal contradictions take primacy over the external factors, and this is also true for*

the crisis of the nation-state in the social formations where one finds
such crisis. Thus, to pose the primacy of internal factors, a primacy
that not only concerns a situation of crisis but goes much further, one
must break with the mechanist and quasi-topological (if not 'geographical') conception of the relation between internal and external
factors. One cannot, in the current phase of imperialism, speak of
external factors that act purely on the 'outside' and 'isolated,' internal
factors that support the former. To accept the primary of internal
factors means that the coordinates of the 'external' imperialist chain to
each country, including the relations of world forces, the role of a
given great power, and so forth, only act on these countries when they
are internalized, that is, when they become inserted in and modify the
relations of force between the classes of these countries and when they
articulate the specific contradictions, contradictions that appear, in
certain of their aspects, as the induced reproduction of contradictions
in the imperialist chain at the centres of the various countries. In this
sense, to speak of the primacy of internal factors is to discover the real
role that imperialism plays – unequal development – in the evolution
of the various social formations and also in their political crisis and the
crises of their own nation-states. This also contributes a fact already
mentioned: the current economic crisis is not necessarily transforming
itself, for all countries involved, into a political crisis–crisis of the
state, and, where this is the case, the various political crises have,
according to the different countries, differences between them and
manifest these under very different forms (in different spaces of
political crises).

The Current Crisis of the State

I will conclude this essay by making, according to the theoretical
directions established above, some remarks on the current political
crisis; where it is taking place, it presents the traditional characteristics
of the political crisis, about which I will here only mention certain new
aspects. In effect, it is situated in the context of an economic crisis
distinct from the simple cyclical crises of capitalism. This poses a
series of problems concerning the economic crisis itself, problems I do
not consider in this essay. But these problems concern: (1) the
accentuation of the generic elements of political-ideological crisis,
and accentuation belonging to the current phase of monopoly capitalism and also touching the ensemble of capitalist countries; (2) the
political-ideological crisis and the crisis of the state in the very sense in
which it is currently experienced in certain capitalist countries, in

brief, the 'structural' character of this crisis in these countries. This
structural character resides, as I have already noted, in the repercussion of the economic crisis in political-ideological crisis (crisis of
hegemony) at the very heart of certain countries, that is, in the current
relations between the economic crisis and the crisis of the state.

1. In effect, one of the most important problems is the fact that,
because of the new economic role of the state and the transformations
of the spaces of politics and economy (transformations in the separation of the state and the economy), a whole series of these state
functions consists of implementing the counter-tendencies to the
tendency of the rate of profit to fall (to some extent to avoid the
crisis), thus becoming themselves involved to a point where the state
cannot avoid committing factors productive of a crisis that, *by this
very fact, goes beyond the simple economic crisis*. I want to call
attention to certain new aspects of the problem.

(a) The considerable accentuation of internal contradictions of the
power bloc (contradictions at the very heart of monopoly capital,
between this and non-monopoly capital, between industrial capital
and bank and commercial capital; etc.) is an important element in the
political crisis insofar as it already has translated itself into an
instability of hegemony. To understand this element in its full impact,
we cannot lose sight of the current conditions of the internationalization of capital: the indirect reproduction and internalization of foreign
capital at the heart of the various social formations produce important
internal dislocations by making a place at the centre of these formations for the emergence of a new division between what I have called
an internal bourgeoisie, which, although linked to external capital (it
is not a true national bourgeoisie), presents important contradictions
with itself, and a comprador bourgeoisie entirely dependent on (and
integrated to) this foreign capital. This line of division does not always
duplicate the 'monopoly capital/non-monopoly capital,' cleavage but
it often cuts across these capitals. This already constitutes a supplementary factor that destabilizes hegemony, especially if interimperialist contradictions, accentuated in a crisis period, are reproduced
directly at the very heart of the power blocs of the various countries.
Now, the current 'economic' functions of the state (devalorization of
certain parts of capital, industrial restructurations to raise the rate of
relative surplus-value, an increasing role in favour of the centralization
of capital, selective aid to certain capitals, the decisive place of the
nation-state in the process of the internationalization of capital) are
accentuated precisely in the context of the economic crisis, favouring

more than ever the severe 'corporate economics' of certain fractions of capital at the expense of others. This direct overlapping of the state in the economic contradictions, with its snowball effects, serves only to increase and deepen the political fissures of the power bloc and becomes, therefore, a direct factor of political crisis in permanently questioning the role of the state in establishing the general political interests of the power bloc.

(b) The organic 'intervention' of the state in a series of domains that, although previously marginal, are now in the process of being integrated into the very space of the reproduction and accumulation of capital (urbanism, transportation, health care, 'environment,' etc.) has considerably politicized the struggle of the popular masses in these fields, insofar as these masses are directly confronted by the state. Already an important element of political crisis, these struggles are accentuated by state interventions, which among other things, aim to raise the rate of (relative) surplus-value by the capitalist reproduction-qualification of the labour force, while casting off their disguise of 'social policy.' These interventions therefore reduce the elements of crisis (a current example of this is aid to the unemployed). This is all the more true since the new petty bourgeoisie or middle-level-salaried workers are, by their nature, particularly sensitive to the objectives of a struggle in these domains; the base of their alliance with the working class is therefore considerably extended. In brief, we are now experiencing the demythification of the providential state or the welfare state.

(c) The role of the state favours foreign or transnational capital, a role accentuated in a context of crisis (look at the current relaxation of the European bourgeoisie under the American economic-political umbrella) and increases the unequal development of capitalism at the heart of each national social formation, where the reproduction of foreign capital occurs, notably by creating new 'poles of development' of certain regions at the expense of others. Arising from this are the phenomena of ruptures of the 'national unity,' of the nation sustained by the state bourgeoisie, by the massive development of regionalist movements that have a political character and that, as ambiguous as they often are, nevertheless constitute important elements of the current political crisis.

(d) In addition, the current role of the state confronts the economic crisis in the strictest sense of the term. It seems to me that the new problem in this regard is the following: Insofar as the state extensively intervenes in the very reproduction of capital and insofar as the economic crises are organic and necessary factors of this reproduction, the state has probably succeeded in limiting the 'wild' aspect of economic crises (like that of the 1930s, for example), but only insofar as it takes charge of the functions formally fulfilled by these 'wild crises'. Without exaggerating this paradox, we can say that all this occurs as if it were henceforth the state that becomes the prime mover of these 'rampant' economic crises (a current example is unemployment and inflation directly orchestrated by the state), even though this should not be seen only, or even principally, as a conscious strategy of the bourgeoisie, but as the objective result of the current role of the state, whereas in the past the state seemed content to limit the social damage of the extreme economic crises. The effect of this, here also, is a considerable politicization (against state policy) of the struggles of the popular masses in the context of the economic crisis.

These remarks, however, are only a beginning; to understand the current political crisis, we must study it in the ensemble of its characteristics while also insisting on certain new forms under which the characteristics currently present themselves; notably the new forms of rupture between the bourgeoisie and the petty bourgeoisie, a particularly important rupture that is taking a totally different form than in the past insofar as it henceforth concerns the new salaried petty bourgeoisie (the famous 'tertiaries'), where the objective polarization on the side of the working class is, because of its class position, altogether more important than was that of the traditional petty bourgeoisie (small merchants and artisans); the emergence of new struggles on fronts often called 'secondary,' the struggles of women, immigrant workers, students, and so forth; the new elements of the ideological crisis, a crisis not experienced before under capitalism, especially in the dominant countries.

Thus, to understand the current political crisis thoroughly, we need a concrete examination of each capitalist country in which it is occurring; in effect, certain facts I just mentioned arise, more generally, from the current phase of capitalism itself: they are concerned with *the accentuation of the generic elements of the crisis*, an accentuation characterizing the ensemble of the current phase, which is marked by a particular instability. But these elements are only translated into a political crisis when they are articulated and condensed in the conjuncture of only certain capitalist countries, while the ensemble of these countries are touched by the accentuation of the generic elements of the crisis.

2. This last remark leads us to wonder about the repercussion of the political crisis, wherever it is taking place, on the crisis of the state,

which in turn compels us to look at the transformations that, to different degrees, currently affect the state apparatuses of the dominant capitalist countries. These transformations also can be understood as state reactions to, among other things, the political crisis, including its own crisis, because it is currently experiencing, in this case, a blockage of its efforts to quietly install itself in the management of its own crisis, an explosion that the English call 'crisis of the crisis management' or 'crisis of the management of the crisis'.

But as I have said, these transformations also are due, among other things, to the crisis of the state, which leads us back to a problem that I posed at the beginning of this text. In effect, certain transformations come from more general factors of the current phase of monopoly capitalism and of its own permanent coordinates (including the accentuation of the elements of crisis and its characteristic instability). These transformations therefore follow the same lines as the adaptation of the state as it is faced with the new realities of the class struggles of this phase and thus lead not simply to an occasional authoritarian turn of the bourgeois state but to the constitution of a new form of the capitalist state with characteristics appropriate to the 'authoritarian state' or 'strong state' that could signify simply that a certain form of 'democratic politics' has come to an end in capitalism. It is under these transformations that we find, in certain of these states, the specific characteristics of the crisis of the state articulated. This not only means that all states undergoing transformations toward this new form of 'authoritarian' state will necessarily experience a crisis of the state but also that their transformation toward an 'authoritarian' state will persist even after this crisis is eventually reabsorbed. Furthermore, in the case of an eventual end to the crisis of the state by its absorption, this crisis will appear to be the way for a transformation-adaptation by specific and necessary means of the capitalist state to the new realities of the class struggle (new form of the capitalist state). The next question, that often comes up – 'Is what is happening a crisis or an adaptation (modernization) of the state?' – poses, in certain respects, a false dilemma: perhaps it is exactly where a crisis is in fact occurring that the capitalist state is led to an adaptation-'modernization.'

Considering the general level of this discussion it is not possible for me to elucidate these transformations of the state that, in a concrete case, are brought up on a first order (new form of the state adapted to the new realities of the phase) or on a second order (reaction of the state faced with the political crisis and its own crisis), I will be content here to call attention to certain aspects of the process in order to reveal the breadth of the problem, without explicitly establishing, much less simplifying, the relations of the process with the coordinates that determine it: processes that accentuate elements of preceding phases and of a series of new elements that coexist in the state of monopoly capitalism.

(a) The prodigious concentration of power in the executive at the expense of not only 'popular' parliamentary representation but also a series of networks founded on popular suffrage, on both central and local or regional levels.

(b) The organic confusion of three powers (executive, legislative, and judicial) and the constant encroachment on the fields of action and competence of the apparatuses or branches that correspond to them (police and justice, for example); the 'separation' of these powers, always somewhat fictional anyway, is really nothing more than a fundamental ideology of bourgeois power.

(c) The accelerated pace of the state's arbitrary policies that restrict citizens' political liberties and that connote, on the one hand, a complete political-ideological overturning of the traditional limits between the 'public' and the 'private' and, on the other, substantial modifications of the very notion of the politics of the 'individual person' that structure a new field, which Michel Foucault in his *Surveiller et punir*, called anatomic politics or the microphysics of power.

(d) The precipitous decline of the role of bourgeois political parties and the displacement of their political-organizational functions (both from the perspective of the power bloc and from that of the dominated classes) in favour of the administration and bureaucracy of the state. This process involves the direct politicization of the personnel of the state apparatuses, which is accompanied by the displacement of the dominant ideology toward 'technocratism' in all its variations, the privileged form by which the state legitimizes itself via the bias of the administrative apparatus.

(e) The accentuation of the use of state violence (both in the sense of physical violence and in that of 'symbolic violence'), which accompanies not only the accentuation of the ideological role of the state (cultural apparatus, mass media, etc., in brief, apparatuses of the 'internalization of repression') but also the displacement of the ideological apparatuses (teaching, family, etc.) in relation to the repressive apparatuses themselves (e.g., the army or the police whose 'civilizing' mission never ceases to be glorified), all of which implies a major reorganization of the repressive apparatuses.

(f) In direct relation with the preceding characteristics, the creation of a vast network of new circuits of 'social control' (extended police surveillance, psychological-psychoanalytic divisions, social welfare controls), which has been subtly and diffusely established in the social texture.

This is how the extension of surveillance takes the form that Robert Castel, in *Le Psychanalysme*,[2] calls, 'deinstitutionalization'; the setting up of ideology and repression and processes of 'non-enclosing' in respect to the special apparatuses (asylums, prisons, and various places of detention) destined to isolate the supposed 'abnormals-deviants-dangerous', opening them by extending their concern to the whole of the social body. This implies, of course, that the ensemble of the social body is considered 'abnormal' and 'dangerous,' guilt passing from accomplished act to mere intent, repression extending from punishment to policies of prevention.

(g) The overthrow of the legal system and of the juridical ideology corresponding to the traditional 'state of law' in order to account for the institutional transformations.

(h) The dislocation in each branch and apparatus of the state (army, police, administration, justice, ideological apparatuses) between formal and open networks, on the one hand, and impervious nuclei indirectly controlled by the summits of the executive, on the other, and the constant displacement of the centres of real power from the former to the latter. This implies transmutation from the principle of public knowledge to that of secrecy, of which the Watergate affair is only a sampling.

(i) The massive development, directly orchestrated by the heights of the state itself, and the increased organizational role of the parallel state networks, paid for publicly, semipublicly, or para-publicly-privately, which must simultaneously function to unify and direct the nuclei of the state apparatuses and which thus also constitute reserves for socio-political confrontations.

(j) The prodigious and characteristic incoherence of the current state policies, which are constantly reduced to contradictory, spasmodic micropolitics, what one calls 'blind piloting' or, more notably, 'absence of a global social project,' on the part of the state and its various governmental majorities. This is characteristic of the state policies from the perspective of both the power bloc and the dominated classes; it is from here that we arrive at the current forms of 'reform-repression' that mark the policies of the Western capitalist states.

13

THE NEW PETTY BOURGEOISIE

I want to focus my attention on the question of the 'new petty bourgeoisie' about which I have already written in *Classes in Contemporary Capitalism*. I want to respond to some of the criticisms that have been made of my position both at this conference and elsewhere.[1] It is important to note that the criticisms that have been levelled are not mutually consistent; for example, Alan Hunt has criticized me for adopting an economistic position, while Stuart Hall claims that I pay insufficient attention to the economic level.

The problem posed by the discussion of the new petty bourgeoisie is that of specifying the boundary of the working class. This is not simply a theoretical problem; it involves political questions of the greatest general importance concerning the role of the working class and of alliances in the transition to socialism. At the outset I should like to make clear what are the political alternatives that confront us. If the working class is defined as embracing all those that sell their labour-power then we must be clear about the implications of such a definition. Without being too polemical I want to insist that this definition of the working class must be viewed in the context of its history in the working-class movement. This definition first emerged in classical social democracy, and has remained the major definition of the working class relied upon by social democracy. We can turn the problem around as much as we wish but the facts remain: the social-democratic position has been one which has defined the working class as the class composed of individuals who are wage-earners, in other words it is a conception of a 'wage-earning class.' This definition can be traced back to Bernstein and to Kautsky. The justification for this definition is presented in the following terms. The working class about

* First published in Alan Hunt (ed.), *Class and Class Struggle*, Lawrence & Wishart, London 1977, pp. 113-24.

which Marx wrote was the 'industrial proletariat' but it is necessary to take account of the actual economic and social transformations that have occurred since that period. These changes make it necessary, it is argued, to recognize that the boundaries of the working class have also been changed. Whenever social democrats seek to make use of Marxism, but at the same time to 'revise' it, they always appeal to changes in capitalism to justify their position. Thus Kautsky argued that because of the actual changes undergone by capitalism the working class is no longer the narrow class that Marx wrote about, and that it is now composed of the whole of the 'wage-earning class'. To define the working class as the whole of the 'wage-earning class' has the effect of reducing the class divisions in society to the division between rich and poor. The class characteristics of the working class become nothing more than the economically poor citizens; class becomes simply a matter of inequality.

The major aspect of the problem to which I wish to draw attention concerns the problem of alliances and the hegemony of the working class in the transition to socialism. This is, as Alan Hunt has made clear, and here I agree with him, the main problem. The main problem is what type of hegemony must the working class achieve in order to achieve the transition to socialism? But we need to examine what the consequences are of adopting the 'broad' definition of the working class. To adopt the broad definition abolishes the problem of alliances; the problem does not exist any more because everyone has become a worker. The whole population, with the exception of a very small minority, are wage-earners. As a consequence, the working class no longer has to play a role of principled leadership over the other classes, because all other classes have been subsumed within the working class. It is in this respect that the major difference is to be found between the Marxist theory of the party, not only that of Lenin, but also of Gramsci, and the social-democratic type of theory which is based on this conception of the large wage-earning class.

To turn to the second problem. Because I am not familiar in detail with the positions of the British Communist Party on this problem, I will concentrate on those adopted by the French and the Italian Communist Parties. These Communist Parties give a relatively restricted definition of the working class, in the sense that they define its limitations as prescribed by immediately or directly productive labour. There are some variations of detail that distinguish the positions of these parties. They do differ as to the precise location of the limits of the working class; for example, the main difference concerns the question of technicians. They do, for example, exhibit somewhat distinct positions concerning the extent to which technicians are to be regarded as being part of the working class, but it is not a fundamental problem for them, since their theoretical positions exclude from the working class most of the salaried non-productive workers. From this point of view, their position differs from the one put forward by Alan Hunt.

There is a further important problem associated with the definition of the working class adopted by the French Communist Party. If the non-productive wage-labourers (whom I will call for convenience 'salaried workers') are excluded from the working class, then it is necessary to determine their class location. The French Communist Party (PCF) does not speak of them as a class, rather it designates them as an 'intermediate strata.' I believe this to be an incorrect position, and here I agree with Alan Hunt, that it is false to imagine that there can exist 'strata' that are outside classes and the class structure, but which nevertheless are regarded as taking part in class struggle. Strata are designations of differentiations within classes, not categories that can exist outside classes. While Alan Hunt goes on to argue that these sections or 'strata' form part of the working class, I have argued that they belong to a specific class, namely the 'new petty bourgeoisie.'

Why have I argued that the new petty bourgeoisie constitutes a separate class? I want, in particular, to stress the political implications of my position. Even if we do not speak of a salaried class but of an intermediate stratum, there is always the danger that we will not see clearly the central problem of revolutionary strategy, which is precisely the problem of the hegemony of the working class within the popular alliance in the transition to socialism.

What difference does it make if we regard salaried workers as an intermediate stratum or as a specific class? The definite characteristic of strata, in comparison to classes, is that strata do not have specific and relatively autonomous class interests. This means that even if we exclude salaried workers from the working class we nevertheless see them as being automatically polarized towards the working class; and we therefore treat them as if they do not have specific interests of their own. Whereas, if we see them as a specific class, distinct from the working class, we must give proper recognition and attention to their specific and distinctive class interests. So the problem of the hegemony of the working class presents itself as exactly how to organize the people, the popular alliance. This popular alliance is made up of *different* classes with specific class interests. If this was not the case the problem would be reduced to an extremely simple one.

Even if we recognize that as a consequence of the transformations of contemporary capitalism they are objectively polarized towards the working class; it is nevertheless important that we understand that this is never an automatic or inevitable process. This is true in two senses: first, that they must be won to alliance with the working class, and in the second sense, even when they have been won, they can be lost as allies and they can turn to the other side. This is what happened in Allende's Chile and also in Portugal. If these salaried non-productive workers can shift from an alliance with the working class to an alliance with the bourgeoisie it is precisely because they are not automatically polarized towards the working class. This is not because they do not have specific class interests, but because they have a very dubious class specificity.

Now, one or two theoretical remarks about this conception of the intermediate salaried stratum. First of all, is it not possible to speak of salaried strata as not having class membership? It points to one of the specific characteristics of Marx's class theory as distinct from other class theories. All bourgeois sociologists speak of classes nowadays, but classes for them are only particular divisions within a more general social stratification in which we find not only classes, but also élites (in the political sphere), status groups, etc. Of course, Marxism recognizes the existence of fractions, and specific categories of classes, but all those are fractions of classes. For example, the commercial bourgeoisie is a fraction of the bourgeoisie, and the labour aristocracy is a specific fraction of the working class itself. In Marxism we cannot admit to the existence of strata, fractions, and significant groupings outside of classes. Nor could one say that, as a result of the development of the mode of production (that is of the pure mode of production, which has two classes, the bourgeoisie and the working class), we would find a tendency within the social formation itself for all the individuals, all the agents, to become part either of the bourgeoisie or of the working class. Such a position is absolutely false because it presupposes that the mode of production is an abstract concept, whereas 'social formation' is a non-abstract concept. A distinction between abstract and non-abstract concepts does not exist. The concept of 'dog' does not bark. All concepts are abstract to a greater or lesser degree. The distinction between the concepts 'social formation' and 'mode of production' revolves around the nature of the object. Mode of production is an abstract formal object and social formation a concrete real object. So this would presuppose that modes of production exist and reproduce themselves as such, and that social formations are nothing other than a geographical topographical place where modes of production, in their abstract reproduction, concretize themselves. So the pure mode of production, the capitalist mode of production (bourgeoisie and working class) reproducing itself in the abstract, would finish by 'revealing itself' like Christ, triumphal in the social formation where finally we would have only bourgeois and proletarian classes.

This position is false because, as Lenin has shown in *The Development of Capitalism in Russia*, the distinction between modes of production and social formations does not have to do with interpretation of Marx, 'young' and 'old Marx', or with the status of the *Communist Manifesto*, it concerns the texts of Lenin, and also the nature of imperialism. One cannot understand imperialism without the distinction between modes of production and social formation. It is not possible to deduce imperialism from the capitalist mode of production itself. Imperialism is a necessary effect of the reproduction and the existence of the mode of production in concrete social formations. Unequal development is not an effect of the simple concretization of the capitalist mode of production conceived as an effect in reality, which develops towards imperialism; rather, it is a constitutive element of imperialism itself. For this reason, the dual conception of society cannot be accepted.

Having developed these theoretical and political points, I would like discuss the major propositions which I have advanced in my text *Classes in Contemporary Capitalism*. These propositions are as follows: (i) that there exists a specific class situation of the salaried non-productive workers which I have called the 'new petty bourgeoisie'; (ii) that there are transformations in the reproduction of capitalism which have to do with extensions of the limits of the working class, but that, nevertheless those transformations do not change the specific class situations of the new petty bourgeoisie; (iii) that these transformations affect the new petty bourgeoisie in the sense that it is increasingly objectively polarized towards the working class, as a specific class, but because the new petty bourgeoisie has a specific class situation this objective polarization does not concern the whole of the class to the same extent. It rather concerns certain fractions of the new petty bourgeoisie which constitute a large majority of it.

We now need to consider if it would be a solution to the problem if one could speak of 'contradictory class locations'? I want to consider the thesis advanced by Erik Wright in his article 'Class Boundaries in Advanced Capitalist Societies'.[2] Can we resolve the theoretical problem by saying that some agents have a contradictory class location? This implies that these agents can occupy different and changing class locations; it suggests that they can occupy a vacuum, a no-man's-land between the bourgeoisie and the working class.

We can approach this theoretical problem by focusing upon the nature of supervision within the capitalist process of production. When Marx spoke about the labour of supervision and direction of the labour process, he insisted upon the double nature of this labour. Indeed, he always used the same expression, saying that, on the one hand, as long as supervisory labour is necessary to every labour process as such, to production in general, then in this sense it is part of productive labour; and, on the other hand, that as long as it concerns the realization of surplus-value, and not the production of it, it constitutes a political control over the working class and, therefore, is not productive labour. I think that this kind of reasoning has to do with what Marx says, very clearly, in those passages in *Capital* in which he discusses 'production in general' and 'production as such', but Marx always says that production in general never exists in reality. The only thing that exists is a production process under given relations of production and within a given class struggle. Classes do not exist at first as such, and then enter into class struggle. Classes exist only as long as they are in struggle with one another. Taking account of these two arguments, I think it is impossible to say that some agents can have, in a given social formation and under given social relations, and in a definite class struggle, contradictory class locations. Marx, after all, made an important statement, in the context of this double nature of the labour process, about the work of the capitalist himself; he says that, for as long as capitalist activity concerns the direction and co-ordination necessary for every labour process and production as such, one can say that the capitalist per- forms productive labour. But can we, therefore, say that the capitalist has a contradictory class location, that he is both 'worker' and 'capitalist'? It would be a perfect absurdity. This set of arguments indicates the general nature of my response to Wright's article.

It has been pointed out that I have a rather limited and restricted definition of the working class. I want now to consider the argument, used by both Wright and Hunt, who draw attention to the fact that, if we make use of the Marxist definition of class which I have proposed and apply it to the United States we find that the working class constitutes less than 20 per cent of the population. Let us examine this argument. First, I think that we cannot speak of classes in contem- porary capitalism referring only to each particular social formation; we must always take into account the imperialist context. So the question of the working class, and the work force that is subject to American capital has not only to do with the domestic working class. We must recognize that the working class which works for American capital includes also those who work, for example, for American firms in Latin America. So the question of the numerical size of the working class, especially when we speak of imperialist countries, must not only be seen in a national, but in a more imperialist context.

Secondly, the issues under discussion raise the very important problem of the transition to socialism, and also the problem of the hegemony of the working class. I want to insist that this cannot be reduced simply to a numerical problem; it is a political problem. It is not by gaining 5 per cent that the political task of winning a majority of the people for the transition to socialism is going to be achieved by the working class.

Third, there is a real problem which revolves around the fact that in the reproduction of capitalism there is a tendency towards a restriction of the importance of the working class in the production process in the imperialist countries, which is associated with the primacy of dead labour over living labour, and has to do with relative surplus-value. It is not my intention to deny any of these facts. To do so would not take us anywhere; but I do not think that this is the important problem. The important problem is the political one. In my analysis of the new petty bourgeoisie, which I have set out here briefly, I began of course with the economic criterion, the distinction between productive and unproductive labour. I simply say somewhat dogmatically that things are perfectly clear for Marx. In *Capital*, the one exception concerns the problem of technicians. It revolves around relative surplus-value, as a counter-tendency to the falling rate of profit, with productivity of labour, and with exploitation mainly through relative surplus labour, and with technological innovations. There is this problem in Marx, but I do not think that there is a problem with the other non-productive workers, workers in the service and commercial sectors, workers involved with circulation, realization or collection of surplus-value. In a very clear way, although Marx might be wrong, he says, in particular in many passages in *Capital*, that commercial employees cannot be conceived as productive labourers. For these purposes it makes little difference if we adopt the criterion of the material or non-material production. If the workers in the commercial sphere are not considered by Marx to perform productive labour, it is not because they do not perform material production; in some instances they do, but it is because they depend on commercial capital and the only capital that produces surplus-value is productive capital. I have demonstrated that this involves the basic elements of Marx's theory of value, and this is why I have based my argument upon it.

I want to insist, nevertheless, that when I speak of productive and unproductive labour, I have tried to show that this is not a technical characteristic of this or that type of labour, but that it has to do with the relations of production, that is, with the forms of exploitation. Productive labour in different modes of production is nothing but that labour which is exploited through the specific type of exploitation that characterizes the mode of production – for example, the production of surplus-value in the capitalist mode of production. It does not mean that salaried unproductive workers are not exploited – they are – which is, of course, extremely important, but not in the specific fashion that constitutes the production of surplus-value.

Now, leaving aside the problem concerning technicians in Marx's treatment, I have tried to show concretely what it means to say that the definition of social classes cannot be limited exclusively to the economic sphere, and that we must take into account politics and ideology. This has been a fundamental thesis advanced in *Political Power and Social Classes*. I want, therefore, to demonstrate why I needed those political and ideological elements. I needed them because, even if the criterion of productive and unproductive labour is sufficient to exclude unproductive workers from the working class, it is not adequate, because it is a negative criterion. It tells us what they are not; that they are not part of the bourgeoisie, in that they do not have either the juridical or the economic ownership of the means of production. Further, it demonstrates that they are not part of the working class. But this economic criterion in itself is not sufficient to tell us to which class they belong. It is in this context that the political and the ideological criteria are important. I want to state briefly what I mean by them, and to indicate why this position has nothing to do with the distinction between 'class in itself' and 'class for itself'.

I agree with Alan Hunt that the economic (the relations of production and of exploitation) is not sufficient in order to define positively the class determination of unproductive salaried workers, and that we must always take into account the political and ideological elements of the social division of labour. To do this I made a distinction between 'structural class determination', which has to do with economic, political and ideological elements, in which the economic level always has the determining role, and 'class position' in a specific conjuncture of class struggle. Political and ideological elements do not only concern the class position in a specific conjuncture. It is very common to find that class in itself – structural class determination – is thought of only at the economic level, and then politics and ideology are introduced in the process of the class struggle in a conjuncture, 'class for itself'.

From the moment that we speak of the structural existence of classes, political and ideological elements are present. This means those political and ideological elements are not to be identified simply with an autonomous political revolutionary organization of the working class, or with a revolutionary ideology. Even when the working class does not have this autonomous political organization – the Communist Party – and does not have revolutionary ideology, it necessarily occupies specific places, not only in the economic sphere, but also in the ideological and political sphere.

This means that we can speak of specific ideological elements of the working class even if this working class does not have a revolutionary ideology and is dominated by bourgeois ideology. The working class always exists in class struggle through specific practices even when no revolutionary organization exists. There always exists an ideology which makes the working class distinct from the bourgeois class. The United States, for example, is a classic example of a country with a working class without a revolutionary ideology and without an autonomous revolutionary party, or mass party. But this does not mean the working class exists only at the economic level. The working class has an autonomous discourse, or at least elements of an autonomous discourse, which Lenin called 'class instinct', which bursts through the envelope that is the domination of bourgeois ideology.

Autonomous political organization and the revolutionary ideology of the working class have to do with the class position in the conjuncture. They are concerned with the making of the working class as a 'social force', which determines the possibility of the working class making a transition to socialism, that is, to make social revolution. So the problem presents itself as to how to locate the political and ideological elements in the structural determination of a class, even if those elements are not the ones traditionally regarded as constituting the 'class for itself'. I have tried to show what these political and ideological elements are in the concrete analysis of the new petty bourgeoisie, and that they stem from its specific characteristics, not only with respect to productive and unproductive labour, but also from its position in the whole of the social division of labour.

I have tried to analyze the implications of the division between manual and mental labour. The division between manual and mental labour is not a physiological or biological division between those who work with their hands and those who work with their brains. It has to do with the social conditions under which the division between mental and manual labour exists, which as Gramsci pointed out, concern the whole series of rituals, 'know how', and symbols. Through this analysis we can define the division between manual and mental labour as being the concrete manifestation of the political and ideological elements in the structural determination of class.

I have tried to show why the new petty bourgeoisie, even its lower strata, are placed on the side of mental labour in the complex political-ideological division that distinguishes this mental labour from manual labour performed by the working class. This does not mean the working class works only with its hands, and the new petty bourgeoisie only with its brain. These divisions between productive and unproductive labour, and between manual and mental labour are tendential divisions. They are not models to be used to determine the position within the class structure of every individual agent; on the contrary, it is concerned with the whole process of class struggle.

The Marxist concept of class is not a statistical category. It is necessary to show concretely, taking account of the detailed division of labour and of skill in the labour process, why even the lower strata of the new petty bourgeoisie are on the side of intellectual or mental labour with respect to their relations with the working class. Gramsci demonstrated in a concrete way that all public servants, all the servants of the state, from head to toe, must be considered as intellectuals in the general sense. I have taken other characteristics, in particular the bureaucratization of labour in the organization of the labour process of unproductive workers in order to show the significance of the distribution of authority. It is these elements, the political and ideological elements, which determine the class position of the new petty bourgeoisie. The new petty bourgeoisie interiorizes the social division of labour imposed by the bourgeoisie throughout the whole of the society. Each level of the new petty bourgeoisie exercises specific authority and ideological domination over the working class, which takes on particular characteristics within the factory division of labour, since the workers do not exert any kind of authority or ideological dominance over other workers, for example, over unskilled workers, that has even remotely the same characteristics as that exercised by the different levels of the new petty bourgeoisie over the working class. These are the political and ideological elements in the social division of labour that I have taken to show the class specificity of the new petty bourgeoisie. It is important to stress that these are elements that have nothing to do with the so-called 'class for itself'.

Finally, I have tried to show the way in which the transformation of contemporary capitalism operates in such a way as to produce an

objective polarization of important fractions of the new petty bourgeoisie towards the working class. I have tried to show that the
division of manual and mental labour, as long as it has to do with the
reproduction of political and ideological elements, reproduces itself
within mental labour on the one hand, and within manual labour on
the other. Some fractions of the new petty bourgeoisie, even if they are
orienting themselves towards the working class, are also orienting
themselves in relation to other fractions of the new petty bourgeoisie.
The objective conditions for polarization become greater as we
approach the barrier of manual labour, with the repetitive type of
labour performed by commercial employees and office workers. The
objective possibilities exist for an alliance of the working class with
certain fractions of the new petty bourgeoisie, and for the realization
of the hegemony of the working class. But it must clearly be understood that because they are members of another class, the new petty
bourgeoisie, they must be *won* by the working class. But this does not
occur automatically; the new petty bourgeoisie does not automatically
adopt the class position of the working class. Even more important: it
must be understood that, when the working class has won them, they
can also be lost again.

14

THE STATE AND THE
TRANSITION TO SOCIALISM

Henri Weber: In a recent book[1] you argue that what is needed is a complete break with the essentialist conceptions of the state. In other words, with those which define it as a simple object-instrument, or as a subject with a will and a rationality of its own to whom the ruling classes obediently defer. Would you say that this essentialist conception was also held by Marx and Lenin?

Nicos Poulantzas: Basically we must examine what we mean by the Marxist theory of the state. Can we find in Marx or Engels a general theory of the state? In my opinion we can no more speak of a general theory of the state than we can of a general theory of the economy, because the concept, content, and terrain of the political and the economic change with the various modes of production. We can certainly find in Marx and Engels the general principles of a theory of the state. We can also find some guidelines concerning the capitalist state. But there is no fully worked out theory, not even of the capitalist state.

The problem is more complex when we come to Lenin. In Marx and Engels's works there are no signs of an instrumentalist conception of the state – I'm thinking now of their political texts on France, etc. – but this is less clear with Lenin. There can be little doubt that some of his analyses fall prey to the instrumentalist conception of the state, that is, as a monolithic bloc without divisions, with almost no internal contradictions, and which can only be attacked globally and frontally from without by establishing the counter-state which would be the dual power, centralized soviets, and so on.

* First published in French as 'L'état et la transition au socialisme' in *Critique communiste*, no. 16 (June 1977). This translation is taken from *International*, vol. 4, no. 1 (Autumn 1977), pp. 3–12.

Does this conception derive from the fact that Lenin was dealing with the Tsarist state (because even when Lenin speaks of the Western democracies he always has in mind the Tsarist state)? Or from the fact that Lenin wrote *State and Revolution* as a polemic against the social-democratic conceptions of the state-subject? Could it be that Lenin was obliged, as he says himself, to 'bend the stick too far in the opposite direction', and to say: no, the state is not an autonomous subject but an instrument, an exclusive tool for the ruling classes.

So I would put a question mark as far as Lenin is concerned, but it is clear all the same that an instrumentalist conception of the state can be found in his texts.

Marxists and the Theory of the State

HW: You put forward a different conception of the state to this essentialist one. You say that the 'state' is no more a thing than 'capital' is an object, that, like capital, it is above all a social relation. It is, to quote you, 'the material condensation of the relation of forces between social classes as it is specifically expressed within the state itself'. You argue that one of the advantages of your conception is that it helps to underline a strategically important fact: that the state is not a solid monolithic bloc which the masses will have to confront from without in a whole series of encounters, and which they will have to destroy *en bloc* through an insurrectional attack bringing about the collapse of the state. Rather, since the state is a 'material condensation of a relation of classes', it is riddled with class contradictions. It is an arena of internal contradictions, and this applies to all its apparatuses – not only those where the masses are present physically (school, army . . .) but also where they are supposedly absent (police, judiciary, civil service). That is your conception, summarized somewhat schematically.

Now I want to ask you a number of questions. First, what is really new in this approach? In other words, I have the impression that Lenin did not consider the state an intrinsic reality, independent of the class struggle and dominating it, any more than did Marx (which brings us back to your first answer). Both of them definitely stress the fact that the nature of the state reflects the relation of forces between the classes (one need only mention the Marxist analysis of Bonapartism). Therefore the state, its institutions and personnel, its type of organization and relationship to the masses, is directly determined by the class structure, the relations between the classes, and the sharpness of the class struggle. I think this is fundamental in determining how Marxists pose the problem of the state.

Furthermore, I don't believe that either Marx or Lenin put forward a theory of the monolithic state, without 'contradictions or divisions' of the kind that you are challenging. Lenin, for example, completely incorporates in his strategy the struggle inside the institutions, even the Tsarist institutions. He argues that communists must be active in the state Duma, the schools, the army . . . In the famous pamphlet *What Is to Be Done?*, he denounces from the start the economist reduction of Marxism and explains that the social revolutionary party has to send its militants into all institutions and all spheres of society. He sees these institutions not only as the stake but also as the terrain of the class struggle.

The difference between these conceptions and those which are 'fashionable' today – I am thinking essentially of the theorizations of the leaders of the Italian Communist Party on the contradictory character of the state system today – is that for Marx, Lenin, and revolutionary Marxists, social classes do not and cannot occupy equivalent positions in the state. The ruling classes control the strategic positions of the state. They hold the real power. The exploited classes occupy or can occupy minor positions as personnel in the various state apparatuses, or as elected representatives in parliament, but these are generally all positions with extremely limited powers. Thus the state which, to use your words, is 'the condensation of a relation of classes', 'riven by internal contradictions', 'a terrain of the class struggle', still remains the primary instrument of bourgeois domination. Therefore the key strategic question of any transition to socialism remains: how do we deal with this state, how do we destroy it?

In fact, Lenin's conception was not so much an instrumentalist one of a monolithic state as one based on the understanding that, whatever its contradictions (and they can be relatively great), the state remains an instrument of domination by one class over another. Lenin does not ignore the Swiss, American and British states. He was perfectly aware of Marx's writings on the possible peaceful passage to socialism in this type of state. I do not accept that his judgement was clouded by the Tsarist state so that he ignored all other reality.

The second question is this: hasn't your constant emphasis on the contradictory character of the modern state had the effect – this is obviously the case with currents like the Italian CP, CERES[2], etc. – of blurring its class character and obscuring the key problem of any strategy for the transition to socialism: the task of smashing the state as the instrument of bourgeois domination?

NP: To return first to the novelty of my conception: we always come up against the same problem. I think that in Marx and Engels, and also in Lenin, not to mention Gramsci, whose contribution is very important, there are certainly elements of what I am trying to develop. In Lenin I still maintain that more than an ambiguity remains, for Lenin was thinking not so much of an internal struggle within the state apparatus as of the presence of revolutionaries within it. That is something quite different.

The main axis of Lenin's political struggle was for the centralization of the parallel powers outside the state, the building of an alternative state apparatus which would replace the bourgeois state at a given moment. Therefore Lenin, it is true, speaks of the presence of revolutionaries within the state, but rather in the sense of a presence that would help, when the time came, to replace this state with an alternative state. You don't seem to appreciate the weight of this intervention as such.

Anyway, what is certain is that within the Third International, I think, there was a tendency to view the state as an instrument that could be manipulated at will by the bourgeoisie. Even if they recognized that certain contradictions existed within it, the idea always persisted that no proper revolutionary struggle could be led in the heart of the state on the basis of these contradictions.

Now, on the other hand, we have the position of the Italian leaders, illustrated by Luciano Gruppi's latest article in *Dialectiques* No. 17 on the contradictory nature of the state. This is totally different from what I am saying. According to this theory of the contradictory nature of the state, which has also been taken up in the French CP, one section of the state corresponds to the development of the productive forces; as a result it embodies neutral, even positive functions of the state, because they correspond to the socialization of the productive forces. In other words, there are two states: a 'good' state, which ultimately corresponds to the growth of popular forces within the state itself, and a 'bad' state. Today the 'bad' state dominates the 'good' state. The super-state of the monopolies, which is the bad side, must be destroyed; but the section of the state that corresponds to the socialization of the productive forces and the popular upsurge must be preserved.

This is a complete false conception. I agree with you: the whole of the present state and all its apparatuses – social security, health, education, administration. etc. – correspond by their very structure to the power of the bourgeoisie. I do not believe that the masses can hold positions of autonomous power – even subordinate ones – within the capitalist state. They act as a means of resistance, elements of corrosion, accentuating the internal contradictions of the state.

This allows us to escape from the false dilemmas in which we are presently stuck: either viewing the state as a monolithic bloc (I am being schematic here), and thus considering the internal struggle as a totally secondary problem – with the main if not exclusive objective being the task of centralizing popular power, the construction of the counter-state to replace the capitalist state; or else seeing the state as contradictory and therefore considering that the essential struggle has to be mounted within the state, within its institutions – thus falling into the classical social-democratic conception of a struggle contained within the state apparatuses.

I believe, on the contrary, that it is necessary to develop some coordination between them:

– on the one hand, a struggle within the state. Not simply in the sense of a struggle enclosed within the physical confines of the state, but a struggle situated all the same on the strategic terrain constituted by the state. A struggle, in other words, whose aim is not to substitute the workers state for the bourgeois state through a series of reforms designed to take over one bourgeois state apparatus after another and thus conquer power, but a struggle which is, if you like, a struggle of resistance, a struggle designed to sharpen the internal contradictions of the state, to carry out a deep-seated transformation of the state.

– on the other hand, a parallel struggle, a struggle outside the institutions and apparatuses, giving rise to a whole series of instruments, means of coordination, organs of popular power at the base, structures of direct democracy at the base. This form of struggle would not aim to centralize a dual power type of counter-state, but would have to be linked with the first struggle.

I think we have to go beyond the classical strategy of dual power without falling into the trap of the Italian CP's strategy, which is, in the last analysis, a strategy located solely within the physical confines of the state.

The State and Dual Power

HW: Let us just concentrate on this aspect of the question, and then perhaps we can come back to the state via a detour. I am convinced that we have to lead a struggle within the institutions, to play as much as we can on the internal contradictions of the state, and that, in the present context, every battle for the democratization of the institutions and the state is a decisive battle. Also that such a struggle within the institutions must link up with a struggle outside to develop mechanisms of popular control and to extend direct democracy. But it seems to me that what is missing from your position, its blind spot, is the antagonism between these external popular committees (in the factories, the neighbourhoods, etc.) and the state apparatus which, whatever struggle you lead within it, won't undergo any change in its nature as a result. Therefore the moment of truth will necessarily arrive when you have a test of strength with the state apparatus. And this state apparatus, however democratized it is, however much it is weakened by the action of the workers movement within its institutions, will nevertheless remain, as we can see in Italy today, the essential instrument of the bourgeoisie's domination over the popular masses.

This test of strength seems unavoidable to me, and the proof of any strategy is the seriousness with which this moment of truth is taken into account. Those who say, a bit like you: there are struggles both inside and outside the institutions, and it is necessary to coordinate the two, and that's all; in reality, they don't take into account the test of strength, this decisive confrontation. This silence speaks for itself. It amounts to considering that the coordination of action outside and inside the institutions can, through a long, gradual process, finally alter the nature of the state and society without a test of strength.

You know, what worries me about your presentation is that you seem to be tilting at windmills, that is, against people who want to make the October Revolution all over again, when that is in no way the case with the far left today. We don't think that the state is a monolith which must be confronted and broken down exclusively from the outside. We are absolutely convinced of the need for a 'war of position', and we know that in the West there will be a whole period of preparation, of conquest of hegemony, etc. But the fundamental line of division, where you have to take a stand, is that some people see this war of position as constituting in itself the transformation of capitalist society and the capitalist state into a socialist society and a workers' state. Whereas, for us, this is only a starting point in establishing the preconditions for the test of strength which seems unavoidable to us whatever the circumstances. To ignore this test of strength is therefore to opt for one strategy over another.

NP: Well, now we are getting somewhere. I agree with you on the questions of the rupture, of the test of strength; but I still think that the repetition of a revolutionary crisis leading to a situation of dual power

is extremely unlikely in the West. However, on the question of the
rupture, this test of strength which you talk about could only take
place between the state and the totally exterior force of the centralized
organization of popular power at the base. That's the problem. I agree
on the necessity of a break. But, ultimately, it is not clear that there can
only be a truly revolutionary test of strength if it takes place between
the state, as such, and forces completely outside it (or identifying as
such), that is, the movement, the organs of popular power, centralized
at the base as an alternative power.

I can give you some very simple examples. For instance, let us look
at what happened in Portugal. You say that nobody wants to repeat
October, etc. But when I read what Daniel Bensaïd has to say in his
book on Portugal . . .

HW: *La Révolution en marche*[3] . . .

NP: But it's exactly this conception that I am fighting. According to
him, the crucial problem in Portugal was that the revolutionaries did
not succeed in centralizing all this experience of popular power at the
base, etc., to establish dual power, an alternative centralized power
which, as such, would have confronted the state. That would be the
unavoidable confrontation, the rupture. I believe that there will be a
rupture, but it's not clear to me that it will necessarily be between the
state *en bloc* and what lies outside it, the structures of popular power
at the base.

It can take place, for example, right inside the state apparatus:
between one fraction of the armed forces which is entirely at the
service of the bourgeoisie and another fraction of the regular army
which, supported also by the popular power at the base, by the
soldiers' unionization struggles or soldiers committees, can break
with its traditional role and pass over – a whole fraction of the state
army – to the side of the people. That's the kind of thing that happened
in Portugal: there was no confrontation between the popular militias
on one side and the bourgeois army on the other. If it didn't work out
in Portugal, it wasn't because the revolutionaries failed to set up a
parallel popular militia which could have totally replaced the state
apparatus at a given moment, but for a whole series of other
reasons . . .

To talk of coordinating the internal struggle with the external
struggle does not mean at all that we necessarily avoid talking of the
rupture. But it means recognizing that the revolutionary break does
not inevitably occur in the form of a centralization of a counter-state

confronting the state itself *en bloc*. It can pass through the state, and I think this is the only way it will happen at present. There will be a rupture, there will be a moment of decisive confrontation, but it will pass through the state. The organs of popular power at the base, the structures of direct democracy, will be the elements which bring about a differentiation inside the state apparatuses, a polarization by the popular movement of a large fraction of these apparatuses. This fraction, in alliance with the movement, will confront the reactionary, counter-revolutionary sectors of the state apparatus backed up by the ruling classes.

Fundamentally, I think that at the moment we cannot repeat the October Revolution under any form. The basis of the October Revolution was not only the opposition pointed out by Gramsci between a war of movement and a war of position. I think that Gramsci, too, basically retains the schema and the model of the October Revolution . . .

HW: Absolutely!

NP: What does Gramsci mean by the war of position? The war of position is to surround the strong castle of the state from outside with the structures of popular power. But in the end it's always the same story. It's a strong castle, right? So either you launch an assault on it – war of movement; or you besiege it – war of position. In any case, there is no conception in Gramsci's work that a real revolutionary rupture, linked to an internal struggle, can occur at this or that point of the state apparatus. It doesn't exist in Gramsci. But I myself find it difficult to believe that a classical situation of dual power can occur again in Europe, precisely because of the development of the state, its power, its integration into social life, into all areas, etc. This development and power make it simultaneously very strong when confronted with a situation of dual power, and also very weak: for now the alternative power, if you like, can somehow also appear within the state; the ruptures can also take place from within the state, and that is its weakness.

HW: The difficulty is in knowing what ruptures we are talking about. What is their nature, their extent? However, we can be sure that breaches of this kind inside the state institutions involve positions that could have been conquered before or during the crisis, but are relatively secondary positions. The essence of the state apparatus, where the reality of power is really concentrated, will not pass to the side of the revolution. And if you think that a revolutionary mass movement can polarize key sectors of the state apparatus – can polarize, for instance, the majority of the officer caste – then in effect you hold that the state is potentially neutral. You are in effect blurring the conception of the class character of this apparatus, and of its leading personnel.

I still think that the best example to take is that of Italy. Here the development of the mass movement, in the factories and elsewhere, has created a democratic movement within the police, the judiciary, the civil service – in all the state apparatuses – but these movements affect only the periphery, the fringe of these apparatuses, and not their core.

I will therefore freely admit that one of the essential functions of a popular movement and a revolutionary strategy is to dislocate the state apparatus and throw it into the crisis, to paralyze it, to turn it as much as possible against bourgeois society. This is relatively easy in the schools, some government services, etc., whose class character is more mediated. It is much more difficult when you come to the apparatuses of direct coercion such as the police, the army, the judiciary, the higher echelons of the civil service, or even the mass media, the television and press – though it's possible, and we have it as an objective. But we must have no illusions on what we can achieve from this angle. There will be no vertical split from top to bottom into two halves. We will not establish dual power inside the state, capturing half the state power from top to bottom and winning everyone from half the ministers to half the postmasters to the side of the popular movement! We will make some inroads, but that won't do away with the continuing existence of the state apparatus, of the state as instrument of domination and general staff of the counter-revolution. Hence the need to deal with it once and for all.

If I remain convinced of the reality of the concept of dual power, clearly under different forms from those in Tsarist Russia, and obviously linked to the growing crisis of the state apparatus, it is because I am convinced that the core of the state apparatus will polarize to the right. We can see it in Italy, we saw it in Chile and Portugal, and we can see it everywhere the ruling class is threatened and where its instrument of domination in consequence throws off its liberal and democratic trappings to reveal the full nakedness of its role.

Direct Democracy and Representative Democracy

NP: You are right on many points, but I think that we are in any case faced with a historical gamble. The new strategy that must be adopted in the concrete situation in the West, where my analyses prompt me to say that there cannot be a situation of dual power, contains in effect the risk, the obvious risk – and everyone is aware of it – that the great majority of the repressive state apparatuses will polarize to the right, and therefore crush the popular movement. Having said that, I think that we must first of all bear in mind that this is a long process. We have to understand the implications of that. We talked about *the* rupture. But it's not clear in fact that there will be *one* big rupture. On the other hand, it's also clear that you risk falling into gradualism if you talk about a series of ruptures. Nevertheless, if we're talking about a long process, we have to come to terms with the fact that it can only mean a series of ruptures, whether you call them successive or not. What matters for me is the idea of a 'long process'. What can you mean by 'long process' if you talk at the same time of *the* rupture?

HW: It means, for example, what we are seeing in Italy. Since 1962, and very sharply since 1968, a relatively long process has been unfolding. It already amounts to ten or fifteen years of a rising popular movement, of the erosion of bourgeois hegemony, it has resulted in the development of forms of direct democracy at the base, a growing crisis of the state apparatuses, and it is ushering in a sharper and sharper crisis, and indeed the test of strength . . .

NP: Yes, but hold on. The process is relatively differentiated all the same, because we've seen also what is happening in Portugal. Then I would say that the most probable hypothesis on which to work in France is the Common Programme. In other words, that the left will move into power, or rather into government, accompanied by a simultaneous huge mobilization of the popular masses. For either there will be no popular mobilization, in which case we will have at best a new social-democratic experience; or else there will be a massive mobilization of the popular classes, coinciding with a left government, which implies already a number of important changes at the top of the state apparatus: in other words, the left, occupying the summit of the state, will be led (willy nilly) to undertake a democratization of the state, also from above. In Italy the PCI finds itself in the corridors of power and yet at the same time it lacks even the slightest means of mobilizing the masses or altering the structure of the state apparatuses which a left government in France would have. There's your first problem.

Second problem. Let's take up the question of dual power and the rupture which must smash the state apparatus, because that's really the heart of the matter. Smashing the state apparatus meant something relatively simple for the Bolsheviks. It meant that the institutions of representative democracy, the so-called formal liberties, etc. are institutions which by their nature are totally under the sway of the bourgeoisie – not only the state, I say, but representative democracy. Smashing the state apparatus therefore meant overthrowing the whole institutional set-up and replacing it with something completely new, a new organization of direct or so-called direct democracy, by means of soviets led by the vanguard party, etc.

This raises the following question. I think that nowadays the perspective of smashing the state remains valid as a perspective for the deep-seated transformation of the state structure. But, in order to be very clear on this point and not treat it lightly, we can no longer speak of smashing the state in the same way, insofar as we are all more or less convinced – and I know your latest views on this question – that a democratic socialism must maintain formal and political liberties: transformed, to be sure, but maintained all the same in the sense that Rosa Luxemburg demanded of Lenin. We musn't forget that. To be honest, Lenin couldn't have cared less about political and formal liberties. And Rosa Luxemburg, a revolutionary who can hardly be accused of social-democratic leanings, took him up on it.

It is easy to say that you have to maintain political and formal liberties. But for me it's clear that this also implies – and here I'm going back to the discussion you had with Jacques Julliard in *Critique communiste* Nos. 8–9 – the maintenance, although profoundly altered, of certain forms of representative democracy.

What is meant by representative democracy as opposed to direct democracy? There are certain criteria. Direct democracy means a compulsory mandate, for instance, with instant recall of the delegates, etc. If you want to preserve political and formal liberties, I think that implies keeping certain institutions which embody them, and also a representative element: that is, centres of power, assemblies which are not directly modelled on the pattern of direct democracy. In other words, national assemblies elected directly by universal suffrage in a secret ballot, and which are not solely ruled by the principles of compulsory mandate and instant recall.

HW: What have you got against the compulsory mandate and instant recall?

NP: Historically, every experience of direct democracy at the base which has not been tied to the maintenance of representative democracy for a certain period has failed. To do away completely with the institutions of so-called representative democracy during a transitional phase, and to think that you will have direct democracy, in the absence of specific institutions of representative democracy, with political liberties as well (plurality of parties, among other things) – well, as far as I know, it's never worked. Direct democracy, by which I mean direct democracy in the soviet sense only, has always and everywhere been accompanied by the suppression of the plurality of parties, and then the suppression of political and formal liberties. Now, to say that that's merely Stalinism seems to me to be going a bit far.

HW: But to say that it is fundamentally tied to the form of direct democracy is to go even further. Because in reality there was an international and national context which meant that it was difficult to conceive of any kind of democratization while the revolution remained isolated. To use the failure of the soviets in Russia in the 1920s to prove your argument is not convincing.

NP: Pardon me, it's not only Russia, it happened again in China . . .

HW: With even more reason . . .

NP: And also in Cuba, not to mention Cambodia; you can't deny all that. I'm quite happy to blame Stalinism or the objective conditions, but it does begin to add up to something in such varied national and international conditions.

To go back to the Russian Revolution, we all know that for Lenin the abolition of other parties was linked to the civil war. That is how it happened concretely. Having said that, I wonder all the same if this abolition of other parties was not already there potentially in Lenin's conception or in certain of his texts. If one conceives that the truth of the proletariat – its political class consciousness – comes from outside the workers' movement, from the theory produced by the intellectuals, then I wonder to what extent that, tied to a certain conception of direct democracy, does not lead directly to the abolition of all democracy in line with the well-known scenario. First of all you say, as Lenin started to say, democracy only for the proletarian parties, the parties of the left. But then, what is a proletarian party? You know what I mean, I don't have to spell it out: which is the real proletarian party? Which is the real proletarian fraction of the proletarian party? I know very well that you can't reduce Lenin's theory of organization to *What Is to Be Done?*, but I believe all the same that a single party is potentially there in the conceptions of *What Is to Be Done?*, which still remains the framework of the Leninist theory . . .

Then, even in Soviet Russia, I wonder if what Rosa Luxemburg said to Lenin ('Beware, isn't that going to lead to . . .'), if even the first comments of Trotsky, the pre-Bolshevik Trotsky, were not more relevant than the explanations of the later Trotsky, the super-Bolshevik Trotsky.

But finally, leaving aside the whole historical debate, I would ask whether today we can talk about political and formal liberties over a long period, the period of transition to socialism, without also having the institutions that can give life to and guarantee this plurality and these liberties? Do you really believe that these liberties will continue to be maintained, simply by their own dynamic, under a soviet democracy at the base (supposing such a system is possible, it's thought of as possible, but I think that dual power, anyway, is a situation that can't recur as such), if there are no institutions that can guarantee these liberties – and, in particular, institutions of representative democracy?

In the debate among Italian Marxists, you know that the discussion was launched by Bobbio.[4] Of course, one clearly can't agree with all Bobbio's social-democratic platitudes, but he did highlight one point. He said: 'If we want to maintain liberties, the plurality of expression, etc., then all I know is that throughout history these liberties have been coupled with a form of parliament'. Certainly he expressed it in a social-democratic form. But yet, I wonder if there isn't a core of truth in that, if the maintenance of formal political liberties doesn't require the maintenance of the institutional forms of power of representative democracy. Obviously they would be transformed; it's not a matter of keeping the bourgeois parliament as it is, etc.

Moreover, we have had some experience of direct democracy in France since 1968. It's a bit too easy to use that as an argument, but you saw how it worked then!

HW: You mean the university?

NP: Yes, I'm thinking mainly of the university, but not just there. Because when I talk about the need for formal and political liberties, it is not just the far left I have in mind, as some people have thought from my article in *Le Monde*; I am thinking also of the CGT and the Communist Party, to say nothing of the leadership of the Socialist Party.

So you would have forms of direct democracy at the base, neighbourhood committees and the like, totally controlled by the official left, without any institutional guarantee of formal liberties . . . well, come on. Even the formal and political liberties of the far left can only be guaranteed by maintaining forms of representative democracy.

Finally, you know that I don't claim to have complete answers. There is a problem traditionally summarized in the expression 'smashing the state', but we're all aware that we have to maintain political liberties and pluralism, and hence also to a certain extent the institutions of representative democracy. I would not hesitate to say also that, precisely because we talk of maintaining rather than purely and simply abolishing the so-called formal liberties, we can no longer use the term 'smashing' to define the problem, but rather that of radically 'transforming' the state. Do you believe in pluralism?

HW: Of course. We believe in it and we practise it.

NP: But for your opponents as well?

HW: Certainly. Even for the bourgeois parties, it's there in writing.

NP: Aha, even for bourgeois parties. Now, not to be too naïve, there are things one has to say, because we fear for ourselves as well . . .

HW: Of course.

NP: It's all very well to say so, but I want to know what forms of institutional guarantee there would be – they are always secondary, of course, but they matter. In what kind of institutions would this pluralism and these liberties be inscribed, in what kind of material institutions would they be sustained and guaranteed? If we're talking only of forms of direct democracy at the base – in other words, structures still massively dominated by the traditional left parties – that hardly eases my misgivings. I can conceive of direct democracy at the base through general assemblies at Renault, or in Marseilles or Rheims . . . but unless we are in a really revolutionary situation where everyone feels totally involved, constantly in the streets, etc., which doesn't happen every day, then I don't know if that is sufficient to guarantee that liberties will be maintained . . .

I certainly wouldn't like to find myself, as I have so often in my past political life, in general assemblies of direct democracy which vote by a show of hands on command and where, after a while, you see X, Y or Z prevented from speaking . . .

HW: No, but your picture of workers' democracy is very one-sided. Democracy is hard to practise in general, and the more democratic it is, the harder it is to practise it. The easiest regime to follow is enlightened despotism, but then you can never be sure of the enlightenment of the despot . . .

Still, on this question, I think first that this counterposition between representative, delegated democracy and democracy at the base is a fraud. There is no such thing as democracy at the base: there is always some delegation. There is a system which aims to resolve a fundamental problem, that of re-rooting politics in the real communities . . .

NP: Henri, I'm sorry to interrupt you, but I think there's some confusion here which we won't get out of through any kind of trick. Take *Critique communiste* Nos. 8–9. On the one hand you have Mandel, who clearly puts forward the soviet system, revised and improved.[5] Then you have the question posed by Jacques Julliard:[6] will we have to have a national-type assembly, based on universal suffrage and periodic elections, without compulsory mandates? Yes, says Julliard while for Mandel there is no such necessity. Julliard poses the question and I tend to agree with him on the necessity for a national assembly, in the form of a parliament – radically transformed, of course.

That wasn't Lenin's view, because Lenin was faced with the Constituent Assembly, if I may remind you! So, once the Constituent Assembly had been elected, well, it was dissolved and never functioned. The drawback was that the majority was held by the Socialist-Revolutionaries, with all the risks that that entailed. So for Lenin it was a simple matter.

Coordinate the Soviets with Parliament?

HW: On this question, I think first of all that this democracy can be codified perfectly easily. There is no reason why it should correspond to the kind of manipulatory sessions that have occurred in the student movement. Clearly so-called direct democracy can be something very grotesque and anti-democratic – a sort of 'assemblyist' democracy. But it can also be something highly codified.

What seems important to me, and it's not a trick, is to root political activity and political life in communities which are real communities and not nominal aggregates of the geographical constituency type. These real communities must be work-communities (in the broadest sense: factories, schools, barracks . . . if any are left) and also neighbourhood communities, in other words, real area units. But that can be codified perfectly easily: the secret ballot can and must be included. The right of recall must exist too, but on a rational basis: you can have immediate recall of factory delegates at any time in the case of problems of work; and you can have annual or biennial recall, as in Italy – because there are already some experiences there – of delegates at a higher level, who are dealing with different kinds of problems which obviously cannot be followed on a day-to-day basis by the worker at the base. All this can be regulated at least as well as bourgeois-democratic procedure.

The problem is not to say whether we are for or against representative democracy: in modern societies, all democracy is representative. It's a question of knowing whether the form of representation means giving up power or the real delegation of it with the possibility of control. I would say that the forms of democracy which carry on bourgeois traditions are actually equivalent to giving up power.

What it boils down to then is handing over power to specialists for a long period and taking no further interest in between two elections. Therefore to struggle for democratization is to try to struggle against this system, which rests on a structure. And the most effective way to struggle against this structure is precisely to root political activity in the real communities. This is what we have to develop. To involve people in political life, they have to feel that they have control over the decisions which affect them: to have control over these decisions, they must form a community, discuss together, be able to carry some weight, etc.

If it is the atomized individual who comes face to face with the political machinery – in other words, the individual as conceived by the bourgeoisie – then they withdraw into the sphere of private life; and every seven years they demonstrate their dissatisfaction or their satisfaction. That is the problem as we see it. That is why we want to change the political system in order to base democracy on real communities – at work or in an area – with duly codified forms of representation which prevent abuses, etc. We think that such a structural alteration would mark a qualitative progress towards political democracy, because it would give people a real chance to run their own affairs. But precondition for this is that it must be one of a whole series of other measures, or else it will be deprived of all content. There must be a significant reduction of working hours, for instance. It is obviously very difficult for people to devote time to management, factory problems, and questions of the economy and society if they have to work more than thirty hours a week.

You say: parliament must change, etc. But it is necessary to explain in what sense it must change. What must be done away with is the system whereby an MP is elected for five years from a vast geographical constituency, thus establishing the conditions for the greatest possible autonomy of the MPs from their electors. In effect, that means another institutional system.

NP: When we talk about coordinating forms of representative democracy with forms of direct democracy, that obviously means that we don't want to continue with the existing system but advance beyond it, that we want to overcome the complete divide between a caste of professional politicians and the rest of the population.

This advance and coordination implies, at least for a long period, the existence of national assemblies as centres of power. For ultimately, if all the power emanates from work-communities and their representatives, then the risk of a corporatist degeneration is obvious. The extension of democracy, the proliferation of decision-taking bodies, poses in fact the problem of centralization, of leadership. And then you have two alternatives. One is that the revolutionary party – or the coalition of left parties dominated by it – does the job. But we all agree that this party does not exist. The only party which could assume this role today is the Communist Party, and we all know what that would mean . . . (to say nothing of the fact that to assign this role to the 'party' is manifestly to open the way to the single party, and even an 'ideal' party which becomes a single party can only end up as Stalinist). The other alternative is a parliament elected by secret, universal suffrage. That is the only alternative I can see. Without the party, the central council of soviets cannot play this role. It has not played it anywhere. If things worked out to some extent in Russia, in China etc., that's because 'the' communist party centralized things, and we know what the ultimate consequences were.

Furthermore, one day we will have to come to terms with the following fact: the complexity of the present economic tasks of the state, a complexity which will not diminish but increase under socialism.

What I'm afraid of is that behind your 'rooting of power in the work-communities' there lurks in reality the restoration of the power of the experts; in other words, that you would escape the dictatorship of the leadership of the single party only to fall captive to the discreet charm of technocratic despotism. Don't you think it's strange that all the technocrats of the Socialist Party swear by self-management! It means for them at most that there are a few discussions, after which the experts take charge of the economic tasks of the state!

And then you have the concrete situation in France today. What you and I are talking about is the ideal model of democracy. We have completely forgotten that we are faced with a concrete situation in France: that of the Common Programme and the likely victory of the Union of the Left.

Faced with that, we can of course conclude that nothing can be expected from the Common Programme, that the united left in power will be devoutly social-democratic to the point of pursuing a new authoritarianism which can only be thwarted by centralized counter-powers at the base, and therefore our only hope is that it takes up office as soon as possible so that the masses understand what reformism is and turn away from it.

My analysis is different: either there will be a tremendous mobilization at the base, or there won't be one. In the latter case, that's it: we are destined to go through a new social-democratic experience. It'll be a bit like it was under Allende, though that experience had a much more shaky electoral foundation than the Common Programme will have. After all, Popular Unity won with only 30 per cent of the vote!

However, if there is a massive mobilization, then things will start to happen. But then we will all find ourselves in a very specific situation. Everyone: both us and the left in power. I don't say us against the left. For there will be two camps and we will be in the orbit of the left, whether we like it or not.

We will then be in a situation characterized by a crisis of the state, but not a revolutionary crisis. The left will be in power, with a programme much more radical than has ever been the case in Italy; committed to implementing it, which will really upset some of its components; already embarked on a process of democratization of the state, faced with an enormous popular mobilization giving rise to forms of direct democracy at the base . . . but at the same time limiting itself to the project of the Common Programme.

So the real problem is to know how we can intervene in this process in order to deepen it. In this context, what does seem clearly impossible is the perspective of centralizing a workers' counter-power, factory council by factory council, soldiers committee by soldiers committee. Furthermore, I must say that this would seem to me to be an extremely dangerous way to proceed. Such a course is the surest road to the total recapture of power by the bourgeoisie, which – as we mustn't forget – remains throughout this period an active (and how!) protagonist in this process.

So what else can we do? How can we force the left to proceed effectively with the democratization of the state, to link up its institutional power with the new forms of the direct democracy? That's the problem. And if one thing's certain, it's that we aren't going to resolve the problem with such hazy notions as the 'real work-communities', metaphysically endowed by their very nature with all the virtues that used to be attributed at one time to the 'Party'.

What Revolutionary Strategy for France?

HW: The situation which it seems to me would definitely lead to the failure of these mobilizations and their defeat is that which would result from the application of the present strategy of the Union of the Left: one where, as you say, the left takes office, and where the mass movement is strong enough to force it to implement the Common Programme. Because then it will attack the bourgeoisie's interests sufficiently to make it angry but not enough to put it out of action. And then we will be in the absolutely classical situation where the ruling class loses patience – both nationally and internationally – and where it still retains the key economic and political levers of control, and in particular the state apparatus; because although part of the state apparatus may break away in France, the bulk of it will on the contrary polarize to the right. The bourgeoisie will therefore have the reasons and the means to retaliate. The popular masses, on the other hand, will be relatively disarmed by decades of sermons on the peaceful road to socialism, the 'contradictory nature' of the bourgeois-democratic state, etc. We risk finding ourselves in the classical situation of being defeated without a fight.

That's our analysis. Like you, though, we say that if there is no mass movement – something which seems inconceivable to me in the medium term . . .

NP: And to me too . . .

HW: Right, then if there is one, I think that the problem will be posed in terms of organizing around objectives – not of immediately destroying the bourgeois state, that would be senseless – but around economic, political and international objectives, what we call transitional objectives, and which are effectively written into the logic of the emergence of dual power . . .

NP: There! You see . . .

HW: But hang on, let me tell you what I mean by that. It clearly means, at the economic level, struggling for the expropriation of big capital and establishing workers' control of production at all levels, culminating in a workers' plan to solve the economic crisis. This is the central axis, which aims not merely to defend the living standards and working conditions of the popular masses but also to oust the bourgeoisie from economic power, both in the factory and in the state, and to organize the working class to take control, to take power.

At the political level, we undoubtedly have to fight for the extension of democracy rather than shouting 'elections are for fools'. We have to fight for proportional representation, regional assemblies, a trade union for soldiers, etc., so as to expand political democracy as much as possible, because this is also the way in which the bourgeois state will be most weakened. At the international level (and I'm summarizing here) we will have to counter the offensive of US imperialism and its allies by developing new relations with the Third World countries and, above all, by involving the popular masses of Southern Europe and beyond . . . That's a necessary condition of success, and it is also possible because a new situation is developing in Europe.

This axis can develop the organization of the masses at the base, in the factories and the neighbourhoods, supporting these objectives and fighting to realize them. And the logic of these objectives is centralization.

The logic of workers' control in the factory is workers' control over the economic policy of the state. The workers who take control in a factory run up against the problems of the market, credit and business practice. And the logic of their action is coordination and centralization at the level of the industry, the region, the nation. Thus you have the emergence of an alternative workers' power against that of the bourgeois state. And the confrontation seems inevitable to me.

I have no doubt that this confrontation will draw support from the internal divisions of the bourgeois state. I even think that the more the mass movement is organized as a powerful pole of attraction outside the state, with its own alternative project, the deeper and more important these divisions will be. But that there will be a confrontation – between this mass movement, organizing and centralizing itself outside the state apparatus, backed up by its representatives and allies within this apparatus, and the bulk of the bourgeois state apparatus, organizing and centralizing the resistance of the ruling classes – seems to me inevitable. You can't finesse indefinitely in such a situation.

Otherwise you have to say, like Amendola and his friends in the Italian Communist Party, that the transition to socialism is not immediately on the cards. Amendola declares that the transition to socialism is not a relevant question today, for reasons of international policy and chiefly for reasons of national policy. He says: most Italians don't want socialism. We have to get that into our heads in order to understand what can be done. We have just had thirty years of unprecedented economic expansion; the Italian people are the freest in the world, they have achieved the greatest gains over the last ten years, and so on. At bottom, most people are attached to the system, and that is why they vote for the right-wing coalition led by the Christian Democrats. They complain, but they are not ultimately prepared to go further and make the sacrifices which would be required by a revolutionary conquest of power. Consequently all talk about the transition must end, we must stop playing little games which consist in pushing people a little further than they want to go, and struggle to democratize and improve Italian society.

Now that's a line which hangs together, it's coherent.

NP: Notice, however, that Ingrao doesn't say the same thing . . .

HW: No, he doesn't. But the politics of the Italian CP are the politics of Amendola using the language of Ingrao. Berlinguer's job is to do the translation . . . Well, it's a coherent policy which considers that for a certain period we are in a historical stalemate. I don't agree, I am ready to argue against it, but I recognize that it is not contradictory within its own terms. What irritates me is, er . . .

NP: What irritates you is what I'm saying.

HW: That's it! [Laughs] It's what CERES and the left of the Italian CP say, because it is incoherent . . .

NP: No, I don't think so, and I'll give you a concrete example. I think the disaster of the Portuguese Revolution occurred precisely because there was a confrontation between the Group of Nine and Otelo de Carvalho, the spokesperson of the workers', neighbourhood and soldiers' commissions. If we are to suppose that there will be a state apparatus essentially mobilized on the right, and Carvalhist-type movements of the base lined up against it, then I say: forget about it, you've lost in advance. So you have to go back to Amendola's position. Amendola's position is certainly coherent, but it is reformist. Your position is very coherent, but totally unrealistic.

Because if you consider the essence of the state apparatus as it is in France, and then the forms of centralization of popular power . . .

Well, it's obvious that it will be crushed before it's taken more than three jumps of a flea! You surely don't think that in the present situation they will let you centralize parallel powers to the state aiming to create a counter-power. Things would be settled before there were even the beginnings of a shadow of a suspicion of such an organization.

So I make a contrary analysis. I think that in the present situation it is possible to undermine much more important fractions of the state apparatus; and I've given the example of Portugal. You can say that it is different. All right. But what interests me in this example is that, particularly in the army, there were much more important divisions than simply between the entire officer corps mobilized in the service of capital on one side and the soldiers committees mobilized alongside the workers' movement on the other.

What happened in Portugal? If it was a disaster, that is because there was a break, a confrontation between the structures of popular power, the Carvalhist-type movements, and the Group of Nine. And Carvalho himself recognized that the form taken by the centralization of these popular counter-powers was in many ways responsible for the disastrous rupture which took place between this movement and the group led by Melo Antunes.

Ruptures in the State Apparatus

HW: I really think that that was a very secondary reason for this rupture. The basic reason was that Melo Antunes and the 'military social democracy', as they were called there, were engaged in the process of stabilizing Portuguese capitalism. He was even one of the spearheads of the operation, the principal military ally of Mario Soares and his international supporters.

The basic reason for the split in the Armed Forces Movement had nothing to do with the SUV movement ('Soldiers United Will Win'). The SUV appeared very late on in the day: after the Group of Nine, in fact, and in reality as a consequence of it. So there is a confusion of causes and effects in your example.

But that isn't the problem. I would like to see you develop your argument further. We don't seek difficulty for difficulty's sake, and the same applies to confrontation. If we were convinced that there could be a majority split in the French state apparatus in favour of the popular movement, then obviously we would be for playing that card for its full worth, even taking some risks in the course of it. But you know this state apparatus. By what miracle would it fall into the camp of the revolution? That's what I would like you to tell me concretely. What reasonable, even risky or daring, hypothesis can be made for a majority rupture in this state apparatus?

NP: I'll tell you. For example, let's look at the army, the police, the judiciary. Because I still base my perspective on the internal crisis of these apparatuses. Take the judiciary: a third of the magistrates are members of the magistrates' union . . . that's very important. And there's a second element: the left in power, even in its own interests, will have to introduce important changes not only in the personnel but also in the structures of the state. After twenty years of Gaullism there is so much patronage, so much institutionalization of the Gaullists or Independent Republicans in the state. Even on the simple basis of ensuring the dominance of its own political élite, the left government will be forced to make changes in the institutional forms as well as the people. In the judiciary, for instance, if they don't want to end up very quickly in an Allende-type situation, they will be forced – I repeat, even from the viewpoint of continuing the élite system – to break the power of the Council of Magistrates, to change the normal rotation of judges, etc.

And then that, linked to the mass movements at the base, will allow you to weigh up the possibilities of a split.

Take Admiral Sanguinetti. Just two years ago he was the head of the French Navy, and an important current of officers share his views. Read his statement in *Politique-Hebdo*: he's in favour of delegates from the ranks, a defence policy independent of the US, etc. . . . In other words, we're talking about an army which is prepared to respect a certain legality, which would not be plotting against the regime from the start.

My hypothesis may be wrong, but I think yours is totally unrealistic . . .

HW: Every revolutionary hypothesis seems unrealistic.

NP: More or less, and everything depends precisely on that nuance.

HW: There was nothing more unrealistic than the Bolshevik hypothesis in 1917, the Maoist hypothesis in 1949, the Castroist hypothesis in 1956! To be realistic is always to be on the side of maintaining the status quo . . .

NP: Don't forget that being unrealistic has frequently led also to disasters and bloody defeats. But you can also make a more realistic hypothesis of the revolutionary possibilities, presented in a different way . . .

To deal also with the problem of the police. After what has happened in the police in the last few years, we can justifiably suppose that a left government will have no alternative but to take significant measures to democratize the police . . .

Then, given that you have the crisis of the state, of which there are indications; given that the left is obliged – again in its own elementary interests – to initiate changes; given that it can proceed to do that because of its powers under the Constitution and the strength it derives from the mass movements at the base; given all that, I think this is the only plausible solution.

It's all the more so because we cannot ignore the actual forces on the ground. In reality, your hypothesis is not based solely on an evaluation of the objective possibilities of a revolutionary crisis in France. *It is also based, implicitly, on the possibility of the extremely rapid and powerful development of a revolutionary party of the Leninist type, to the left of the French Communist Party. Your whole hypothesis is based on that.* It's there in black and white in Mandel's interview on revolutionary strategy in Europe.

But I don't think that this is at all likely. First, because of what I said before about the new reality of the state, the economy, the international context, etc. And then, because of the weight of the political forces of the traditional left, particularly in a country like France.

Your hypothesis implies, for instance, that the LCR[7] will grow from 7,000 militants to ten or twenty times that number in a few months! That's never happened anywhere! Not in Chile, not . . .

HW: In Portugal, and still more in Spain, we've seen something not so far off it.

NP: You're joking! Compared with the Communist Party, especially in Spain, these forces are insignificant. But it's not just that. If you analyze the Communist Party as a simple social-democratic party, organizationally as well as politically, then you can certainly reckon on a rapid and massive recomposition of the workers' movement, as you say. But the fact is that they are not social-democratic parties.

While there remains a mass Communist Party, a rapid and structured growth of the independent revolutionary left is out of the question. We saw that with the MIR in Chile.

So, if we stick with your hypothesis, perhaps it is coherent and realistic, but it's fifty or sixty years ahead of its time. We must not blind ourselves to the failure of the far left (from this point of view) over the last few years in Europe.

HW: You are right to underline that our perspective is based on the hypothesis of a profound recomposition of the workers' movement. But it seems to me that you look too statically at the movement as it exists. It's a movement which has already evolved a great deal in the space of five or ten years from the point of view of its restructuring. I agree with you that the CPs are not social-democratic parties, but they have entered a phase of crises and flux, of internal differentiations, of which only the first signs are apparent today.

Of course, if you start from a static hypothesis, by saying: that is the relation of forces for a whole historical period, then obviously you can only be right. Because the reformists are largely hegemonic, and the revolutionaries – apart from their lack of preparedness, their disunity, etc. – do not have a sufficient implantation in any case. Then only a reformist perspective has any credibility. The only hope, in these conditions, would be to act to push the reformists as far left as possible, and eventually to straighten them out. This is the perspective adopted by CERES. But as I see it, this depends on a fixed conception of the workers' movement, something which is largely belied by its recent evolution in Italy as well as France, not to mention Portugal and Spain.

Take the results of the far left in the French municipal elections in March 1977: they were a surprise, but a surprise which should make us think. What does it mean when the far left wins eight or ten per cent of the vote in the most working-class areas of certain cities? It is a vote of no confidence in the policies of the main left parties. The relation of forces inside the workers' movement isn't just a question of parties and organizations. You must also take into account the attitudes of tens of thousands of worker militants, politically unorganized, or organized in the CP or SP, who have developed a sound distrust of the existing leaderships through a series of experiences since 1968. In the event of a victory of the Union of the Left, and the worsening of the crisis of the system, these militants and many others might well refuse to take a 'pause', and seek a socialist solution instead.

If the far left manages to link up with these militants, to present them with a serious anti-capitalist alternative, then there could be a drastic change in the relation of forces with the reformists.

This is all the more true since, I repeat, the entry of the CP and the SP into government, the implementation of the Common Programme, will bring their internal contradictions to boiling point. There is in fact no chance of achieving the transition to socialism in France if a large number of CP and SP militants are not polarized to the left and don't opt at the crucial moment for a 'leap forward' rather than a 'retreat'.

But for them to do that, you must precisely have a credible anti-capitalist alternative to the left of the CP. Otherwise, critical as they are, they will follow their leadership. It is this alternative pole, based in the mass movement, equipped with a strategy and programme for a socialist solution, working to recompose the whole workers movement, that we are fighting to build.

In reality, we're probably getting to the bottom of our disagreement. Perhaps it's not so much to do with the need to break up the bourgeois state apparatus – including from within, through the internal rupture of its apparatuses – as with the means of achieving it. Some people think that to reach this goal it is necessary to avoid doing anything which could cement the social cohesion of the state and polarize it to the right. For them it is moderation and 'responsibility' which is most likely to expose the internal contradictions. In reality, what they have in mind here is the top level of the state apparatus.

For us, on the contrary, it is the development of a vast anti-capitalist movement, its independent organization and activity – outside the state apparatuses, though also within them – which creates the conditions for a rupture.

NP: For me, a significant movement of the far left, critical and autonomous, is essential to influence the very course of the experience of the Union of the Left. But not for the same reasons as you. Not because the far left could constitute a real alternative political and organizational pole, as you say; on the one hand, it's incapable of it, and on the other hand, because I no longer think that there is a real anti-capitalist alternative outside or alongside the road of the Common Programme. *There is currently no other way possible.* So the question is not of acting in such a way that the left abandons its reformist road and opts for the good and pure revolutionary road, a road for which the far left would act as a signpost. The question is to extend and deepen the road of the Common Programme and to prevent social-democratic stagnation, which is not necessarily written into it like original sin.

The far left can thus play a role not as a pole of attraction leading somewhere else but as a stimulus, a force opening up the perspectives of the Common Programme and raising its horizons. Then, because the far left is not limited to its organizational aspect (which ultimately is the least important), it can take up a series of new problems that the united and institutional left is quite incapable of dealing with. There is a final reason why the far left is absolutely essential: as an active reminder at all times of the need for direct democracy at the base – in short, as a safeguard, let us say, against any eventual temptation by the left government to seek an authoritarian solution. In other words, a role more of criticizing than of outflanking.

15

TOWARDS A
DEMOCRATIC SOCIALISM

The question of socialism and democracy, of the democratic road to socialism, is today posed with reference to two historical experiences, which in a way serve as examples of the twin limits or dangers to be avoided: the traditional social-democratic experience, as illustrated in a number of West European countries, and the Eastern example of what is called 'real socialism'. Despite everything that distinguishes these cases, despite everything that opposes social democracy and Stalinism to each other as theoretico-political currents, they nevertheless exhibit a fundamental complicity: both are marked by *statism* and profound distrust of mass initiatives, in short by suspicion of democratic demands. In France, many now like to speak of two traditions of the working-class and popular movements: the statist and Jacobin one, running from Lenin and the October Revolution to the Third International and the Communist movement; and a second one characterized by notions of self-management and direct, rank-and-file democracy. It is then argued that the achievement of democratic socialism requires a break with the former and integration with the latter. In fact, however, this is a rather perfunctory way of posing the question. Although there are indeed two traditions, they do not coincide with the currents just mentioned. Moreover, it would be a fundamental error to imagine that mere integration with the current of self-management and direct democracy is sufficient to avoid statism.

The Leninist Legacy and Luxemburg's Critique

First of all, then, we must take yet another look at Lenin and the October Revolution. Of course, Stalinism and the model of the

* First published in French as the postscript to *L'État, le pouvoir, le socialisme*, Paris 1978; translated as *State, Power, Socialism*, London 1978. This version is taken from *New Left Review* 109 (1978), pp. 75–87. Translated by Patrick Camiller.

transition to socialism bequeathed by the Third International differ from Lenin's own thought and action. But they are not simply a deviation from the latter. Seeds of Stalinism were well and truly present in Lenin – and not only because of the peculiarities of Russia and the Tsarist state with which he had to grapple. The error of the Third International cannot be explained simply as an attempt to universalize in an aberrant manner a model of socialism that corresponded, in its original purity, to the concrete situation of Tsarist Russia. At the same time, these seeds are not to be found in Marx himself. Lenin was the first to tackle the problem of the transition to socialism and the withering away of the state, concerning which Marx left only a few general observations on the close relationship between socialism and democracy.

What then was the exact import of the October Revolution for the withering away of the state? Out of the several problems relating to the seeds of the Third International in Lenin, one seems here to occupy a dominant position. For all Lenin's analyses and actions are traversed by the following *leitmotif*: the state must be entirely destroyed through frontal attack in a situation of *dual power*, to be replaced by a second power – soviets – which will no longer be a state in the proper sense of the term, since it will already have begun to wither away. What does Lenin mean by this destruction of the bourgeois state? Unlike Marx, he often reduces the institutions of representative democracy and political freedoms to a simple emanation of the bourgeoisie: representative democracy = bourgeois democracy = dictatorship of the bourgeoisie. They have to be completely uprooted and replaced by direct, rank-and-file democracy and mandated, recallable delegates – in other words, by the genuine proletarian democracy of soviets.

I am intentionally drawing a highly schematized picture: Lenin's principal thrust was not at first towards a variant of authoritarian statism. I say this not in order to leap to Lenin's defence, but to point up the simplistic and befogging character of that conception according to which developments in Soviet Russia resulted from Lenin's 'centralist' opposition to direct democracy – from a Leninism which is supposed to have carried within it the crushing of the Kronstadt sailors' revolt, in the way that a cloud carries the storm. Whether we like it or not, the original guiding thread of Lenin's thought was, in opposition to the parliamentarianism and dread of workers' councils characteristic of the social-democratic current, the sweeping replacement of 'formal' representative democracy by the 'real', direct democracy of workers' councils. (The term 'self-management' was not yet used in Lenin's time.) This leads me on to the real question. Was it not this very line (sweeping substitution of

rank-and-file democracy for representative democracy) which principally accounted for what happened in Lenin's lifetime in the Soviet
Union, and which gave rise to the centralizing and statist Lenin whose
posterity is well enough known?

I said that I am posing the question. But, as a matter of fact, it was
already posed in Lenin's time and answered in a way that now seems
dramatically premonitory. I am referring, of course, to Rosa Luxemburg, whom Lenin called an eagle of revolution. She also had the eye of
an eagle. For it was she who made the first correct and fundamental
critique of Lenin and the Bolshevik Revolution. It is decisive because it
issues not from the ranks of social democracy, which did not want
even to hear of direct democracy and workers' councils, but precisely
from a convinced fighter who gave her life for council democracy,
being executed at the moment when the German workers' councils
were crushed by social democracy.

Now, Luxemburg reproaches Lenin not with neglect or contempt of
direct, rank-and-file democracy, but rather with *the exact opposite* –
that is to say, *exclusive* reliance on council democracy and complete
elimination of representative democracy (through, among other
things, dissolution of the Constituent Assembly – which had been
elected under the Bolshevik government – in favour of the soviets
alone). It is necessary to re-read *The Russian Revolution*, from which I
shall quote just one passage.

> In place of the representative bodies created by general, popular
> elections, Lenin and Trotsky have laid down the soviets as the only
> true representation of the labouring masses. But with the repression
> of political life in the land as a whole, life in the soviets must also
> become more and more crippled. Without general elections, with-
> out unrestricted freedom of press and assembly, without a free
> struggle of opinion, life dies out in every public institution, becomes
> a mere semblance of life, in which only the bureaucracy remains as
> the active element.[1]

This is certainly not the only question to be asked concerning Lenin.
An important role in subsequent developments was played by the
conception of the party contained in *What Is to Be Done?*; by the
notion of theory being brought to the working class from outside by
professional revolutionaries, and so on. But the fundamental question
is the one posed by Luxemburg. Even if we take into account Lenin's
positions on a series of other problems, as well as the historical
peculiarities of Russia, what ensued in Lenin's own lifetime and above

all after his death (the single party, bureaucratization of the party, confusion of party and state, statism, the end of the soviets themselves, etc.) was already inscribed in the situation criticized by Luxemburg.

The Third-International Model

Be that as it may, let us now look at the 'model' of revolution that was bequeathed by the Third International, having already been affected by Stalinism in certain ways. We find the same position with regard to representative democracy, only now it is combined with statism and contempt for direct, rank-and-file democracy – in short, the meaning of the entire council problematic is twisted out of shape. The resulting model is permeated by the instrumental conception of the state. The capitalist state is still considered as a mere object or instrument, capable of being manipulated by the bourgeoisie of which it is the emanation. According to this view of things, the state is not traversed by internal contradictions, but is a monolithic bloc without cracks of any kind. The struggles of the popular masses cannot pass through the state, any more than they can become, in opposition to the bourgeoisie, one of the constituent factors of the institutions of representative democracy. Class contradictions are located *between* the state and the popular masses standing outside the state. This remains true right up to the crisis of dual power, when the state is effectively dismantled through the centralization at national level of a parallel power, which becomes the real power (soviets). Thus:

1. The struggle of the popular masses for state power is, in essence, a frontal struggle of manoeuvre or encirclement, taking place outside the fortress-state and principally aiming at the creation of a situation of dual power.
2. While it would be hasty to identify this conception with an assault strategy concentrated in a precise moment or 'big day' (insurrection, political general strike, etc.), it quite clearly lacks the strategic vision of a *process* of transition to socialism – that is, of a long stage during which the masses will act to conquer power and transform the state apparatuses. It presents these changes as possible only in a situation of dual power, characterized by a highly precarious balance of forces between the state/bourgeoisie and the soviets/working class. The 'revolutionary situation' is itself reduced to a crisis of the state that cannot but involve its breakdown.
3. The state is supposed to hold pure power – a quantifiable substance that has to be seized from it. 'To take' state power therefore means to

occupy, during the interval of dual power, all the parts of the instrument-state: to take charge of the summit of its apparatuses, assuming the commanding positions within the state machinery and operating its controls in such a way as to replace it by the second, soviet power. A citadel can be taken only if, during the dual power situation, ditches, ramparts and casemates of its instrumental structure have already been captured and dismantled in favour of something else (soviets); and this something else (the second power) is supposed to lie entirely outside the fortified position of the state. This conception, then, is still marked by permanent scepticism as to the possibility of mass intervention within the state itself.

4. How does the transformation of the state apparatus appear during the transition to socialism? It is first of all necessary to take state power, and then, after the fortress has been captured, to raze to the ground the entire state apparatus, replacing it by the second power (soviets) constituted as a state of a new type.

Here we can recognize a basic distrust of the institutions of representative democracy and of political freedoms. But if these are still regarded as creations and instruments of the bourgeoisie, the conception of soviets has in the meantime undergone significant changes. What is to replace the bourgeois state *en bloc* is no longer direct, rank-and-file democracy. The soviets are now not so much an anti-state as a *parallel state* – one copied from the instrumental model of the existing state, and possessing a proletarian character in so far as its summit is controlled/occupied by a 'single' revolutionary party which itself functions according to the model of the state. Distrust of the possibility of mass intervention within the bourgeois state has become distrust of the popular movement as such. This is called strengthening the state/soviets, the better to make it wither away in the future . . . *And so was Stalinist statism born.*

We can now see the deep complicity between this Stalinist kind of statism and that of traditional social democracy. For the latter is also characterized by basic distrust of direct, rank-and-file democracy and popular initiative. For it too, the popular masses stand in a relationship of externality to a state that possesses power and constitutes an essence. Here the state is a subject, bearing an intrinsic rationality that is incarnated by political élites and the very mechanism of representative democracy. Accordingly, occupation of the state involves replacing the top leaders by an enlightened left élite and, if necessary, making a few adjustments to the way in which the existing institutions function; it is left as understood that the state will thereby bring socialism to the popular masses from above. *This then is the techno-bureaucratic statism of the experts.*

Stalinist state-worship, social-democratic state-worship: this is indeed one of the traditions of the popular movement. But to escape from it through the other tradition of direct, rank-and-file democracy or self-management would really be too good to be true. We should not forget the case of Lenin himself and the seeds of statism contained in the original workers' councils experience. The basic dilemma from which we must extricate ourselves is the following: *either* maintain the existing state and stick exclusively to a modified form of representative democracy – a road that ends up in social-democratic statism and so-called liberal parliamentarianism; *or* base everything on direct, rank-and-file democracy or the movement for self-management – a path which, sooner or later, inevitably leads to statist despotism or the dictatorship of experts. The essential problem of the democratic road to socialism, of democratic socialism, must be posed in a different way: *how is it possible radically to transform the state in such a manner that the extension and deepening of political freedoms and the institutions of representative democracy* (which were also a conquest of the popular masses) *are combined with the unfurling of forms of direct democracy and the mushrooming of self-management bodies?*

Not only did the notion of dictatorship of the proletariat fail to pose this problem; it ended by obscuring it. For Marx, the dictatorship of the proletariat was a notion of applied strategy, serving at most as a signpost. It referred to the class nature of the state and to the necessity of its transformation in the transition to socialism and the process of withering away of the state. Now, although the object to which it referred is still real, the notion has come to play a precise historical role: it obscures the fundamental problem of combining a transformed representative democracy with direct, rank-and-file democracy. It is for these reasons, and not because the notion eventually became identified with Stalinist totalitarianism, that its abandonment is, in my opinion, justified. Even when it took on other meanings, it always retained the historical function in question – both for Lenin, at the beginning of the October Revolution, and, nearer our own time, for Gramsci himself.

Of course, there is no disputing Gramsci's considerable theoretical-political contributions, and we know the distance he took from the Stalinist experience. Still, even though he is currently being pulled and pushed in every conceivable direction, the fact remains that Gramsci was also unable to pose the problem in all its amplitude. His famous analyses of the differences between war of movement (as waged by the

Bolsheviks in Russia) and war of position are essentially conceived as the application of Lenin's model/strategy to the 'different concrete conditions' of the West. Despite his remarkable insights, this leads him into a number of blind alleys, which we do not have space to discuss here.

The Democratic Socialist Imperative

This then is the basic problem of democratic socialism. It does not concern only the so-called developed countries, for there is no strategic model exclusively adapted to these countries. In fact, there is no longer a question of building 'models' of any kind whatsoever. All that is involved is a set of signposts which, drawing on the lessons of the past, point out the traps to anyone wishing to avoid certain well-known destinations. The problem concerns every transition to socialism, even though it may present itself quite differently in various countries. This much we know already: socialism cannot be democratic here and of another kind over there. The concrete situation may of course differ, and the strategies undoubtedly have to be adapted to the country's specific features. But democratic socialism is the only kind possible.

With regard to this socialism, to the democratic road to socialism, the current situation in Europe presents a number of peculiarities: these concern at one and the same time the new social relations, the state form that is being established, and the precise character of the crisis of the state. For certain European countries, these particularities constitute so many chances – probably unique in world history – for the success of a democratic socialist experience, articulating transformed representative democracy and direct, rank-and-file democracy. This entails the elaboration of a new strategy with respect both to the capture of state power by the popular masses and their organizations, and to the transformations of the state designated by the term 'democratic road to socialism'.

Today less than ever is the state an ivory tower isolated from the popular masses. Their struggles constantly traverse the state, even when they are not physically present in its apparatuses. Dual power, in which frontal struggle is concentrated in a precise moment, is not the only situation that allows the popular masses to carry out an action in the sphere of the state. The democratic road to socialism is a long process, in which the struggle of the popular masses does not seek to create an effective dual power parallel and external to the state, but brings itself to bear on the internal contradictions of the state. To be sure, the seizure of power always presupposes a crisis of the state (such as exists today in certain European countries); but this crisis, which sharpens the very internal contradictions of the state, cannot be reduced to a breakdown of the latter. To take or capture state power is not simply to lay hands on part of the state machinery in order to replace it with a second power. Power is not a quantifiable substance held by the state that must be taken out of its hands, but rather a series of relations among the various social classes. In its ideal form, power is concentrated in the state, which is thus itself the condensation of a particular class relationship of forces. The state is neither a thing-instrument that may be taken away, nor a fortress that may be penetrated by means of a wooden horse, nor yet a safe that may be cracked by burglary: it is the heart of the exercise of political power.

For state power to be taken, a mass struggle must have unfolded in such a way as to modify the relationship of forces within the state apparatuses, themselves the strategic site of political struggle. For a dual-power type of strategy, however, the decisive shift in the relationship of forces takes place not within the state but between the state and the masses outside. In the democratic road to socialism, the long process of taking power essentially consists in the spreading, development, reinforcement, coordination and direction of those diffuse centres of resistance which the masses always possess within the state networks, in such a way that they become the real centres of power on the strategic terrain of the state. It is therefore not a question of a straight choice between frontal war of movement and war of position, because in Gramsci's use of the term, the latter always comprises encirclement of a fortress state.

I can already hear the question: have we then given in to traditional reformism? In order to answer this, we must examine how the question of reformism was posed by the Third International. As a matter of fact, it regarded every strategy other than that of dual power as reformist. The only radical break allowing the seizure of state power, the only meaningful break making it possible to escape from reformism was the break between the state (as a simple instrument of the bourgeoisie external to the masses) and a second power (the masses/soviets) lying wholly outside the state. By the way, this did not prevent the emergence of a reformism peculiar to the Third International – one bound up precisely with the instrumental conception of the state. Quite the contrary! You corner some loose parts of the state machinery and collect a few isolated bastions while *awaiting* a dual power situation. Then, as time passes, dual power goes by the board: all that remains is the instrument-state which you capture cog by cog or whose command posts you take over.

Now, reformism is an ever-latent danger, not a vice inherent in any strategy other than that of dual power – even if, in the case of a democratic road to socialism, the criterion of reformism is not as sharp as in the dual-power strategy, and even if (there is no point in denying it) the risks of social-democratization are thereby increased. At any event, to shift the relationship of forces within the state does not mean to win successive reforms in an unbroken chain, to conquer the state machinery piece by piece, or simply to occupy the positions of government. It denotes nothing other than a *stage of real breaks*, the climax of which – and there has to be one – is reached when the relationship of forces on the strategic terrain of the state swings over to the side of the popular masses.

The State as a Battleground

This democratic road to socialism is therefore not simply a parliamentary or electoral road. Waiting for an electoral majority (in parliament or for a presidential candidate) can be only a moment, however important that may be; and its achievement is not necessarily the climax of breaks within the state. The shift in the relationship of forces within the state touches its apparatuses and mechanisms as a whole; it does not affect only parliament or, as is so often repeated nowadays, the ideological state apparatuses that are supposed to play the determining role in the 'contemporary' state. The process extends also, and above all, to the repressive state apparatuses that hold the monopoly of legitimate physical violence: especially the army and the police. But just as we should not forget the particular role of these apparatuses (as is frequently done by versions of the democratic road that are founded on a misinterpretation of some of Gramsci's theses), so we should not imagine that the strategy of modifying the relationship of forces within the state is valid only for the ideological apparatuses, and that the repressive apparatuses, completely isolated from popular struggle, can be taken only by frontal, external attack. In short, we cannot add together two strategies, retaining the dual-power perspective in relation to the repressive apparatuses. Obviously, a shift in the balance of forces within the repressive apparatuses poses special, and therefore formidable, problems. But as the case of Portugal showed with perfect clarity, these apparatuses are themselves traversed by the struggles of the popular masses.

Furthermore, the real alternative raised by the democratic road to socialism is indeed that of a struggle of the popular masses to modify the relationship of forces within the state, as opposed to a frontal, dual-power type of strategy. The choice is not, as is often thought, between a struggle 'within' the state apparatuses (that is, physically invested and inserted in their material space) and a struggle located at a certain physical distance from these apparatuses. *First*, because any struggle at a distance always has effects within the state: it is always there, even if only in a refracted manner and through intermediaries. *Second*, and most importantly, because struggle at a distance from the state apparatuses, whether within or beyond the limits of the physical space traced by the institutional *loci*, remains necessary at all times and in every case, since it reflects the autonomy of the struggles and organizations of the popular masses. It is not simply a matter of entering state institutions (parliament, economic and social councils, 'planning' bodies, etc.) in order to use their characteristic levers for a good purpose. In addition, struggle must always express itself in the development of popular movements, the mushrooming of democratic organs at the base, and the rise of centres of self-management.

It should not be forgotten that the above points refer not only to transformations of the state, but also to the basic question of state power and power in general. The question of *who* is in power *to do what* cannot be isolated from these struggles for self-management or direct democracy. But if they are to modify the relations of power, such struggles or movements cannot tend towards centralization in a second power; they must rather seek to shift the relationship of forces on the terrain of the state itself. This then is the real alternative, and not the simple opposition between 'internal' and 'external' struggle. In the democratic road to socialism, these two forms of struggle must be combined. In other words, whether or not one becomes 'integrated' in the state apparatuses and plays the game of the existing power is not reducible to the choice between internal and external struggle. Such integration does not necessarily follow from a strategy of effecting changes on the terrain of the state. To think that it does is to imagine that political struggle can ever be located wholly outside the state.

This strategy of taking power leads on directly to the question of transformations of the state in a democratic road to socialism. Authoritarian statism can be avoided only by combining the transformation of representative democracy with the development of forms of direct, rank-and-file democracy or the movement for self-management. But this in turn raises fresh problems. In the dual-power strategy, which envisages straightforward replacement of the state apparatus with an apparatus of councils, taking state power is treated as a preliminary to its destruction/replacement. Transformation of the state apparatus does not really enter into the matter: first of all the existing state power is taken, and then another is put in its place. This view of things can no longer be accepted. If taking power denotes a shift in the relationship of forces within the state, and if it is recognized that this will involve a long process of change, then the seizure of state power will entail concomitant transformations of its apparatuses. It is true that the state retains a specific materiality: not only is a shift in the relationship of forces within the state insufficient to alter that materiality, but the relationship itself can crystallize in the state only to the extent that the apparatuses of the latter undergo transformation. In abandoning the dual-power strategy, we do not throw overboard, but pose in a different fashion, the question of the state's materiality as a specific apparatus.

In this context, I talked above of a *sweeping transformation* of the state apparatus during the transition to democratic socialism. Although this term certainly has a demonstrative value, it seems to indicate a general direction, before which – if I dare say so – stand two red lights. First, the expression 'sweeping transformation of the state apparatus in the democratic road to socialism' suggests that there is no longer a place for what has traditionally been called *smashing* or *destroying* that apparatus. The fact remains, however, that the term smashing, which Marx too used for indicative purposes, came in the end to designate a very precise historical phenomenon: namely, the eradication of any kind of representative democracy or 'formal' liberties in favour purely of direct, rank-and-file democracy and so-called real liberties. It is necessary to take sides. If we understand the democratic road to socialism and democratic socialism itself to involve, among other things, political (party) and ideological pluralism, recognition of the role of universal suffrage, and extension and deepening of all political freedoms including for opponents, then talk of smashing or destroying the state apparatus can be no more than a mere verbal trick. What is involved, through all the various transformations, is a real permanence and continuity of the institutions of representative democracy – not as unfortunate relics to be tolerated for as long as necessary, but as an essential condition of democratic socialism.

Mass Intervention

Now we come to the second red light: the term 'sweeping transformation' accurately designates both the direction and the means of changes in the state apparatus. There can be no question of merely secondary adjustments (such as those envisaged by neo-liberal conceptions of a revived *de jure* state), nor of changes coming mainly from above (according to the vision of traditional social democracy or liberalized Stalinism). There can be no question of a statist transformation of the state apparatus. *Transformation of the state apparatus tending towards the withering away of the state* can rest only on increased intervention of the popular masses in the state: certainly through their trade-union and political forms of representation, but also through their own initiatives within the state itself. This will proceed by stages, but it cannot be confined to mere democratization of the state – whether in relation to parliament, political liberties, the role of parties, democratization of the union and political apparatuses themselves, or to decentralization.

This process should be accompanied with the development of new forms of direct, rank-and-file democracy, and the flowering of self-management networks and centres. Left to itself, the transformation of the state apparatus and the development of representative democracy would be incapable of avoiding statism. But there is another side to the coin: a unilateral and univocal shift of the centre of gravity towards the self-management movement would likewise make it impossible, in the medium term, to avoid techno-bureaucratic statism and authoritarian confiscation of power by the experts. This could take the form of centralization in a second power, which quite simply replaces the mechanisms of representative democracy. But it would also occur in another variant that is quite frequently envisaged today. According to this conception, the only way to avoid statism is to place oneself outside the state, leaving that radical and eternal evil more or less as it is and disregarding the problem of its transformation. The way forward would then be, without going as far as dual power, simply to block the path of the state from outside through the construction of self-management 'counter-powers' at the base – in short, to quarantine the state within its own domain and thus halt the spread of the disease.

Such a perspective is currently formulated in numerous ways. It appears first in the neo-technocratic talk of a state which is retained because of the complex nature of tasks in a post-industrial society, but which is administered by left experts and controlled simply through mechanisms of direct democracy. At the most, every left technocrat would be flanked by a self-management commissar – a prospect which hardly frightens the various specialists, who are even manifesting a sudden passion for self-management because they know that, at the end of the day, the masses will propose and the state will decide. It also appears in the language of the new libertarians, for whom statism can be avoided only by breaking power up and scattering it among an infinity of micro-powers (a kind of guerrilla warfare conducted against the state). In each case, however, the Leviathan-state is left in place, and no attention is given to those transformations of the state without which the movement of direct democracy is bound to fail. The movement is prevented from intervening in actual transformations of the state, and the two processes are simply kept running along parallel lines. The real question is of a different kind: how, for example, can an organic relationship be created between citizens' committees and universal suffrage assemblies that will themselves have been trans-formed as a function of the relationship?

As we see then, the task is really not to 'synthesize' or stick together the statist and self-management traditions of the popular movement, but rather to open up a *global perspective of the withering away of the state*. This comprises *two* articulated processes: transformation of the state and unfurling of direct, rank-and-file democracy. We know the consequences of the formal split between the two traditions that has arisen out of the disarticulation of these processes. However, while it alone is capable of leading to democratic socialism, this path has a reverse side: two dangers are lying in wait for it.

The first of these is the *reaction of the enemy*, in this case the bourgeoisie. Although old and well-known, this danger appears here in a particularly acute form. The classical response of the dual-power strategy was precisely destruction of the state apparatus – an attitude which in a certain sense remains valid, since truly profound breaks are required, rather than secondary modifications of the state apparatus. But it remains valid in one sense only. In so far as what is involved is no longer destruction of that apparatus and its replacement with a second power, but rather a long process of transformation, the enemy has greater possibilities of boycotting an experience of democratic socialism and of brutally intervening to cut it short. Clearly, the democratic road to socialism will not simply be a peaceful changeover.

It is possible to confront this danger through active reliance on a broad, popular movement. Let us be quite frank. As the decisive means to the realization of its goals and to the articulation of the two preventives against statism and the social-democratic impasse, the democratic road to socialism, unlike the 'vanguardist' dual-power strategy, presupposes the continuous support of a mass movement founded on broad popular alliances. If such a movement (what Gramsci called the active, as opposed to the passive, revolution) is not deployed and active, if the left does not succeed in arousing one, then nothing will prevent social-democratization of the experience: however radical they may be, the various programmes will change little of relevance. A broad popular movement constitutes a guarantee against the reaction of the enemy, even though it is not sufficient and must always be linked to sweeping transformations of the state. That is the dual lesson we can draw from Chile: the ending of the Allende experience was due not only to the lack of such changes, but also to the fact that the intervention of the bourgeoisie (itself expressed in that lack) was made possible by the breakdown of alliances among the popular classes, particularly between the working class and the petty bourgeoisie. Even before the coup took place, this had broken the momentum of support for the Popular Unity government. In order to arouse this broad movement, the left must equip itself with the necessary means, taking up especially new popular demands on fronts that used to be wrongly called 'secondary' (women's struggles, the ecological movement, and so on).

The second question concerns the *forms of articulation* of the two processes: transformations of the state and of representative democracy, and development of direct democracy and the movement for self-management. The new problems arise as soon as it is no longer a question of suppressing the one in favour of the other, whether through straightforward elimination or – which comes to the same thing – through integration of the one in the other (of, for example, self-management centres in the institutions of representative democracy); that is to say, as soon as it is no longer a question of assimilating the two processes. How it is possible to avoid being drawn into mere parallelism or juxtaposition, whereby each follows its own specific course? In what fields, concerning which decisions, and at what points in time should representative assemblies have precedence over the centres of direct democracy: parliament over factory committees, town councils over citizen's committees – or vice versa? Given that up to a point conflict will be inevitable, how should it be resolved without leading, slowly but surely, to an embryonic or fully fledged situation of *dual power*?

This time, dual power would involve two powers of the left – a left government and a second power composed of popular organs. And, as we know from the case of Portugal, even when two forces of the left are involved, the situation in no way resembles a free play of powers and counter-powers balancing one another for the greatest good of socialism and democracy. It rather quickly leads to open opposition, in which there is a risk that one will be eliminated in favour of the other. In one case (e.g. Portugal), the result is social-democratization, while in the other variant – elimination of representative democracy – it is not the withering of the state or the triumph of direct democracy that eventually emerges, but a new type of authoritarian dictatorship. But in either case, the state will always end up the winner. Of course, there is a strong chance that, even before dual power reaches that outcome, something else will happen – something that Portugal just managed to avoid – namely, the brutal, fascist-type reaction of a bourgeoisie that can always be relied upon to stay in the game. Thus, open opposition between these two powers seriously threatens, after a first stage of real paralysis of the state, to be resolved by a third contender, the bourgeoisie, according to scenarios that are not difficult to imagine. I said third contender, but it will not have escaped the reader's notice that in all these cases (fascist-type intervention, social-democratization, authoritarian dictatorship of experts on the ruins of direct democracy) this contender is in one form or another ultimately the same: the bourgeoisie.

What then is the solution, the answer to all that? I could, of course, point to the observations made above, to the numerous works, research projects and discussions under way more or less throughout Europe, as well as to the partial experiences now taking place at regional, municipal or self-management level. But these offer no easy recipe for a solution, since the answer to such questions does not yet exist – not even as a model theoretically guaranteed in some holy text or other. History has not yet given us a successful experience of the democratic road to socialism: what it has provided – and that is not insignificant – is some negative examples to avoid and some mistakes upon which to reflect. It can naturally always be argued, in the name of realism (either by proponents of the dictatorship of the proletariat or by the others, the orthodox neoliberals), that if democratic socialism has never yet existed, this is because it is impossible. Maybe. We no longer share that belief in the millennium founded on a few iron laws concerning the inevitability of a democratic socialist revolution; nor do we enjoy the support of a fatherland of democratic socialism. But one thing is certain: socialism will be democratic or it will not be at all. What is more, optimism about the democratic road to socialism should not lead us to consider it as a royal road, smooth and free of risk. Risks there are, although they are no longer quite where they used to be: at worst, we could be heading for camps and massacres as appointed victims. But to that I reply: if we weigh up the risks, that is in any case preferable to massacring other people only to end up ourselves beneath the blade of a Committee of Public Safety or some Dictator of the proletariat.

There is only one sure way of avoiding the risks of democratic socialism, and that is to keep quiet and march ahead under the tutelage and the rod of advanced liberal democracy. But that is another story.

16

IS THERE A CRISIS IN MARXISM?

Before entering into the discussion of our subject, the crisis in Marxism, we should stop to notice that there are many people talking about that crisis right now. The political, ideological, and theoretical meaning of the crisis varies, of course, according to who is doing the talking. Naturally, the old – but also the newly-converted – opponents of Marxism talk the loudest, exploiting certain problems in Marxism to declare that Marx is dead and Marxism is obsolete. This is nothing new. Throughout the history of Marxism, its opponents, and rightist intellectuals in general, have worked hard to present it as a discredited theory. But in some countries of Western Europe today, that standard tactic is assuming new and extreme forms. In fact, after a long period in which the dominant ideology was in retreat on every front – a retreat which began in Europe with the rise of labour and countercultural movements (May 1968), but which was already evident in the US with the movement against the war in Vietnam – we now see a kind of regrouping of the dominant ideology in new forms. This regrouping coincides with a general attack on Marxism on all fronts. Both the reshaping and the counterattack of the dominant ideology involve contradictions, as is always the case with ideology. But these contradictions are much sharper than before because the reproduction and diffusion of the dominant ideology are not systematic but dissociated. This is so because the centre of gravity of the ideological apparatuses which reproduce it tends to be displaced from institutionally organized discourse (schools, universities, books, etc.) to the mass media (radio, television, the mass press, etc.).

* First published in Greek in the 19 March and 20 March 1979 editions of the Athens daily, *Ta Nea*; subsequently published in a revised and expanded form in *O politis*, no. 25 (March–April, 1979). This translation is taken from the *Journal of the Hellenic Diaspora*, vol. 6, no. 3 (1979), pp. 7–16. Translated by Sarah Kafatou.

The Contemporary Dominant Ideology

We can, very schematically, identify three determining elements of the contemporary dominant ideology. First, *irrationalism*, which takes extreme form in the thought of the 'New Philosophers,' but is not confined to them. The attack on Marxism is part of a more general attack on rationalism, including the philosophy of the Enlightenment (viewed as a precursor of Marxism), in the name of fantasy and 'impulse' or in connection with the revival in Western Europe of religious cultism in various forms.

Second, *neoliberalism*: this amounts to an attempt by the dominant ideology to exploit and distort the legitimate struggle for human rights, as well as to return to the myth of 'Western civilization' as the touchstone of democracy and political progress. On the socio-economic level and in the context of the present economic crisis, neoliberalism propagandizes the need to free the economy from state intervention. Thus, it reveals the bankruptcy of Keynesianism and the welfare state, that is to say, it reveals the retreat of the state from social policies. Neoliberalism combats Marxism by arguing that the latter's theoretical premises imply the Gulag archipelago just as surely as clouds bring rain. For isn't the USSR, they say, a country where Marxism is in power? And don't the USSR and the other 'socialist' countries have clearly totalitarian regimes which shamelessly violate civil rights and political freedoms?

Third, *authoritarianism*: paternalistic reason which stresses discipline and restraint from over-indulgence in democratic freedoms. The themes of authoritarianism come across clearly in the 1975 Report of the Trilateral Commission, the famous expert committee which included President Carter before his election, the Prime Minister of France, Raymond Barre, the Italian industrialist, Giovanni Agnelli, and the president of the Japanese banking consortium, Mitsubishi. The rise of authoritarian reason encompasses the decline of democratic institutions in modern societies, the increased importance of bureaucracy, and the particular importance of the ideological state apparatuses to an oppression based less, perhaps, on the use of physical force and more on its internalization by individuals as symbolic violence.

These elements, however mutually contradictory they seem, have an internal consistency and cohere into a single world view. We know, after all, that liberalism has often coexisted with authoritarianism throughout the history of bourgeois political philosophy. For example, for Rousseau, liberalism in social relations was compatible with the view that 'every citizen should be as independent as possible of other citizens and as dependent as possible on the state'. The English Physiocrats were simultaneously devotees of liberalism in economic affairs and advocates of despotism in politics, so that the state could preserve social peace in the interest of private enterprise.

It is still not clear why the convergence of liberalism and authoritarianism is no longer completed by rationalism but by irrationalism. I think the explanation is that the centre of gravity has shifted from organized brute force to internalized oppression, a fact which is translated in a complex way onto the symbolic-ideological level. A further reason is the ever-intensifying technocratic logic of sociopolitical relations, creating in individual subjects a tendency to flight from reality which expresses itself symbolically in irrationalism.

We should emphasize as well that the regrouping of the dominant ideology in recent years is related to a major defeat of the working-class movement, in particular to last year's parliamentary elections in France and the deadlock of the strategy of the historic compromise in Italy, and in general to the relative weakening of the political aspect of labour struggles in Europe. The relative retreat of Marxism from the ideological forefront has been a consequence of the defeat or decline of the working-class movement, especially in countries such as France and Italy, where defeat was experienced more intensely, but also in Germany and Spain. Marxism is somehow less fashionable now than it was two or three years ago. As a result we face a raging anti-Marxist counterattack by the entire right and 'liberal' establishment in every area of public life. The reactionary backlash is facilitated by the political retreat of the working-class movements.

The Theoretical Orientation of the
Anti-Marxist Counterattack

The anti-Marxist counterattack within the social sciences is not always overt, but frequently takes complicated and disguised forms. Specifically, there is a revival of fossilized Weberian positivism on the one hand and Anglo-Saxon empiricism on the other. Denial of the crucial importance of *theory* in the social sciences is a typical feature of the attack on Marxism. We see a revival of empiricism and a denial of the organic relation between the social sciences and politics; that is, value judgements and judgements as to fact are dissociated, as in the thought of Max Weber.

Among the epochal contributions of Marxist thought to the social sciences is the close relationship it established between a *systematic theoretical approach* (which, as the most authoritative contemporary epistemology affirms, is the only route by which to arrive at a specific analysis of a given situation) and an emphasis on the organic connection between a political standpoint and intellectual work. It is clear that, although positivism-empiricism on the one hand and irrationalism on the other seem mutually contradictory, they both exclude theory, and hence represent elements of a unified world view, namely, the contemporary reorganized dominant ideology which opposes itself now, as in the past, to Marxism.

Another characteristic element of the present situation is the wave of opportunism sweeping over a large part of the intelligentsia of Western Europe. When Marxism was fashionable these people rushed to present themselves as authorities on the subject, or at least kept quiet about their disagreements. Today the same people compete to see who can be more anti-Marxist, who can claim more categorically to have 'gone beyond' Marx. Indeed many indulge in shameless self-criticism of their 'Marxist past': the 'New Philosophers' are typical examples of this since some of them, such as André Glucksmann, were previously Maoists.

Of course, the ideological conjuncture is still different in Greece, where Marxist concepts gained considerable influence among young intellectuals and students after the fall of the dictatorship. But I think that the conjuncture will soon change in our country as well, both because outside influence is always important (particularly now that our need for Europeanization is being trumpeted everywhere) and because Marxist concepts have not grafted themselves satisfactorily onto the social sciences in our country. We don't have an adequate native production of Marxist works capable of counterposing themselves to the ideologies of irrationalism, empiricism, and neoliberalism. Already, neo-Weberian positivism and, especially, Anglo-Saxon empiricism are gaining ground, although they lack the courage to identify themselves. And since, in our country, anyone is what he says he is, these tendencies seem at present to coexist 'creatively' with Marxism.

The further development of these tendencies will be particularly harmful not only because of their profoundly anti-Marxist character but, above all, because they will inhibit the development of original Greek theory. A new and very promising development following the fall of the dictatorship was that people began to feel the need for a serious theoretical standpoint such as is essential if we are to emerge from the 'illusionary reality of everyday life' and the narrow scope of fragmentary empiricism, and construct scientific analyses. But those anti-Marxist tendencies flatter demagogically the spirit of seeking the easy way which has been cultivated among Greeks for so long, even though we know that there is no 'royal road' to knowledge, as Marx said. For some young Greek intellectuals in Greece and abroad, Marxism amounts to no more than an oversimplified affectation, or the rhetorical display of a pseudo-Marxist vocabulary. In their work, theoretical concepts are reduced to empirical categories, thereby opening the door to a series of compromises with the dominant ideology. For example, certain recent studies of Greek reality which refer rhetorically and *a priori* to the need for class analysis are unable to support their specific conclusions with a minimally serious account of the class struggle in Greece.

We also encounter ever more often a kind of anti-Marxism which is not perceived as such by its advocates, as in the views expressed in publications which move in the ambience of the Parisian 'New Philosophers.' The interesting but dangerous aspect of this phenomenon is that it objectively facilitates the dissemination of the official ideology and of the neoliberalism through which one sector of the 'up-to-date, progressive' intelligentsia supports and promotes the rightist authoritarian state.

Is There a Crisis in Marxism?

The rise of the themes of irrationalism, empiricism, and authoritarianism is not in itself a symptom of the crisis in Marxism. I think that the ideological break between Marxist and anti-Marxist thought, insofar as it exists, is actually a very positive development. For the recent establishment of Marxism at the forefront of the ideological conjuncture, and in particular its confused coexistence with anti-Marxist tendencies, amounted, in my opinion, to a rather unhealthy situation for Marxism itself: there was the danger of the academicization of Marxism and of its conversion into an established ideology.

We should also not enclose ourselves in a Eurocentric vision, oblivious to what is happening on a world scale. Regardless of current developments in Western Europe, Marxism has profoundly marked contemporary thought (Sartre called it the unsurpassable horizon of our age), and it is not only gaining ground steadily in the underdeveloped countries (in Latin America for example), but is also advancing in Anglo-Saxon countries such as Britain and the US. Paradoxically, Anglo-Saxon empiricism is appearing in Western Europe just as progressive intellectuals in its place of origin begin to turn massively toward Marxism. But there is today a crisis in Marxism which is quite unrelated to the crisis its opponents proclaim. On that point, in spite of all the disagreements between us as to the nature of the crisis, I agree with [Louis] Althusser, who recently spoke of a *creative and hopeful* crisis in Marxism.

To say that the crisis in Marxism contains creative elements is not, of course, to imply that its underlying causes are positive. On the contrary, it was the major negative aspect of the countries of the so-called 'actually existing socialism,' where lip-service to Marxism is the official state dogma, that precipitated a collapse – which had been threatening for a long time – in Marxist thought. Yet that collapse can be salutary if, through it, Marxism can overcome the dogmatic torpor and dessication into which it has been led.

The first underlying cause of the crisis in Marxism is the by-now general recognition, to which we have been led by history itself, that the regimes which exist in the countries of 'actually existing socialism' have suspended democratic liberties. This realization has induced almost all the Western European Communist parties to adopt a critical stance and to distinguish their own positions from those of the Soviet Union. The second cause of the crisis, inextricably intertwined with the first, is the very profound division of the international working-class movement, which had already begun to appear at the time of the first Sino-Soviet split.

These issues gave the first jolt to the kind of Marxism which is not a crystallized dogma or official state ideology. But through them we came to the realization, among others, that we do not have an adequate Marxist explanation, based on serious theory and scientific evidence, for the situation which prevails in the countries of 'actually existing socialism' and for the by-now armed conflict between them. Even though many Marxist scholars – from the classic Trotskyists to Ellenstein and Bettelheim – have studied the Eastern European countries, we still do not have a satisfactory account of those regimes. This means that the political right and the specialists in the Gulag archipelago are free to exaggerate the confusion and unreliability of Marxism.

We should view this situation in the context of the present conjuncture in Western Europe. Until a few years ago, the Communist parties and the left socialists (such as the French Socialist Party, which differs from classic social democracy) were confined to an oppositional role within the political systems of their countries, but now, for the first time, and in spite of all their recent failures, there is a real possibility of their participation in state power. In this context it has become clear that dogmatic Marxism is not only unable to devise a new strategy for the conquest of or participation in state power in contemporary conditions – that is, to find a way to the democratic transition to democratic socialism – but is also completely incapable of creating new insights into contemporary reality.

More specifically, certain dominant views of Marxism itself have been discredited, above all the view of Marxism as a complete and perfect system of interpretation of all human phenomena codified in the form of 'laws' (mainly the famous laws of 'dialectical materialism' institutionalized during the Stalinist period) which are really nothing but dogmas formulated in the crudest way and backed up with quotations from the so-called 'classics' of Marxism. Such is the kind of Marxism which is known as 'Marxism-Leninism' and which was utilized, as we know, by Stalinism and by Stalin himself.

I have made this point repeatedly, and most recently in my interview in the newspaper *Ta Nea* of 17–18 August 1978. But even though my statement was, I think, completely unambiguous, my friend George Katiforis thought it appropriate to attack me in the same newspaper, emphasizing that Marx and Engels never presented their analyses as a totalized theory. His comment is completely correct, but I don't believe I ever maintained the contrary. It is in any case undeniable, and should be stressed, that the Stalinists thought of Marxism as a universal dogma, and that by calling it 'Marxism-Leninism,' codifying it and raising it to the status of a religion, they imposed it upon the world working-class movement for entire decades, excommunicating every other voice, objection, or question.

That 'Marxism' is definitely in crisis. Even the French Communist Party, one of the most backward of European Communist parties with respect to Eurocommunism, whose recently published theses for its up-coming congress represent, from that point of view, an actual step back from its earlier positions, has abandoned the expression 'Marxism-Leninism' to denote its official theory, and replaced it with the expression 'scientific socialism.'

Thus, even within the Communist parties, the view begins to prevail that not only is Marxism not a complete and universal system, but that it cannot function other than *creatively*. This does not mean that Marxists should simply 'adapt' the same old theoretical concepts to new conditions. Marxism is creative when it succeeds in transforming, or even abandoning – in line with historical and theoretical developments and always within the bounds of its own intellectual structure – certain concepts (for example, the dictatorship of the proletariat) and creating new ones.

A second point, less obvious than the first, is that the crisis of Marxism as a totalized theory of human phenomena calls upon us to perceive breaks, omissions, and contradictions both in its theoretical apparatus and in its specific analyses. There is no such thing as a science of sciences, 'dialectical materialism,' which dictates to the entirety of the social sciences and to which historical materialism is a tributary – a view which, as we know, pervaded even the natural sciences under Stalinism (Lysenko). Marxism, if it wishes to be creative and not dogmatic, must open itself to the other disciplines. It must be both open to the other social sciences and aware of the boundaries which define it as a discipline. This opening involves serious theoretical problems. We must avoid an eclectic attitude which views the various disciplines, 'including' Marxism, as mutually complementary. Say, a little psychoanalytic theory, a little linguistics, and a bit more Marxism. One of the great errors of so-called 'Freudian Marxism' is that it regards the various disciplines as different ways of observing the same object. In fact we can only speak of a discipline when a theory, by raising certain problems, has defined its own specific, unique object.

The specific object of Marxism is the class struggle on all levels: economic, political, ideological. Marxism is required by its object to construct a theory of the *history of social formations*. The specific object of psychoanalytic theory is the individual subject. Psychoanalysis does not complement Marxism by investigating a different aspect of the same object, that is, the individuals who make up a society. If that were so, there could then be an eclectic discipline, Freudian Marxism: Marxism for the society as a whole, psychoanalysis for the individuals who compose it. The specific object of psychoanalytic theory is the *unconscious*. We can say the same of linguistics, which becomes a discipline in relation to its own object, namely, language and discourse. It follows that the direct intervention of one discipline through the theoretical investigation of the object of another discipline is not possible. Consequently, the terms 'Marxism and psychoanalysis,' 'Marxism and linguistics' and so on are, from this point of view, fundamentally in error. This is not to say that every special discipline should be closed upon itself, ignoring all others. On the contrary, undogmatic and creative Marxism, like every discipline, should be in touch with many other disciplines in order to grasp the universality and complexity of human phenomena. But that contact should respect the limits of the specific objects which constitute the other disciplines as such. And if we Marxists think of Marxism as the fundamental discipline of our age, that is not because it defines in a dominant way every object of intellectual inquiry, whereas the other disciplines are merely subsidiary, but because we believe that the class struggle, the specific object of Marxism, is the central element in history and social reality.

The same issue reappears in a different light when we come to theories which treat the specific object of Marxism, namely, social reality in its historical dimension, but which examine it from another perspective. To what extent can Marxist political science 'borrow' elements from systems theory or Marxist economics borrow elements from Keynesianism?

This problem, which is related to the crisis of dogmatic Marxism, is a complex one. How can Marxism emancipate itself from dogmatism without falling into eclecticism? The issue poses itself in Greece with unsettling frequency. Many self-styled Marxists uncritically incorporate elements of neo-Weberian positivism and Anglo-Saxon empiricism into their analyses, while others who work entirely within the bounds of those tendencies add to their analyses, with greater or less dexterity, a little Marxist sauce in order to follow the crowd.

The issue, as I emphasized in my debate with Ralph Miliband is the following: we must always keep in mind that concepts and methodological approaches do not exist in isolation but are woven into a certain intellectual problematic, whether a given scholar is conscious of that problematic or not, whether or not it is manifest in his or her work. Even Anglo-Saxon empiricism has an epistemology which consists precisely in its exclusion of theoretical consistency in the name of direct experiential truth.

Marxism obviously cannot borrow isolated concepts from other disciplines and use them in its own problematic without first seeing to what degree the philosophy underlying those concepts is compatible with its own. A Marxism which did so would be reduced to eclecticism and pseudo-intellectual babbling; the borrowed concepts would not only not enrich it, but they would operate within it as linguistic barriers or even disorienting forces.

Often, however, there is the possibility of harmonizing other theoretical approaches with Marxism, that is to say, with the fundamental conceptual system of historical materialism. This possibility can take many forms. The most important are the following:

1) Some scholars have an approach which explicitly agrees with Marxism on basic issues. A case in point is *Annales*, the well-known French school of historiography. In such a case some concepts and conclusions can certainly be incorporated into the conceptual apparatus of historical materialism.

2) Some scholars work without a clear theoretical framework whereas their procedures and results can only be understood with the aid of an implicit logic compatible with Marxism.

3) Some scholars profess to be anti-Marxist, but are really opposed only to a caricature of Marxism such as Stalinist economism, whereas their operative intellectual philosophy is perfectly compatible with an authentic Marxist approach.

4) Some scholars have an anti-Marxist problematic which is extrinsic to their work. Their work is actually grounded on theoretical presuppositions which are concealed by their overt argument and coincide with Marxism on fundamental points.

The last two of these categories, as I argued in my last book (*State, Power, Socialism*), apply to the work of Michel Foucault. Indeed, some of Foucault's analyses enrich Marxism greatly, even though in his latest book (*The History of Sexuality*) he expounds an explicitly anti-Marxist problematic, but one directed against a caricature of Marxism. In any event, Foucault's anti-Marxism is by and large not related organically to his intellectual conclusions, but gives the impression of something tacked on.

Within the limits of these categories, then, Marxism can be enriched with elements of theories concerning its own object. In that sense, our recognition of the omissions, disjunctions, and contradictions in Marxism and of the crisis of Marxism is indeed hopeful and can be creative.

The Renewal of Marxism

The crisis is not limited to dogmatic Marxism. It affects creative Marxism as well, although the two crises are not the same. Contemporary epistemology has demonstrated that a discipline does not progress except through crises, breaks, and conflicts. Such is the case with creative Marxism. The crisis of the kind of Marxism which was dominant until recently is a crisis of all Marxism. We begin to perceive the fetters of dogmatism on us still, on us who have overcome it, who rejected it long ago.

The weight of dogmatism manifests itself even today in *delays and omissions* concerning a number of basic issues, delays and omissions which have facilitated the current resurgence of the dominant ideology in as much as we have failed to occupy a certain area of the theoretical-ideological field. I don't shrink from the conclusion that the crisis of dogmatic Marxism has revealed the nakedness of us all in the presence of fundamental problems. Overthrowing a dogma is one thing, but finding something to put in its place is another and much more difficult matter.

Let me review some of the areas in which we still have no adequate answers. In respect to problems of social classes and of the state I think that creative Marxism has advanced satisfactorily. The same cannot be said of the study of ideology in general and of ideological constructs. I do not think that creative Marxism has succeeded in constructing a real theory of ideology, although it has successfully criticized the traditional dogmatic view of ideology as 'false consciousness.' This delay is due in part to the difficulty which Marxism has had in understanding cultural tendencies and problems of our time such as the youth movement, the women's movement, the environmentalist movement, and so forth. The same can be said of the study of legal systems and of the law in general; although we have cast off traditional dogmas as to the merely 'formal' nature of democratic freedoms, we still do not have a real theory of justice. As a result we are unable to formulate a positive concept of human rights and freedoms clearly distinct from neoliberalism. We have not developed theoretically the need to deepen and transform representative democracy and to establish new institutions of self-management and direct democracy at the base.

The same holds for the nation, which is still a real puzzle for Marxism. Although we have rejected the dogmatic, economistic accounts of nationalism which ignore its special role in the shaping of social reality and the transition to socialism, we are only beginning to suspect what direction an authentic Marxist study of the subject would take. Not to mention the immense gaps which exist in regard to a new revolutionary strategy that will be distinct both from Stalinism and traditional social democracy.

I have emphasized the inadequacies and weaknesses of creative Marxism. I want to add that they must be seen as new horizons opening up with the crisis of dogmatic Marxism. Through its questions, its negations, and its conquests, Marxism can turn its crisis into a creative and salutary experience.

17

INTERVIEW WITH
NICOS POULANTZAS

Marxism Today: Your books are now widely influential in Britain but I think that it would be useful for people here to know something more about your personal political and intellectual development.[1]

Nicos Poulantzas: Well let us say that I first met Marxism through French culture and through Sartre, as did many people of my class situation and of my age in Greece. At that time I was beginning to be able to work for myself at the age of seventeen or eighteen. We were in the post-Civil War situation, with the Communist Party declared illegal, which lasted until 1974. The conditions for the circulation of Marxist ideas were extremely difficult. It was impossible even to acquire the classical texts of Marxism and as a result I came to Marxism through French philosophy and through Sartre in particular. When I was at University I became involved in my first political activity on the left, with the student unions or syndicates and then I joined EDA (United Democratic Left), that being a broad legal form of the Communist Party. At that time, however, I was not a member of the Communist Party.

After my law studies, I came to Western Europe and at that time I continued to be actively involved in membership of EDA. But the big problem within EDA was that some of them were Communists and some were not; it was a kind of popular front organization, but absolutely under the dominance of the Communist Party and without any real autonomy.

Developing an interest in Marxism through Sartre, I was much influenced by Lucien Goldmann and by Lukács. My doctoral thesis was undertaken in the philosophy of law, in which I tried to develop a conception of law drawing on Goldmann and Lukács. It was published

* First published in *Marxism Today* (July 1979), pp. 198–205.

in 1964; but from the moment it was published I began to feel the
limitations of that orientation within Marxism. At this time I began to
encounter Gramsci through *Critica Marxista* which was the most
important journal of Marxism at that time.

I began also to work with Althusser, while still being influenced – as
I always am – by Gramsci – which created a kind of agreement and
disagreement, from the beginning, with Althusser. It would take too
long now to explain the kind of differences I had, which were not so
much with Althusser but rather more with Balibar. With Althusser's
first texts, which were mainly philosophical and methodological, I
profoundly agreed and I always felt that Althusser has a kind of
understanding in relation to the class struggle and its problems. The
problem of structuralism was more a problem with Balibar than with
Althusser. In *Political Power and Social Classes* there are definite
differences between the text of Balibar and my text. I have spoken a
little about these differences in *Classes in Contemporary Capitalism*.

Meanwhile, I joined the Greek Communist Party before the split in
1968, which came one year after the colonels' coup and since then I
have been in the Communist Party of the Interior. The Communist
Party of the Interior has moved towards the Eurocommunist line. The
Greek Communist Party of the Exterior, on the other hand, is one of
the last Stalinist parties in Europe. I mean that in the strongest sense –
in the sense of theoretical dogmatism, the total absence of internal
democracy, and total dependency towards the Soviet Union.

MT: Your theoretical writings suggest that political alliances play a
very central role in the project for a democratic socialism. Yet the
alliance between the Communist Party of France (PCF) and the
Socialist Party (PS) has proved to be very fragile. What lessons do
you think can be learnt?

NP: Well, I think that the main problem is not so much that of political
alliances between political organizations. The main problem, as we
know, is the political alliance between the classes and class fractions
which are represented by those parties, because one of the lessons of
the failure of this alliance in France is exactly that it has mainly been
seen and constructed as an alliance from the top. One cannot say it
was a pure electoral alliance: it was not, because the 'Common
Programme of the Left' is a very significant fact in the history of
the European Left. It was not a pure conjunctural electoralist type of
alliance; but nevertheless it was very significant that neither of these
parties tried to found this alliance in the base – that is, amongst the

masses – by creating common organizations. We had some type of common actions in some organizations, between those organized by the parties and the trade unions, but we never achieved an original or specific type of organization at the base which could crystallise this type of alliance. This was also a traditional failure of the 'popular front' type of alliance. In the Third International strategy, Dimitrov was always saying that we must have specific types of base organization, crystallizing this type of alliance. This was not achieved during that period, nor has it been achieved by the Communist Party of France or the Socialist Party. But nevertheless your question goes much further. I think that the realization of this type of alliance is only possible, given a change within the Communist Parties themselves. It is very clear that as long as you are working with the conception of the 'dictatorship of proletariat' you are not going to be able to make a durable alliance with a partner who knows he is going to be eliminated during the transition to socialism when that dictatorship is implemented. So I think that revolutionary strategy towards democratic socialism requires the changes that have occurred in some Communist Parties of Western Europe and this is one of the conditions for achieving new forms of political alliance.

Now we come to the problem of social democracy, which is a very specific problem and which demonstrates that this question of alliances has much to do with the actual conditions of the specific country; and consequently that we must be cautious about making generalizations because we see that social democracy plays quite different political roles in the different countries in which it exists. For example, I do not see any possibility of political alliances with the type of social democracy you have in West Germany, or in Sweden. The situation is different in countries where social democracy is not a governmental party, as it has not been for many years in France. Then, in the present structural crisis of capitalism, we can see a shift of social democracy towards the left and this is one of the conditions for a more durable alliance between the Communist Party and the Socialist Party. I do not think we can speak of social democracy in general any more, given this structural crisis of capitalism. We cannot find, I think, a general tendency of the bourgeoisie to employ social democracy as a solution to the crisis. Nor does the bourgeoisie have the economic power in all societies to offer to the working class the types of compromises that are needed for social democracy to have its political function fulfilled when it is in government, especially in the context of the austerity programmes we have now in Europe. It is not clear at all that a social-democratic solution, which involves compromises with the working class, can be realized by the bourgeoisie through social democracy in the particular circumstances of each individual country in Europe. In these circumstances social democracy does not have any other solution than alliance with the Communist Party. In this specific type of situation (which is very different from the other types of situation) you find the integration of social democracy in the governmental apparatus, as in West Germany. I do not wish to comment on the situation in Britain but in Germany it is a very peculiar situation because Germany plays a dominating economic role in the Common Market, and so it still has possibilities of compromise with its working class. This is not the case at all in Italy or France and most probably also not the case in Spain. We should not speak nowadays, given the structural crisis of capitalism, of social democracy in general.

MT: Do you think this means that there is no longer a problem of 'reformism' in general for the Left?

NP: No, I do not mean that; especially given the double character of the social democracy – that is, on the one-hand trying to achieve a modernization of capitalism but nevertheless, on the other, having deep roots in the working class. The problem confronting social democracy is to make the combination of the two; and given the structural crisis of capitalism, the inter-imperialist contradictions, and the uneven developments, the situation of social democracy in Europe is extremely different from one country to another. This game can be played in economically dominant countries in Europe like West Germany, and Sweden; but it cannot be played by social democracy in France or in Italy. In such conjunctures I think that one of the solutions for the social-democratic parties is the left turn towards an alliance with the Communist parties.

MT: You have already mentioned the question of Eurocommunism. It is becoming increasingly apparent that Eurocommunism is not a single phenomenon but that there are a number of diverse trends within what is called Eurocommunism. Do you think that it is helpful to distinguish between trends that can be labelled left and right?

NP: We speak here of general tendencies and one must not first personalize and then make a fetish of this distinction in a phenomenon which is relatively new. Now, in the strategy of the Third International, which was a strategy of dual power and frontal smashing of the state, the problem of reformism was in some sense a clear and an easy one.

Everything was 'reformist' which did not lead to the creation of dual power and achieving the possibilities of a frontal clash with the state. Now, when we speak of a democratic road to democratic socialism, such a strategy must not only profoundly transform but also maintain forms of representative democracy and forms of liberties (what we have called for a long time 'formal liberties' but which are not just 'formal'). This representative democracy must, at the same time, go hand in hand with the creation of direct democracy at the base. But the first point is important; if we can no longer speak of a sudden clash with the state but of the maintenance of and profound deepening of institutions of representative democracy under socialism, then the distinction between reformism and a revolutionary road becomes much more difficult to grasp, even if nevertheless it continues to exist.

It is very clear that in Eurocommunism you can find the reformist tendency and in this sense I think one can speak of a left-wing and of a right-wing Eurocommunism. For example, I think that when Ellein-stein speaks of a gradual, peaceful, legal, progressive revolution, this is exactly the classical Kautskian way of posing these questions. But what would be the proper distinction between a left-wing and a right-wing Eurocommunism? There are a number of them. First of all, the question of the importance given to direct and workers' council democracy, which has always been a decisive continuum between reformist and a revolutionary road to socialism. Left-wing Euro-communism gives a much greater significance to rank-and-file democ-racy. The second one is the types of ruptures and the types of transformation envisaged in the very state itself: because even if we do not speak about 'smashing the state', nevertheless left Eurocommu-nism is very conscious of the problem of the necessity of radical transformation, not only the ideological apparatuses of the state but also of the repressive apparatuses themselves: whereas right-wing Eurocommunism tends to see those apparatuses more or less as neutral apparatuses and consequently does not attach the same importance to their transformation. Left Eurocommunism retains the insistence on the moment of rupture in the state itself. It does not speak of a gradual progressive transformation of the state. It is very conscious that there will be a decisive turning point, which is not going to be a civil war but is nevertheless going to be a profound crisis of the state, with a shift in the balance of forces inside the state itself. Right-wing Eurocommu-nism does not examine this alternative very seriously. To be concrete whenever I have read Carrillo I have seen more right-wing Euro-communism positions and whenever I have read Ingrao of the PCI I have found more left-wing Eurocommunism positions.

I think more and more that Eurocommunism is a specific phenomenon of *advanced* capitalist social formations. The whole problematic
of the democratic road to socialism, of the revolutionary road to
democratic socialism, is closely related to the specific stage of capitalist development.

MT: For you and for us the Italian experiment of the 'historic
compromise' is of enormous importance. Now in such a situation
what sort of importance do you attach to the need for the establishment of some kind of national consensus?

NP: I do not have much confidence in this conception of national
consensus. The Italian Communists themselves have never presented
the historical compromise as a type of transition to socialism. Sometimes they have come close to saying this, but most of the time they
have presented it as a specific strategy in a specific conjuncture in Italy;
they have not presented it as a general model for the transition to
socialism. Now, we have a second question, which is the famous
question posed by Berlinguer after the Chile coup, about the importance of a broad national consensus. Well, I am very dubious about
this position. There is a kind of analysis that derives from the
Gramscian tradition and which is one of the most disputed points
in Gramsci, where he suggests that the working class can have an
ideological and political hegemony *before* achieving political power.
To me the question of national consensus must be seen much more in
the process of democratic socialism rather than as a *precondition* of
democratic socialism itself. To say that one needs 80 per cent of the
people in order to create the unity necessary for a left government is a
contradiction in terms.

MT: You yourself are a member of the Greek Communist Party of the
Interior and perhaps we can now turn our attention to the situation in
Greece. In last year's elections the alliance in which your party
participated suffered a serious electoral setback, particularly at the
hands of the orthodox Greek Communist Party. What is your analysis
of this experience and how do you account for the attraction of the
oppositionist strategy of the orthodox party? What lessons can you
derive from this?

NP: Well there are some general reasons and there are reasons which
have to do more specifically with Greece. The general reasons have
to do with the insufficient analysis and insufficiently coherent

strategy within Eurocommunism itself. If the Eurocommunist turning point is taken by a constituted Communist party, there is no
possible contestation of this turning point, apart from that by the
extreme left. But if you have a situation of split, with the majority of
the party being in an orthodox position, the lack of sufficient
analysis of revolutionary strategy on the part of Eurocommunism
becomes much more critical when you have to cope with the
dogmatic fractions of the party. Then we have reasons which have
to do very specifically with Greece and which are linked to the
question of the Greek Civil War. I refer to the whole imagery and
symbolic position of revolution during the Civil War. It has been the
Communist Party of the Exterior, most of whose members were very
active in the Civil War and who were exiled in other countries and
have come back after 1974, which has been best able to mobilize this
popular imagery of the Civil War. Let us say that they have
succeeded in what Lister failed to do in Spain because – exactly
as I said before – Carrillo has been able to make the turning point
towards Eurocommunism in the Communist Party itself. It also has
to do with the social conditions in Greece.

The Greek working class is a very feeble working class because most
of Greek capital is not indigenous capital, it is a bourgeoisie rooted in
the Mediterranean area and big shipping capital and so on. So the
Greek working class does not have a very high level of class consciousness. You very rarely find in Greece a family where father and
son are workers. We have a high social mobility into the petty
bourgeoisie. We have some of the working class who become petty
bourgeois and who migrate and become agents of the international
Greek bourgeoisie. Either they come here to London and work in the
shipping companies or they go to America. To me there is a feebleness
of the Greek working class which has a relationship to the success of
dogmatism in Greece nowadays. And of course it has to do with the
errors of the Greek Communist Party – for example, the fact that, for
long, we have tried to seek the official approval of the Soviet Union –
not being able to make real criticisms of the Soviet Union and not
being able to take a real alliance for the democratic road to socialism,
because we hoped that the Soviet Union would choose between the
two parties! This has been a very negative factor in the development of
the Greek Party of the Interior.

MT: Can we turn to some theoretical questions? It seems as if there
has been at some point a quite decisive turn with respect to Leninism.
Would you like to comment on that?

NP: That is absolutely true. I think that if there is a turning point it has been expressed in my book *The Crisis of Dictatorships* and it comes from very definite positions I took during the period of the Greek dictatorship. During that period we had two lines in the Greek Communist Party of the Interior. The one was the line of a (violent or less violent) frontal opposition to the dictatorship regime of external frontal opposition. The other line was one that thought that one could employ or utilize the internal contradiction between the fractions of the dominant class and the internal contradictions of the military regime.

After six or seven years of dictatorship I began to grasp theoretically and politically that these conceptions of the military dictatorship were associated with some views held by Marxists about the state itself. The state is seen as a kind of closed place which can be taken only by an external type of strategy, whether it be the Leninist frontal type of strategy or the Gramscian type of encircling of the state. In its place I began to think of the state as a condensation, a relation of forces, I developed this idea in *Classes in Contemporary Capitalism*. At the same time I was beginning to see the significance that this could have for the strategy of opposition to the military regimes. Also I began to apply this conception of the state to the problem of the transition to socialism, which became clearer in my last book, *State, Power, Socialism*. It is clear to me that there is a crisis, and that crisis involves Leninism as such.

I think that the position with regard to Lenin is not exactly what my position is towards Leninism. I do not think that one can simply say that Lenin was only right with respect to the Soviet Union. I think one of the big insights of Lenin, as a strategist, and in which I believe, is not Leninist centralism, it is that Lenin was a convinced supporter of the rank and file and of the direct democracy of the soviets. The thing that Rosa Luxemburg opposed in Lenin was not that he was too much of a centralist, or too oppressive toward the working class; it was much more that he crushed all the institutions of representative democracy and left only the institution of direct democracy of the soviets. I think this is the Lenin that we can still employ. This is the Lenin of *The State and Revolution*, which is the most important Lenin: I think this is the positive aspect of Lenin.

The negative aspect involves the whole question of the application and the theorization of the dictatorship of proletariat which revolves around the total smashing of representative democracy. It is not true to say that Lenin was not able to do anything else because of the conditions of the civil war in the Soviet Union; nor that he could not do otherwise because of the different trends within the party. I think that there are some theoretical elements in Leninism itself that were related to both the situation during Lenin's period and afterwards under Stalin. There were definitely elements of centralization and a conception of the party as bringing consciousness to the working class from the outside. This includes *What Is to Be Done?*, which is an aspect of Leninism in which I do not believe any more. Further, I think that this conception of the party leads directly to the conception of 'the State Party' and then to statism.

MT: Can we return to the question of Althusser. In *Fascism and Dictatorship* you make this specific criticism of Althusser, that he does not give the class struggle the place it deserves. Is it possible in Marxist structuralism of the Althusserian kind, to give the class struggle the place it deserves?

NP: In the way you posed the question, you have already given the answer, because you have spoken of structuralism. I have not. You would have to accept, first of all, that there is a global Althusserian conception, which I do not believe myself; most of us had so many differences between Balibar, Althusser and myself, not to mention others; we had huge differences at the beginning.

For Althusser himself, or what one can still retain from Althusserianism, I think that the problematic of structuralism is a false problematic applied to the basic guidelines of Althusserian thought. I do not think that it is true that Althusser, in his epistemological guidelines really has – in the theoretical conception itself – an absence, due to a theoretical impossibility, of history and of class struggle. I think there is a problem in this respect with Balibar, but not even with all of Balibar. So I would say that structuralism has not been the very essence of Althusserianism but it has been the *maladie infantile*. There are some remnants of structuralism in Althusser and in the rest of us, in the theoretical conjuncture in which we were working; it was structuralism against historicism; it was Lévi-Strauss against Sartre. It has been extremely difficult for us to make a total rupture, from those two problematics. We insisted that for Marxism the main danger was not structuralism but historicism itself, so we directed all our attention against historicism – the problematic of the subject; against the problematics of Sartre and of Lukács, and as a result we 'bent the stick'; and of course this had effects in our theory itself. For example, it has had effect in my books in the distinction I made between 'structures' and 'practices' in *Political Power and*

Social Classes which I did not pursue afterwards in *Classes in Contemporary Capitalism*.

The remark I made in *Fascism and Dictatorship* with reference to Althusser concerned the ideological state apparatuses; it was a reproach I made to Althusser in the specific context of the discussion of the ideological state apparatuses and not a reproach about the core of the problematic with which we were then concerned. So I would still stand by the critical role of Althusserianism rather than with the substantive analysis.

MT: Much of your writing has been directed towards questions of the state and of politics, based upon the concept of 'relative autonomy'. What is your assessment of the capacity of a theory based on a concept of 'relative autonomy' to grapple with the problems of the specificity of the state and of politics?

NP: I will answer this question very simply because we could discuss it for years. It is very simple. One must know whether one remains within a Marxist framework or not; and if one does one accepts the determinant role of the economic in the very complex sense; not the determination of forces of production but of relations of production and the social division of labour. In this sense, if we remain within this conceptual framework, I think that the most that one can do for the specificity of politics is what I have done. I am sorry to have to speak like that.

I am not absolutely sure myself that I am right to be Marxist; one is never sure. But if one is Marxist, the determinant role of relations of production, in the very complex sense, must mean something; and if it does, one can only speak of 'relative autonomy' – this is the only solution. There is, of course, another solution, which is not to speak of the determinant role of the economic at all. The conceptual framework of Marxism has to do with this very annoying thing which is called 'relations of production' and the determinant role of relations of production. If we abandon it then, of course, we can speak of the autonomy of politics or of other types of relations between politics and economics.

MT: But I suppose that one way of staying somewhere within the Marxist framework for understanding the relation between politics and economics without attempting to derive one from the other, even in a very complex way, is to posit the notion of 'the conditions of existence' which one practice forms for another. What do you think of this alternative?

NP: For example if one talks not of relative autonomy, but of 'conditions of existence', such a position does not escape the difficulty; all that it achieves is to translate the same difficulty into other words. If you say that something is the condition of existence or the necessary pre-conditions of existence of another instance you are still within the relative autonomy framework. Whatever type of formulation you give to it you still have the same core problem. Do we believe or not in a determinant role of a relations of production? And if we do you are always going to be limited in the autonomy of politics in whatever way you can express it. The problem still remains, how to find the specificity and the autonomy without falling into the absolute autonomy of politics. It is the core of the Marxist problematic. Now we can probably formulate it better but this question of determination is the central core of Marxism.

The question was posed concerning the relation between 'economics' and 'politics', but of course the question also requires us to ask what we mean by 'economics'. Once you include class struggle and then you examine the relative autonomy of the state with respect to the dominant classes and to the class struggle then the problem of economics is different. The question has two terms, politics and economics, which we had to clarify in advance. When I speak of the final determination by the economic I already include the relations of production of social classes and of class struggle. There is no 'economy as such' and then class struggle on another level. So when I speak of 'the relative autonomy of the economic' already the economic has this other sense which embraces the presence of class struggle.

In addition we should note a further danger. If we speak only in terms of apparatuses we have another danger, that of institutionalization. Apparatuses, after all, are material condensations of relations. In the famous example, it is not the church that created religion, it is religion that created the church. So if we speak in terms of apparatuses, of course, we can clarify the debate: but still we displace it, because we can speak only in terms of enterprises and apparatuses which already presuppose the relations of production themselves.

MT: In your latest book you seek to develop a notion of 'authoritarian statism' which I understand as being the intensification of state control associated with the decline in political democracy. Is this theory simply a more sophisticated version of the much more traditional Leninist thesis that monopoly capitalism necessarily tends towards authoritarianism? Is it not true that the political reality of the experience of European and North American capitalism is that intensified state control has developed alongside an expanding area of political democracy?

NP: This question raises a more general problem: can we find significant differences between *forms* of state that correspond to different stages of capitalism? It is certain that under monopoly capitalism, as seen by Lenin, the state has gone through very significant modifications which existed under fascism and also in the New Deal; you can find some common characteristics without resorting to a simple identification of these different regimes. In this sense you can speak in general of the fascist state and the parliamentary state as being two forms of capitalist state. You can find some common characteristics alongside the essential differences. What I tried to say about 'authoritarian statism' was to find the general characteristics of a new phase of the state because I think that we are at a turning point in the organization of the capitalist state. My object was to find a formulation that could designate the general characteristics of this turning point, without identifying it with a specific regime. So when I speak of 'authoritarian statism' it does not mean that political democracy or representative democracy is going to end. 'Authoritarian statism' can take extremely different forms. It can take neoliberal forms as in France, or it can take a much more authoritarian form as in Germany. Nevertheless we are witnessing a decline of representative democracy in the classical sense without implying that there is a trend towards fascism. I tried therefore to distinguish between 'authoritarian statism' and fascism.

MT: I think my anxiety can be expressed in terms of the political implications that flow from your conception of 'authoritarian statism'. The democratic transition to socialism to which you are committed depends upon the possibility, prior to any advance towards socialism itself, of creating the conditions for an expanded democracy. Yet the possibility of achieving this democratic advance would seem to be more remote as a result of the advance of 'authoritarian statism'.

NP: This is the whole problem. It is the question of rupture. The thing that I want to point out is that what democratic socialism requires is a deepening and an extension of liberties, of representative institutions and so on. This can not occur without a deep transformation of social and economic conditions. This is the conclusion that I draw: that you cannot struggle to expand political rights and liberties is a defensive position against the authoritarian tendency of today's capitalism. But I believe that we cannot save political democracy any more without profound modifications of the social and economic structures of capitalism itself.

MT: Can I ask you to clarify your idea of 'authoritarian statism'. Is it merely a phase of the 'interventionist state' or is it a distinct new type of state succeeding the liberal and the interventionist state?

NP: I am not entirely clear myself because there is a general difficulty about the stages of capitalism. The Leninist conception was of two stages, the first that of industrial capitalism, the second stage that of monopoly capitalism. I have held the view that in these stages we can have different phases but we cannot speak of a third stage. But I am no longer so certain about this position. Within this framework, 'authoritarian statism' could not be a distinct stage as long as we retained the commitment to two stages. But now I think the problems are much more complicated. My earlier discussion of them very much revolved around the theory of state monopoly capitalism, and the debate within the PCF on this topic. Now I think that, even if we speak of phases of interventionist states, the contemporary transformations of the capitalist state are not therefore simply a phase; something much more important is involved in the emergence of 'authoritarian statism'.

MT: You tend to talk about the current stage of 'authoritarian statism' in the context of the intensification of generic elements of political crisis as well as economic crisis. This begins to sound as if you are suggesting that the final stage of capitalism has arrived.

NP: Yes, I see the problem. It is a danger which I was not very conscious of and now I see when you speak of it. I see very clearly that there is a danger but I want to stress that it requires us to consider what we mean by the structural crisis of capitalism. In my text 'The Crisis of the State', I try to analyze this structural crisis of capitalism, taking issue with some of the conceptions of the French Communist Party, and insist that the existence of such a crisis does not imply that it cannot be resolved.

MT: What is the connection between this discussion of the state and the emphasis which you place on the role of the single dominant mass party?

NP: I have tried to say that even if you do not have the massive, dominant governmental party what you do find is a relationship between two parties that are able to exchange political power between themselves. I had in mind the German model or even the British model, where even within the core of the state apparatus you could find a mixing of forces of Labour or Conservative, or of Social Democrats and of Christian Democrats, which tends to function as a single mass party of the bourgeoisie, in spite of the differences that might exist between them. Even if we do have ordinary governmental changes in this sense they are superficial changes in the face of an institutionalized core of forces belonging to both parties.

MT: Can we turn to the question of your conception of socialism. You now oppose a simple Leninist or vanguardist conception of 'the party'. In the concluding chapter of *State, Power, Socialism*, you talk about the need to combine forms of direct democracy and forms of representative democracy. But you do not explicitly discuss how these two different forms are to be articulated or combined.

NP: The problem is that these are extremely new questions, and we are increasingly becoming aware that we do not have any positive theory of democracy in Marx. We have the theory of capitalist democracy and the theory of dictatorship of the proletariat. But we do not really have this positive evaluation and theoretical foundation for the type of the articulation between direct and representative democracy. Now it is clear that, as long as we speak of representative democracy, the relative separation is still going to exist between the public and private sphere. This leads us to the more complex problem of the relative separation of the state not being simply a question relating only to *capitalist* relations of production. If it is not necessarily tied to capitalist relations of production then perhaps the very question of the relative separation in capitalist relations of production itself becomes much more problematic. This is the first problem.

   The second problem is about the vanguard party. We must be very clear. As soon as we speak of a plurality of parties in the transition to socialism and as long as we take this conception seriously, it is evident that you cannot 'have your cake and eat it'. It is very clear that in the Leninist tradition (although Lenin himself did not have a conception of the one-party system) the conception of the vanguard party goes hand in hand with the conception of the dictatorship of the proletariat and the one-party system. You cannot, at the same time, say we are going to have a pluralism of parties and maintain the Leninist conception of the vanguard party because such a conception of the party implies or even requires the single party system. You cannot have both of them.

Consider the political party; I am not sure that a political party is the best form of organizing even, in their differences, the new forms of social movements. For example, I am not sure at all that we must ask a revolutionary political party to take under consideration the ecological problem, the feminist problem and so on. So the problem is not only to have a party so good that it is not only going to be political but take up every sphere of social life and economic life. I think that this conception of the party as the unique centralizer, even if it is a very subtle centralization, is not necessarily the best solution. I think more and more that we must have autonomous social movements whose type of organization cannot be the same as that of a political party organization. There must be a feminist movement outside the most ideal possible party because the most ideal party cannot include such types of social movements even if we insist that the revolutionary party must have certain conceptions of the woman question.

Secondly, does the party have a central role? Of course it has a central role as long as it believes that politics has a central role, and as long as the state has a central role. But then as long as we need some type of organization, we must have a type of centralism or a type of homogenization of differentiations if we must make this articulation between representative democracy and direct democracy. If, up to the present, this centralizing role has been played by the single party, in future some aspects of this role must be transferred from the party itself to the representative organs where many parties can play their own role. We must have this differentiation and non-identification between party and the state. And if representative institutions can really play their full role, the type of relations, or articulation will not have to be transmitted as in the past, through the party itself. In Italy, for example, in the regional assemblies with Communist and Socialist majorities, the co-ordination between forms of direct democracy, movements of citizens, ecological movements on the one hand and the representative democracy does not pass through the centralization provided by the Communist Party itself.

An interesting problem, to which we do not have definite answers is (and of this I am profoundly confident) that pluralism of parties in the democratic road to socialism means necessarily changes in the function of the party itself. You cannot have, at the same time, the traditional Leninist conception of the party, and simply say that there ought to be other parties also. This does not work.

What must be the differentiation, what must be the transformation of the party? I do not believe that the party should be lost in or amalgamated with the different types of social movements. But nor can the party, as a cadre apparatus, successfully link the many different social or economic movements. We must also reconsider the classical view of Leninist centralism in which everything political is primary and the remainder is secondary. What is the feminist movement, what is the ecological movement, what are the other types of social movement? These are not mere secondary movements in relation to the working-class movement or to the party. Otherwise, everything becomes secondary. This question of primary and secondary relations must be rethought.

If Eurocommunism, like Marxism itself, is in crisis, it is because we are in an experimental stage where parties are trying to work out this different type of strategy. We see what is happening in Spain for example, we see what is happening in Italy; even in France we are in crisis; in France it is perhaps more difficult because the PCF functions as the French party has always functioned. It is also the party which sometimes makes the biggest breaks and then swings back; it goes from the most open party (for example, you have never seen any Communist Party so open to the question of women as the PCF), to the other side.

In this process there is a drawing back towards a traditional response, we see this clearly in the PCF. The changing conception of the party lies at the heart of these responses. There is an important response within the different parties which says 'where are these new positions leading us' and they draw back in alarm. You find it also in Italy, you find it in Spain and in the other parties. This is not surprising because as yet there are no definite answers to these problems. But these are the problems which we must tackle; they will not go away, nor can we simply retreat to the old orthodoxy.

RESEARCH NOTE ON
THE STATE AND SOCIETY

The object of this paper is to point out the essential problems and outline the themes which, in my opinion, should guide research on the state and society in the world today.

It seems evident that the two objects of study, 'state' and 'society', can on no account be equated or dealt with at the same level without running the risk of considerably enlarging the scope of the research.

It is, of course, impossible to speak of the contemporary state without referring to the society underlying it, nor can society be divorced from the state which governs it. The fact remains, however, that according to whether we choose the state or society as the focal point of our research, our approach to the other term will necessarily be different. If we consider the problem from the standpoint of society, the state will indeed come into it, but not so much for its own sake as in terms of its effects on, and its presence in society.

I propose here to focus research on the state, for three main reasons:

First, because of the much broader role of the state and the development of state structures in the world today, a phenomenon that is not altogether new but which differs qualitatively from what it has been in the past.

Second, the comparative lag in research on the state as opposed to studies on society that characterized the three main trends in social science thinking up until about 1965–70:

The dominant Anglo-Saxon tradition in the social sciences – a melting-pot of trends from functionalism to systemism – a marked feature of which has been a neglect of the peculiar role and specific character of the 'state' which has been absorbed into a very broad

* First published in the *International Social Science Journal*, vol. 32, no. 4 (1980), pp. 600–608.

concept of the 'political system' and into one dividing up power into a multitude of 'power pluralisms' and micro-powers.

In official Marxism, there has also been a marked neglect of the inherent role and specific nature of the state. For a long time the state was regarded as no more than the so-called 'superstructural' envelope surrounding the 'basis' to which it was entirely subordinated and was, therefore, no more than a tool to be manipulated at will by the ruling class.

Social sciences in Western Europe, particularly in France, the Federal Republic of Germany and Italy. Although in these countries the state has always been a primary object of research (one of the reasons for this no doubt being the role of the European states in the democratic-bourgeois revolutions), they have nearly always been confined to a 'juridical' conception of the state, hence European juridico-political science, the predominant feature of which was the study of constitutional law and juridico-political philosophy.

Third, the choice of the state as the central object of research is prompted by the fact that it is becoming – and this is no coincidence – one of the main themes in the present trend in ideologico-theoretical thinking in what is held to be important in the social sciences today.

Taking the state as the main focus for research alters the lines along which the latter is to be conducted, and analyses of social phenomena and of society in the broad sense (economic, social and ideological structures, the class struggle, social movements, etc.), indispensable though they are, will be approached in terms of their relevance to change within the state and in state structures. Obvious, typical examples are multinational corporations or the current world economic crisis, but seen in terms of their impact on, and relation to the nation-state, and to state policies with regard both to that crisis and to the crisis of the state.

In short, it is a matter of deciding upon an approach and adhering to it for both practical purposes (research constraints) and scientific reasons, for if all things are inexorably bound up (state-society), the only way of arriving at a scientific result is to circumscribe the subject under study, albeit allowing oneself the greatest possible leeway.

Research should concentrate on five or six broad fields, each comprising several main themes. I shall restrict myself initially to outlining them before embarking on questions of method (interdisciplinarity, schools of thought, order in which they may be dealt with, etc.), it being understood that at the first stage of research these fields and themes should be seen in their overall perspective and only subsequently dealt with in detail through case-studies.

The first of these broad subject headings concerns general problems pertaining to the theory of the state, its purpose being to clear the theoretical terrain. There is in fact a series of *common theoretical issues* with which all disciplines and schools of thought are faced in analyzing the state, even if they differ as to the solutions they propose. These questions of theory arise in the current crisis in, and explosion of, traditional thinking on the state in the social sciences: (a) the crisis in the Anglo-Saxon tradition of social science which can be seen quite clearly in the United States with the trend among the members of the academic establishment away from this traditional way of thought; (b) the crisis in Marxism, most obvious in the revival of Marxist thinking on the state; (c) the crisis in the juridico-constitutionalist conception of the state in Western Europe and the revival of sociologico-political analyses of the state; (d) the emergence of schools of thought in the analysis of power: the Foucault school, the anti-psychiatry school, the psycho-analytical school going beyond classic Freudo-Marxism, the anti-institutional school, new research into the 'totalitarian phenomenon', etc.

What are these new themes and the questions they raise?

The state, the political, powers. Is power reduced to the state? Is power reduced to the political? Is the political reduced to the state? Is the state composed of government machinery under formal state control, or does it go beyond that and include institutions which in terms of their form are 'private' (such as the family)? These issues are fundamental in present-day societies and are relevant in defining and designating the subject and scope of the state.

The connection between the economico-social sphere and the political-state sphere: questions as to the specific nature of state structures. Is there an order of determination between the state and the mode of production, and if so, what is it? According to what theoretical frame can current state intervention into the economy be comprehended?

The state and forms of organization of hegemony. Is there a correlation, and if so what is it, between the state and class domination? Is the state merely a tool-object of the ruling classes, is it an independent entity overlying class, or is it more a field of manoeuvre within which power relations between classes are condensed? What are the relations between the 'ruling classes' type of organization and the institutional framework of the state? Is the position of the state *vis-à-vis* the general public that of an isolated, impregnable fortress, or do the struggles of the people permeate the state?

The state and politico-social consensus. Does the state dominate through sheer repression? If not, is it enough to simply combine repression with ideological apparatus, thereby enabling the state to 'deceive' the people? Should one also speak of a power technology (Foucault) which would consist of physical procedures going far beyond the repression + ideology combination? Does state domination correspond to the people's wish to be dominated, to a 'master wish' (psycho-analytical concept)? How exactly does it come about that the people sometimes say no to oppression?

State machinery and class relations. If indeed there is a correlation between state and class relations, can that correlation alone, even if approached in a complex and subtle way, be accepted as an exhaustive explanation for state machinery? Does state machinery have a specific physical make-up (disciplinary and authoritarian structures, bureaucratization, etc.) which cannot be broken down into class relations of one kind or another?

These questions are important for they are encountered constantly in any concrete analysis, and in some respects are the key to all further research. It remains to be seen whether these theoretical problems should be dealt with separately and as a preliminary or in the course of investigation into the other fields.

The second field consists of a breakdown of some of the areas of research into broad *theoretical headings.*

There are three that I can see: (a) the state of developed capitalism; (b) the state in independent capitalist countries; and (c) the state in socialist countries.

I should like to make a preliminary comment based on a theoretical premise of my own; it is increasingly clear, for all or nearly all current research, that what were thought to be decisive differences between capitalist and socialist states are narrowing, in the sense that there are certain structural similarities, or at least related elements in the problems they are confronted with and also in their way of dealing with them – in the field of welfare, technological problems, aspects of bureaucratization, etc. The reasons for this are widely discussed today. Whatever the case may be, without falling in with the theories of Raymond Aron or even Alain Touraine as to the affinitive nature of post-industrial societies, it does appear that the supposed radical difference between these two types of state (capitalist societies and those practising really existing socialism) does not stand up to a close examination, which leads us to the conclusion that investigation into areas of common ground in these states is not to be discarded, indeed quite the reverse.

From a scientific point of view, however, the distinction must be made between these different types of state if we are to avoid confusion. Even if their basic structures are in some respects related, they nevertheless have their own specific features. Phenomena such as bureaucratization, technological constraints, the movement of elites, etc., appear in a different light in the two types of state, both as regards their present-day form and as they emerged and have been reproduced historically.

There is a particular problem with regard to the distinction to be made within the capitalist states, between the central and the peripheral, dependent states. Indeed, the degree to which capital and labour processes are now internationalized, widening the gulf between the imperialist centre and the so-called Third World, makes any overall theory on the capitalist state of today an inadequate basis for the study of these states. A theory on the new type of state that has developed in the countries of dependent capitalism is called for, all the more urgently in that, whereas a great deal of research has been done into the economies of dependent countries (trade inequalities, technological dependency, neo-colonialism, etc.), no 'general theory' on the political system peculiar to these countries has so far been evolved. The only general studies we have are those establishing the relationship between political institutions and the dependent countries' efforts towards 'modernization', and adhere to the ideology of 'under-development', viewing the situation in the Third World countries not as one of structural exploitation and oppression by the dominant countries, but merely as a matter of 'making up the leeway' between these and the 'developed' countries. But all the current theories on dependency are radically opposed to this approach, of which a typical protagonist in the economic field is Walter Rostow.

A particular effort should therefore be made in research to work out general analytical principles in dealing with the type of state prevalent in the dependent countries, reaching beyond concrete case-studies on one or other of them.

Which leads me to a further problem which arises again in the fourth field below. What form do the structural links between today's three main types of state (central capitalist, dependent capitalist and socialist states) take?

This question goes far beyond the simple issue of international relations between these states. It is clear, for example, that if the actual institutions prevalent in each of these types of state are what they are today, it is partly (and the question is just how much) because of the very existence of the other types of state. It is probably a complex structural link going beyond the mere 'external' influence of each state on the others.

To continue on the subject of concretizing and narrowing down research, which should however otherwise be kept at a fairly general level, another distinction should be made.

It concerns present-day 'capitalist' countries and is the distinction to be made between *exceptional state forms* (fascist states and military dictatorships) and those which are more or less typically representative of hegemony, roughly corresponding, in so far as the countries of the centre are concerned, to the 'parliamentary democracy' model.

This distinction is, of course, clearer in the countries belonging to the centre than those of the periphery, where there is a tendency for exceptional forms of government to become the rule, and this brings us back to the previous point, i.e. an analysis of the actual form of state in dependent countries. But there, too, there is a clear distinction to be made, for there is a marked difference between Mexico and Chile or between India and Argentina.

Whatever the case may be, I wish to emphasize this point in order to stress the need to pin-point one field of research in particular, and that is *fascist states or military dictatorships*. In the first place because it is a phenomenon that is as topical now as it has been in the past. Secondly, and above all because the principles guiding research into these types of state cannot be the same as those applied to the 'other' state forms. They are phenomena with a character entirely of their own, with their own structures. The problem cannot be eluded by vague considerations as to the spread of 'totalitarianism' throughout the world. The phenomenon of totalitarianism is none the less real and must be dealt with in its proper context. But this does not mean one should entertain the illusion that fascist states and military dictatorships are inherently and entirely different from others states, for they are structurally alike in many respects, and this explains why they may be analyzed as part of one and the same research project.

As my study of the contemporary state proceeds, I shall set aside a chapter on the international aspect, along the lines set forth in the second field above. Although this issue crops up again in the subsequent fields, it deserves special attention, notably on the following topics:

The first concerns the state, nation, nation-state and the present phase of imperialism. Does the current internationalization of capital and labour processes call in question the existence of the nation-state? Does the present phase in imperialism bring about such profound changes in the nation as to challenge the constitutive link between state and nation? Are we moving towards the decline of the nation-state, to be superseded by institutional inter-state, para-state or supra-state forms of government? If so, to what extent does the nation-state still carry any weight, and what is its role? If not, assuming that the nation-state is still the core, and the kingpin of domination, as I personally hold it to be, what changes is it nevertheless undergoing as a result of the current phase of imperialism? For the fact that the nation-state still actively persists (and does not merely survive) and is reproduced does not mean that it is immune to change brought about by internationalization.

The second topic concerns the nation. A problem that is unavoidable and must be tackled, the blind spot in the social sciences today, the importance of which is becoming increasingly clear. What are the effects of internationalization on the nation? Is the nation really on the path to decadence or is it more a case of a rupture of the 'national unity' imposed by various states and a resurgence of a variety of national entities hitherto kept down by the dominant nation-states? Whence the question of the revival of national minority struggles the world over and their effects on the state.

Third, the state and multinational corporations, a problem which may be dealt with here (for it comes up again) from a particular standpoint: is it a question here of the declining power of the nation-state giving way not to supra-state forms of government, but directly to fractions of capital in the shape of multinational companies? If not, what bearing do multinational corporations actually have on the present changes in nation-states? What connection is there between multinational capital and domestic capital in each country?

The fifth field concerns the present institutional changes in the state. I would suggest the following as the main line of research:

Are the capitalist countries today undergoing such profound changes as to make it possible to speak of a new state form different qualitatively from any they have had in the past? I personally think this is so, and would describe this *form* of government as 'authoritarian statism'. The following points may be made in this connection, and are central to current research in this field.

To what extent do the growing economic functions of the state, which are plainly to be seen in the vastly increased state intervention in all spheres of social life, bring about significant changes in the state? Is the economic planning machinery of the state, leading to pronounced state control over social life, an inevitable consequence of the development of capitalism? Does this machinery succeed in overcoming economico-social contradictions or are we witnessing the downfall of the welfare state founded on Keynesian illusions on organized planned capitalism which is supposed to have succeeded in mastering these contradictions?

A marked shift in the organizing role of the state away from political parties towards state bureaucracy and administration, and the overall decline of the representative role of political parties. This is a subject which today goes much further than the relatively old phenomenon of dwindling parliamentary prerogatives and a more powerful executive. What are the consequences for political institutions as a whole, of this new phenomenon of centralism and bureaucratization? And consequently how do the political parties now fit in structurally with the political system?

The new hegemonic organization of the bloc in power and its effects on the diverse machinery of state. Significance of the massive shift in hegemony towards powerful monopolistic capital and the restructuring of the repressive machinery of state: example of the army within the framework of the military-industrial complex. The crisis of the ideological hegemony of the ruling classes and consequent shift in the role of consensus-building away from ideological apparatus such as schools or universities towards the media.

The new forms of social control: replacement of the clear-cut social pattern previously based mainly on places of confinement (prisons, homes, etc.) by a whole new flexible far-reaching set of expedients cutting across the whole social system (a more dispersed police force, psychologico-psychiatric sectorization, networks for social work and unemployment benefits, etc.). One important result of this is a decisive process of 'de-institutionalization' of the ideologico-repressive machinery, and a process of 'de-confinement' in so far as the special machinery (homes, prisons, various places of collective confinement) intended to 'isolate' those who are thought to be 'abnormal, deviant or dangerous' is opening up and extending its influence to the whole of the social body, thus implying that the whole of society is potentially 'abnormal' and 'dangerous', guilt now being shifted away from the actual deed committed towards the intention inherent in people's mental make-up, and repression now encompassing both punishment and prevention. The disruption of the existing legal system and juridical ideology, as represented by the 'state of law' in order to make allowance for these institutional changes.

The new forms of social control and aids to sustain a new technology of power: computerization, electronics and political freedoms.

The mechanization and breaking down of the state machinery (army, police, administration, justice, ideological devices) into formal, overt networks, on the one hand, and tightly sealed nuclei controlled closely by the highest executive authorities, on the other, and the constant transfer of real power from the former to the latter, entailing the spread of the principle of secrecy. The deployment of a whole system of unofficial state networks operating concurrently with the official ones (para-state machinery) with no possible check by the representatives of the people.

The new forms of protest and social struggles (urban, ecological, feminist, student movements, struggles to improve the quality of life) and the new policies to control them. New methods of organizing social 'consensus' against these 'dissident' movements. Neo-liberalism and new state 'reform' practices, co-existing alongside authoritarian statism and akin to it in content.

Special attention should be given here to issues pertaining to the present economic crisis, the political crisis and the state crisis. This means setting out from the theoretical premise that the present world economic crisis is not simply due to the overall economic situation at the present time but is an actual structural and macro historical issue. Whence the following questions:

The modern state faced with the economic crisis. Crisis of state policies in the face of crisis; it now appears that the classic palliatives used by the state to deal with the crisis are themselves directly conducive to economic crisis. Hence what is known as 'crisis of the crisis-management'. Effects of this situation on the machinery of government, social control, organization of the consensus.

Is this economic crisis as well as the crisis in the way in which the state handles this crisis leading to a crisis of the state at the present time? For it is now known that economic crises on their own, of whatever kind they may be, do not necessarily bring about a crisis of the state. If so, does this crisis occur in all capitalist states and with equal sharpness? What role does it play in the reorganization of state machinery? What is the exact nature of the crisis? Is it a crisis leading to the disruption and weakening of the state, or one giving rise to a further crisis foreshadowing the strengthening and modernization of the state? Do the weakening and replacement of the present state constitute two alternatives, or are they rather a dual, contradictory tendency characteristic of the state today?

Finally, I feel that a special sixth field should be set aside for questions pertaining to the state and democracy today: (a) towards a decline in representative democracy and civil liberties; (b) the new claims for self-management or direct democracy in the world today, and how they relate to representative democracy.

NOTES

Introduction

1. *State, Power, Socialism*, Verso Classics Edition, London and New York 2000, p. 123.
2. The best available account of Poulantzas's life and work in English is Bob Jessop, *Nicos Poulantzas: Marxist Theory and Political Strategy*, Basingstoke 1985.
3. See *Nature des choses et droit: essai sur la dialectique du fait et de la valeur*, Paris 1965.
4. Ibid., p. 348.
5. See this volume, p. 65.
6. See Louis Althusser, *For Marx*, trans. Ben Brewster, London 1969 and Louis Althusser and Etienne Balibar, *Reading 'Capital'*, trans. Ben Brewster, London 1970.
7. The best discussion of Althusser's intellectual arrival is Gregory Elliott, *Althusser: the Detour of Theory*, Revised edition, Leiden 2007.
8. See Ibid., pp. 38-53.
9. See the articles reproduced in Perry Anderson, *English Questions*, London and New York 1992 and Tom Nairn, *The Break-Up of Britain: Crisis and Neo-Nationalism*, London 1977.
10. See E.P. Thompson, 'The Peculiarities of the English' (1965), republished in *The Poverty of Theory and Other Essays*, London 1978.
11. See this volume, p. 388.
12. *Pouvoir politique et classes sociales*, Paris 1968. English translation: *Political Power and Social Classes*, London 1973.
13. Personal communication from Poulantzas to Bob Jessop. I am grateful to Bob for making this known to me.
14. *Political Power*, p. 19.
15. Ibid., p. 77 and 84.
16. Ibid., p. 92.
17. See Ralph Miliband, *The State in Capitalist Society*, London 1969.
18. See Ralph Miliband, 'The Capitalist State: Reply to Nicos Poulantzas', *New Left Review* 59 (1970); 'Poulantzas and the Capitalist State', *New Left Review* 82 (1973). Selections of these texts, as well as the original review by Poulantzas, were republished in Robin Blackburn (ed.), *Ideology in Social Sciences*, London 1972.
19. Miliband, 'The Capitalist State', p. 57.

20. Ibid., p. 58.
21. Miliband, 'Poulantzas and the Capitalist State', p. 86.
22. Ibid., pp. 87–89.
23. See Ibid., pp. 89–92.
24. See Ernesto Laclau, 'The Specificity of the Political: the Miliband-Poulantzas Debate', *Economy and Society*, no. 1 (1975), republished as Chapter 2 of *Politics and Ideology in Marxist Theory*, London and New York 1977. I have drawn on this latter version.
25. Laclau, *Politics and Ideology*, p. 60.
26. Ibid., p. 63.
27. Ibid., p. 64.
28. Ibid., p. 70.
29. Ibid., p. 73.
30. See this volume, p. 282.
31. See *Fascisme et dictature: la troisième internationale face au fascisme*, Paris 1970. English translation: *Fascism and Dictatorship: the Third International and the Problem of Fascism*, London 1974.
32. Poulantzas's critical remarks are largely contained in footnotes. See, especially, *Fascism and Dictatorship*, pp. 300–7, notes 2, 5, 6 and 9.
33. See *La Crise des dictatures: Portugal, Grèce, Espagne*, Paris 1975. English translation: *The Crisis of the Dictatorships: Portugal, Greece, Spain*, New Left Books, London 1976.
34. See *Les Classes sociales dans le capitalisme aujourd'hui*, Paris 1974. English translation: *Classes in Contemporary Capitalism*, London 1975.
35. See *Classes*, Part Three, pp. 191-331.
36. See *L'État, le pouvoir, le socialisme*, Paris 1978. English translation: *State, Power, Socialism*, London 1978.
37. See Nicos Poulantzas, ed., *La Crise de l'état*, Paris 1976. The volume included chapters by, among others, Christine Buci-Glucksmann, Manuel Castells and Joachim Hirsch.
38. See, for example, James O'Connor, *The Fiscal Crisis of the State*, New York 1973; Jürgen Habermas, *Legitimation Crisis*, London 1976; and Claus Offe, *Contradictions of the Welfare State*, ed. John Keane, Cambridge, Mass. 1984.
39. Poulantzas's prediction of increased authoritarianism was directly influential on Stuart Hall's seminal analyses of the emergence of 'authoritarian populism' in the UK in the form of 'Thatcherism'. See Stuart Hall *et al.*, *Policing the Crisis: Mugging, the State, and Law and Order*, Basingstoke 1978 and the essays in Stuart Hall, *The Hard Road to Renewal: Thatcherism and the Crisis of the Left*, London 1988. For a definitive account of Thatcherism as a 'strong state' project, see Andrew Gamble, *The Free Economy and the Strong State: the Politics of Thatcherism*, Basingstoke 1988. A more 'Poulantzasian' breakdown of the phases of the Thatcher period, including an important debate with Hall, can be found in Bob Jessop *et al.*, *Thatcherism: A Tale of Two Nations*, Cambridge 1988.
40. See *State, Power, Socialism*, pp. 36–7, 43–6.
41. Ibid., p. 44.
42. Ibid., p. 148. Emphases in the original.
43. Jessop reviews Poulantzas's political alignments in *Nicos Poulantzas*, pp. 15–23.

44. See Norberto Bobbio, *Which Socialism? Marxism, Socialism and Democracy*, ed. Richard P. Bellamy, Cambridge 1988.

45. See this volume, p. 367.

46. See this volume, p. 391.

47. See Louis Althusser, *The Future Lasts Forever: A Memoir*, eds Oliver Corpet and Yann Moulier Boutang, trans. Richard Veasey, London 1993, p. 260.

48. See, for example, the republication of interviews and articles on the state by Poulantzas, *Repères: hier et aujourd'hui. Textes sur l'état*, Paris 1980; the essays in honour in Christine Buci-Glucksmann, ed., *La gauche, le pouvoir, le socialisme: hommage à Nicos Poulantzas*, Paris 1983; and Jessop, *Nicos Poulantzas*.

49. See, for example, the work of Bob Jessop, particularly *State Theory: Putting the Capitalist State in its Place*, Cambridge 1990; and Leo Panitch, *Working-Class Politics in Crisis: Essays on Labour and the State*, London 1986, and 'The New Imperial State', *New Left Review* (II) 2 (2000), pp. 5–20.

50. These problems are noted by Jessop, *Nicos Poulantzas*, pp. 184 and 191.

51. See, for example, two recent collections that take up Poulantzas's legacy: Stanley Aronowitz and Peter Bratsis (eds), *Paradigm Lost: State Theory Reconsidered*, Minneapolis 2002; and Lars Bretthauer *et al* (eds), *Poulantzas lesen: Zur Aktualität marxistischer Staatstheorie*, Hamburg 2006. See also, Alex Demirovic, *Nicos Poulantzas - Aktualität und Probleme materialistischer Staatstheorie*, Second edition, Münster 2007.

1. Marxist Examination of the Contemporary State and Law and the Question of the 'Alternative'

1. For Marx, Engels and Lenin, as we shall see later, there is no significant historical distinction, *genetic* or *specific*, between law and state.

2. Karl Marx and Frederick Engels, 'The German Ideology', in *Collected Works*, vol. 5, London 1976, p. 90; translation modified.

3. A conclusion at which Althusser also arrives, by a different route: see 'On the Materialist Dialectic' (*La Pensée*, no. 110, 1963), in *For Marx*, trans. Ben Brewster, London 1969.

4. See especially 'The German Ideology', pp. 59, 320–30 and the 'Economic and Philosophical Manuscripts' (in Karl Marx, *Early Writings*, trans. Rodney Livingstone and Gregor Benton, Harmondsworth 1975), pp. 352–4 (where Marx conceives man as a unity of being and thought). Moreover, the reality of the superstructure in Marx is suggested by the very term – *Entwirklichung* – that he uses in connection with alienation in general. This term, which means negation as well as 'de-realization', can thus be considered equally valid for the superstructure. However, in concrete circumstances a phenomenon can be *derealized* – this term always being employed in the framework of the polemical problematic we have referred to – *only if it is genetically conceived as real*. The reality of the superstructural sphere is more tangible in the Preface to *A Contribution to the Critique of Political Economy* and in *Capital* (especially in the passages in Volume Three where Marx clarifies the relations between essence and phenomenon). We may conclude with a phrase of Gramsci's, underscoring 'the necessary reciprocity between structure and superstructure, a reciprocity which is nothing other than the real dialectical process' (Antonio

Gramsci, *Selections from the Prison Notebooks*, ed. and trans. Quintin Hoare and Geoffrey Nowell Smith, London 1971, p. 366).

5. Thus, Marx's 'false ideology' and 'superstructural system distorting the base' are *not analogous* to Hegel's 'perverted existence'. We know that the latter, in order to respond to those who accused him of identifying the logical ideal state with the existing real state, *and of thus slipping into an axiological worship of the fait accompli*, maintained that an existing state is only in part real, and hence logical, and in part remains a mere phenomenal *existence*. To that extent, it does not ontologically conform to the real-Idea; in this sense, it constitutes an *ontologically* perverted existence and *accordingly* can be condemned *axiologically*. However, given that the real in Hegel ended up being 'essentially' *identified with*, 'historically' *absorbed into*, the Idea-Logic, how can an unreal existence, one not *totalized-identified* with the Idea, only exist *ontologically*? On what ontological 'site' and 'ground' can this factually perverted existence be situated historically, and thus subsequently condemned axiologically? The ontological impossibility of a perverted existence does not allow us, in the framework of Hegelian thought, to question the axiological legitimation of *any* existing reality. (See, moreover, Marx's conception of the Idea as an axiological ideal in his first writings on the philosophy of law, which predate his *Contribution to the Critique of Hegel's Philosophy of Right*.) For Marx, by contrast, a false ideology or a superstructural system that distorts the base, and which concerns (and this is what we are interested in here) the normative superstructures, remains wholly real (real-ideal), can exist ontologically as such, and possesses a historical effectivity, *while not being 'adequate'* – monism of contradiction – *to the real-material*. Precisely to the extent that they are not adequate, they are axiologically invalid. In effect, *although genetically 'grounded'*, as historical values, *in the base* – whence the fact that, in existing socially, they remain real – they do not, or they no longer, conform to the *true meaning* immanent in the real-material. Thus they are not – or are no longer – *legitimated* and *validated* by those material realities of the base that structure, at this particular moment, its *historical meaning*. It is this differentiation in Marx between the *genetic foundation* and *historical effectivity* of values on the one hand, and their *axiological validation* or *legitimation* on the other, which precludes pure and simple worship of the *fait accompli* in his thought.

6. Marx's texts on these issues are numerous, but scattered throughout his work. See especially the article of 25 October 1842 on the debates on the law on the theft of wood, in the *Rhenish Gazette*; the *German Ideology*; the *Contribution to the Critique of Political Economy*; the *Grundrisse der Kritik der politischen Oekonomie*; and Volume One of *Capital*.

7. The value of volition is thus not constitutively bound up with the value of liberty. For Roman law, will, even when expressed in circumstances of direct physical constraint, sufficed to create an obligation, according to the maxim: 'Although, if free, I would have refused, the fact remains that, albeit constrained, I willed it.' On the philosophical problems of juridical voluntarism, see Michel Villey, *Leçons d'histoire de philosophie du droit*, 2nd edn, and H. Battifol, *La Philosophie du droit*.

8. *Inter alia*, in Marx's *Critique of Hegel's Doctrine of the State*.

9. This is particularly clear in the *Communist Manifesto*.

10. See Marx, *Contribution to the Critique of Hegel's Philosophy of Right*.

Introduction, published in the *Franco-German Yearbooks*, and the 1844 *Manuscripts*.

11. See, *inter alia*, Jean Piaget, *Introduction à l'épistémologie génétique*, vol. 3.

12. Letter of 27 October 1890 to Conrad Schmidt, in Marx and Engels, *Selected Correspondence*, trans. I. Lasker, Moscow 1975, p. 399.

13. In this sense, the methodological concept of institution should be reserved exclusively for phenomena pertaining to the state political *superstructure*. It is interesting to note that in French and German 'institutionalist' theories we find, as early as the pre-war period, the epistemological and methodological problematic of the contemporary 'structuralist' tendency being applied to the juridical-state domain. Several of these theories thus distinguish between the concept–tool of institution and those of category, classification or system, indicating that an institution constitutes a social and economic reality possessing an autonomous existence, predating and relatively independent of its integration into law, the other concepts representing *purely* scientific tools. However, in a Marxist reflection on the base-superstructure relationship, because every superstructural phenomenon evinces a substratum in the base which *already* attains *a degree of totalization or structuration* there, no difference *in kind* exists between the concept of institution and the other concepts. There is only a difference of degree of *superstructural* totalization or structuration between them, every methodological concept being adequate to a real 'object' and to the latter's substratum in the base.

14. See *The State and Revolution*.

15. On this point, see André Gorz, Introduction to *Strategy for Labour* (1964), trans. Martin A. Nicolaus and Victoria Ortiz, Boston 1968.

2. Sartre's *Critique of Dialectical Reason* and Law

1. See Ludwig Feuerbach, 'Principles of the Philosophy of the Future' (in *The Fiery Brook: Selected Writings of Ludwig Feuerbach*, New York 1972).

2. See 'Le droit naturel comme dépassement du droit positif', *Archives de philosophie du droit*, 1963.

3. More specifically, *Critique of Hegel's Doctrine of the State* (1841–42); *On the Jewish Question* (1843); *Contribution to the Critique of Hegel's Philosophy of Right* (1843–44).

4. Marx, 'Economic and Philosophical Manuscripts', in *Early Writings*, trans. Rodney Livingstone and Gregor Benton, Harmondsworth 1975, pp. 385–86.

5. On this, see Louis Althusser, 'On the Young Marx' (*La Pensée*, no. 96, 1961) and 'On the Materialist Dialectic' (*La Pensée*, no. 110, 1963), both reprinted in *For Marx*, trans. Ben Brewster, London 1969; Galvano della Volpe, *Rousseau and Marx and Other Writings* (1964), trans. John Fraser, London 1978; Umberto Cerroni, *Marx e il diritto moderno*, Bologna 1962; and K. Stoyanovitch, *Marxisme et droit*, Paris 1964.

6. See, for example, L. Landgrebe, 'Hegel und Marx', in *Marxismus-Studien*, vol. 1. Husserl's basic text lending itself to these interpretations – a text that is virtually unknown to phenomenological jurists, despite the fact that it is the only one where Husserl deals systematically with the problematic of social values – is Edmund Husserl, *Ethische Untersuchungen* (notes of courses taken by A. Roth), The Hague 1960.

7. See, for example, J. Hommes, *Zwiespältiges Dasein. Die existentiale Onto-logie von Hegel bis Heidegger*, Freiburg 1953.

8. Jean-Toussaint Desanti, *Phénoménologie et praxis*, Paris 1963, p. 17.

9. G.W.F. Hegel, *Elements of the Philosophy of Right*, ed. Allen W. Wood, trans. H.B. Nisbet, Cambridge 1991, pp. 73 ff.

10. Jean-Paul Sartre, *Critique of Dialectical Reason*, vol. 1, trans. Alan Sheridan-Smith, ed. Jonathan Rée, London 1976, pp. 45 and 47.

11. Ibid, p. 80.

12. Ibid, p. 216.

13. As regards reviews of and critical texts on the *Critique*, see particularly those of J. Freund, in *Archives de philosophie du droit*, 1961; Roger Garaudy, *Lettre ouverte à J.-P. Sartre*, Paris 1962; and Georges Gurvitch, in *Dialectique et sociologie*, Paris 1962. pp. 157 ff.

14. See especially Werner Maïhofer, *Recht und Sein* (1954) and *Vom Sinn menschlicher Ordnung* (1956).

15. See 'Notes sur la phénoménologie et l'existentialisme juridiques', *Archives de philosophie du droit*, no. 8, 1963.

16. See his already cited article and also 'Konkrete existenz, Versuch über die philosophische Anthropolgie L. Feuerbachs', in *Festschrift E. Wolf*, 1962.

17. Sartre, *op. cit.*, pp. 80 and 90.

18. Ibid., p. 197.

19. Ibid., pp. 79–341.

20. Ibid., pp. 345–404.

21. Ibid., pp. 405–44.

22. Ibid., pp. 599–607.

23. Ibid., p. 161.

24. Ibid., p. 219.

25. Ibid., pp. 257–8.

26. Ibid., p. 262.

27. Ibid., p. 472.

28. Ibid., p. 374.

29. Ibid., p. 564.

30. Ibid., pp. 417–28.

31. Ibid., pp. 431–2.

32. Ibid., p. 425.

33. Ibid., p. 448.

34. Ibid., p. 441.

35. Ibid., p. 449.

36. Ibid., p. 450.

37. Ibid., p. 452

38. Ibid., pp. 197 ff.

39. Ibid., p. 331.

40. Ibid., pp. 599 ff.

41. Ibid., p. 635.

42. 'Le droit, l'*a priori*, l'imaginaire et l'expérience', *Archives de philosophie du droit*, 1962.

43. See his *Sociologie juridique*, duplicated lecture course, 1961.

44. In this respect, we may regard Sartre's position as vitiated by a 'surplus ontologism'. His ontological analyses constantly duplicate and overlap with socio-economic analysis. Thus, one often wonders whether the concrete

results of his analyses of law and the state, rather than having a single
foundation – that is to say, an ontological foundation that translates, from
level to level, into a socio-economic foundation – do not emerge as having a
dual foundation – on the one hand ontological and on the other socio-
economic. Were this to be the case, the Sartrean enterprise would, of course,
be broken-backed.

3. Preliminaries to the Study of Hegemony in the State

1. On these epistemological issues, see Galvano della Volpe, *Logic as a Positive Science* (1950) (trans. Jon Rothschild, New Left Books, London 1980) and *Rousseau and Marx and Other Writings* (1956) (trans. John Fraser, London 1978).
2. See Stalin, 'Marxism and Linguistics' (1950) (in Bruce Franklin, ed., *The Essential Stalin*, London 1973).
3. Karl Marx, 'Critique of Hegel's Philosophy of Right. Introduction', in *Early Writings*, trans. Rodney Livingstone and Gregor Benton, Harmondsworth 1975, pp. 253–4.
4. It is in *The Eighteenth Brumaire* that we find this clear distinction in Marx between the 'political' interest of the bourgeois class and its private 'eco-nomic-corporate' interest. And it is precisely in this text that Marx *expressly* adopts the theme of the separation between civil society and the state.
5. Marx's analyses are to be found in numerous passages scattered throughout his work – *inter alia*, in *The German Ideology*, *The Poverty of Philosophy*, the *Grundrisse*, *Capital* (especially Volume One) – and also in Engels's *Anti-Dühring*. This major phenomenon for any study of political science, parti-cularly as regards issues of capitalist 'democracy' – i.e. the atomization of civil society as a necessary precondition, as a 'synchronic' condition of possibility, of its socialization – has been almost completely ignored by Marxist thought. By way of a well-nigh unique exception, we might cite Umberto Cerroni, particularly in *Marx e il diritto moderno* (1962) and 'Per una teoria del partito politico', *Critica marxista*, December 1963.
6. The relations between Marx's analyses and Gramsci's theses concerning the concept of the 'economic-corporate' – the transposition in Gramsci of Lenin's thematic of 'trade unionism' – have gone virtually unnoticed. *In this context, we shall indicate below why we continue to employ the concept of civil society.*
7. Despite their selective and limited character, the *Oeuvres choisies* published by Éditions Sociales contain the main texts of Gramsci that furnish the basis for our analysis of hegemony.
8. Here we are concerned with an attempt at a general scientific definition of the level of the political, which we apply to power and the practices aimed at the preservation of the class-division of society. As regards proletarian power and practice, the problematic of the political and the concept of hegemony in fact assume different forms.
9. By way of indications for an examination of ideologies, see Louis Althusser, 'Marxism and Humanism' (*La Nouvelle Critique*, March 1965), reprinted in Althusser, *For Marx*, trans. Ben Brewster, London 1969; and Pierre Macher-ey, 'Lenin, Critic of Tolstoy' (*La Pensée*, June 1965), reprinted in Macherey, *A Theory of Literary Production*, trans. Geoffrey Wall, London 1978.

10. Antonio Gramsci, *Selections from the Prison Notebooks*, ed. and trans. Quintin Hoare and Geoffrey Nowell Smith, London 1971, p. 56 n. However, in connection with the fact that Lenin regarded the institution of the state as the contradictory unity of organization and force, see his discussion with Struve in 'The Economic Content of Narodnism and the Criticism of it in Mr Struve's Book' (in Lenin, *Collected Works*, Volume 1, Moscow 1963).

11. 'The Poverty of Philosophy', in Karl Marx and Frederick Engels, *Collected Works*, volume six, Lawrence and Wishart, London 1976, p. 185. However, we must point out that a Marxist study of political science concerning the concept of power remains to be carried out, the only existing one (to my knowledge) being Sartre's in the *Critique of Dialectical Reason*, which belongs to a different problematic from the one I am setting out. It is in the context of this study that we could decide whether it is necessary definitively to reject the concept of 'civil society', which is too hastily condemned today (here I am referring to Althusser's articles). Actually, the concept of civil society both can and cannot coincide with that of mode of production, depending upon the conception of the mode of production itself which, in any event, obviously cannot be conceived as inter-subjective relations. At any rate, civil society comprises a specific level of class *'struggle'* – *power relations* – the economic-corporate-trade-unionist level, the *'economic struggle' that is systematically and expressly conceptualized by Lenin, Luxemburg and Gramsci as distinct from the 'political struggle'*. By contrast, from Althusser's standpoint the mode of production is *necessarily* translated at the level of every class *'struggle'* by its 'political' investment. There is no doubt that this discussion has far-reaching implications and its political consequences are clear.

12. On this subject, see, *inter alia*, Champaud, *Le Pouvoir de concentration dans les sociétés par actions* (1962).

13. Nicolai Bukharin, *Theorie des historischen Materialismus*, Hamburg 1962, pp. 259 f.

14. Thus, if we distinguish *schematically* between the objective coordinates of the formation of the state – and also of the dominant class – and the domains in which it performs its specific functions – *in short, the relations between the state and 'society as a whole', as Engels puts it* – we shall be able to identify the technico-economic, the socio-economic, and the political, *but always in their respective relations within a determinate social formation*. The *technico-economic* concerns labour productivity – the 'general direction of labour', as Engels put it – within the set of the relations of production. The *socio-economic* concerns class exploitation and relates, among other things and via numerous mediations, to the fact that within the general social division of labour the management of the 'common interests' of the members of a social formation is entrusted to a limited number of individuals, who monopolize it to serve class interests. The *political* concerns the political class struggle and the state's function in this struggle. However, to the extent that the technico-economic and socio-economic – in short, civil society as a whole – *are invested in and overdetermined by the political level*, as an objective ensemble of relations, both the various factors in state formation and the state's various specific functions are overdetermined by the political level. *It is precisely in this sense that we are here considering the relations between the state and the 'whole set' of coordinates of a social formation, contrary to any*

functionalist conception, at the political level of the relations between the state, the dominant classes, and the dominated classes. (In connection with the concept of 'overdetermination', I refer readers, bearing in mind the reservations I have expressed, to Althusser's work.) As for the questions posed by the state in the Asiatic mode of production, hobby horse of those who believe that they have discovered in Marx a view of the state as independent of class struggle in the Marxist sense, but which in fact form part of the schema outlined above, see the clarification by Maurice Godelier in *Les Temps Modernes*, May 1965.

15. The notions of 'technico-economic' and 'socio-economic' are used here in a provisional fashion. Given the still far from clear state of the discussion I have referred to over the concepts of 'civil society' and 'relations of production', I understand by socio-economic the level of economic 'class struggle' encompassed in civil society. I have borrowed these notions from Martynov, who previously distinguished between '*Arbeitstechnische Produktionsverhältnisse*' and '*sozialökonomische Produktionsverhältnisse*' ('Die Theorie des beweglichen Gleichgewichts der Gesellschaft', in *Unter dem Banner des Marxismus*, vol. 4, no.1, pp. 103 ff.).

16. Maurice Duverger, *Introduction à la politique*.

17. Gorz, *Strategy for Labour*, pp. 65–6.

4. Marxist Political Theory in Great Britain

1. *New Left Review* 23, January–February 1964.
2. *New Left Review* 27 and 28, September–October and November–December 1964.
3. *New Left Review* 32, July–August 1965.
4. *The Socialist Register* 1965.
5. 'Origins of the Present Crisis', *New Left Review* 23, pp. 38–9.
6. *New Left Review* 23 and *New Left Review* 27 and 28.
7. *New Left Review* 23 and *New Left Review* 27 and 28.
8. *New Left Review* 23 and *New Left Review* 27 and 28.
9. 'Problemi della teoria marxista del partito rivoluzionario', *Critica Marxista*, September–December 1963.
10. *New Left Review* 23, p. 41.
11. For the relation between Weber's and Lukács's theories of class, which has passed almost unnoticed in France, see Weber, *Gesammelte Politische Schriften*, Tübingen 1958, pp. 294–431 (in particular his text 'Parlament und Regierung in neugeordneten Deutschland', written in 1918). As far as the relation between Weber and Parsons is concerned, there is no doubt that Parsons misinterprets Weber's work in certain respects (see *The Social System*, New York 1964, pp. 100 ff. and 519 ff.). It nevertheless remains true that the relation he establishes between Weber and functionalism is ultimately correct. As to the problem of Weber's historicism, it may be said that he explicitly undertook a critique of the historicist 'totality', particularly in his analyses of the work of Eduard Mayer (*Gesammelte Aufsätze zur Wissenschaftslehre*). Yet his own theory must, despite his warnings, be considered a typical historicist theory. For the relation between the concepts of the 'ideal type' and the 'concrete universal', see among others, Leo Strauss, *Droit naturel et histoire*, Paris 1957, pp. 55 ff. and K. Larenz, *Methodenlehre*

de Rechtswissenschaft, Berlin 1960, pp. 336 ff. There is an interesting 'Marxization' of Weber's theory of classes, in a completely different sense from that of Lukács, in Dahrendorf, *Class and Class Conflict in Industrial Society*, London 1959.

12. There is no better example of this perspective, applied to political analysis, than the work of Marcuse – although it leads to different results. As long ago as 1935, for instance, he admitted that the unity of a social formation, in opposition to a purely functionalist conception, lay in the 'dominance' of a certain element of this formation over the others. However, he represented this element by the 'consciousness-conception of the world' of *one* class *ideologically* dominant in these formations (*Kultur und Gesellschaft*, Frankfurt 1965, pp. 34 ff.). Marcuse now argues that a global de-ideologization characterizes industrial societies, and hence he logically reaches the conception of a social formation as an integrated Hegelian-functionalist 'totality', in the absence of a proletarian 'class consciousness' which 'would countervail the whole'. (*One-Dimensional Man*, London 1964 p. 51 ff.) One may note in passing the manifestly un-critical use by Anderson of Sartre's concept of 'detotalized totality' in a Lukácsian perspective, one which Sartre himself has criticized.

13. This *functionalist perspective*, applied to the modern state, results in a conception of a state which corresponds to the 'vital needs' of the 'whole society': the conception of a class state is thus abandoned in favour of an integrationist theory (cf. J. Goldthorpe: 'Social Stratification in Industrial Society', *Sociologial Review Monograph* no. 8 and 'Le développement de la politique sociale en Angleterre de 1800 à 1914', *Sociologie du Travail* no. 2 1963; R. Titmuss: *Essays on the Welfare State*, London 1958, etc.). It is surely significant that the *epistemological principles* of the integrationist theory of the superstructures and those of a historicist-Marxist theory of the over-politicization of these superstructures are the same in both cases.

14. Among others, Marx: 'The Elections in Britain and British Constitution', in *Marx and Engels on Britain*, Moscow 1953, and Engels: *Zur Wohnungsfrage* in M/E *Ausgewählten Schriften* Berlin 1951/2, vol. I.

15. *Histoire et conscience de classe*, trans. Paris 1960, pp. 76 et seq. Appeals to Lukács to establish the relation between dominant class and dominant ideology last appeared in France with Ziegler: *Sociologie de l'Afrique Noire* (Paris 1964). A striking example of the errors to which a historicist-subjectivist perspective can lead in this field is provided elsewhere by Touraine: *Sociologie de l'action* (Paris 1965) which, while criticizing Lukács, explicitly appeals to the conception of an historical 'subject'.

16. Tom Nairn: 'The British Political Elite', *New Left Review* 23, pp. 21–22.

17. *The Socialist Register* 1965, p. 320.

18. We have ourselves derived the notion of the aristocracy as a class 'fraction' from an *interpretation* of the analyses of Anderson and Nairn. For the latter, even after the constitution of the 'power bloc' in England, the aristocracy is still expressly considered either as a class *distinct* from the bourgeoisie, or as having 'fused' with the bourgeoisie within the bloc. However, their analyses enable us to perceive this aristocracy precisely as a 'fraction' of the capitalist class: they point out that the process of capitalization of ground rent was accomplished, but that the interests of this fraction were distinct from those of the industrial or financial fractions. Further, this *'power bloc'* may exist not simply when it is composed of *fractions* of one class, as in Britain since

the 19th century, but also when there are *several ruling classes* as appears to have been the case in Britain before the 19th century, the aristocratic and bourgeois *classes* then forming a bloc *under the aegis of the bourgeoisie*. In fact, if the perspective of the class consciousness-subject, *sole* will in history, is abandoned, the possibility not simply of *one* ruling class with several fractions, but also of 'several ruling *classes*' of which one retains hegemony, can be admitted. But we have seen that for Anderson and Nairn, before the 19th century the bourgeois class did not seem to be the hegemonic class in a power bloc of two classes, but a 'class dominated politically' by the ruling aristocracy.

19. Here it is only possible to point out the importance of this problem of 'periodization': it concerns the delimitation of a temporal minimum necessary if political 'practices' are to be *susceptible to a rigorous theoretical conceptualization*. This *political* 'period' might for example, as Engels seems to suggest in his introduction to Marx's *The Class Struggle in France*, comprise at least a decade within the context of a capitalist formation. The concepts – e.g. of 'stage' and 'phase' – which can be applied to this periodization remain to be defined; the length of the periods will also depend on the *particular temporality* of the *political* level in a determined situation. In this sense, the periodization does not necessarily or perfectly coincide with that required for the 'economic' transformation of a social formation. For example, in Engels's periodization it does not coincide with the so-called 'decennial' cyclical crises of the system of capitalist production. *The political periodization is related among other things to the general periodization of the 'global' transformations of a social formation.*

20. Anderson, *op. cit.*, p. 1.

21. Contemporary political science raises this notion of 'compromise' to the level of a 'concept' within a functionalist approach. This considers the forces present at the political level as 'homogeneous', 'equivalent' and in principle 'autonomous' elements whose strategic *play* is situated in the framework of an integrative *pluralism*. See Helge Pross: 'Zum Begriff der pluralistischen Gesellschaft', *Zeugnisse Theodor Adorno* (Neuwied 1960), pp. 439 ff.; Abendroth: 'Innergewerkschaftliche Willensbildung, Urabstimmung und "Kampfmassnahmen" ', *Arbeit und Recht*, VII, 1959, pp. 261 ff.; J. Habermas: *Strukturwandel der Öffentlichkeit* (Neuwied 1965) pp. 217 ff.

22. 'Problems of Socialist Strategy', in *Towards Socialism*, p. 242. André Gorz quotes these observations on Anderson in 'Contradictions of Advanced Capitalism', *International Socialist Journal* 10. But Gorz seems to have situated the problematic of the 'revolutionary bloc' correctly: 'This explains the crucial importance of the *cultural and political work* of part of the working-class . . . in *welding* the non-proletariat of scientific and technical workers, students and teachers, to the working-class by the perspective and the nature of the solutions which it is able to pursue for *their specific problems*, which must be respected precisely in their relative specificity and autonomy.' (Our italics.)

5. *Towards a Marxist Theory*

1. This article was written prior to the publication of *Reading 'Capital'*. However, it takes account of Althusser's text on the concept of history

published in *La Pensée* in June 1965 and reproduced in *Reading 'Capital'*. It is appearing today as written, on the one hand in order to indicate some of the questions that need to be posed to *Reading 'Capital'* and to see how far it answers them; and on the other, because *Reading 'Capital'* contains texts of varying significance, which doubtless cannot all be related to Althusser's own problematic.

2. Louis Althusser, *For Marx*, trans. Ben Brewster, London 1969, p. 168.
3. Ibid., pp. 201–2.
4. Louis Althusser and Etienne Balibar, *Reading 'Capital'*, trans. Ben Brewster, London 1970, p. 94.
5. Ibid., p. 96.
6. Ibid., p. 108.
7. *For Marx*, pp. 195–6.
8. Ibid., pp. 205–6.
9. Ibid., p. 213.
10. 'Esquisse d'un concept d'histoire', p. 19. [Editorial Note: This passage was cut from the second edition (1968) of *Lire 'le Capital'* – the one translated into English in 1970.]
11. Gilles Gaston Granger, *Pensée formelle et sciences de l'homme*, pp. 18f.
12. See Roland Barthes, 'L'activité structuraliste', *Lettres Nouvelles*, no. 32, February 1963.
13. 'Perhaps, however, the problem is badly posed and it is pointless to seek to privilege either structures, which are always-already constituted and thus presuppose something else, or individual praxis, which is certainly totalizing. Maybe we should ask whether they could not be coordinated within a broader totalization that would render the relationship between them fully intelligible. But what would its nature be? Neither Sartre nor Lévi-Strauss offers a developed answer to this question. But it is curious that both of them end up posing it in terms whose convergence underscores the simultaneously radical and paradoxical character of the previous contrasts' (Jean Pouillon, 'Sartre and Lévi-Strauss', *L'Arc*, no. 26).
14. Jean-Paul Sartre, *Critique of Dialectical Reason*, vol. 1, trans. Alan Sheridan-Smith, ed. Jonathan Rée, London 1976, p. 480.
15. Now reprinted in *Situations VI* (Jean-Paul Sartre, 'Reply to Claude Lefort', in *The Communists and Peace*, trans. Irene Clephane, London 1969).
16. *Reading 'Capital'*, pp. 95–6.
17. In addition to the theme of structure and history, we could certainly also uncover the *common* problematic of Sartre and Lévi-Strauss, in contrast to Althusser's, in their *epistemological* positions concerning the specificity of 'theory' and its 'object' – positions treated in the 'dialectical reason/analytical reason' controversy. Their epistemological problematic would emerge even more clearly if related to the famous analogous controversy in Germany between Adorno (dialectical reason) and Popper (analytical reason) in the *Kölner Zeitschrift für Soziologie* in 1962–63. However, this would be tendentious, given that Althusser's *epistemological* positions are still at an undeveloped stage. In any event, here too the merit of Sartre and Lévi-Strauss is to have established, from their standpoint, the *problematic* character of the relationship between 'theory' and its 'object'.
18. *For Marx*, p. 37.

19. See Galvano della Volpe, *Rousseau and Marx and Other Writings* (1964), trans. John Fraser, London 1978, p. 173, n. 3.

20. *For Marx,* p. 213.

21. Ibid., p. 215.

22. In the context of this article, we cannot go into this problem in greater depth and attempt to offer solutions.

23. [Editorial note: unfortunately, the copy is corrupted here.]

24. [Editorial note: unfortunately, the copy is corrupted here.]

25. [Editorial note: unfortunately, the copy is corrupted here.]

26. *For Marx,* p. 179.

27. I stress, and we shall see, that this over-politicization is only an *apparent* means of avoiding gestaltism. Let us see what Talcott Parsons, the master of functionalism, has to say about the political (does his position not seem similar to Althusser's?): 'political reality cannot be studied according to a specific conceptual scheme . . . because the political component of the social system is a centre of integration for all the aspects of this system which analysis can separate, and not the sociological scene of a particular class of social phenomena': *The Social System,* Glencoe 1951, pp. 126–27.

28. Antonio Gramsci, *Selections from the Prison Notebooks,* ed. and trans. Quintin Hoare and Geoffrey Nowell Smith, London 1971, p. 137.

29. To try to encapsulate these remarks, I shall say that the problematic of *structural 'overdetermination'* risks signifying, through the political, the sliding of the element of the 'development of forms', conceived in *historicist* fashion, 'into' the systematic matrix of a formation. To avoid this trap, it must be shown why the political, a *specific level of structures* of a formation, is *as such* the 'motor' of this formation in the process of development of forms.

30. *For Marx,* p. 99.

6. *The Political Forms of the Military Coup d'État*

1. [Editorial Note: According to the editor of *Politis*, this text was written just one month after the coup of 21 April 1967. At that time, Poulantzas was a member of the still united Communist Party of Greece (KKE). The text must be situated in the context of the then current debates in the Greek Left about the nature of the coup and the perspectives of the resistance. As its main thrust went against the dominant position that accommodated the military dictatorship of the colonels under the *passe-partout* of 'neo-fascism', this text was 'ignored' by the official channels of the Left.]

2. [Editorial Note: Poulantzas is referring here to the modalities of the 'white terror' exercised by the so-called 'para-state' that persisted long after the termination of the Civil War, especially in the countryside. The phrase 'violence and fraud' was coined with reference to the general elections of 1961 in which Karamanlis mobilized not only the para-state to intimidate the opponents of the Right but also the dead to vote for him.]

3. See Antonio Gramsci, *Selection from the Prison Notebooks,* ed. and trans. Quintin Hoare and Geoffrey Nowell Smith, London 1971, p. 219.

4. [Editorial Note: A bourgeois party with roots in the Liberal party of Venizelos. Led by Papandreou, the Centre Union (CU) attracted a mass following as the official opposition to the governing ERE of Karamanlis. Its

electoral victory in 1963 was the first successful challenge of the rule of the right since the termination of the Civil War (1949). Although it never challenged the status quo, once in power, the CU adopted a more independent position on the Cyprus issue, started to renegotiate the status of the foreign capital, and attempted to check the omnipotence of the para-state. In 1965, Papandreou's government was undermined by the right. Two years later, a greater electoral victory of the CU, based on the upsurge of the anti-right movement, was prevented by the coup.]

5. [Editorial Note: A junta of high-ranking royalist officers of the extreme right that was formed in the early 1960s. One of the surprising characteristics of the coup was that it was carried out not by the 'generals' and the palace, but by the 'colonels' – different circuits, different scenarios.]

6. [Editorial Note: 'United Democratic Left', the broad, legal substitute of the KKE, although their membership did not coincide. The KKE maintained a clandestine structure within EDA.]

7. [Editorial Note: General Confederation of Workers of Greece.]

7. The Problem of the Capitalist State

1. London 1969.
2. Paris 1968.
3. Miliband, pp. 24 ff. and 47.
4. 'Marxist Political Theory in Great Britain', *New Left Review* 43. See this volume, Chapter 4.
5. Miliband, *op. cit.*
6. Miliband, p. 34.
7. Bettelheim, *La Transition vers l'économie socialiste*, and Poulantzas, *Pouvoir Politique et classes sociales*, pp. 23 ff.
8. Miliband, pp. 48–68.
9. Ibid., pp. 69–145, especially 119–145.
10. Ibid., pp. 68–118.
11. Ibid., pp. 96 ff.
12. Ibid., pp. 119–45.
13. Ibid., p. 93.
14. Ibid., pp. 119 ff.
15. Ibid., pp. 130 ff.
16. Ibid., expecially pp. 123 ff.
17. See the acts of the colloquy at Choisy-le-Roi on 'State Monopoly Capitalism' in *Economie et Politique*, Special Number.
18. Poulantzas, *op. cit.* pp. 297 ff.
19. *Les Temps Modernes*, August–September 1968.
20. Miliband, pp. 50 ff.

8. On Social Classes

1. This text was originally produced at the request of the trade-union federation CFDT (*Confederation Française Democratique de Travail*). It was circulated in roneoed form by the CFDT-BRAEC Centre (document no. 9) for use by CFDT cadres. It is therefore an attempt at a brief presentation for working-class militants of elements of theoretical analysis applied to the present

conjuncture. These elements are drawn from my two works, *Political Power and Social Classes* and *Fascism and Dictatorship*.
2. *Le capitalisme monopoliste, Traité d'économie marxiste*, Paris 1972, 2 vols.
3. Trade union of teachers in higher education [Trans.].
4. Gaullist Minister of the Interior [Trans.].

9. Internationalization of Capitalist Relations and the Nation-State

1. Paul M. Sweezy and Paul A. Baran, *Monopoly Capital*, Harmondsworth 1968. See also Sweezy's many articles in *Monthly Review*.
2. Harry Magdoff, 'The Age of Imperialism', *Monthly Review*, October 1968; Martin Nicolaus, 'USA: the Universal Contradiction', *New Left Review*, No. 59, 1970; Pierre Jalée, *The Pillage of the Third World*, New York 1970.
3. Robin Murray 'Internationalization of Capital and the Nation-State', *New Left Review*, No. 67, 1971.
4. The most important reference in this respect is Ernest Mandel, *Europe versus America? Contradictions of Imperialism*, London 1970.
5. Michael Kidron, *Western Capitalism Since the War*, London 1968; Bill Warren, 'How International is Capital?', *New Left Review*, No. 68, 1971; Bob Rowthorn, 'Imperialism in the Seventies: Unity or Rivalry', *New Left Review*, No. 68, 1971; and Jacques Valier, 'Impérialisme et révolution permanente', *Critique de l'Economie Politique*, 1971, No. 198.
6. See the Treatise *Le Capitalisme monopoliste d'Etat*, and the works of Philippe Herzog, *Politique économique et planification en régime capitaliste*, Paris 1971; Philippe Herzog, 'Nouveaux développements de l'internationalisation du capital', *Economie et Politique*, No. 212, 1971; Jean-Pierre Delilez, *Les Monopoles*, Paris 1970 and Jean-Pierre Delilez, 'Internationalisation', *Economie et Politique*, No. 212, 1972.
7. Charles Bettelheim, 'Theoretical Comments', in *Unequal Exchange: A Study of the Imperialism of Trade*, Arghiri Emmanuel (ed.), London 1972.
8. Manuel Castells, *La Question urbaine*, Paris 1972, pp. 62 f.
9. Among others see Samir Amin, *L'Accumulation à l'échelle mondiale*, Paris 1970 and the various works of Faletto, dos Santos, Quijano, Torres Rivas, Weffort, etc. In particular, see Fernando H. Cardoso, 'Notes sur l'état actuel des études de la dépendence' (mimeographed in August), 1972.
10. See John Dunning, 'Capital Movements in the Twentieth Century', in *Studies in International Investment*, London 1970 and Gilles Y. Bertin, *L'Investissement public international*, Paris 1971, pp. 26f., and the French information document: 'Les investissements directs des Etats-Unis dans le monde', pp. 7 f.
11. See John Dunning, *The Multinational Enterprise*, London 1971.
12. See B. Balassa, article in Maurice Byé (ed.), *La Politique industrielle de l'Europe intégrée et l'apport des capitaux extérieurs*, Paris 1968.
13. See the French information document cited in Note 10, and see B. Balassa, *op cit*.
14. See S. Hymer, 'The Efficiency (Contradictions) of Multinational Corporations', in Gilles Paquet (ed.), *The Multinational Firm and the Nation State*, Dunn Mills 1972.
15. See John Dunning, *American Investments in British Manufacturing Industry*, London 1958.

16. See Samir Amin, *op. cit.*

17. See F. Braun, article in Maurice Byé (ed.), *op. cit.*

18. In connection with these concepts, see Charles Bettelheim, *Calcul économique et formes de propriété*, Paris 1970.

19. This is the conclusion of Harvard research, as shown by R. Vernon, 'International Investment and International Trade in the Product Cycle', *Quarterly Journal of Economics*, 1966, May.

20. See Dunning, *The Multinational Enterprise*, pp. 19, 297f.

21. In this connection see the first section of Christian Palloix, 'Le Procès d'internationalisation', 1972 (duplicated text), and the many research works of the IREP.

22. Manuel Janco and Daniel Furjot, *Informatique et capitalisme*, Paris 1971.

23. André Gorz, 'Technique, techniciens, et lutte des classes', *Les Temps Modernes*, 1971, September–October and 'Le dispotisme et ses lendermains', *Les Temps Modemes*, 1972, September–October.

24. Ernest Mandel, *Europe versus America? Contradictions of Imperialism*, London 1970, p. 57.

25. Ibid., p. 58.

26. Ibid., p. 60.

27. Philippe Herzog, 'Nouveaux développements de l'internationalisation du capital', *Economie et Politique*, No. 212, 1971, p. 148.

28. This position emerges from all the analyses in the treatise cited above. On this question, see my article 'On Social Classes'.

29. Robin Murray, 'Internationalization of Capital and the Nation-State', *New Left Review*, No. 67, 1971.

30. See Jean-Pierre Delilez, 'Internationalisation', p. 69.

31. See in particular Philippe Herzog, *Politique économique et planification en régime capitaliste*, Paris 1971, pp. 35, 65, 139 f.

10. On the Popular Impact of Fascism

1. [Editorial Note: Text amended by translator. In the original, Poulantzas mistakenly inserted 'Second World War'.]

11. The Capitalist State: A Reply to Miliband and Laclau

1. Nicos Poulantzas, 'The Problem of the Capitalist State', *New Left Review* 58, November–December 1969; Ralph Miliband, 'The Capitalist State – Reply to Nicos Poulantzas', *New Left Review* 59, January–February 1970. This exchange of articles has been republished in Robin Blackburn (ed.), *Ideology in Social Science*, London 1972, and in J. Urry and J. Wakeford (eds), *Power in Britain: Sociological Readings*, London 1973.

2. *Pouvoir Politique et Classes Sociales*, Paris 1968, English edition *Political Power and Social Classes*, London 1973.

3. Ralph Miliband, 'Poulantzas and the Capitalist State', *New Left Review* 82, November–December 1973.

4. Nicos Poulantzas, *Fascism and Dictatorship*, London 1974; *Classes in Contemporary Capitalism*, London 1975.

5. Ernesto Laclau, 'The Specificity of the Political: Around the Poulantzas-Miliband Debate', *Economy and Society*, vol. 5, no. 1, February 1975.

6. 'Origins of the Present Crisis', *New Left Review* 23, January–February 1964, p. 40.
7. Louis Althusser, 'The Materialist Dialectic', in *For Marx*, London 1969; *Political Power and Social Classes*, pp. 18 ff.
8. *New Left Review* 82, p. 86.
9. *Political Power and Social Classes*, pp. 79 ff.
10. Ibid. ch. 2 and thereafter.
11. Ibid. ch. 4.
12. Nicos Poulantzas, *La Crise des dictatures: Portugal, Grèce, Espagne*, Paris 1975.
13. *New Left Review* 82, pp. 87 ff.
14. M. Castells, *Monopolville: l'entreprise, l'état, l'urbain*, Paris 1974; J. Hirsch, *Staatsapparat und Reproduktion des Kapitals*, Frankfurt 1974.
15. Among others: A. Wolfe, 'New Directions in the Marxist Theory of Politics', and A.B. Bridges, 'Nicos Poulantzas and the Marxist Theory of the State', both in *Politics and Society*, vol. 4, no. 2, 1974; J. Mollenkopf, 'Theories of the State and Power Structure Research', special issue of *The Insurgent Sociologist*, vol. 5, no. 3, 1975; G.E. Anderson and R. Friedland, 'Class Structure, Class Politics and the Capitalist State', roneo document, Department of Sociology, University of Wisconsin 1975; etc.
16. But only to some extent. I disagree with Laclau in particular when he sometimes identifies formalism and 'descriptive functioning of concepts'. I would also note that Laclau's article presents some patent structuralist connotations. He often comes to my defence against Miliband, but nonetheless sometimes accepts Miliband's criticism of me for 'structuralism'; he seems to be saying that I am indeed guilty of structuralism but that he (Laclau) thinks this a good thing, because this structuralism does not prevent me – quite the contrary – from carrying out concrete analyses, from examining the relative autonomy of the state, from establishing the distinction between fascism and the other forms of bourgeois state, etc.
17. A first version appeared in English: Etienne Balibar, 'Self-criticism – an Answer to Questions from *Theoretical Practice*', *Theoretical Practice*, no. 7/8, January 1973.
18. Etienne Balibar, *Cinq études de matérialisme historique*, Paris 1974, p. 240.
19. Ibid. p. 229.
20. In *Lire 'le Capital'*, 1st French edn, Paris 1966, p. 189.
21. *Political Power and Social Classes*, p. 13.
22. *Cinq études de matérialisme historique*, p. 231.
23. *Political Power and Social Classes*, pp. 13 ff.
24. Ibid. pp. 87 ff.
25. Ibid. p. 24.
26. *Lineages of the Absolutist State*, London 1974, p. 19.
27. See *Fascism and Dictatorship*, pp. 302 ff; Althusser's essay is in *Lenin and Philosophy and Other Essays*, London 1971.
28. Emanuel Terray, *Marxism and 'Primitive' Societies*, New York 1972.
29. *Political Power and Social Classes*, pp. 85 ff.

12. The Political Crisis and the Crisis of the State

1. [Editorial Note: Two of the 'Grandes Ecoles' that educate France's élite, particularly its 'technocrats.']
2. Paris 1973.

13. The New Petty Bourgeoisie

1. It should be borne in mind that I did not have an opportunity to read the papers presented by Stuart Hall, Alan Hunt and Paul Hirst before the conference.
2. *New Left Review* 98, pp. 3–41.

14. The State and the Transition to Socialism

1. *La Crise de l'Etat*, Paris 1976.
2. [Editorial Note: CERES (Centre d'Etudes, de Recherches, et d'Education Socialistes – Centre for Socialist Studies, Research and Education) was the organized form taken by the left wing in the French Socialist Party.]
3. *Portugal: La Révolution en marche*, by Daniel Bensaïd, Carlos Rossi and Charles-André Udry, Paris 1975.
4. [Editorial Note: Norberto Bobbio was Professor of Political Sciences at the University of Turin and editor of the Italian Socialist Party's theoretical journal, *Mondoperaio*. In September 1975 he published a special issue of the journal on 'Socialism and Democracy' which sparked off a huge and continuing debate on this subject.]
5. [Editorial Note: This interview, 'Revolutionary Strategy In Europe', has also been published in *New Left Review* 100.]
6. [Editorial Note: Jacques Julliard was a former national executive member of the social-democratic trade union federation, the CFDT, and joint author with its general secretary, Edmond Maire, of a book entitled *The CFDT Today*.]
7. [Editorial Note: The LCR (Ligue Communiste Révolutionnaire – Revolutionary Communist League) is the French section of the Fourth International.]

15. Towards a Democratic Socialism

1. Mary-Alice Waters (ed.), *Rosa Luxemburg Speaks*, New York 1970, p. 391.

17. Interview with Nicos Poulantzas

1. This interview took place in Coventry on 5 April 1979 and was conducted by Stuart Hall and Alan Hunt. Thanks are due to Phil Jones and Bob Jessop for assistance with the interview and to Sheila Ford for transcribing and typing the original interview.

INDEX

Adler, Max 29
Adorno, Theodor 94
Agnelli, Giovanni 377
alienation 78, 81, 93, 94
Allende, Salvador 300, 326, 351, 374
Althusser, Louis
  Balibar and 273, 290
  class struggle and 388, 395
  'theoretical practice' 273
  on unity 141–4
  Poulantzas and 1–2, 6–8
  Poulantzas on 10, 381, 396
  on Theory 139–40, 143
  For Marx 7, 139–65
  Reading 'Capital' (with Balibar) 7
  see also 'epistemological break';
    structuralism
Amendola, Giorgio 353–4
Anderson, Perry 8–9, 125–38, 272,
  290
  on aims of socialism 138
  on English class system 120–3
Annales school 384
Antunes, Melo 355
Argentina 408
Aron, Raymond 178, 406
authoritarianism 377, 397–9
autonomy 4, 105, 14, 290, 396
  'conditions of existence' and 397
  of law 4, 28, 105
  misconstrued by Miliband 279–82
  of state 1, 28, 180, 283, 284–5, 308,
    311

Bachelard, Gaston 140
Balibar, Étienne 273, 290, 388, 395
  Reading 'Capital' (with Althusser)
    7, 287–8
Baran, Paul 254
Barre, Raymond 377
Barthes, Roland 7, 148
base/superstructure 25–8, 38–40, 68,
  77
  hegemony and 72, 98
Bensaïd, Daniel 340
Berlinguer, Enrico 354, 391
Bernstein, Eduard 323
Bettelheim, Charles 177, 287, 381
'Bismarckism' 128–9, 179
Bobbio, Norberto 22, 346
Bonapartism 105–6, 179, 180, 207,
  335
  in Greece 168–9
bourgeoisie
  comprador/national 200–1, 242–
    3
  divisions of 206
  see also petty bourgeoisie
Britain 120–38, 400
Bukharin, Nikolai 112
bureaucracy 106, 179, 202–4
  Luxemburg on 363
  Trotsky on 202

Cambodia 345
capitalism